Machine Learning Techniques for Text

Apply modern techniques with Python for text processing, dimensionality reduction, classification, and evaluation

Nikos Tsourakis

BIRMINGHAM—MUMBAI

Machine Learning Techniques for Text

Copyright © 2022 Packt Publishing

Publishing Product Manager: Ali Abidi

Content Development Editor: Shreya Moharir

Technical Editor: Rahul Limbachiya

Copy Editor: Safis Editing

Project Coordinator: Farheen Fathima

Proofreader: Safis Editing

Indexer: Manju Arasan

Production Designer: Vijay Kamble

Marketing Coordinator: Shifa Ansari

First published: October 2022

Production reference: 3111122

Published by Packt Publishing Ltd.
Livery Place
35 Livery Street
Birmingham
B3 2PB, UK.

ISBN 978-1-80324-238-5

www.packt.com

This book is dedicated to my parents, Vasileios and Zoi

Acknowledgments

Why bother writing a book on topics for which there is already a vast amount of information available? My main driving force was to share knowledge in a beloved field in a way I would have liked to have been exposed to several years ago. Creating a book for a single reader who has long ago ceased to exist (my past self) has no merit. Instead, we wanted to offer a practical resource to a broader audience, which required feedback from colleagues in active conversations, who also functioned as a sounding board for our ideas. These people directly or indirectly affected the current book's structure and content, and to these people I am overwhelmingly indebted.

Initially, I would like to thank Vassilis Digalakis, for opening the door and welcoming me to a new playground. Nikos Chatzichrisafis, for providing a unique landing point in the field. Pierrette Bouillon, for enlarging the space with more toys, and Manny Rayner for the company during gameplay.

Special thanks go to my colleagues at the International Institute in Geneva, and particularly to Dogan Guven (for architecting our Business Analytics program), Andrea di Mauro (for the inspiration), and Ioanna Liouka (for the opportunity).

It would be negligent to omit my master's students in the Text Mining and Python course, who unwittingly became testing subjects for a large part of the content.

Many thanks to my colleagues at the University of Geneva for fostering a productive multidisciplinary work environment. The technologies described in this book find practical usage in our research tasks. My daily interaction with such competent researchers in the field is hopefully reflected in the quality of the current book.

I can only recall positive sentiments from my collaboration with the Packt team. Their professionalism and interpersonal interaction gave me the freedom to create a book as I imagined. But, on the other hand, they provided a large bounding box and direction that prevented unintended ricochets. In particular, I would like to thank Shreya Moharir (for making the book appropriate for a global audience), Aparna Nair (for maintaining the right pace), and Ali Abidi (for orchestrating the whole process). In addition, the two reviewers, Ved Mathai and Saurabh Shahane, did their utmost to highlight all the unintentional pitfalls in my initial drafts and provided a genuine quality boost to the outcome. Finally, I would also like to thank Costas Boulis for reading part of this work and providing valuable feedback.

Last but not least, I would like to acknowledge my wife Kyriaki and my son Vassili for their love and support during the compilation of this work. Without them, the book would have finished a little earlier, but it wouldn't have meant nearly as much.

All these people have assisted me in one way or another in creating a better book.

Enjoy the ride!

Contributors

About the author

Nikos Tsourakis is a professor of computer science and business analytics at the International Institute in Geneva, Switzerland, and a research associate at the University of Geneva. He has over 20 years of experience designing, building, and evaluating intelligent systems using speech and language technologies. He has also co-authored over 50 research publications in the area. In the past, he worked as a software engineer, developing products for major telecommunication vendors. He also served as an expert for the European Commission and is currently a certified educator at the Amazon Web Services Academy. He holds a degree in electronic and computer engineering, a master's in management, and a PhD in multilingual information processing.

About the reviewers

Ved Mathai is a graduate of Manipal Institute of Technology and has a postgraduate degree in information technology from the International Institute of Information Technology, Bangalore. He has worked on numerous start-ups. He worked on semantics and machine learning at DataWeave, as a senior NLP engineer for 4 years at Slang Labs, and, most recently, as the CTO at Navanc Data Sciences. When he is not programming, he can be found watching Formula One or running in the park while listening to a podcast.

Saurabh Shahane is a data scientist-turned-entrepreneur. Currently, he is the CEO of **The Machine Learning Company** (**TMLC**). With TMLC, he is creating a data science ecosystem for both industries and educational organizations. He is an adjunct professor at the AI faculty at Symbiosis Institute of Technology and is also a Kaggle Grandmaster. He has a blend of academic and industry experience having worked with industrialists and researchers from domains such as pharmaceuticals, sports, finance, and business to promote and release research work and practical data strategies.

Table of Contents

3

Classifying Topics of Newsgroup Posts   63

4

Extracting Sentiments from Product Reviews   113

5

Recommending Music Titles   165

6

Teaching Machines to Translate   213

7

Summarizing Wikipedia Articles   261

8

Detecting Hateful and Offensive Language   301

9

Generating Text in Chatbots   341

10

Clustering Speech-to-Text Transcriptions   375

Preface

Crafting machines that can learn from data to perform intelligent decisions is becoming the dominant paradigm in many areas of technology. Acquiring the necessary skill set to perform this task will definitely boost your career. *Machine Learning Techniques for Text* aims to help you in this endeavor, focusing specifically on text data and human language. The book will show you how to analyze text data, get started with machine learning, and work effectively with the Python libraries often used for these tasks, such as pandas, NumPy, matplotlib, seaborn, and scikit-learn. You will also have the opportunity to work with state-of-the-art deep learning frameworks such as TensorFlow, Keras, and PyTorch.

There is a plethora of resources for mastering the field of machine learning for text, including complex theoretical concepts often expressed in a demanding mathematical language. Conversely, other resources focus disproportionately on Python code, and the theoretical foundations behind the design choices remain shallow. This book steers a middle path to keep the right balance between theory and practice. A good metaphor the book's content builds upon is the relationship between an experienced craftsperson and their trainee. Based on the problem, the craftsperson picks a tool from the toolbox, explains its utility, and puts it into action. This approach will help you to identify at least one practical usage for the method or technique presented.

In each chapter, we focus on one specific case study using real-world datasets. For that reason, the book is solution oriented, and it's accompanied by Python code in the form of Jupyter notebooks to help you obtain hands-on experience. This case study approach will allow you to engage more readily in learning and not just passively absorb information. Each time, the problem statement is set from the beginning, and everybody is aware of the challenge. Even if the discussion temporarily diverts from the principal aim, for instance, presenting some fundamental concept, you will be easily reoriented on the problem under study. A recurring pattern in the chapters is that we first try to gain some intuition on the data and then implement and contrast various solutions.

By the end of this book, you'll be able to understand and apply various techniques with Python for text preprocessing, text representation, dimensionality reduction, machine learning, language modeling, visualization, and evaluation. This diverse skillset will allow you to work on similar problems seamlessly.

Who this book is for

The target audience of this book is professionals in the areas of computer science, programming, data science, informatics, business analytics, statistics, language technology, and more who aim for a gentle career shift in machine learning for text. Students of relevant disciplines that seek a textbook in the field will benefit from the practical aspects of the content and how the theory is presented. Finally, professors teaching a similar course can pick pertinent topics in terms of content and difficulty. Beginner-level knowledge of Python programming is needed to learn from this book.

What this book covers

Chapter 1, Introducing Machine Learning for Text, presents the main techniques for machine learning for text, the relevant terminology, and the implications while using text corpora. You will familiarize yourself with the basic concepts behind text processing and the special challenges encountered while treating human language. We also discuss the notion of what a machine can learn, along with a taxonomy of different types of learning. The chapter completes by introducing the importance of visualization and evaluation techniques.

Chapter 2, Detecting Spam Emails, presents a typical exercise in machine learning for text: spam detection. The aim is to create classifiers that distinguish between spam and non-spam emails using an open source dataset. The chapter elaborates on why it is difficult to feature select on this kind of problem and introduces the basic techniques for representing text data and preprocessing it. The chapter focuses on supervised learning using the Naïve Bayes and SVM algorithms that are evaluated on standard performance metrics.

Chapter 3, Classifying Topics of Newsgroup Posts, deals with the problem of assigning a topic label to some piece of text. Again, new concepts and techniques are presented using an open source dataset. The exploratory data analysis step is formalized, and you become acquainted with the notion of dimensionality reduction using PCA and LDA. The chapter focuses on unsupervised learning. Word embedding is the new text representation introduced in the chapter, and the analysis is based on the KNN and Random Forests algorithms.

Chapter 4, Extracting Sentiments from Product Reviews, presents an analysis of how to extract the sentiment from a given corpus. You will learn how to extend the exploratory data analysis and how to use dimensionality reduction not only for visualization but also for feature selection. The focus is now on deep learning techniques, and to facilitate their explanation, the chapter discusses linear and logistic regression. Concepts related to minimizing loss and gradient descent constitute part of this discussion. You will learn how to construct, train, and test a deep neural network model in Keras for sentiment analysis.

Chapter 5, Recommending Music Titles, deals with recommender systems and how they can be incorporated to suggest music titles to customers. Systems of this kind can be categorized into content-based and collaborative-filtering types, and both are presented throughout the chapter. Using an open source dataset, we apply t-SNE and RBM to provide meaningful recommendations for the problem under study. Tuning is also an essential part of any machine learning algorithm, and this chapter dedicates some discussion on grid search for identifying the optimal combination of the hyperparameters.

Chapter 6, Teaching Machines to Translate, presents various techniques for machine translation. Rule-based and statistical machine translation constitute an excellent way to introduce fundamental concepts on the topic. You will become familiar with typical NLP methods such as POS tagging, parse trees, and NER. The discussion on deep learning models becomes more challenging as the focus is now on sequence-to-sequence learning. An extended section describes in detail the famous encoder/decoder architectures using RNN and LSTM. A seq2seq model is put into action to create an English-to-French translator, and the chapter ends with a typical evaluation of machine translation systems based on the BLEU score.

Chapter 7, Summarizing Wikipedia Articles, performs text summarization with data scraped from the internet and Wikipedia, and for this task, you will learn how to incorporate web scraping tools. After presenting a few basic text summarization techniques and applying them to the scraped data, the discussion moves to more advanced topics. You will learn the concept of attention, frequently encountered in deep learning models, and become accustomed with state-of-the-art models such as the Transformer. We train a Transformer network on Wikipedia articles to extract their summaries. The ROUGE score is used to assess the summarization quality as a measure of performance.

Chapter 8, Detecting Hateful and Offensive Language, deals with how to identify hate and offensive language on Twitter. We use the BERT language model based on the Transformer architecture, which permits the fine-tuning of pre-trained models, with our custom datasets. We also examine the role of the validation set to fine-tune the model's hyperparameters and the strategies for dealing with imbalanced data. The classification tasks are based on boosting algorithms and CNN.

Chapter 9, Generating Text in Chatbots, focuses on the implementation of retrieval-based and generative chatbots. A gamut of NLP techniques is presented throughout the chapter starting from simple regular expressions. Then, we move into more sophisticated solutions based on deep learning. We present how to create language models from scratch or fine-tune a pre-trained one. You will also become acquainted with reinforcement learning and also how to create GUIs that can host the implemented chatbot. Finally, we present perplexity as an evaluation metric and discuss TensorBoard, which helps us shed light on the internal mechanics of deep neural networks.

Chapter 10, Clustering Speech-to-Text Transcriptions, performs clustering on transcribed speech to assign them into different groups. We use a system that can automatically transform human speech into text and examine how to assess its performance using WER. The clustering methods introduced are hierarchical clustering, k-means, and DBSCAN. Finally, there is a relevant discussion on how to choose the optimal number of clusters. The chapter concludes by applying soft clustering and LDA to identify the topics in the dataset.

To get the most out of this book

You will need a version of Python installed on your computer—the latest version, if possible. All code examples have been tested using Python 3.10 on Windows. However, they should work with future version releases too.

Software/hardware covered in the book	Operating system requirements
Python 3.10	Windows, macOS, or Linux
Microsoft C++ Build Tools	Windows

The Python examples in the book are available as Jupyter notebooks, and you need to use an IDE such as Visual Studio Code (https://code.visualstudio.com/) to run them. You also need a Gmail account to download specific resources.

If you are using the digital version of this book, we advise you to type the code yourself or access the code from the book's GitHub repository (a link is available in the next section). Doing so will help you avoid any potential errors related to the copying and pasting of code.

In certain notebooks, the code uses reduced versions of the datasets to limit the run time to an acceptable level. Feel free to adjust the size of the datasets based on your system configuration. At the end of each chapter, you are strongly urged to re-execute the code by alternating the configuration of each machine learning algorithm.

Download the example code files

You can download the example code files for this book from GitHub at https://github.com/PacktPublishing/Machine-Learning-Techniques-for-Text. If there's an update to the code, it will be updated in the GitHub repository.

We also have other code bundles from our rich catalog of books and videos available at https://github.com/PacktPublishing/. Check them out!

Conventions used

There are a number of text conventions used throughout this book.

`Code in text`: Indicates code words in text, database table names, folder names, filenames, file extensions, pathnames, dummy URLs, user input, and Twitter handles. Here is an example: "The `CountVectorizer` class takes the token pattern argument as the input `[a-zA-Z]+`, which identifies words with lowercase or uppercase letters."

A block of code is set as follows:

```
import numpy as np
from sklearn.model_selection import train_test_split

# Create the train and test sets.
X_train, X_test, y_train, y_test = train_test_
split(data['tweet'], data['class'], test_size=0.1,
stratify=data['class'], random_state=123)
```

When we wish to draw your attention to a particular part of a code block, the relevant lines or items are set in bold:

```
Epoch 7/15
628/628 [==============================] - 753s 1s/step - loss:
0.2343 - accuracy: 0.9388 - val_loss: 0.3681 - val_accuracy:
0.8991
```

Bold: Indicates a new term, an important word, or words that you see onscreen. For instance, words in menus or dialog boxes appear in **bold**. Here is an example: "For example, **muscles** can be transformed into **mussels** with a minimum of **3** substitutions."

> **Tips or important notes**
> Appear like this.

Get in touch

Feedback from our readers is always welcome.

General feedback: If you have questions about any aspect of this book, email us at customercare@packtpub.com and mention the book title in the subject of your message.

Errata: Although we have taken every care to ensure the accuracy of our content, mistakes do happen. If you have found a mistake in this book, we would be grateful if you would report this to us. Please visit www.packtpub.com/support/errata and fill in the form.

Piracy: If you come across any illegal copies of our works in any form on the internet, we would be grateful if you would provide us with the location address or website name. Please contact us at copyright@packt.com with a link to the material.

If you are interested in becoming an author: If there is a topic that you have expertise in and you are interested in either writing or contributing to a book, please visit authors.packtpub.com.

Share Your Thoughts

Once you've read *Machine Learning Techniques for Text*, we'd love to hear your thoughts! Scan the QR code below to go straight to the Amazon review page for this book and share your feedback.

https://packt.link/r/1-803-24238-8

Your review is important to us and the tech community and will help us make sure we're delivering excellent quality content.

Download a free PDF copy of this book

Thanks for purchasing this book!

Do you like to read on the go but are unable to carry your print books everywhere?

Is your eBook purchase not compatible with the device of your choice?

Don't worry, now with every Packt book you get a DRM-free PDF version of that book at no cost.

Read anywhere, any place, on any device. Search, copy, and paste code from your favorite technical books directly into your application.

The perks don't stop there, you can get exclusive access to discounts, newsletters, and great free content in your inbox daily!

Follow these simple steps to get the benefits:

1. Scan the QR code or visit the link below:

https://packt.link/free-ebook/9781803242385

2. Submit your proof of purchase

3. That's it! We'll send your free PDF and other benefits to your email directly

1
Introducing Machine Learning for Text

The language phenomenon is still shrouded in mystery despite the recent achievements in various scientific disciplines in terms of understanding how and why it works. Yet, surprisingly, homo sapiens are the only species to develop this complex medium for exchanging information, which has led to the most striking accomplishments of humankind. Although the oral and gestural forms of language were the driving forces over millennia, their written counterpart decisively spread knowledge worldwide. Inspired by the expressive power of human texts, this introductory chapter sets the scene for the discussion in the following chapters, where we examine how to teach machines to extract meaningful interpretations from text corpora.

Building machines that learn from observations is becoming the dominant paradigm due to the ever-increasing amount of data that cannot be processed using traditional methods. For instance, text data is produced in vast quantities through social network interactions, scientific publications, and transcribing multimedia streams, among other things. These resources pose fewer challenges in terms of access and storage, which have become relatively inexpensive. Conversely, we need techniques to extract, visualize, and analyze text data to leverage this massive amount of unstructured information.

The content of this chapter is meant to introduce the main techniques for **machine learning** (**ML**) for text, the relevant terminology, and the implications while using text corpora. For that reason, you might need to revisit its content while navigating through the book.

In this chapter, we go through the following topics:

- Introducing the human language as a data resource
- Understanding how machines learn
- Identifying the basic taxonomy of machine learning algorithms
- Understanding the importance of visualization and evaluation techniques

The language phenomenon

Human language is a structured communication system based on grammar and vocabulary. Although other animals can incorporate some form of communication, human language has a distinctive feature; it is *compositional*. We can combine or recombine sets of words and create new sentences with little effort. With the odd exception of the waggle dance of honeybees for sharing information about the direction and distance to patches of flowers, no other animal communication system puts messages together like this. Human language is also *referential* in that we can refer to people, objects, or situations that occurred in the past or could occur in the future. Language's ability to transmit information about things that aren't physically or temporally present is unique. Another fascinating characteristic is that it is *modality-independent*. A spoken language, for instance, uses the auditive modality for communication, while the Braille system used by visually impaired people is based on the tactile modality. Similarly, we use the visual modality in writing and the sign language of deaf people.

The reasons for the emergence of language are so far unknown. Still, hypotheses contend that it occurred as a vehicle for exchanging information, as a byproduct of our tool development, or as a way to keep human groups cohesive. It is also not clear when human language evolved. Based on the current scientific data, we can trace its origin back to 150,000 to 200,000 years ago in eastern or southern Africa. It is suggested that it evolved from earlier pre-linguistic systems among our pre-human ancestors and increased in complexity through cultural transmission over many generations of speakers. During this process, many languages disappeared, and there are currently over 570 known extinct cases. More than 7,000 languages are spoken worldwide, some by millions and some by a few dozen people, endangered by extinction.

> **Interesting fact**
>
> It is believed that an Italian cardinal, Giuseppe Gasparo Mezzofanti (1774-1849), who spoke some fifty or sixty languages of the most widely separated families with considerable fluency, holds the record for multilingualism.

Linguistics is the main field for studying human languages and applying scientific methods to questions about their nature and function. Nevertheless, many of these questions overlap with other fields in the life sciences, social sciences, and humanities, making the study of languages a multidisciplinary undertaking. Besides theoretical inquiry, there is also an urgent need for practical applications. Applying computational approaches to linguistic questions requires a different mixture of disciplines, focusing more on language technology.

In the new machine age era, delegating the effort of analyzing human language to a computer is an attractive option simply because it can process a more significant amount of data in a fraction of the time, but the execution of this task is not merely quantitative. We can also teach a machine to perform it efficiently. The focus of the current book is to present techniques in practical scenarios that allow a machine to extract meaningful insights from text data and act intelligently to solve a particular problem.

The data explosion

We live in a data-driven world that steadily becomes even more data-driven. The innate tendency of humans to impart information, especially in written form, has caused an abundance of data for various languages and domains. Besides people's willingness to share information, advances in computer connectivity and storage have paved the way for an explosion in the volume of text data. For instance, hundreds of billions of emails are sent daily, and thousands of tweets are posted per second. Frantically, people and businesses are churning out lots of unstructured data with an increased *volume*, *velocity*, and *variety*, but with less *veracity*. The four *Vs* are defining properties of *big data* and shape our digital world. For that reason, they need some attention:

- **Volume**: Big data is about this volume now reaching unprecedented heights. Digital storage has become so cheap and vast in its capacity that we can practically keep all the digital data we're creating.

- **Velocity**: The speed at which data is generated, transmitted, and changed happens at an increasing velocity. It becomes hard to manage the data flow to make the best decisions. For instance, an online store should capture and process every mouse click while its users browse the website and provide instant recommendations.

- **Variety**: Big data consists of different forms; this is where variety comes into the scene. For example, interacting with an online chatbot entails structured data, such as the connection time or the user ID, and unstructured data, such as what is typed during the interaction.

- **Veracity**: This refers to the trustworthiness of data when making crucial decisions. Does it include biases, duplication, or inconsistencies?

Thus, confronting an overwhelmingly large amount of unstructured text data is unavoidable in most industries, and being able to cope is an essential skill. You can check out `https://www.internetlivestats.com/` for a real-time sense of big data.

The era of AI

At the end of the first section of this chapter, we mentioned that we are interested in teaching machines to act intelligently. This task entails the simulation of human intelligence in machines to make them think and act like real humans, but, of course, this is far more than a modest goal. Even from the creation of the first computers in the 1940s, the expectation was that machines would match humans in general intelligence. Back then, there was a great degree of optimism that this could happen in the foreseeable future. These great expectations paved the way for an emerging field called **artificial intelligence (AI)** that has faced several hype and investment cycles ever since, followed by periods of disappointment in the mid-70s and mid-90s. The great promise of AI has been recorded in myriad science fiction novels and movies. Since then, the high expectations inspired by this vision have not been fully met. Also, the term *intelligent* is still controversial due to whether a machine can actually exhibit human-level intelligence or just mimic a few of its manifestations.

Anyway, AI, once considered to be science fiction, has now partially become a reality. Although achieving human-level intelligence or even superintelligence seems hopelessly complicated, AI applications are ubiquitous in several sectors and activities of human life. You are probably using these applications even if you are unaware of this fact. According to Andrew Ng, a pioneer in the field, AI is the new electricity and has the potential to liberate humanity from a lot of mental drudgery, just as the industrial revolution emancipated many people from physical labor.

Nevertheless, if AI has been around for decades, why did it just start taking off now? Three main reasons were the driving forces for this situation:

- **Data availability**: Digital devices, such as laptops and smartphones, are now an extension of the human body, generating vast amounts of data we can feed our learning algorithms – for example, email text, tweet posts, or video and audio transcriptions.

- **Computational scale**: The advancement in hardware permitted the creation of intelligence models that are big enough to take advantage of the huge datasets currently available.

- **New algorithms**: The AI community has grown significantly, which has led to the creation of more powerful algorithms.

According to their ability to imitate human behavior, AI systems can be categorized into three main types:

- **Artificial narrow intelligence** (**ANI**): ANI, also known as *narrow AI* or *weak AI*, is goal-oriented with a limited range of abilities. All current AI applications, such as Siri, chatbots, and self-driving cars, fall under this category.

- **Artificial general intelligence** (**AGI**): AGI, also called *strong AI*, will be achieved when the relevant applications exhibit human-level intelligence.

- **Artificial superintelligence** (**ASI**): ASI is where things become scary and machines are more capable than humans in every possible way. According to a dystopian view, this might even lead to our extinction!

The list of AI applications is endless. To provide a few related examples, consider extracting the sentiment from a piece of text, recommending products based on user reviews, translating a sentence to another language, or creating a summary from a document. These are part of the case studies presented in the next chapters.

Relevant research fields

Parallel to AI, another field has continuously gained traction over the past decades. ML is how a computer system develops its intelligence, used by AI to carry out its tasks. Their relation is shown in *Figure 1.1*:

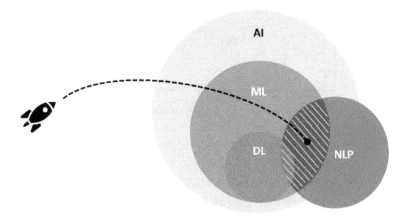

Figure 1.1 – How AI, ML, DL, and NLP are related

ML is a subset of AI and its intelligence is encompassed by a model trained over several iterations on a large amount of data. With minimal human intervention, the ML algorithm tries to identify patterns from past experiences and develop an efficient model to make predictions. As the ML algorithm is exposed to more data over time, its performance improves.

> **Interesting fact**
>
> The term *machine learning* was coined in 1959 by Arthur Samuel as the field of study that allows computers to learn without being explicitly programmed.

One way to perform training is to use a special kind of architecture stemming from **deep learning** (**DL**). DL algorithms mimic the human brain to incorporate intelligence into a machine. The output of these algorithms has been shown to offer better performance, especially when the amount of data becomes very large. The reason is that the performance of traditional ML algorithms reaches a plateau as you add more data. In the case of DL, on the other hand, the performance continues to increase – see *Figure 1.2*:

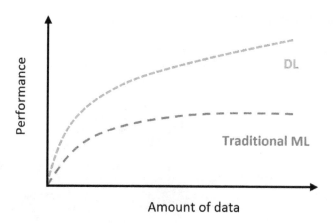

Figure 1.2 – Performance versus the amount of data for traditional ML and DL

In any case, keep in mind this well-known aphorism: *all models are wrong, but some are useful*. In simple terms, all models fall short of the complexities of real-world problems and are our best effort for a given task. As an ML expert, your job is to minimize the error of any trained model as possible.

Finally, *Figure 1.1* includes another large field of research called **natural language processing** (**NLP**), which, as the name suggests, deals with processing natural language data. The term *natural* is related to the fact that NLP works with languages that have evolved naturally in humans without conscious planning. As a counter-example, consider any programming language, which is artificially constructed. Human text data is usually available through a **corpus** (or **corpora** if plural) that consists of a collection of texts. When there is only one language, it is called a *monolingual* corpus; for more than one language, it is referred to as a *multilingual* corpus.

NLP must overcome many challenges related to the peculiarities of human language. For example, when we speak or write, we tend to omit a lot of common sense knowledge, assuming that the reader possesses it. The inherent ambiguity of natural language can also not be resolved without the proper context. Consider, for example, the word *break*, which can be interpreted as a pause from doing something. Still, it can also refer to a personal or social separation. Besides lexical ambiguity, we can encounter syntactic ambiguity, as in the following phrase: *The fish is ready to eat*. Is the fish ready to be fed, or can we eat the fish now?

Many other phenomena introduce more limitations and problems to NLP. For instance, identifying irony and sarcasm is a typical example where certain positive or negative words actually connote the opposite, such as *yeah, sure*. In the same way, slang terms might not be available in a dictionary, making it difficult to process the text that includes them. Even worse, human texts can contain stereotypes and biases that prohibit their use in systems for the general public. Finally, when dealing with low-resource languages, we lack sufficient resources to implement complex systems. These are a few of the possible problems when dealing with natural languages.

Note that NLP does not necessarily involve ML; we can program computers to process and analyze large amounts of natural language data without ML. However, the sweet spot lies where the two fields overlap, and our playground is the intersection of ML, DL, and NLP (check *Figure 1.1* and the area with the grid texture).

The following section provides more insight into ML.

The machine learning paradigm

The essence behind computer programming is to dictate to machines how to perform laborious tasks quickly and without errors. Calculating the average value of a series of numbers, resizing a photograph, streaming a video clip, and many other tasks are well-defined processes that require sophisticated software to execute. When performing more complex tasks, however, providing all the execution steps is error-prone and can often lead to brittle and buggy programs. Unsurprisingly, regular updates of our favorite computer programs claim to fix various problems – until, of course, the next update.

In the last two decades, we are experiencing a strong paradigm shift in commercial software development based on ideas that have been available for several decades. Instead of explicitly defining all the execution steps for a program, we can give pairs of examples in the form of possible input and the desired output. In this configuration, the machine tries to create (learn) its representation (model) on the examples so that the correct output is emitted when a new input arrives. Consider the example in *Figure 1.3*, which shows two processes for creating cakes:

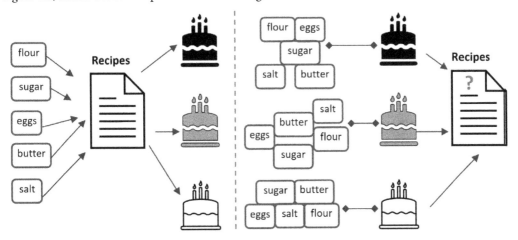

Figure 1.3 – Traditional (left) versus new software development paradigm (right)

In the traditional paradigm, the machine (in this case, a human) takes the ingredients and creates different cake variants by following the recipes. Conversely, in the new software development paradigm, they are given multiple combinations of ingredient-cake pairs. After many trial-and-error iterations of baking cakes, they can presumably identify the recipe for each type. Then, it is straightforward to create similar cakes in the future.

So what is the benefit of the second approach? Following a readymade recipe and obtaining a delicious cake seems much easier in this contrived example – and, in fact, it is! However, there is a catch. In most practical problems, we are never given complete recipes. Suppose, for example, the pastry chef does not reveal all the preparation steps. It is, therefore, better to exploit the abundance of data (if possible) to train a model that elicits all the intermediate steps in preparing the cakes.

On the other hand, when there is a lack of data or the task is well-defined, the traditional paradigm is still the direction to follow.

Taxonomy of machine learning techniques

The discussion in the previous section should have helped you understand the reason behind the ML paradigm. However, it only corresponds to one type of learning. ML algorithms can be trained differently, with each method having advantages and disadvantages. Broadly, they can be categorized into four main types: **supervised learning**, **unsupervised learning**, **semi-supervised learning**, and **reinforcement learning**. Let's examine each one in the following sections.

Supervised learning

In supervised learning, also called **inductive learning**, we work with labeled data that teaches the model to yield the desired output. For example, a dataset with emails labeled as either spam or non-spam can be used to train a model for spam filtering. It's called *supervised* because by knowing the correct label for each sample, we can supervise the learning process and correct the model during training, just like a teacher in the classroom. This type of learning is extremely powerful in extracting cause-and-effect relationships from the data, but we need to contemplate the cost of creating the initial dataset. Labeling observations from scratch is not a trivial task and requires considerable effort most of the time. In the following sections, we provide more details about this method.

Predictive modeling

In ML, the main aim is to create a model that can make predictions using data from the past. There are infinite examples of this kind – for instance, warning of potential health risks based on current health factors, predicting the future value of apartments in some geographical regions, determining the probability of bankruptcy before approving a loan, and so on. These tasks are part of **predictive modeling**, which uses mathematical and computational methods to calculate the probability of various outcomes. The process typically starts with data collection and the formulation of one or more statistical models. Then, these models are used to make predictions and can be adjusted as new data becomes available.

The simplest form of mathematical predictive modeling approximates function f from an input variable x to an output variable y. The example of *Figure 1.4* shows how a curve fits various data points in a two-dimensional space. In this case, the parameters of the curve, like its order, are well-defined and can explain how a new input x is mapped to an output y. Computational predictive modeling, on the other hand, produces models that are not easy to explain because they do not provide insight into the factors that lead to a specific input or output result:

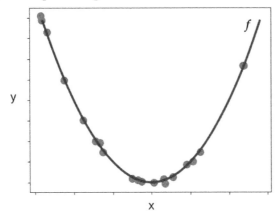

Figure 1.4 – Mathematical prediction model

Generally, we can have two types of predictive modeling depending on the output variable. First, we refer to classification when the output is a discrete variable, such as a list with categories or labels. Then, we refer to regression for continuous output variables, such as real numbers. In the following sections, we discuss the two methods.

Classification

Let's put aside the mechanics of the learning algorithm for the moment and concentrate on the available information and the result we want it to produce. Having a dataset with labeled examples at our disposal, we can split the classification process into two phases: *training* and *inference*. The process is summarized in *Figure 1.5*:

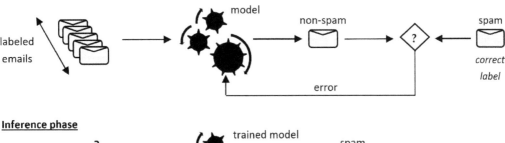

Figure 1.5 – Typical training and inference phases in supervised ML

During the training phase, the samples of the labeled dataset are used to train the model. Note that other names for a sample are *row, instance record, observation,* or *example.* The model generates a prediction for each instance in the dataset that we compare to the correct label. The specific comparison yields an error value—each time, the error is used as feedback to the model, which improves itself after many training iterations. The process terminates when the model only makes a few mistakes on the labeled data. Finally, during the inference phase, the trained model is used to make predictions on unseen data, which hopefully should be correct. Next, we will shed more light on the actual learning process during classification.

How machines learn

Suppose that *Figure 1.6* includes a set of labeled emails in a two-dimensional space based on two hypothetical characteristics, **T1** and **T2**. A spam email is denoted with the **o** symbol, whereas a non-spam email is denoted with the symbol **x**:

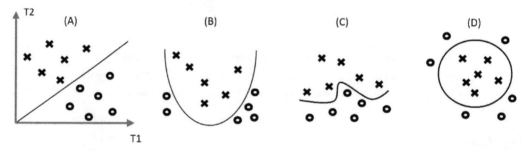

Figure 1.6 – Different layouts of labeled data in the two-dimensional space

During the training phase, the ML algorithm examines the annotated corpus to identify patterns that separate spam from non-spam. The simplest way to separate these points in *Figure 1.6 (A)* is to draw a line between the two groups. An ML algorithm can learn the equation of this line (mathematically expressed as $y = x$). Everything above the line denotes non-spam and everything under the line is the opposite. Clear, isn't it?

In many practical situations, however, the layout of the points is less than ideal. Consider, for example, *Figure 1.6 (B)*. In this case, the algorithm needs to identify a second-order polynomial that is described by the equation $y = x^2$. What about the situation in *Figure 1.6 (C)*? Now, a higher-order polynomial should be estimated, and the situation becomes even more complicated in *Figure 1.6 (D)*. This time, the separation line is not even a function. In practical situations, the difficulty of finding the best separation line scales very quickly, so another kind of trick must be employed.

How about experimenting with the coordinates of the space? Imagine moving the data points from the lower dimensional space they currently belong to into a higher order one. The assumption is that if the correct transformation were applied, the points would be much easier to separate in the new coordinate system. Thus, the problem concerns finding the right transformation for a specific dataset. The three examples in *Figure 1.7* demonstrate this process visually:

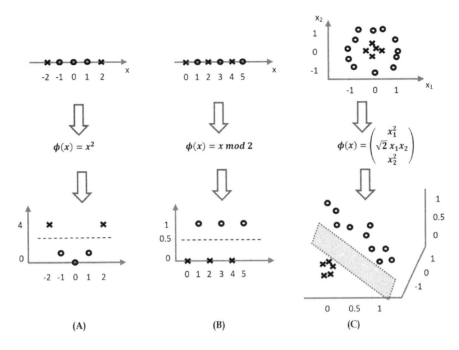

Figure 1.7 – Examples of transformation of data points to a higher-dimensional space

Let's apply a transformation function ϕ to each one of the data points. In plots **(A)** and **(B)**, the data is transformed from one-dimensional to two-dimensional, whereas in plot **(C)**, it's transformed from two-dimensional to three-dimensional. Notice that for **(B)**, the modulo operator (**mod**) produces the remainder of an integer division. After this step, we can immediately identify the points as linearly separable using the dashed line (or hyperplane). The line and the hyperplane are called **decision boundaries** and partition the underlying space into different areas.

We have seen a transformation in 3D, but ML algorithms typically work in much higher dimensions. For that reason, our human brain, wired to think in 3D, finds it difficult to conceptualize how data is transformed in a multi-dimensional space. In practice, however, ML algorithms use sophisticated approaches to look for the decision boundaries without the need to increase the already high dimensions of their space. The problem with mapping the data points to higher dimensional spaces is that it can be very compute-intensive. The key point to retain is that these algorithms aim to transform the input data in a way that can easily help identify the boundaries.

In the following sections, we will briefly discuss the other types of learning.

Regression

Regression is used to understand the relationship between dependent and independent variables. Regression models allow the prediction of numerical values based on different data points, such as stock prices, sale profits, population, and more. As in classification, there is a training and inference phase. However, these processes output continuous values instead of discrete ones.

Unsupervised learning

Unsupervised learning can work with unlabeled data, which is usually easier to acquire. For that reason, it is used mainly to discover hidden patterns in a set of observations without any human intervention. Unfortunately, unsupervised learning techniques are hard to evaluate because, without any reference, we cannot tell what is good learning and what is not. Next, we will present the three typical unsupervised learning techniques.

Clustering

Clustering is a convenient technique when looking for meaningful groups or collections from unlabeled observations. In theory, data points in the same cluster exhibit similar features, while data points in different clusters should have highly dissimilar properties. Clustering can be used, for example, to identify the topics of discussion in social media posts or to identify groups of households that are similar to each other. These observations are organized into groups in both cases based on a similarity metric.

Association analysis

Association analysis is a methodology that helps us discover interesting relationships hidden in large datasets. These relationships can be represented in two forms: association rules or sets of frequent items. The rules can identify, for example, that there is a strong relationship between certain products in a supermarket because customers frequently buy them together. This information is important to these stores and opens new opportunities for cross-selling their products. For example, they can place these products together in a basket, advertise the whole list to people that buy a fraction of these products, or offer discounts when they are all bought in one purchase. In addition, when dealing with text data, association analysis can assist in identifying dependencies between words and mining keywords that appear together frequently.

Dimensionality reduction

Dimensionality reduction is another typical unsupervised learning technique. It applies a transformation of data from a high-dimensional space to a low-dimensional one. The specific transformation retains most of the data's initial information with minimal loss. The utility of the method is twofold – first, to remove redundant information from the samples and thus increase the performance of the learning task, and second, to help visualize the samples in 1D, 2D, or 3D, to provide a better intuition on the data before starting the analysis.

Semi-supervised learning

Semi-supervised learning represents the intermediate category between supervised and unsupervised learning algorithms. It can be considered a method that helps alleviate the effort needed for data labeling by using a small number of labeled samples and a large pool of unlabeled data for model training. The process can be summarized as follows. First, we train a model using the smaller set of labeled examples. Then, we apply it to the bigger number of unlabeled instances, keeping the most confident predictions. The labels generated for the samples in the large pool are called *pseudo labels*. Then, we train a new model using the extended dataset and repeat the process, adding more pseudo labels in each iteration. If the data is appropriate to the task, we should experience a steady increase in performance.

Reinforcement learning

Reinforcement learning problems are markedly different from the ones of supervised, unsupervised, and semi-supervised categories. Reinforcement learning is the task of learning through trial and error, having an agent take actions within an environment – see *Figure 1.8*:

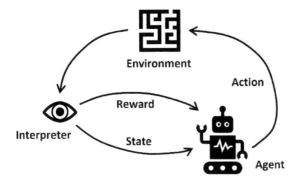

Figure 1.8 – The reinforcement learning loop

The agent is most commonly an algorithm that must discover through interaction with its environment which sequence of actions is the best to accomplish a given goal. Specifically, the agent acts in an environment, and its actions yield a reward and a new state. Contrary to the other forms of learning, the agent directly affects the information provided by the environment. In supervised learning problems, for example, the model just consumes the underlying data and cannot impact it in any way.

Let's examine the following example to understand this ambitious type of learning better. First, consider yourself an agent and the world around you the environment you can interact with. Performing the action of *going to college* led to the state of *getting a job* with a *high salary* as a reward, but, in the same way, we can also have negative rewards. For instance, *staying up late* as an action led to the state of *being sleepy* and obtaining the *reward* of *failing the exam*. The next two sections will conclude the chapter with two recurring topics appearing throughout the book.

Visualization of the data

The vast majority of all human communication is visual. The reason is that we are wired to understand images instantly while we need to process text. For instance, visual artifacts such as maps have been around for centuries to help understand data, so it is not surprising that most people are visual learners and can easily retain the information they see. In addition, visuals make it much easier to spot patterns and identify anomalies, which is critical to people working with data. Technology ignited the need for better data visualizations to represent and present data.

A good visualization should encompass three characteristics: *being trustworthy*, *accessible*, and *elegant*. By saying it is trustworthy, we refer to the fact that the data is honestly portrayed. For example, if the visual suggests a relationship, trend, or correlation, the data should support that relationship; otherwise, we are just deceiving the audience. An accessible visualization refers to whether we understand our audience and how they perceive and interpret the information presented. For instance, using technical notation for a non-technical audience reduces their capacity to benefit from the presentation. Finally, the visualization should be clear and aesthetically beautiful.

There are four types of information visuals:

- **Conceptual-declarative**: They aim to simplify complex concepts using visual metaphors. For example, the food pyramid and the water cycle visualizations fall under this category.

- **Conceptual-exploratory**: They are used for brainstorming sessions and have an informal type. They aim to gather ideas from multiple people either on a whiteboard or on a piece of paper.

- **Data-driven-exploratory**: They are the most complex type and have a formal character. They aim to find trends and provide an in-depth analysis of the underlying data.

- **Data-driven-declarative**: They are the most common type, typically found in newspapers, magazines, and the internet. They have a formal style but are generally simple.

This book uses visualization techniques from the data-driven categories extensively to attack two main problems – first, to extract some evident information or identify possible problems with the data before resorting to analysis, and second, to report on the performance of the implemented systems. We have deliberately incorporated different libraries and plot types to expose the reader to as many options as possible.

Evaluation of the results

Determining the value or worth of something in terms of quantity and quality is the process of *evaluation*. The increasing sophistication of text systems necessitates evaluation frameworks that measure the stated objectives and anticipated results. These frameworks serve a dual role – assessing different versions of the same product and also comparing similar systems. The topic of evaluation has grown into an essential part of systems development and a research field of its own.

Numerous convenient methods have been put forth to evaluate ML systems, which frequently make use of various computer- and human-centered metrics, most commonly known as objective and subjective evaluation. For example, using objective metrics allows us to measure something consistently and typically defies interpretation; either the spam detector achieved an accuracy above a threshold or didn't. On the other hand, subjective evaluations are more expensive and time-consuming to set up but reflect the system's actual performance with real users.

It is not uncommon that during the optimization of one metric, performance has deteriorated on another one. In the following chapters, we will have the opportunity to discuss the trade-offs during this situation. In addition, each metric typically evaluates a specific aspect of the system. Thus, combining multiple evaluation results for a fair comparison is often essential.

Another crucial aspect is prioritizing the errors based on their severity for the given problem. For instance, suppose that you take a test for COVID-19, and the result is erroneous. Then, one possible faulty outcome is that the test says you have coronavirus when you don't (**type I error**). Otherwise, it says you don't have coronavirus when you actually do (**type II error**). Which of the two errors is more critical to minimize? The type II error, most probably, and similar questions arise for many practical problems.

In each chapter, we will introduce relevant metrics to measure the performance of the systems implemented. Moreover, we will discuss different implications and how to avoid possible pitfalls.

Summary

In this introductory chapter, we provided a high-level description of the themes covered in the book. First, we discussed different aspects of human language and what makes it such a unique resource. On the other hand, it can pose many challenges when processing human text, with ambiguity being the most serious threat.

Then, the discussion went into the current data explosion identifying the defining properties of big data. For AI, we presented its main types and the driving forces that led to its take-off. We also introduced the cutting-edge topics of ML, DL, and NLP. In this context, we set our own playground at the intersection of these fields.

A large part of the chapter was dedicated to the new paradigm shift in software programming imposed by ML. We also discussed the basic taxonomy of this emerging field. Finally, we concluded with the visualization and evaluation topics encountered many times throughout the book.

The next chapter deals with the first case study, *spam detection*.

2

Detecting Spam Emails

Electronic mail is a ubiquitous internet service for exchanging messages between people. A typical problem in this sphere of communication is identifying and blocking unsolicited and unwanted messages. Spam detectors undertake part of this role; ideally, they should not let spam escape uncaught while not obstructing any non-spam.

This chapter deals with this problem from a **machine learning** (**ML**) perspective and unfolds as a series of steps for developing and evaluating a typical spam detector. First, we elaborate on the limitations of performing spam detection using traditional programming. Next, we introduce the basic techniques for text representation and preprocessing. Finally, we implement two classifiers using an open source dataset and evaluate their performance based on standard metrics.

By the end of the chapter, you will be able to understand the nuts and bolts behind the different techniques and implement them in Python. But, more importantly, you should be capable of seamlessly applying the same pipeline to similar problems.

We go through the following topics:

- Obtaining the data
- Understanding its content
- Preparing the datasets for analysis
- Training classification models
- Realizing the tradeoffs of the algorithms
- Assessing the performance of the models

Technical requirements

The code of this chapter is available as a Jupyter Notebook in the book's GitHub repository: `https://github.com/PacktPublishing/Machine-Learning-Techniques-for-Text/tree/main/chapter-02`.

The Notebook has an in-built step to download the necessary Python modules required for the practical exercises in this chapter. Furthermore, for Windows, you need to download and install *Microsoft C++ Build Tools* from the following link: `https://visualstudio.microsoft.com/visual-cpp-build-tools/`.

Understanding spam detection

A **spam detector** is software that runs on the mail server or our local computer and checks the inbox to detect possible spam. As with traditional letterboxes, an inbox is a destination for electronic mail messages. Generally, any spam detector has unhindered access to this repository and can perform tens, hundreds, or even thousands of checks per day to decide whether an incoming email is spam or not. Fortunately, spam detection is a ubiquitous technology that filters out irrelevant and possibly dangerous electronic correspondence.

How would you implement such a filter from scratch? Before exploring the steps together, look at a contrived (and somewhat naive) spam email message in *Figure 2.1*. Can you identify some key signs that differentiate this spam from a non-spam email?

```
From:      kmitnick@jakqd.com
To:        tjones@tsourakis.net
Subject:   Urgent!

Dear MR tjones,

You have noticed lately that your laptop is runing slow!
This is because I gained access to your machine, and I
installed a harmful VIRUS!!!

Even if you change your password my virus CANNOT BE
intercept!

The only SOLUTION is to following my instractions here:
https://bit.ly/33rhdNM

You have 48 hour before the virus is activated!
...OTHERWISE...GOOD LUCK!!!!
```

Figure 2.1 – A spam email message

Even before reading the content of the message, most of you can immediately identify the scam from the email's subject field and decide not to open it in the first place. But let's consider a few signs (coded as T1 to T4) that can indicate a malicious sender:

- T1 – The text in the subject field is typical for spam. It is characterized by a manipulative style that creates unnecessary urgency and pressure.

- T2 – The message begins with the phrase **Dear MR tjones**. The last word was probably extracted automatically from the recipient's email address.

- T3 – Bad spelling and the incorrect use of grammar are potential spam indicators.

- T4 – The text in the body of the message contains sequences with multiple punctuation marks or capital letters.

We can implement a spam detector based on these four signs, which we will hereafter call *triggers*. The detector classifies an incoming email as spam if T1, T2, T3, and T4 are *True* simultaneously. The following example shows the pseudocode for the program:

```
IF (subject is typical for spam)
    AND IF (message uses recipients email address)
        AND IF (spelling and grammar errors)
            AND IF (multiple sequences of marks-caps) THEN
                print("It's a SPAM!")
```

It's a no-brainer that this is not the best spam filter ever built. We can predict that it blocks legitimate emails and lets some spam messages escape uncaught. We have to include more sophisticated triggers and heuristics to improve its performance in terms of both types of errors. Moreover, we need to be more specific about the cut-off thresholds for the triggers. For example, how many spelling errors (T3) and sequences (T4) make the relevant expressions in the pseudocode *True*? Is T3 an appropriate trigger in the first place? We shouldn't penalize a sender for being bad at spelling! Also, what happens when a message includes many grammar mistakes but contains few sequences with capital letters? Can we still consider it spam? To answer these questions, we need data to support any claim. After examining a large corpus of messages annotated as spam or non-spam, we can safely extract the appropriate thresholds and adapt the pseudocode.

Can you think of another criterion? What about examining the message's body and checking whether certain words appear more often? Intuitively, those words can serve as a way to separate the two types of emails. An easy way to perform this task is to visualize the body of the message using **word clouds** (also known as **tag clouds**). With this visualization technique, recurring words in the dataset (excluding articles, pronouns, and a few other cases) appear larger than infrequent ones.

One possible implementation of word clouds in Python is the word_cloud module (https://github.com/amueller/word_cloud). For example, the following code snippet presents how to load the email shown in *Figure 2.1* from the spam.txt text file (https://github.com/PacktPublishing/Machine-Learning-Techniques-for-Text/tree/main/chapter-02/data), make all words lowercase, and extract the visualization:

```
# Import the necessary modules.
import matplotlib.pyplot as plt
```

```
from wordcloud import WordCloud

# Read the text from the file spam.txt.
text = open('./data/spam.txt').read()

# Create and configure the word cloud object.
wc = WordCloud(background_color="white", max_words=2000)

# Generate the word cloud image from the text.
wordcloud = wc.generate(text.lower())

# Display the generated image.
plt.imshow(wordcloud, interpolation='bilinear')
plt.axis("off")
```

Figure 2.2 shows the output plot:

Figure 2.2 – A word cloud of the spam email

The image suggests that the most common word in our spam message is **virus** (all words are lowercase). Does the repetition of this word make us suspicious? Let's suppose yes so that we can adapt the pseudocode accordingly:

```
        . . .
        AND IF (multiple sequences of marks-caps) THEN
            AND IF (common word = "virus") THEN
                print("It's a SPAM!")
```

Is this new version of the program better? Slightly. We can engineer even more criteria, but the problem becomes insurmountable at some point. It is not realistic to find all the possible suspicious conditions and deciphering the values of all thresholds by hand becomes an unattainable goal.

Notice that techniques such as word clouds are commonplace in ML problems to explore text data before resorting to any solution. We call this process **Exploratory Data Analysis (EDA)**. EDA provides an understanding of where to direct our subsequent analysis and visualization methods are the primary tool for this task. We deal with this topic many times throughout the book.

It's time to resort to ML to overcome the previous hurdles. The idea is to train a model from a corpus with labeled examples of emails and automatically classify new ones as spam or non-spam.

Explaining feature engineering

If you were being observant, you will have spotted that the input to the pseudocode was not the actual text of the message but the information extracted from it. For example, we used the frequency of the word **virus**, the number of sequences in capital letters, and so on. These are called **features** and the process of eliciting them is called **feature engineering**. For many years, this has been the central task of ML practitioners, along with calibrating (fine-tuning) the models.

Identifying a suitable list of features for any ML task requires **domain knowledge** – comprehending the problem you want to solve in-depth. Furthermore, how you choose them directly impacts the algorithm's performance and determines its success to a significant degree. Feature engineering can be challenging, as we can overgenerate items in the list. For example, certain features can overlap with others, so including them in the subsequent analysis is redundant. On the other hand, specific features might be less relevant to the task because they do not accurately represent the underlying problem. *Table 2.1* includes a few examples of good features:

Problem	Features
Classify movie reviews as positive or negative	Count the number of times words such as good, excellent, bad, or horrible appear in a review
Separate images that contain either forests or the sea	Count the number of pixels in an image with almost green colors versus blue ones
Classify flowers into specific categories	Calculate the sepal length, sepal width, petal length, and petal width of each flower
Identify angry customers from telephone recordings	Calculate the mean amplitude of the recorded signal
Predict the value of an apartment in a specific area	Extract the size in square meters, number of rooms, floor number, and postal code of each apartment

Table 2.1 – Examples of feature engineering

Given the preceding table, the rationale for devising features for any ML problem should be clear. First, we need to identify the critical elements of the problem under study and then decide how to represent each element with a range of values. For example, the value of an apartment is related to its size in square meters, which is a real positive number.

This section provided an overview of spam detection and why attacking this problem using traditional programming techniques is suboptimal. The reason is that identifying all the necessary execution steps manually is unrealistic. Then, we debated why extracting features from data and applying ML is more promising. In this case, we provide hints (as a list of features) to the program on where to focus, but it's up to the algorithm to identify the most efficient execution steps.

The following section discusses how to extract the proper features in problems involving text such as emails, tweets, movie reviews, meeting transcriptions, or reports. The standard approach, in this case, is to use the actual words. Let's see how.

Extracting word representations

What does a word mean to a computer? What about an image or an audio file? To put it simply, nothing. A computer circuit can only process signals that contain two voltage levels or states, similar to an on-off switch. This representation is the well-known *binary system* where every quantity is expressed as a sequence of 1s (high voltage) and 0s (low voltage). For example, the number 1001 in binary is 9 in decimal (the numerical system humans employ). Computers utilize this representation to encode the pixels of an image, the samples of an audio file, a word, and much more, as illustrated in *Figure 2.3*:

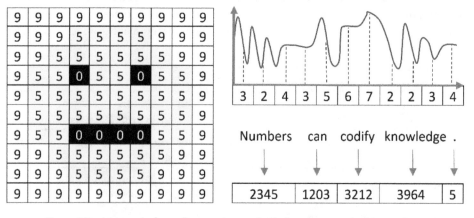

Figure 2.3 – Image pixels, audio samples, and words represented with numbers

Based on this representation, our computers can make *sense* of the data and process it the way we wish, such as by rendering an image on the screen, playing an audio track, or translating an input sentence into another language. As the book focuses on text, we will learn about the standard approaches for representing words in a piece of text data. More advanced techniques are a subject in the subsequent chapters.

Using label encoding

In ML problems, there are various ways to represent words; **label encoding** is the simplest form. For example, consider this quote from Aristotle: *a friend to all is a friend to none*. Using the label-encoding scheme and a dictionary with words to indices (*a:0, all:1, friend:2, is:3, none:4, to:5*), we can produce the mapping shown in *Table 2.2*:

Input								
a	friend	to	all	is	a	friend	to	none
0	2	5	1	3	0	2	5	4

Table 2.2 – An example of using label encoding

We observe that a numerical sequence replaces the words in the sentence. For example, the word **friend** maps to the number **2**. In Python, we can use the LabelEncoder class from the sklearn module and feed it with the quote from Aristotle:

```
from sklearn.preprocessing import LabelEncoder

# Create the label encoder and fit it with data.
labelencoder = LabelEncoder()
labelencoder.fit(["a", "all", "friend", "is", "none", "to"])

# Transform an input sentence.
x = labelencoder.transform(["a", "friend", "to", "all", "is",
"a", "friend", "to", "none"])
print(x)
>> [0 2 5 1 3 0 2 5 4]
```

The output is the same array as the one in *Table 2.2*. There is a caveat, however. When an ML algorithm uses this representation, it implicitly considers and tries to exploit some kind of order among the words, for example, a<friend<to (because 0 < 2 < 5). This order does not exist in reality. On the other hand, label encoding is appropriate if there is an ordinal association between the words. For example, the good, better, and best triplet can be encoded as 1, 2, and 3, respectively. Another example is online surveys, where we frequently use categorical variables with predefined values for each question, such as disagree=-1, neutral=0, and agree=+1. In these cases, label encoding can be more appropriate, as the associations good<better<best and disagree<neutral<agree make sense.

Using one-hot encoding

Another well-known word representation technique is **one-hot encoding**, which codifies every word as a vector with zeros and a single one. Notice that the position of the one uniquely identifies a specific word; consequently, no two words exist with the same one-hot vector. *Table 2.3* shows an example of this representation using the previous input sentence from Aristotle:

	Input								
Unique words	A	friend	to	all	is	a	friend	to	none
a	1	0	0	0	0	1	0	0	0
all	0	0	0	1	0	0	0	0	0
friend	0	1	0	0	0	0	1	0	0
is	0	0	0	0	1	0	0	0	0
none	0	0	0	0	0	0	0	0	1
to	0	0	1	0	0	0	0	1	0

Table 2.3 – An example of using one-hot encoding

Observe that the first column in the table includes all unique words. The word `friend` appears at position 3, so its one-hot vector is [0, 0, 1, 0, 0, 0]. The more unique words in a dataset, the longer the vectors are because they depend on the vocabulary size.

In the code that follows, we use the `OneHotEncoder` class from the `sklearn` module:

```
from sklearn.preprocessing import OneHotEncoder

# The input.
X = [['a'], ['friend'], ['to'], ['all'], ['is'], ['a'],
['friend'], ['to'], ['none']]

# Create the one-hot encoder.
onehotencoder = OneHotEncoder()

# Fit and transform.
enc = onehotencoder.fit_transform(X).toarray()
print(enc.T)
>> [[1. 0. 0. 0. 0. 1. 0. 0. 0.]
 [0. 0. 0. 1. 0. 0. 0. 0. 0.]
```

```
[0. 1. 0. 0. 0. 0. 1. 0. 0.]
[0. 0. 0. 0. 1. 0. 0. 0. 0.]
[0. 0. 0. 0. 0. 0. 0. 0. 1.]
[0. 0. 1. 0. 0. 0. 0. 1. 0.]]
```

Looking at the code output, can you identify a drawback to this approach? The majority of the elements in the array are zeros. As the corpus size increases, so does the vocabulary size of the unique words. Consequently, we need bigger one-hot vectors where all other elements are zero except for one. Matrixes of this kind are called **sparse** and can pose challenges due to the memory required to store them.

Next, we examine another approach that addresses both ordinal association and sparsity issues.

Using token count encoding

Token count encoding, also known as the **Bag-of-Words (BoW)** representation, counts the absolute frequency of each word within a sentence or a document. The input is represented as a *bag* of words without taking into account grammar or word order. This method uses a **Term Document Matrix (TDM)** matrix that describes the frequency of each term in the text. For example, in *Table 2.4*, we calculate the number of times a word from a minimal vocabulary of seven words appears in Aristotle's quote:

Unique words							
a	all	friend	is	me	none	to	world
2	1	2	1	0	1	2	0

Table 2.4 – An example of using token count encoding

Notice that the corresponding cell in the table contains the value **0** when no such word is present in the quote. In Python, we can convert a collection of text documents to a matrix of token counts using the CountVectorizer class from the sklearn module, as shown in the following code:

```
from sklearn.feature_extraction.text import CountVectorizer

# The input.
X = ["a friend to all is a friend to none"]

# Create the count vectorizer.
vectorizer = CountVectorizer(token_pattern='[a-zA-Z]+')

# Fit and transform.
x = vectorizer.fit_transform(X)
```

```
print(vectorizer.vocabulary_)
>> {'a': 0, 'friend': 2, 'to': 5, 'all': 1, 'is': 3, 'none': 4}
```

Next, we print the token counts for the quote:

```
print(x.toarray()[0])
>> [2 1 2 1 1 2]
```

The `CountVectorizer` class takes the token pattern argument as the input `[a-zA-Z]+`, which identifies words with lowercase or uppercase letters. Don't worry if the syntax of this pattern is not yet clear. We are going to demystify it later in the chapter. In this case, the code informs us that the word a (with id 0) appears twice, and therefore the first element in the output array `[2, 1, 2, 1, 1, 2]` is 2. Similarly, the word `none`, the fifth element of the array, appears once.

We can continue by extending the vectorizer using a property of human languages: the fact that certain word combinations are more frequent than others. We can verify this characteristic by performing Google searches of various word combinations inside double quotation marks. Each one yields a different number of search results, an indirect measure of their frequency in language.

When reading a spam email, we don't usually focus on isolated words and instead identify patterns in word sequences that trigger an alert in our brain. How can we leverage this fact in our spam detection problem? One possible answer is to use **n-grams** as tokens for `CountVectorizer`. In simple terms, n-grams illustrate word sequences, and due to their simplicity and power, they have been extensively used in **Natural Language Processing (NLP)** applications. There are different variants of n-grams depending on the number of words that we group; for a single word, they are called *unigrams*; for two words, *bigrams*, and three words *trigrams*. *Figure 2.4* presents the first three order n-grams for Aristotle's quote:

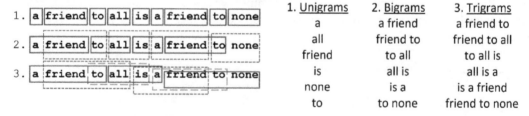

Figure 2.4 – Unigrams, bigrams, and trigrams for Aristotle's quote

We used unigrams in the previous Python code, but we can now add the `ngram_range` argument during the vectorizer construction and use bigrams instead:

```
from sklearn.feature_extraction.text import CountVectorizer


# The input.
```

```
X = ["a friend to all is a friend to none"]


# Create the count vectorizer using bi-grams.
vectorizer = CountVectorizer(ngram_range=(2,2), token_
pattern='[a-zA-Z]+')


# Fit and transform.
x = vectorizer.fit_transform(X)
print(vectorizer.vocabulary_)
>> {'a friend': 0, 'friend to': 2, 'to all': 4, 'all is': 1,
'is a': 3, 'to none': 5}
```

Next, we print the token counts for the quote:

```
print(x.toarray()[0])
>> [2 1 2 1 1 1]
```

In this case, the `friend to` bigram with an ID of 2 appears twice, so the third element in the output array is 2. For the same reason, the `to none` bigram (the last element) appears only once.

In this section, we discussed how to utilize word frequencies to encode a piece of text. Next, we will present a more sophisticated approach that uses word frequencies differently. Let's see how.

Using tf-idf encoding

One limitation of BoW representations is that they do not consider the value of words inside the corpus. For example, if solely frequency were of prime importance, articles such as *a* or *the* would provide the most information for a document. Therefore, we need a representation that *penalizes* these frequent words. The remedy is the **term frequency-inverse document frequency (tf-idf)** encoding scheme that allows us to weigh each word in the text. You can consider tf-idf as a heuristic where more common words tend to be less relevant for most semantic classification tasks, and the weighting reflects this approach.

From a virtual dataset with 10 million emails, we randomly pick one containing 100 words. Suppose that the word *virus* appears three times in this email, so its **term frequency (tf)** is $\frac{3}{100}$ = 0.03. Moreover, the same word appears in 1,000 emails in the corpus, so the **inverse document frequency (idf)** is equal to $\log(\frac{10000000}{1000})$ = 4. The tf-idf weight is simply the product of these two statistics: $0.03 \cdot 4 = 0.12$. We reach a high tf-idf weight when we have a high frequency of the term in the random email and a low document frequency of the same term in the whole dataset. Generally, we calculate tf-idf weights with the following formula:

$$w_{i,j} = tf_{i,j} \cdot \log(\frac{N}{df_i})$$

Where:

- $w_{i,j}$ = *Weight of word i in document j*
- $tf_{i,j}$ = *Frequency of word i in document j*
- N = *Total number of documents*
- df_i = *Number of documents containing word i*

Performing the same calculations in Python is straightforward. In the following code, we use `TfidfVectorizer` from the `sklearn` module and a dummy corpus with four short sentences:

```python
from sklearn.feature_extraction.text import TfidfVectorizer

# Create a dummy corpus.
corpus = [
        'We need to meet tomorrow at the cafeteria.',
        'Meet me tomorrow at the cafeteria.',
        'You have inherited millions of dollars.',
        'Millions of dollars just for you.']

# Create the tf-idf vectorizer.
vectorizer = TfidfVectorizer()

# Generate the tf-idf matrix.
tfidf = vectorizer.fit_transform(corpus)
```

Next, we print the result as an array:

```python
print(tfidf.toarray())
>> [[0.319  0.319    0.         0.        0.         0.
   0.        0.        0.319     0.        0.404     0.
   0.319     0.404    0.319     0.404     0.]
  [0.388     0.388    0.         0.        0.         0.
   0.        0.493    0.388     0.        0.         0.
   0.388     0.        0.388     0.        0.]
  [0.        0.        0.372     0.        0.472     0.472
   0.        0.        0.        0.372     0.         0.372
   0.        0.        0.         0.       0.372]
  [0.        0.        0.372     0.472    0.         0.
```

```
 0.472        0.          0.         0.372      0.        0.372
 0.           0.          0.         0.         0.372]]
```

What does this output tell us? Each of the four sentences is encoded with one tf-idf vector of 17 elements (this is the number of unique words in the corpus). Non-zero values show the tf-idf weight for a word in the sentence, whereas a value equal to zero signifies the absence of the specific word. If we could somehow compare the tf-idf vectors of the examples, we can tell which pair resembles more. Undoubtedly, `'You have inherited millions of dollars.'` is *closer* to `'Millions of dollars just for you.'` than the other two sentences. Can you perhaps guess where this discussion is heading? By calculating an array of weights for all the words in an email, we can compare it with the reference arrays of spam or non-spam and classify it accordingly. The following section will tell us how.

Calculating vector similarity

Mathematically, there are different ways to calculate vector resemblances, such as **cosine similarity** (**cs**) or **Euclidean distance**. Specifically, cs is the degree to which two vectors point in the same direction, targeting orientation rather than magnitude (see *Figure 2.5*).

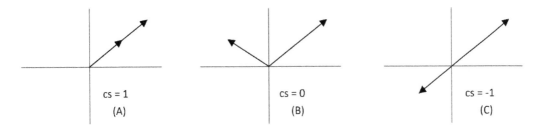

Figure 2.5 – Three cases of cosine similarity

When the two vectors point in the same direction, the cs equals 1 (in **A** in *Figure 2.5*); when they are perpendicular, it is 0 (in **B** in *Figure 2.5*), and when they point in opposite directions, it is -1 (in **C** in *Figure 2.5*). Notice that only values between 0 to 1 are valid in NLP applications since the term frequencies cannot be negative.

Consider now an example where A, B, and C are vectors with three elements each, so that A = (4, 4, 4), B = (1, 7, 5), and C = (-5, 5, 1). You can think of each number in the vector as a coordinate in an *xyz-space*. Looking at *Figure 2.6*, **A** and **B** seem more similar than **C**. Do you agree?

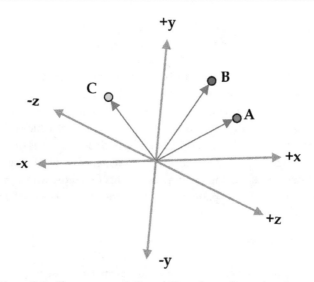

Figure 2.6 – Three vectors A, B, and C in a three-dimensional space

We calculate the *dot product* (signified with the symbol •) between two vectors of the same size by multiplying their elements in the same position. $V = (v_1, v_2, v_3)$ and $U = (u_1, u_2, u_3)$ are two vectors, so their dot product is $V \bullet U = v_1 \cdot u_1 + v_2 \cdot u_2 + v_3 \cdot u_3$ In our example, $A \bullet B = 4 \cdot 1 + 4 \cdot 7 + 4 \cdot 5 = 52$, $A \bullet C = 4 \cdot (-5) + 4 \cdot 5 + 4 \cdot 1 = 4$ and $B \bullet C = 1 \cdot (-5) + 7 \cdot 5 + 5 \cdot 1 = 35$ Additionally, the *magnitude* of the vector V is defined as $\|V\| = \sqrt{v_1^2 + v_2^2 + v_3^2}$ and in our case, $\|A\| = \sqrt{4^2 + 4^2 + 4^2} = \sqrt{48}$, $\|B\| = \sqrt{75}$, and $\|C\| = \sqrt{51}$.

Therefore, we obtain the following:

$$\cos(A, B) = \frac{52}{\sqrt{48} \times \sqrt{75}} \approx 0.87, \cos(A, C) = \frac{4}{\sqrt{48} \times \sqrt{51}} \approx 0.08, \text{ and } \cos(B, C) = \frac{35}{\sqrt{75} \times \sqrt{51}} \approx 0.57.$$

The results confirm our first hypothesis that A and B are more similar than C.

In the following code, we calculate the cs of the tf-idf vectors between the corpus's first and second examples:

```
from sklearn.metrics.pairwise import cosine_similarity

# Convert the matrix to an array.
tfidf_array = tfidf.toarray()
```

```
# Calculate the cosine similarity between the first amd second
example.
print(cosine_similarity([tfidf_array[0]], [tfidf_array[1]]))
>> [[0.62046087]]
```

We also repeat the same calculation between all tf-idf vectors:

```
# Calculate the cosine similarity among all examples.
print(cosine_similarity(tfidf_array))
>> [[1.          0.62046     0.          0.          ]
   [0.62046     1.          0.          0.          ]
   [0.          0.          1.          0.5542      ]
   [0.          0.          0.5542      1.          ]]
```

As expected, the value between the first and second examples is high and equal to 0.62. Between the first and the third example, it is 0, 0.55 between the third and the fourth, and so on.

Exploring tf-idf has concluded our discussion on the standard approaches for representing text data. The importance of this step should be evident, as it relates to the machine's ability to create models that better understand textual input. Failing to get good representations of the underlying data typically leads to suboptimal results in the later phases of analysis. We will also encounter a powerful representation technique for text data in *Chapter 3, Classifying Topics of Newsgroup Posts*.

In the next section, we will go a step further and discuss different techniques of preprocessing data that can boost the performance of ML algorithms.

Executing data preprocessing

During the tf-idf discussion, we mentioned that articles often do not help convey the critical information in a document. What about words such as *but, for,* or *by*? Indeed, they are ubiquitous in English texts but probably not very useful for our task. This section focuses on four techniques that help us remove *noise* from the data and reduce the problem's complexity. These techniques constitute an integral part of the **data preprocessing** phase, which is crucial before applying more sophisticated methods to the text data. The first technique involves splitting an input text into meaningful chunks, while the second teaches us how to remove low informational value words from the text—the last two focus on mapping each word to a root form.

Tokenizing the input

So far, we have used the term *token* with the implicit assumption that it always refers to a word (or an n-gram) independently of the underlying NLP task. **Tokenization** is a more general process where we split textual data into smaller components called *tokens*. These can be words, phrases, symbols, or other meaningful elements. We perform this task using the `nltk` toolkit and the `word_tokenize` method in the following code:

```
# Import the toolkit.
import nltk
nltk.download('punkt')


# Tokenize the input text.
wordTokens = nltk.word_tokenize("a friend to all is a friend to
none")

print(wordTokens)
>> ['a', 'friend', 'to', 'all', 'is', 'a', 'friend', 'to',
'none']
```

As words are the tokens of a sentence, sentences are the tokens of a paragraph. For the latter, we can use another method in `nltk` called `sent_tokenize` and tokenize a paragraph with three sentences:

```
# Tokenize the input paragraph.
sentenceTokens = nltk.sent_tokenize("A friend to all is a
friend to none.
A friend to none is a friend to all. A friend is a friend.")

print(sentenceTokens)
>> ['A friend to all is a friend to none.', 'A friend to none
is a friend to all.', 'A friend is a friend.']
```

This method uses the full stop as a **delimiter** (as in, a character to separate the text strings) and the output in our example is a list with three elements. Notice that using the full stop as a delimiter is not always the best solution. For example, the text can contain abbreviations; thus, more sophisticated solutions are required to compensate for this situation.

In the *Using token count encoding* section, we saw how `CountVectorizer` used a pattern to split the input into multiple tokens and promised to demystify its syntax later in the chapter. So, it's time to introduce **regular expressions** (**regexp**) that can assist with the creation of a tokenizer. These expressions are used to find a string in a document, replace part of the text with something else, or examine the conformity of some textual input. We can improvise very sophisticated matching patterns and mastering this skill demands time and effort. Recall that the unstructured nature of text data means that it requires preprocessing before it can be used for analysis, so regexp are a powerful tool for this task. The following table shows a few typical examples:

regexp	matches
[A-Za-z0-9]	Any character, letter, or digit, in the range A to Z, a to z, or 0 to 9 – for example, G.
[A-Za-z0-9]+	Any sequence of characters, letters, or digits, in the range A to Z, a to z, or 0 to 9. The plus sign signifies at least one occurrence – for example, Hello2You.
[a-z]{2,5}	Any sequence of lowercase letters containing two to five characters – for example, hello.
^([0-9][a-z]+)	Any sequence of characters beginning with a number and followed by lowercase letters – for example, 4ever.
([A-Z]+[0-9])$	Any sequence of characters with uppercase letters that ends with a number – for example, ME2.

Table 2.5 – Various examples of regular expressions

A pattern using square brackets (*[]*) matches character ranges. For example, the [A-Z] regexp matches Q because it is part of the range of capital letters from A to Z. Conversely, the same lowercase character is not matched. Quantifiers inside curly braces match repetitions of patterns. In this case, the [A-Z] {3} regexp matches a sequence of BCD. The ^ and $ characters match a pattern at the beginning and end of a sentence, respectively. For example, the ^[0-9] regexp matches a 4ever string, as it starts with the number four. The + symbol matches one or more repetitions of the pattern, while * matches zero or more repetitions. A dot, ., is a wildcard for any character.

We can go a step further and analyze a more challenging regexp. Most of us have already used web forms that request an email address input. When the provided email is not valid, an error message is displayed. How does the web form recognize this problem? Obviously, by using a regexp! The general format of an email address contains a *local-part*, followed by an @ symbol, and then by a *domain* – for example, local-part@domain. *Figure 2.7* analyzes a regexp that can match this format:

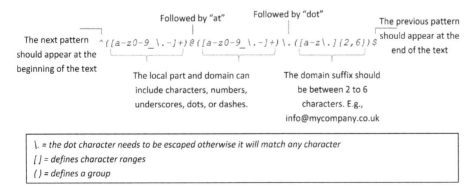

Figure 2.7 – A regexp for checking the validity of an email address

This expression might seem overwhelming and challenging to understand, but things become apparent if you examine each part separately. Escaping the dot character is necessary to remove its special meaning in the context of a regexp and ensure that it is used literally. Specifically, ., a regexp, matches *any word*, whereas \. matches only a *full stop*.

To set things into action, we tokenize a valid and an invalid email address using the regexp from *Figure 2.7*:

```
# Create the Regexp tokenizer.
tokenizer = nltk.tokenize.
RegexpTokenizer(pattern='^([a-z0-9_\.-]+)@([a-z0-9_\.-]+)\.([a-
z\.]{2,6})$')

# Tokenize a valid email address.
tokens = tokenizer.tokenize("john@doe.com")

print(tokens)
>> [('john', 'doe', 'com')]
```

The output tokens for the invalid email are as follows:

```
# Tokenize a non-valid email address.
tokens = tokenizer.tokenize("john-AT-doe.com")
print(tokens)
>> []
```

In the first case, the input, john@doe.com, is parsed as expected, as the address's local-part, domain, and suffix are provided. Conversely, the second input does not comply with the pattern (it misses the @ symbol), and consequently, nothing is printed in the output.

There are many other situations where we need to craft particular regexps for identifying patterns in a document, such as HTML tags, URLs, telephone numbers, and punctuation marks. However, that's the scope of another book!

Removing stop words

A typical task during the preprocessing phase is removing all the words that presumably help us focus on the most important information in the text. These are called **stop words** and there is no universal list in English or any other language. Examples of stop words include determiners (such as another and the), conjunctions (such as but and or), and prepositions (such as before and in). Many online sources are available that provide lists of stop words and it's not uncommon to adapt their content according to the problem under study. In the following example, we remove all the stop words from a spam text using a built-in set from a `wordcloud` module named `STOPWORDS`. We also include three more words in the set to demonstrate its functionality:

```
from wordcloud import WordCloud, STOPWORDS

# Read the text from the file data.txt.
text = open('./data/spam.txt').read()

# Get all stopwords and update with few others.
sw = set(STOPWORDS)
sw.update(["dear", "virus", "mr"])

# Create and configure the word cloud object.
wc = WordCloud(background_color="white", stopwords=sw, max_
words=2000)
```

Next, we generate the word cloud plot:

```
# Generate the word cloud image from the text.
wordcloud = wc.generate(text.lower())

# Display the generated image.
plt.imshow(wordcloud, interpolation='bilinear')
plt.axis("off")
```

The output is illustrated in *Figure 2.8*:

Figure 2.8 – A word cloud of the spam email after removing the stop words

Take a moment to compare it with the one in *Figure 2.2*. For example, the word **virus** is missing in the new version, as this word was part of the list of stop words.

The following section will cover another typical step of the preprocessing phase.

Stemming the words

Removing stop words is, in essence, a way to extract the *juice* out of the corpus. But we can squeeze the lemon even more! Undoubtedly, every different word form encapsulates a special meaning that adds richness and linguistic diversity to a language. These variances, however, result in data redundancy that can lead to ineffective ML models. In many practical applications, we can map words with the same core meaning to a central word or symbol and thus reduce the input dimension for the model. This reduction can be beneficial to the performance of the ML or NLP application.

This section introduces a technique called **stemming** that maps a word to its root form. Stemming is the process of cutting off the end (suffix) or the beginning (prefix) of an inflected word and ending up with its stem (the root word). So, for example, the stem of the word `plays` is `play`. The most common algorithm in English for performing stemming is the **Porter stemmer**, which consists of five sets of rules (`https://tartarus.org/martin/PorterStemmer/`) applied sequentially to the word. For example, one rule is to *remove the "-ed" suffix from a word to obtain its stem only if the remainder contains at least one vowel*. Based on this rule, the stem of `played` is `play`, but the stem for `led` is still `led`.

Using the `PorterStemmer` class from `nltk` in the following example, we observe that all three forms of `play` have the same stem:

```
# Import the Porter stemmer.
from nltk.stem import PorterStemmer


# Create the stemmer.
stemmer = PorterStemmer()


# Stem the words 'playing', 'plays', 'played'.
stemmer.stem('playing')
>> 'play'
```

Let's take the next word:

```
stemmer.stem('plays')
>> 'play'
```

Now, check `played`:

```
stemmer.stem('played')
>> 'play'
```

Notice that the output of stemming doesn't need to be a valid word:

```
# Stem the word 'bravery'
stemmer.stem('bravery')
>> 'braveri'
```

We can even create our stemmer using regexps and the `RegexpStemmer` class from `nltk`. In the following example, we search for words with the ed suffix:

```
# Import the Porter stemmer
from nltk.stem import RegexpStemmer

# Create the stemmer matching words ending with 'ed'.
stemmer = RegexpStemmer('ed')

# Stem the verbs 'playing', 'plays', 'played'.
stemmer.stem('playing')
>> 'playing'
```

Let's check the next word:

```
stemmer.stem('plays')
>> 'plays'
```

Now, take another word:

```
stemmer.stem('played')
>> 'play'
```

The regexp in the preceding code matches `played`; therefore, the stemmer outputs `play`. The two other words remain unmatched, and for that reason, no stemming is applied. The following section introduces a more powerful technique to achieve similar functionality.

Lemmatizing the words

Lemmatization is another sophisticated approach for reducing the inflectional forms of a word to a base root. The method performs morphological analysis of the word and obtains its proper lemma (the base form under which it appears in a dictionary). For example, the lemma of *goes* is *go*. Lemmatization differs from stemming, as it requires detailed dictionaries to look up a word. For this reason, it's slower but more accurate than stemming and more complex to implement.

WordNet (https://wordnet.princeton.edu/) is a lexical database for the English language created by Princeton University and is part of the nltk corpus. Superficially, it resembles a thesaurus in that it groups words based on their meanings. WordNet is one way to use lemmatization inside nltk. In the example that follows, we extract the lemmas of three English words:

```
# Import the WordNet Lemmatizer.
from nltk.stem import WordNetLemmatizer
nltk.download('wordnet')
nltk.download('omw-1.4')


# Create the lemmatizer.
lemmatizer = WordNetLemmatizer()


# Lemmatize the verb 'played'.
lemmatizer.lemmatize('played', pos='v')
>> 'play'
```

Observe that the lemma for played is the same as its stem, play. On the other hand, the lemma and stem differ for led (lead versus led, respectively):

```
# Lemmatize the verb 'led'.
lemmatizer.lemmatize('led', pos='v')
>> 'lead'
```

There are also situations where the same lemma corresponds to words with different stems. The following code shows an example of this case where good and better have the same lemma but not the same stem:

```
# Lemmatize the adjective 'better'.
lemmatizer.lemmatize('better', pos='a')
>> 'good'
```

The differences between lemmatization and stemming should be apparent from the previous examples. Remember that we use either method on a given dataset and not both simultaneously.

The focus of this section has been on four typical techniques for preprocessing text data. In the case of word representations, the way we apply this step impacts the model's performance. In many similar situations, identifying which technique works better is a matter of experimentation. The following section presents how to implement classifiers using an open source corpus for spam detection.

Performing classification

Up until this point, we have learned how to represent and preprocess text data. It's time to make use of this knowledge and create the spam classifier. First, we put all the pieces together using a publicly available corpus. Before we proceed to the training of the classifier, we need to follow a series of typical steps that include the following:

1. Getting the data
2. Splitting it into a training and test set
3. Preprocessing its content
4. Extracting the features

Let's examine each step one by one.

Getting the data

The *SpamAssassin* public mail corpus (`https://spamassassin.apache.org/old/publiccorpus/`) is a selection of email messages suitable for developing spam filtering systems. It offers two variants for the messages, either in plain text or HTML formatting. For simplicity, we will use only the first type in this exercise. Parsing HTML text requires special handling – for example, implementing your own regexps! The term coined to describe the opposite of spam emails is *ham* since the two words are related to meat products (spam refers to canned ham). The dataset contains various examples divided into different folders according to their complexity. This exercise uses the files within these two folders: spam_2 (`https://github.com/PacktPublishing/Machine-Learning-Techniques-for-Text/tree/main/chapter-02/data/20050311_spam_2/spam_2`) for spam and hard_ham (`https://github.com/PacktPublishing/Machine-Learning-Techniques-for-Text/tree/main/chapter-02/data/20030228_hard_ham/hard_ham`) for ham.

Creating the train and test sets

Initially, we read the messages for the two categories (ham and spam) and split them into training and testing groups. As a rule of thumb, we can choose a 75:25 (https://en.wikipedia.org/wiki/Pareto_principle) split between the two sets, attributing a more significant proportion to the training data. Note that other ratios might be preferable depending on the size of the dataset. Especially for massive corpora (with millions of labeled instances), we can create test sets with just 1% of the data, which is still a significant number. To clarify this process, we divide the code into the following steps:

1. First, we load the ham and spam datasets using the `train_test_split` method. This method controls the size of the training and test sets for each case and the samples that they include:

```
import email
import glob
import numpy as np
from operator import is_not
from functools import partial
from sklearn.model_selection import train_test_split


# Load the path for each email file for both categories.
ham_files = train_test_split(glob.glob('./data/20030228_
hard_ham/hard_ham/*'), random_state=123)
spam_files = train_test_split(glob.glob('./data/20050311_
spam_2/spam_2/*'), random_state=123)
```

2. Next, we read the content of each email and keep the ones without HTML formatting:

```
# Method for getting the content of an email.
def get_content(filepath):
    file = open(filepath, encoding='latin1')
    message = email.message_from_file(file)


    for msg_part in message.walk():
        # Keep only messages with text/plain content.
        if msg_part.get_content_type() == 'text/plain':
            return msg_part.get_payload()


# Get the training and testing data.
ham_train_data = [get_content(i) for i in ham_files[0]]
```

```
ham_test_data = [get_content(i) for i in ham_files[1]]
spam_train_data = [get_content(i) for i in spam_files[0]]
spam_test_data = [get_content(i) for i in spam_files[1]]
```

3. For our analysis, we exclude emails with empty content. The `filter` method with `None` as the first argument removes any element that includes an empty string. Then, the filtered output is used to construct a new list using `list`:

```
# Keep emails with non-empty content.
ham_train_data = list(filter(None, ham_train_data))
ham_test_data = list(filter(None, ham_test_data))
spam_train_data = list(filter(None, spam_train_data))
spam_test_data = list(filter(None, spam_test_data))
```

4. Now, let's merge the spam and ham training sets into one (do the same for their test sets):

```
# Merge the train/test files for both categories.
train_data = np.concatenate((ham_train_data, spam_train_data))
test_data = np.concatenate((ham_test_data, spam_test_data))
```

5. Finally, we assign a class label for each of the two categories (ham and spam) and merge them into common training and test sets:

```
# Assign a class for each email (ham = 0, spam = 1).
ham_train_class = [0]*len(ham_train_data)
ham_test_class = [0]*len(ham_test_data)
spam_train_class = [1]*len(spam_train_data)
spam_test_class = [1]*len(spam_test_data)

# Merge the train/test classes for both categories.
train_class = np.concatenate((ham_train_class, spam_train_class))
test_class = np.concatenate((ham_test_class, spam_test_class))
```

Notice that in *step 1*, we also pass `random_state` in the `train_test_split` method to make all subsequent results reproducible. Otherwise, the method performs a different data shuffling in each run and produces random splits for the sets.

In this section, we have learned how to read text data from a set of files and keep the information that makes sense for the problem under study. After this point, the datasets are suitable for the next processing phase.

Preprocessing the data

It's about time to use the typical data preprocessing techniques that we learned earlier. These include tokenization, stop word removal, and lemmatization. Let's examine the steps one by one:

1. First, let's tokenize the train or test data:

```
from nltk.stem import WordNetLemmatizer
from nltk.tokenize import word_tokenize
from sklearn.feature_extraction.text import ENGLISH_STOP_
WORDS

# Tokenize the train/test data.
train_data = [word_tokenize(i) for i in train_data]
test_data = [word_tokenize(i) for i in test_data]
```

2. Next, we remove the stop words by iterating over the input examples:

```
# Method for removing the stop words.
def remove_stop_words(input):
    result = [i for i in input if i not in ENGLISH_STOP_
WORDS]
    return result

# Remove the stop words.
train_data = [remove_stop_words(i) for i in train_data]
test_data = [remove_stop_words(i) for i in test_data]
```

3. Now, we create the lemmatizer and apply it to the words:

```
# Create the lemmatizer.
lemmatizer = WordNetLemmatizer()

# Method for lemmatizing the text.
def lemmatize_text(input):
    return [lemmatizer.lemmatize(i) for i in input]
```

```
# Lemmatize the text.
train_data = [lemmatize_text(i) for i in train_data]
test_data = [lemmatize_text(i) for i in test_data]
```

4. Finally, we reconstruct the data in the two sets by joining the words separated by a space and return the concatenated string:

```
# Reconstruct the data.
train_data = [" ".join(i) for i in train_data]
test_data = [" ".join(i) for i in test_data]
```

As a result, we have at our disposal two Python lists, namely `train_data` and `test_data`, containing the initial text data in a processed form suitable for proceeding to the next phase.

Extracting the features

We continue with the extraction of the features of each sentence in the previously created datasets. This step uses tf-idf vectorization after training the vectorizer with the training data. There is a problem though, as the vocabulary in the training and test sets might differ. In this case, the vectorizer ignores unknown words, and depending on the mismatch level, we might get suboptimal representations for the test set. Hopefully, as more data is added to any corpus, the mismatch becomes smaller, so ignoring a few words has a negligible practical impact. An obvious question is – why not train the vectorizer with the whole corpus before the split? However, this engenders the risk of getting performance measures that are too optimistic later in the pipeline, as the model has *seen* the test data at some point. As a rule of thumb, always keep the test set separate and only use it to evaluate the model.

In the code that follows, we vectorize the data in both the training and test sets using tf-idf:

```
from sklearn.feature_extraction.text import TfidfVectorizer

# Create the vectorizer.
vectorizer = TfidfVectorizer()

# Fit with the train data.
vectorizer.fit(train_data)

# Transform the test/train data into features.
train_data_features = vectorizer.transform(train_data)
test_data_features = vectorizer.transform(test_data)
```

Now, the training and test sets are transformed from sequences of words to numerical vectors. From this point on, we can apply any sophisticated algorithm we wish, and guess what? This is what we are going to do in the following section!

Introducing the Support Vector Machines algorithm

It's about time that we train the first classification model. One of the most well-known supervised learning algorithms is the **Support Vector Machines** (**SVM**) algorithm. We could dedicate a whole book to demystifying this family of methods, so we will visit a few key elements in this section. First, recall from *Chapter 1*, *Introducing Machine Learning for Text*, that any ML algorithm creates decision boundaries to classify new data correctly. As we cannot sketch high-dimensional spaces, we will consider a two-dimensional example. Hopefully, this provides some of the intuition behind the algorithm.

Figure 2.9 shows the data points for the spam and ham instances along with two features, namely x_1 and x_2:

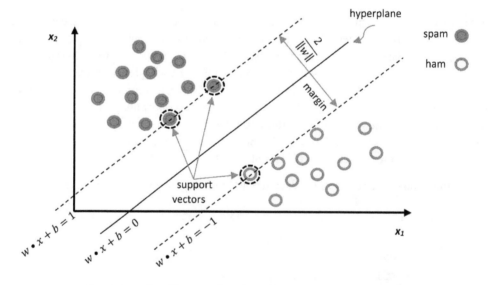

Figure 2.9 – Classification of spam and ham emails using the SVM

The line in the middle separates the two classes and the dotted lines represent the borders of the margin. The SVM has a twofold aim to find the optimal separation line (a one-dimensional hyperplane) while maximizing the margin. Generally, for an n-dimensional space, the hyperplane has (n-1) dimensions. Let's examine our space size in the code that follows:

```
print(train_data_features.shape)
>> (670, 28337)
```

Each of the 670 emails in the training set is represented by a feature vector with a size of 28337 (the number of unique words in the corpus). In this sparse vector, the non-zero values signify the tf-idf weights for the words. For the SVM, the feature vector is a point in a 28,337-dimensional space, and the problem is to find a 28,336-dimensional hyperplane to separate those points. One crucial consideration within the SVM is that not all the data points contribute equally to finding the optimal hyperplane, but mostly those close to the margin boundaries (depicted with a dotted circle in *Figure 2.9*). These are called **support vectors**, and if they are removed, the position of the dividing hyperplane alters. For this reason, we consider them the critical part of the dataset.

The general equation of a line in two-dimensional space is expressed with the formula $y = a \cdot x + b$. Three examples are shown in *Figure 2.10*:

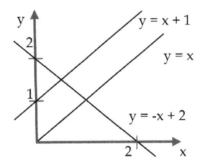

Figure 2.10 – Examples of line equations

In the same sense, the middle line in *Figure 2.9* and the two margin boundaries have the following equations, respectively:

$$a \cdot x_1 - x_2 + b = 0, \ a \cdot x_1 - x_2 + b = 1 \text{ and } a \cdot x_1 - x_2 + b = -1$$

Defining the vectors $x = (x_1, x_2)$ and $w = (a, -1)$, we can rewrite the previous equations using the *dot product* that we encountered in the *Calculating vector similarity* section:

$$w \bullet x + b = 0, \ w \bullet x + b = 1, \text{ and } w \bullet x + b = -1$$

To find the best hyperplane, we need to estimate w and b, referred to as the **weight** and **bias** in ML terminology. Among the infinite number of lines that separate the two classes, we need to find the one that maximizes the margin, the distance between the closest data points of the two classes. In general, the distance between two parallel lines $Ax + By + C_1 = 0$ and $Ax + By + C_2 = 0$ is equal to the following:

$$\frac{|C_1 - C_2|}{\sqrt{A^2 + B^2}}$$

So, the distance between the two margin boundaries is the following:

$$\frac{|(b - 1) - (b + 1)|}{\sqrt{a^2 + (-1)^2}} = \frac{2}{\|w\|}$$

To maximize the previous equation, we need to minimize the denominator, namely the quantity $\|w\|$ that represents the **Euclidean norm** of vector w. The technique for finding w and b is beyond the scope of this book, but we need to define and solve a function that penalizes any misclassified examples within the margin. After this point, we can classify a new example, x', based on the following model (the *sign* function takes any number as input and returns +1 if it is positive or -1 if it is negative):

$$f(x') = sign(w \bullet x' + b) = \begin{cases} +1, & (spam) \\ -1, & (ham) \end{cases}$$

The example we are considering in *Figure 2.9* represents an ideal situation. The data points are arranged in the two-dimensional space in such a way that makes them linearly separable. However, this is often not the case, and the SVM incorporates **kernel functions** to cope with nonlinear classification. Describing the mechanics of these functions further is beyond the scope of the current book. Notice that different kernel functions are available, and as in all ML problems, we have to experiment to find the most efficient option in any case. But before using the algorithm, we have to consider two important issues to understand the SVM algorithm better.

Adjusting the hyperparameters

Suppose two decision boundaries (straight lines) can separate the data in *Figure 2.11*.

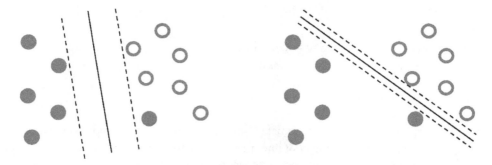

Figure 2.11 – Two possible decision boundaries for the data points using the SVM

Which one of those boundaries do you think works better? The answer, as in most similar questions, is that it depends! For example, the line in the left plot has a higher classification error, as one opaque dot resides on the wrong side. On the other hand, the margin in the right plot (distance between the dotted lines) is small, and therefore the model lacks generalization. In most cases, we can tolerate a small number of misclassifications during SVM training in favor of a hyperplane with a significant margin. This technique is called **soft margin classification** and allows some samples to be on the wrong side of the margin.

The SVM algorithm permits the adjustment of the training accuracy versus generalization tradeoff using the hyperparameter C. A frequent point of confusion is that **hyperparameters** and model parameters are the same things, but this is not true. Hyperparameters are parameters whose values are used to control the learning process. On the other hand, model parameters update their value in every training iteration until we obtain a good classification model. We can direct the SVM to create the most efficient model for each problem by adjusting the hyperparameter C. The left plot of *Figure 2.11* is related to a lower C value compared to the one on the right.

Let's look at another dataset for which two possible decision boundaries exist (*Figure 2.12*). Which one seems to work better this time?

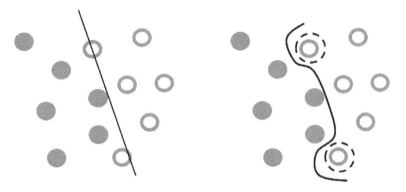

Figure 2.12 – Generalization (left) versus overfitting (right)

At first glance, the curved line in the plot on the right perfectly separates the data into two classes. But there is a problem. Getting too specific boundaries entails the risk of **overfitting**, where your model learns the training data perfectly but fails to classify a slightly different example correctly.

Consider the following real-world analogy of overfitting. Most of us have grown in a certain cultural context, trained (overfitted) to interpret social signals such as body posture, facial expressions, or voice tone in a certain way. As a result, when socializing with people of diverse backgrounds, we might fail to interpret similar social signals correctly (generalization).

Besides the hyperparameter C that can prevent overfitting, we can combine it with *gamma*, which defines how far the influence of a single training example reaches. In this way, the curvature of the decision boundary can also be affected by points that are pretty far from it. Low *gamma* values signify far reach of the influence, while high values cause the opposite effect. For example, in *Figure 2.12* (right), the points inside a dotted circle have more weight, causing the line's intense curvature around them. In this case, the hyperparameter *gamma* has a higher value than the left plot.

The takeaway here is that both *C* and *gamma* hyperparameters help us create more efficient models but identifying their best values demands experimentation. Equipped with the basic theoretical foundation, we are ready to incorporate the algorithm!

Putting the SVM into action

In the following Python code, we use a specific implementation of the SVM algorithm, the **C-Support Vector Classification**. By default, it uses the **Radial Basis Function (RBF)** kernel:

```
from sklearn import svm


# Create the classifier.
svm_classifier = svm.SVC(kernel="rbf", C=1.0, gamma=1.0,
probability=True)


# Fit the classifier with the train data.
svm_classifier.fit(train_data_features.toarray(), train_class)


# Get the classification score of the train data.
svm_classifier.score(train_data_features.toarray(), train_
class)
>> 0.9970149253731343
```

Now, use the test set:

```
# Get the classification score of the test data.
svm_classifier.score(test_data_features.toarray(), test_class)
>> 0.8755760368663594
```

Observe the classifier's argument list, including the kernel and the two hyperparameters, *gamma* and *C*. Then, we evaluate its performance for both the training and test sets. We are primarily interested in the second result, as it quantifies the accuracy of our model on unseen data – essentially, how well it generalizes. On the other hand, the performance on the training set indicates how well our model has learned from the training data. In the first case, the accuracy is almost 100%, whereas, for unseen data, it is around 88%.

Equipped with the necessary understanding, you can rerun the preceding code and experiment with different values for the hyperparameters; typically, $0.1 < C < 100$ and $0.0001 < gamma < 10$. In the following section, we present another classification algorithm based on a fundamental theorem in ML.

Understanding Bayes' theorem

Imagine a pool of 100 shapes (including squares, triangles, circles, and rhombuses). These can have either an opaque or a transparent fill. If you pick a circle shape from the pool, what is the probability of it having a transparent fill? Looking at *Figure 2.13*, we are interested to know which shapes in set **A** (circles) are also members of set **B** (all transparent shapes):

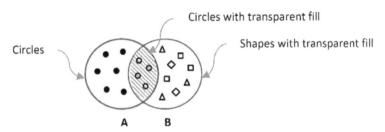

Figure 2.13 – The intersection of the set with circles with the set of all transparent shapes

The intersection of the two sets is highlighted with the grid texture and mathematically written as A∩B or B∩A. Then, we construct *Table 2.6*, which helps us perform some interesting calculations:

	Opaque fill	Transparent fill	#count
Circle	10	30	40
Not circle	20	40	60
#count	30	70	100

Table 2.6 – The number of shapes by type and fill

First, notice that the total number of items in the table equals 100 (the number of shapes). We can then calculate the following quantities:

- The probability of getting a circle is $P(circle) = \dfrac{10 + 30}{100} = 40\%$
- The probability of getting a transparent fill is $P(transparent) = \dfrac{30 + 40}{100} = 70\%$
- The probability of getting a transparent fill when the shape is a circle is

  $P(transparent|circle) = \dfrac{30}{10 + 30} = 75\%$
- The probability of getting a circle when the fill is transparent is

  $P(circle|transparent) = \dfrac{30}{30 + 40} = 43\%$

The symbol | signifies **conditional probability**. Based on these numbers, we can identify a relationship between the probabilities:

$$P(transparent|circle)P(circle) = P(circle|transparent)P(transparent)$$

The previous equation suggests that if the probability *P(transparent|circle)* is unknown, we can use the others to calculate it. We can also generalize the equation as follows:

$$P(A|B)P(B) = P(A \cap B) = P(B \cap A) = P(B|A)P(A)$$

Exploring the different elements, we reach the famous formula known as **Bayes' theorem**, which is fundamental in information theory and ML:

$$P(A|B) = \frac{P(B|A)P(A)}{P(B)}$$

The exercise in *Table 2.6* was just an example to introduce the fundamental reasoning behind the theorem; all quantities are available to calculate the corresponding probabilities. However, this is not the case in most practical problems, and this is where Bayes' comes in handy. For example, consider the following situation: you are concerned that you have a severe illness and decide to go to the hospital for a test. Sadly, the test is positive. According to your doctor, the test has 99% reliability; for 99 out of 100 sick people, the test is positive, and for 99 out of 100 healthy people, the test is negative. So, what is the probability of you having the disease? Most people logically answer 99%, but this is not true. The Bayesian reasoning tells us why.

We have a population of 10,000 people, and according to statistics, 1% (so, 100 people) of this population has the illness. Therefore, based on a 99% reliability, this is what we know:

- Of the 100 sick subjects, 99 times (99%), the test is positive, and 1 is negative (1% and therefore wrong).

- Of the 9,900 healthy subjects, 99 times (1%), the test is positive, and 9,801 is negative (99% and therefore correct).

As before, we construct *Table 2.7*, which helps us with the calculations:

	sick	healthy	
positive test	99	99	198
negative test	1	9801	9802
	100	9900	10000

Table 2.7 – The number of people by health condition and test outcome

At first glance, the numbers suggest that there is a non-negligible likelihood that you are healthy and that the test is wrong ($99/10000{\approx}1\%$). Next, we are looking for the probability of being sick given a positive test. So, let's see the following:

$$P(sick|positive\ test) = \frac{P(positive\ test|sick)P(sick)}{P(positive\ test)} = \frac{\frac{99}{100} \times 0.01}{\frac{198}{10000}} = 0.5 = 50\%$$

This percentage is much smaller than the 99% initially suggested by most people. What is the catch here? The probability *P(sick)* in the equation is not something we know exactly, as in the case of the shapes in the previous example. It's merely our best estimate on the problem, which is called **prior probability**. The knowledge we have before delving into the problem is the hardest part of the equation to figure out.

Conversely, the probability *P(sick|positive test)* represents our knowledge after solving the problem, which is called **posterior probability**. If, for example, you retook the test and this showed to be positive, the previous posterior probability becomes your new prior one – the new posterior increases, which makes sense. Specifically, you did two tests, and both were positive.

Takeaway

Bayesian reasoning tells us how to update our prior beliefs in light of new evidence. As new evidence surfaces, your predictions become better and better.

Remember this discussion the next time you read an article on the internet about an illness! Of course, you always need to interpret the percentages in the proper context. But let's return to the spam filtering problem and see how to apply the theorem in this case.

Introducing the Naïve Bayes algorithm

Naïve Bayes is a classification algorithm based on Bayes' theorem. We already know that the features in the emails are the actual words, so we are interested in calculating each posterior probability P(spam|word) with the help of the following theorem:

$$P(spam|word) = \frac{P(word|spam)P(spam)}{P(word)}$$

where $P(word) = P(word|spam)P(spam) + P(word|ham)P(ham)$.

Flipping a coin once gives a ½ probability of getting tails. The probability of getting tails two consecutive times is ¼, as P(tail first time)P(tail second time)=(½)(½)=¼. Thus, repeating the previous calculation for each word in the email (*N* words in total), we just need to multiply their individual probabilities:

$$\prod_{i=1}^{N} P(spam|word_i) = \prod_{i=1}^{N} \frac{P(word_i|spam)P(spam)}{P(word_i)}$$

As with the SVM, it is straightforward to incorporate Naïve Bayes using `sklearn`. In the following code, we use the algorithm's `MultinomialNB` implementation to suit the discrete values (word counts) used as features better:

```
from sklearn import naive_bayes

# Create the classifier.
nb_classifier = naive_bayes.MultinomialNB(alpha=1.0)

# Fit the classifier with the train data.
nb_classifier.fit(train_data_features.toarray(), train_class)

# Get the classification score of the train data.
nb_classifier.score(train_data_features.toarray(), train_class)
>> 0.8641791044776119
```

Next, we incorporate the test set:

```
# Get the classification score of the test data.
nb_classifier.score(test_data_features.toarray(), test_class)
>> 0.8571428571428571
```

The outcome suggests that the performance of this classifier is inferior. Also, notice the result on the actual training set, which is low and very close to the performance on the test set. These numbers are another indication that the created model is not working very well.

Clarifying important key points

Before concluding this section, we must clarify some points concerning the Naïve Bayes algorithm. First of all, it assumes that a particular feature in the data is unrelated to the presence of any other feature. In our case, the assumption is that the words in an email are conditionally independent of each other, given that the type of the email is known (either spam or ham). For example, encountering the word *deep* does not suggest the presence or the absence of the word *learning* in the same email. Of course, we know that this is not the case, and many words tend to appear in groups (remember the discussion about n-grams). Most of the time, the assumption of independence of words is false and *naive*, and this is what the algorithm's name stems from. In reality, of course, the assumption of independence allows us to solve many practical problems.

Another issue is when a word appears in the ham emails but is not present in the spam ones (say, *covid*). Then, according to the algorithm, its conditional probability is zero, *P("covid"|spam) = 0*, which is rather inconvenient since we are going to multiply it with the other probabilities (making the outcome equal to zero). This situation is often known as the **zero-frequency** problem. The solution is to apply smoothing techniques such as **Laplace smoothing**, where the word count starts at 1 instead of 0.

Let's see an example of this problem. In a corpus of 10,000 emails, 6,000 are ham and 4,000 are spam. The word *heritage* appears in 37 emails of the first category and 453 of the second one. Its conditional probabilities are the following:

$$P("heritage"|ham) = \frac{37}{6000} \approx 0.61\% \quad and$$

$$P("heritage"|spam) = \frac{453}{4000} \approx 11\%$$

Moreover:

$$P("covid"|spam) = \frac{0}{4000} = 0\%$$

For an email that contains both words (*heritage* and *covid*), we need to multiply their individual probabilities (the symbol "..." signifies the other factors in the multiplication):

$$... P("heritage"|spam)P("covid"|spam) ... = 0\%$$

To overcome this problem, we apply Laplace smoothing, adding 1 in the numerator and 2 in the denominator. As a result, the smoothed probabilities now become the following:

$$P(\text{"heritage"}|ham) = \frac{38}{6002} \approx 0.63\%,$$

$$P(\text{"heritage"}|spam) = \frac{454}{4002} \approx 11\% \qquad and$$

$$P(\text{"covid"}|spam) = \frac{1}{4002} \approx 0.02\%$$

Notice that Laplace smoothing is a hyperparameter that you can specify before running the classification algorithm. For example, in the Python code used in the previous section, we constructed the `MultinomialNB` classifier using the `alpha=1.0` smoothing parameter in the argument list.

This section incorporated two well-known classification algorithms, the SVM and Naïve Bayes, and implemented two versions of a spam detector. We saw how to acquire and prepare the text data for training models, and we got a better insight into the trade-offs while adjusting the hyperparameters of the classifiers. Finally, this section provided some preliminary performance scores, but we still lack adequate knowledge to assess the two models. This discussion is the topic of the next section.

Measuring classification performance

The standard approach for any ML problem incorporates different classification algorithms and examines which works best. Previously, we used two classification methods for the spam filtering problem, but our job is not done yet; we need to evaluate their performance in more detail. Therefore, this section presents a deeper discussion on standard evaluation metrics for this task.

Calculating accuracy

If you had to choose only one of the two created models for a production system, which would that be? The spontaneous answer is to select the one with the highest accuracy. The argument is that the algorithm with the highest number of correct classifications should be the right choice. Although this is not far from the truth, it is not always the case. **Accuracy** is the percentage of correctly classified examples by an algorithm divided by the total number of examples:

$$Accuracy = \frac{Number\ of\ correctly\ classified\ examples}{Total\ number\ of\ examples}$$

Suppose that a dataset consists of 1,000 labeled emails. *Table 2.8* shows a possible outcome after classifying the samples:

	spam	ham
spam	True Positive (TP) Reality: spam Prediction: spam Total number: 15	False Positive (FP) Reality: ham Prediction: spam Total number: 20
ham	False Negative (FN) Reality: spam Prediction: ham Total number: 85	True Negative (TN) Reality: ham Prediction: ham Total number: 880

Table 2.8 – A confusion matrix after classifying 1,000 emails

Each cell contains information about the following:

- The correct label of the sample (**Reality**)
- The classification result (**Prediction**)
- **Total number** of samples

For example, **85** emails are labeled as **ham**, but they are, in reality, **spam** (in the bottom-left cell). This table, known as a **confusion matrix**, is used to evaluate the performance of a classification model and provide a better insight into the types of error. Ideally, we would prefer all model predictions to appear in the main diagonal (**True Positive** and **True Negative**). From the matrix, we can immediately observe that the dataset is imbalanced, as it contains 100 spam emails and 900 ham ones.

We can rewrite the formula for accuracy based on the previous information as follows:

$$Accuracy = \frac{TP + TN}{TP + TN + FP + FN} = \frac{15 + 880}{15 + 880 + 20 + 85} = 0.895$$

89.5% of accuracy doesn't seem that bad, but a closer look at the data reveals a different picture. Out of the 100 spam emails (**TPs + FNs**), only 15 are identified correctly, and the other 85 are labeled as ham emails. Alas, this score is a terrible result indeed! To assess the performance of a model correctly, we need to make this analysis and consider the type of errors that are most important within the task. Is it better to have a strict model that can block a legitimate email for the sake of fewer spam ones (increased **FPs**)? Or is it preferable to have a lenient model that doesn't block most ham emails but allows more undetected spam in your mailbox (increased **FNs**)?

Similar questions arise in all ML problems and generally in many real-world situations. For example, wrong affirmative decisions (**FPs**) in a fire alarm system are preferable to wrong negative ones (**FNs**). In the first case, we get a false alert of a fire that didn't occur. Conversely, declaring innocent a guilty prisoner implies higher **FNs**, which is preferable to finding guilty an innocent one (higher **FPs**). Accuracy is a good metric when the test data is balanced and the classes are equally important.

In the following Python code, we calculate the accuracy for a given test set:

```
from sklearn import metrics


# Get the predicted classes.
test_class_pred = nb_classifier.predict(test_data_features.
toarray())


# Calculate the accuracy on the test set.
metrics.accuracy_score(test_class, test_class_pred)
>> 0.8571428571428571
```

Accuracy is a prominent and easy-to-interpret metric for any ML problem. As already discussed, however, it poses certain limitations. The following section focuses on metrics that shed more light on the error types.

Calculating precision and recall

Aligned with the previous discussion, we can introduce two evaluation metrics: **precision** and **recall**. First, precision tells us the proportion of positive identifications that are, in reality, correct, and it's defined as the following (with the numbers as taken from *Table 2.8*):

$$Precision = \frac{TP}{TP + FP} = \frac{15}{15 + 20} = 0.43$$

In this case, only 43% of all emails identified as spam are actually spam. The same percentage in a medical screening test suggests that 43% of patients classified as having the disease genuinely have it. A model with zero FPs has a precision equal to 1.

Recall, on the other hand, tells us the proportion of the actual positives that are identified correctly, and it's defined as the following:

$$Recall = \frac{TP}{TP + FN} = \frac{15}{15 + 85} = 0.15$$

Here, the model identifies only 15% of all spam emails. Ditto, 15% of the patients with a disease are classified as having the disease, while 85 sick people remain undiagnosed. A model with zero FNs has a recall equal to 1. Improving precision often deteriorates recall and vice versa (remember the discussion on strict and lenient models in the previous section).

We can calculate both metrics in the following code using the Naïve Bayes model:

```
# Calculate the precision on the test set.
metrics.precision_score(test_class, test_class_pred)
>> 0.8564814814814815
```

After calculating precision, we do the same for recall:

```
# Calculate the recall on the test set.
metrics.recall_score(test_class, test_class_pred)
>> 1.0
```

Notice that in this case, recall is equal to 1.0, suggesting the model captured all spam emails. Equipped with the necessary understanding of these metrics, we can continue on the same path and introduce another typical score.

Calculating the F-score

We can combine precision and recall in one more reliable **F-score** metric: their harmonic mean, given by the following equation:

$$F\text{-}score = 2 \cdot \frac{precision \cdot recall}{precision + recall} = 2 \cdot \frac{0.43 \cdot 0.15}{0.43 + 0.15} = 0.22$$

When precision and recall reach their perfect score (equal to 1), the F-score becomes 1. In the following code, we calculate the F-score comparing the actual class labels in the test set and the ones predicted by the model:

```
# Calculate the F-score on the test set.
metrics.f1_score(test_class, test_class_pred)
>> 0.9226932668329177
```

As we can observe, the Naïve Bayes model has an F-score equal to 0.92. Running the same code for the SVM case gives an F-score of 0.93.

The following section discusses another typical evaluation metric.

Creating ROC and AUC

When the classifier returns some kind of confidence score for each prediction, we can use another technique for evaluating performance called the **Receiver Operator Characteristic (ROC) curve**. A ROC curve is a graphical plot that shows the model's performance at all classification thresholds. It utilizes two rates, namely the **True Positive Rate** (TPR), the same as recall, and the **False Positive Rate** (FPR), defined as the following:

$$TPR = \frac{TP}{TP + FN} \quad and \quad FPR = \frac{FP}{FP + TN}$$

The benefit of ROC curves is that they help us visually identify the trade-offs between the TPR and FPR. In this way, we can find which classification threshold better suits the problem under study. For example, we need to ensure that no important email is lost during spam detection (and consequently, label more spam emails as ham). But, conversely, we must ascertain that all ill patients are diagnosed (and consequently, label more healthy individuals as sick). These two cases require a different trade-off between the TPR and FPR.

Let's see how to create a ROC curve plot in *Table 2.9* using a simplified example with 10 emails and 7 thresholds:

Reality •ham ○spam	Pred. prob.	Threshold						
		0.0	0.55	0.65	0.75	0.85	0.95	1.0
•	0.1	○	•	•	•	•	•	•
•	0.2	○	•	•	•	•	•	•
•	0.3	○	•	•	•	•	•	•
•	0.4	○	•	•	•	•	•	•
•	0.5	○	•	•	•	•	•	•
○	0.6	○	○	•	•	•	•	•
•	0.7	○	○	○	•	•	•	•
•	0.8	○	○	○	○	•	•	•
○	0.9	○	○	○	○	○	•	•
○	0.99	○	○	○	○	○	○	•
		3 7	3 2	2 2	2 1	2 0	1 0	0 0
		0 0	0 5	1 5	1 6	1 7	2 7	3 7
	TPR	1	1	0.67	0.67	0.67	0.33	0
	FPR	1	0.29	0.29	0.14	0	0	0

Table 2.9 – Calculating the TPR and FPR scores for different thresholds

For each sample in the first column of the table, we get a prediction score (probability) in the second one. Then, we compare this score with the thresholds. If the score exceeds the threshold, the example is labeled as ham. Observe the first sample in the table, which is, in reality, ham (represented by a black dot). The model outputs a prediction probability equal to **0.1**, which labels the sample as ham for all thresholds except the first one. Repeating the same procedure for all samples, we can extract the confusion matrix in each case and calculate the TPR and FPR. Notice that for a threshold equal to **0**, the two metrics are equal to **1**. Conversely, if the threshold is **1**, the metrics are equal to **0**.

Figure 2.14 shows the different possible results of this process. The grayed area in these plots, called the **Area Under the ROC Curve (AUC)**, is related to the quality of our model; the higher its surface, the better it is:

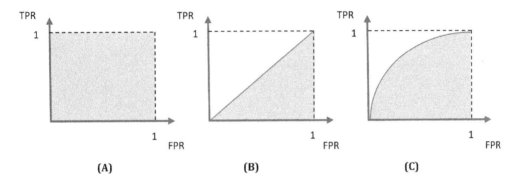

Figure 2.14 – Different ROC curves and their corresponding AUCs

> **Interesting fact**
>
> Radar engineers first developed the **ROC curve** during World War II for detecting enemy objects on battlefields.

A in *Figure 2.14* represents the ideal situation, as there are no classification errors. **B** in *Figure 2.14* represents a random classifier, so if you end up with a similar plot, you can flip a coin and decide on the outcome, as your ML model won't provide any additional value. However, most of the time, we obtain plots similar to **C** in *Figure 2.14*. To summarize, the benefit of ROC curves is twofold:

- We can directly compare different models to find the one with a higher AUC.
- We can specify which TPR and FPR combination offers good classification performance for a specific model.

We can now apply the knowledge about the ROC and AUC to the spam detection problem. In the following code, we perform the necessary steps to create the ROC curves for the two models:

```
# Create and plot the ROC curves.
nb_disp = metrics.plot_roc_curve(nb_classifier, test_data_
features.toarray(), test_class)

svm_disp = metrics.plot_roc_curve(svm_classifier, test_data_
features.toarray(), test_class, ax=nb_disp.ax_)
svm_disp.figure_.suptitle("ROC curve comparison")
```

Figure 2.15 shows the output of this process:

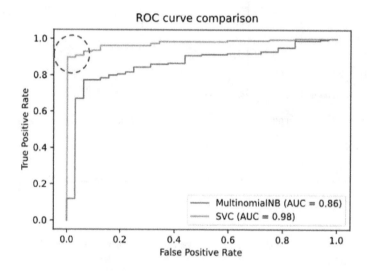

Figure 2.15 – The AUC for the SVM and the Naïve Bayes model

According to the figure, the AUC is **0.98** for the SVM and **0.87** for Naïve Bayes. All results so far corroborate our initial assumption of the superiority of the SVM model. Finally, the best trade-off between the TPR and FPR lies in the points inside the dotted circle. For these points, the TPR is close to **1.0** and the FPR close to **0.0**.

Creating precision-recall curves

Before concluding the chapter, let's cover one final topic. ROC curves can sometimes perform too optimistically with imbalanced datasets. For example, using the TN factor during the FPR calculation can skew the results; look at the disproportional value of **TN** in *Table 2.8*. Fortunately, this factor is not part of the precision or recall formulas. The solution, in this case, is to generate another visualization called the **Precision-Recall curve**. Let's see how to create the curves for the Naïve Bayes predictions:

1. Initially, we extract the ROC:

    ```
    # Obtain the scores for each prediction.
    probs = nb_classifier.predict_proba(test_data_features.
    toarray())
    test_score = probs[:, 1]


    # Compute the Receiver Operating Characteristic.
    fpr, tpr, thresholds = metrics.roc_curve(test_class,
    test_score)


    # Compute Area Under the Curve.
    roc_auc = metrics.auc(fpr, tpr)


    # Create the ROC curve.
    rc_display = metrics.RocCurveDisplay(fpr=fpr, tpr=tpr,
    roc_auc=roc_auc, estimator_name='MultinomialNB')
    ```

2. Let's use the same predictions to create the precision-recall curves:

    ```
    # Create the precision recall curves.
    precision, recall, thresholds = metrics.precision_recall_
    curve(test_class, test_score)
    ap = metrics.average_precision_score(test_class, test_
    score)
    pr_display = metrics.
    PrecisionRecallDisplay(precision=precision,
    recall=recall, average_precision=ap, estimator_
    name='MultinomialNB')
    ```

3. We can combine and show both plots in one:

    ```
    # Plot the curves.
    fig, (ax1, ax2) = plt.subplots(1, 2, figsize=(10, 5))
    rc_display.plot(ax=ax1)
    pr_display.plot(ax=ax2)
    ```

The output in *Figure 2.16* presents the ROC and precision-recall curves side by side:

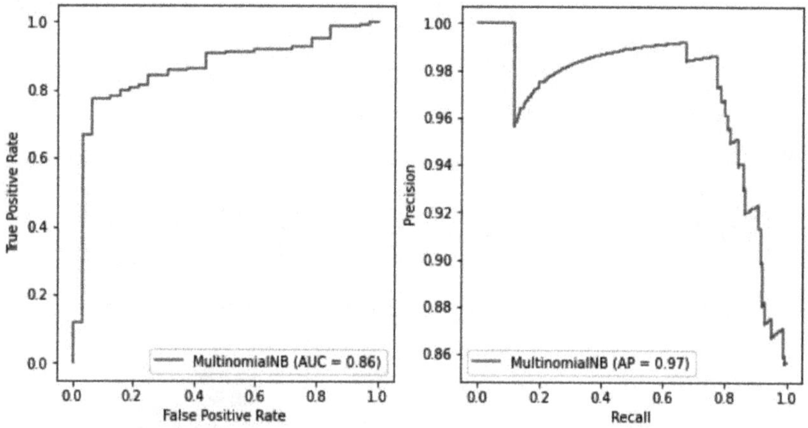

Figure 2.16 – The ROC curve (left) versus the precision-recall curve (right) for the Naïve Bayes model

Both plots summarize the trade-offs between the rates on the *x* and *y* axes using different probability thresholds. In the right plot, the average precision (**AP**) is **0.97** for the Naïve Bayes model and **0.99** for the SVM (not shown). Therefore, we do not observe any mismatch between the ROC and the precision-recall curves concerning which model is better. The SVM is the definite winner! One possible scenario when using imbalance sets is that the TN factor can affect the choice of the best model. In this case, we must scrutinize both types of curves to understand the models' performance and the differences between the classifiers. The takeaway is that a metric's effectiveness depends on the specific application and should always be examined from this perspective.

Summary

This chapter introduced many fundamental concepts, methods, and techniques for ML in the realm of text data. Then, we had the opportunity to apply this knowledge to solve a spam detection problem by incorporating two supervised ML algorithms. The content unfolded as a pipeline of different tasks, including text preprocessing, text representation, and classification. Comparing the performance of different models constitutes an integral part of this pipeline, and in the last part of the chapter, we dealt with explaining the relevant metrics. Hopefully, you should be able to apply the same process to any similar problem in the future.

Concluding the chapter, we need to make it clear that spam detection in modern deployments is not just a static binary classifier but resembles an adversarial situation. One party constantly tries to modify the messages to avoid detection, while the other party constantly tries to adapt its detection mechanisms to the new threat.

The next chapter expands on the ideas introduced in this chapter but focuses on more advanced techniques to perform *topic classification*.

3

Classifying Topics of Newsgroup Posts

The large volumes of unstructured text that large corporations and organizations need to sort daily necessitate automatizing tedious and time-consuming manual tasks. The good news is that **machine learning (ML)** is also of assistance when analyzing this type of data. This chapter will educate us on how to tag a text document using a list of predefined topics. The aim is to assign each sample to one and only one label, which becomes more challenging as the number of topics increases.

We will attack the problem by utilizing supervised and unsupervised ML techniques. First, we expand on the basic exploratory data analysis presented in the previous chapter and create richer visualizations with extra meaning and depth. The transformation of data from a high-dimensional space into a low-dimensional one assists in this task, so we will discuss pertinent techniques throughout the chapter. Then, we will implement two classifiers using one of Python's built-in datasets and compare the different models. Finally, we will introduce state-of-the-art word representation techniques comprising unique properties.

Notice that the content of the first two chapters complemented each other. So, the presented methods and techniques can be applied across the problems presented in both chapters. By the end of this one, you will enhance your arsenal with additional theoretical knowledge and the skills to implement topic classifiers in Python.

We will cover the following topics:

- Creating comprehensive plots
- Reducing the complexity of data either for visualization or classification
- Setting up a baseline model
- Training the classification models
- Fine-tuning the hyperparameters
- Understanding state-of-the-art word representation techniques

Technical requirements

The code is available as a Jupyter notebook in the book's GitHub repository: `https://github.com/PacktPublishing/Machine-Learning-Techniques-for-Text/tree/main/chapter-03`.

The notebook has an in-built step to download the necessary Python modules required for the practical exercises in this chapter. Additionally, you need a Google account to download the `GoogleNews-vectors-negative300.bin.gz` pre-trained vectors from the following link: `https://code.google.com/archive/p/word2vec/`.

Understanding topic classification

In *Chapter 2, Detecting Spam Emails*, we learned how to classify incoming emails as either spam or ham. Undoubtedly, quarantining unwanted correspondence in the spam folder is an excellent feature for any email application. But is that enough? Still, ending up with a large number of emails stacked in your inbox can be an equally unpleasant situation. For this reason, creating personalized folders to accommodate each item and facilitate either responding to or archiving email threads is common. This necessity is even more acute for companies or large organizations that offer a generic contact account for external people. Hence, the appropriate personnel or department must process a large volume of incoming questions, announcements, offers, and complaints. This task can be cumbersome for a single person, while an automated system can check every email and decide who its recipient should be.

Besides emails, businesses deal with many other unstructured texts, such as news posts, support tickets, or customer reviews. Failing to glean this data efficiently can lead to missed opportunities or, even worse, angry customers. The time factor is also crucial, as the company can have a real-time view of the different issues and react accordingly. Moreover, manual classification engenders the risk of labeling each document using slightly different criteria. Applying consistent system guidelines means that all text data is processed similarly. So again, an automated system that can process a vast amount of data is a more scalable solution than manual scanning.

In the spam detection problem, we had to assign precisely one of two labels to the samples, a task known as **binary classification**. The two labels implicitly specified a desirable (*non-spam*) and an unwanted (*spam*) state, a common assumption for the binary classifiers. Contrary to this approach, other applications need to perform fine-grained categorization using more than two classes. In the case of **multiclass classification**, there is no notion of positive versus negative states, and the task is to predict the correct label among a range of available classes. Note that the methods presented in the previous chapter and those discussed in the current one can be applied to both binary and multiclass classification problems.

In this chapter, we focus on the problem of **topic classification**, intending to assign a label (or topic) to a piece of text. For this task, we use the `20 newsgroups` dataset available in the `scikit-learn` module, which comprises around 18,000 news posts on 20 topics. As the list of topics is predefined, we are still in the realm of supervised learning. In *Chapter 10, Clustering Speech-to-Text Transcriptions*, we deal with situations where the topics are unknown. The analysis can have a different level of granularity and take place at the document, sentence, or sub-sentence level. In our case, however, we use the whole text inside the post to create the training and test instances. Let's first start with the **Exploratory Data Analysis** (EDA).

Performing exploratory data analysis

During the EDA phase in *Chapter 2, Detecting Spam Emails*, we saw how word clouds could provide some basic intuition on text data by identifying the most frequent words in a document. Another primary concern during EDA is to verify that the dataset is appropriately formatted before resorting to the subsequent analysis. For instance, it is not uncommon to encounter missing or out-of-the-range values. Plotting the data or extracting various statistics can reveal this unpleasant situation. Other times, we need to transform or exclude part of the data. Having an imbalanced dataset where one class monopolizes the whole corpus is also a source of concern. In this case, the ML algorithm is overexposed and subsequently learns data of one class type well while having difficulty with samples from the less frequent classes. All the previous issues must be addressed early to avoid any nasty surprises when treating the data later in the pipeline.

In the following code, we load and extract some basic statistics from the `fetch_20newsgroups` corpus, starting with the total number of samples:

```
from sklearn.datasets import fetch_20newsgroups


# Load the news data and print the names of the categories.
news = fetch_20newsgroups(subset='all')


# Print various information about the data.
print("Number of articles: " + str(len(news.data)))
>> Number of articles: 18846
```

Let's get the number of the different news post categories:

```
print("Number of different categories: " + str(len(news.target_
names)))
>> Number of different categories: 20
```

Now, we obtain the topic names of all categories:

```
print(news.target_names)
>> ['alt.atheism', 'comp.graphics', 'comp.os.ms-windows.misc',
'comp.sys.ibm.pc.hardware', 'comp.sys.mac.hardware', 'comp.
windows.x', 'misc.forsale', 'rec.autos', 'rec.motorcycles',
'rec.sport.baseball', 'rec.sport.hockey', 'sci.crypt', 'sci.
electronics', 'sci.med', 'sci.space', 'soc.religion.christian',
'talk.politics.guns', 'talk.politics.mideast', 'talk.politics.
misc', 'talk.religion.misc']
```

The output suggests that the posts deal with diverse topics, including *technology*, *politics*, *religion*, and *sports*. Next, we print the content of one sample:

```
print("\n".join(news.data[6].split("\n")[:]))
>> From: lpa8921@tamuts.tamu.edu (Louis Paul Adams)
Subject: Re: Number for Applied Engineering
Organization: Texas A&M University, College Station
Lines: 9
NNTP-Posting-Host: tamuts.tamu.edu


>Anyone have a phone number for Applied Engineering so I can
give them
>a call?



AE is in Dallas...try 214/241-6060 or 214/241-0055. Tech
support may be on
their own line, but one of these should get you started.

Good luck!
```

Notice that each sample contains metadata besides the actual post message (such as `From` and `Subject`). Later in the chapter, we will discuss whether to consider this metadata in the analysis. But for the time being, let's continue the EDA.

Visualization methods offer a competitive advantage over other techniques by enhancing the richness of data with additional meaning and depth. This is why they are extensively used when exploring the input or reporting results. We discuss different plot types throughout the book and implement them in Python. Thus, in the following code snippet, we create and show a pie chart; each slice represents the percentage of one of the news categories in the corpus:

```python
import matplotlib.pyplot as plt


# Keep track of the number of samples per category.
samples_per_category = {}


# Iterate over all data.
for i in range(len(news.data)):
    # Get the category for the specific sample.
    category = news.target_names[news.target[i]]
    # Increase the category index by one.
    if category in samples_per_category:
        samples_per_category[category] += 1
    else:
        samples_per_category[category] = 1


# Create and show the distribution pie chart.
slices = []


# Obtain the slices of the pie.
for key in samples_per_category:
    slices.append(samples_per_category[key])


fig, ax = plt.subplots(figsize=(10, 10))
ax.pie(slices, labels=news.target_names, autopct='%1.1f%%',
startangle=90)
```

Figure 3.1 shows the pie chart:

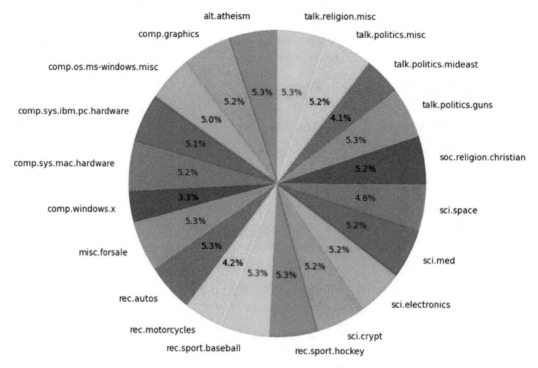

Figure 3.1 – A pie chart of the distribution of all categories

Looking at *Figure 3.1*, we immediately observe a balance between the number of samples per category (around 5% each). This observation is essential, as we want to avoid categories that might dominate the dataset and skew our analysis. If this were the case, we could use a subset of samples in the dominant category to balance it against the rest.

Another helpful visualization is the frequency of the n-grams, which directly indicates the most common word combinations in any news category. In the following code, we decide to extract the 30 most frequent bi-grams for the `misc.forsale` topic:

```
import pandas as pd
from sklearn.feature_extraction.text import CountVectorizer

# Samples for the 'misc.forsale' category.
news_misc_forsale = []

# Iterate over all data.
for i in range(len(news.data)):
```

```
    # Get the samples.
    if news.target_names[news.target[i]] == 'misc.forsale':
        news_misc_forsale.append(news.data[i])


# Create the count vectorizer using bi-grams.
vectorizer = CountVectorizer(ngram_range=(2, 2))


# Fit and transform
x = vectorizer.fit_transform(news_misc_forsale)
```

Next, we get the 30 most frequent bigrams:

```
sum_words = x.sum(axis=0)
words_freq = [(word, sum_words[0, idx]) for word, idx in
vectorizer.vocabulary_.items()]
words_freq = sorted(words_freq, key=lambda x:x[1],
reverse=True)
words = words_freq[:30]
```

We can now visualize their frequency with a bar plot:

```
# Create and show the bar chart.
df = pd.DataFrame(words, columns=['Bigram', 'Frequency'])
df = df.set_index('Bigram')
df.plot(figsize=(10, 5), kind='bar', title='Bigram frequency
chart')
```

Figure 3.2 shows the output plot:

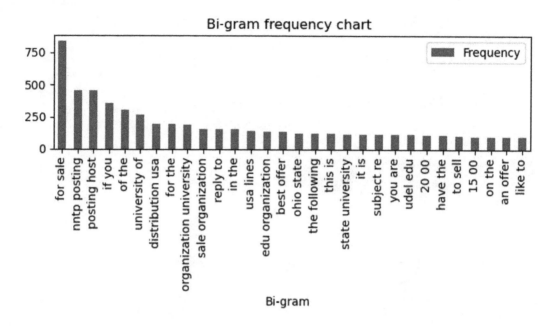

Figure 3.2 – A bar chart of the 30 most frequent bi-grams in the misc.forsale category

In *Figure 3.2*, we can observe several bi-grams relevant to the topic, such as **for sale**, **best offer**, and **to sale**, while others can appear just as much in all categories. One possible utility of the plot is identifying and removing less relevant or meaningless frequent bi-grams. Although this is not the case in our example, it is not uncommon to encounter this situation when dealing with human texts.

In this section, we performed an initial investigation of the 20 newsgroups dataset with the help of summary statistics and graphical representations. This process is the first typical phase of resolving any ML problem, and it is essential for identifying directions for analysis, detecting patterns or anomalies, and avoiding possible pitfalls. In the subsequent chapters, we see that avoiding proper EDA can lead to erroneous analyses.

The discussion in the following section involves another typical step in the pipeline for reducing the dimensions of a ML problem for visualization or classification purposes. For this reason, we present two quantitative techniques and apply them to the 20 newsgroups corpus.

Executing dimensionality reduction

In the *Explaining feature engineering* section of *Chapter 2, Detecting Spam Emails*, we defined a *feature* of a ML problem as an attribute or a characteristic that describes it. Accumulating many features together creates a vector of attributes and each sample in a dataset is a unique combination of vector values. Consequently, adding more features to a specific problem implies increasing the vector's dimensions. It is logical to think that having more features will provide a better description of the underlying data and alleviate the work of any ML algorithm that follows. But unfortunately, there are other implications.

In our discussion about **Support Vector Machines** (**SVM**) in *Chapter 2, Detecting Spam Emails*, we saw that each sample is a point in a high-dimensional space. More similar samples are closer than others and using the cosine similarity or Euclidean distance metrics, we can obtain their proximity. If we expand the dimensions of the feature space, we should also increase the number of data points in the set. The reason is that each point obtains a more *unique* combination of features after the expansion, and the feature space as a whole becomes sparse (emptier). As a result, the distance between the points grows, and supervised learning algorithms have difficulty making predictions for new data samples. There are not enough observations for all combinations of the features and there is a risk of overfitting to noise. Consequently, the model does not work well for unseen data and lacks generalization performance. We need more data samples to compensate for this problem – as a rule of thumb, at least five training examples for each dimension. This phenomenon in high-dimensional spaces is known as the **curse of dimensionality** (https://en.wikipedia.org/wiki/Curse_of_dimensionality) and appears in different domains besides ML.

But is the constant addition of more features a good idea in the first place? The curse of dimensionality is used interchangeably with the **peaking phenomenon**. This principle states that the performance of a model steadily increases as more features (or dimensions) are added and starts to deteriorate after a certain threshold is reached (see *Figure 3.3*):

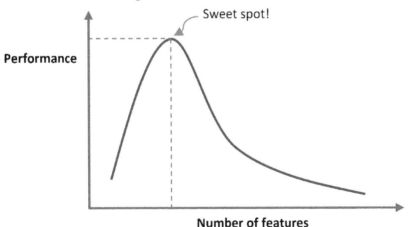

Figure 3.3 – The peaking phenomenon

Let's expand this discussion further. In the *Explaining feature engineering* section of *Chapter 2, Detecting Spam Emails*, we argued that selecting the appropriate features for a given problem is not easy. One reason is that we can end up with redundant or highly correlated features that unnecessarily tangle the ML algorithm. For example, consider the task of classifying planets based on two attributes, radius (*r*) and circumference ($2\pi r$). Jupiter and Saturn are classified as *big* planets, whereas Mars and Mercury are labeled *small*. So, what is the caveat here? Essentially, we are using two highly correlated quantities, and there is no extra benefit to including both in the feature space. The solution is to either keep one of them or introduce a new feature that is a linear combination of radius and circumference. This process is called **dimensionality reduction** and proves to be very helpful for speeding up the training of ML algorithms, filtering noise out of the data, performing feature extraction, and data visualization. Furthermore, working with fewer dimensions often makes the analysis more efficient and can help ML algorithms offer more accurate predictions.

As part of the EDA, it can be helpful to visualize high-dimensional spaces in a way that our limited human brains can comprehend. This way, we can identify patterns in the data and possible directions for analysis. In this section, we will apply dimensionality reduction to visualize the samples in the `20 newsgroups` dataset. For this reason, you can consider it part of the exploratory data analysis discussed earlier. Later in this chapter and in *Chapter 5, Recommending Music Titles*, we will use it for feature extraction during the classification phase. In the next section, we examine two typical algorithms for dimensionality reduction.

Understanding principal component analysis

Principal component analysis (**PCA**) deals with unlabeled data, and for this reason, it is an **unsupervised learning** method. Contrary to supervised learning methods, PCA tries to identify relationships between the data samples without knowing the class each belongs to. The method creates a new coordinate system with a new set of orthogonal axes (principal components); the first axis goes toward the highest variance in the data, while the second one goes toward the second-highest variance. The number of principal components is a hyperparameter for the algorithm and we can calculate more components if needed. We will experiment with different values for the principal components throughout the chapter.

PCA aims to retain the maximum amount of variation (information) about how the original data is distributed, but bear in mind that a certain level of information is lost during the process. Intuitively, the method performs lossy compression on the data, just as an image is compressed using photo editing software to reduce its size in bytes. As a result, part of the image quality is forever lost. Conversely, zipping a file is lossless compression, as we can recover the original data without wasting any information.

> **Note**
>
> **Variance** is a statistical measure of dispersion that shows how far data points are spread out from their mean value. The variance is high when the data points are far from each other and very spread from the mean. Conversely, the variance is small when the points gravitate toward the mean.

We will examine the basic steps of this method using an example. *Figure 3.4* shows a plot of 20 random points in a three-dimensional space (the table includes the *xyz* coordinates of each point):

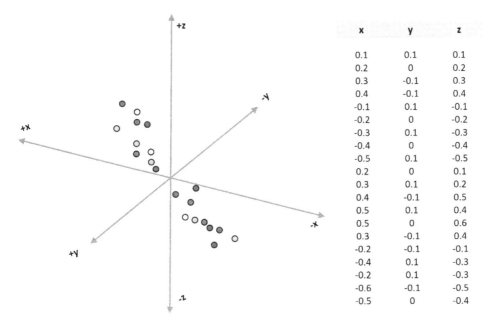

x	y	z
0.1	0.1	0.1
0.2	0	0.2
0.3	-0.1	0.3
0.4	-0.1	0.4
-0.1	0.1	-0.1
-0.2	0	-0.2
-0.3	0.1	-0.3
-0.4	0	-0.4
-0.5	0.1	-0.5
0.2	0	0.1
0.3	0.1	0.2
0.4	-0.1	0.5
0.5	0.1	0.4
0.5	0	0.6
0.3	-0.1	0.4
-0.2	-0.1	-0.1
-0.4	0.1	-0.3
-0.2	0.1	-0.3
-0.6	-0.1	-0.5
-0.5	0	-0.4

Figure 3.4 – A plot of 20 random points in a three-dimensional space

Rotating the axes at various angles provides different views of the data points and possibly helps us understand how they relate. For example, two snapshots of this rotation along the *xy* and *xz* planes are presented in *Figure 3.5*:

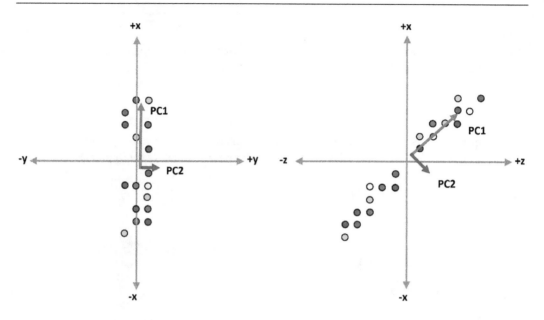

Figure 3.5 – The principal components on the xy and xz planes

The points in both plots are now projected in a two-dimensional space, which helps us identify where the variance occurs. Specifically, the first principal component axis, called **PC1**, is in the direction where the most variance takes place. Perpendicular to **PC1** is the second principal component axis called **PC2**. The length of the vector is a measure of the variance of the data when projected onto that axis. Theoretically, we can even transform each of the two-dimensional into a one-dimensional line with 20 points using just one principal component axis.

Let's programmatically calculate the first three principal components of the points in *Figure 3.4*. In the code that follows, we create the array with the points and standardize their values:

```
import numpy as np
from sklearn.preprocessing import StandardScaler
from sklearn.decomposition import PCA

# Our random data points.
points = np.array([[0.1,0.1,0.1], [0.2,0,0.2], [0.3,-
0.1,0.3], [0.4,-0.1,0.4], [-0.1,0.1,-0.1], [-0.2,0,-0.2],
[-0.3,0.1,-0.3], [-0.4,0,-0.4], [-0.5,0.1,-0.5], [0.2,0,0.1],
[0.3,0.1,0.2], [0.4,-0.1,0.5], [0.5,0.1,0.4], [0.5,0,0.6],
[0.3,-0.1,0.4], [-0.2,-0.1,-0.1], [-0.4,0.1,-0.3], [-0.2,0.1,-
0.3], [-0.6,-0.1,-0.5], [-0.5,0,-0.4]])
```

```
# Standardize the points.
spoints = StandardScaler().fit_transform(points)
```

The standardization step is necessary; otherwise, PCA becomes biased towards features with high variance, leading to false results.

Normalization versus standardization

There is a common misconception about normalization and standardization. Both are data rescaling techniques to transform the values of the features into the same scale. For instance, if a feature set has data expressed in units of kilograms, dollars, or light-years, ML algorithms cannot use them, or they are less effective. Normalization is preferable when the data does not follow a Gaussian distribution and standardization is preferable in the opposite case.

Normalization is the process of rescaling real-valued numbers to the range of 0 and 1. If X_{min} and X_{max} are the minimum and maximum values of a feature, then the normalized value of X is given by the following:

$$X_{norm} = \frac{X - X_{min}}{X_{max} - X_{min}}$$

Standardization is the process where the values are centered around the mean (μ) with a unit standard deviation (σ), given by the following:

$$X_{std} = \frac{X - \mu}{\sigma}$$

Next, we calculate the components:

```
# Calculate 3 principal components.
pca = PCA(n_components=3)
pcaComponents = pca.fit_transform(spoints)


# Generate the scatter plot.
x1 = [1]*20
x2 = [2]*20
x3 = [3]*20
```

Notice the usage of the n_components=3 argument, as it permits defining the number of components for the PCA. Let's now visualize them:

```
# Plot the figure.
pcaFigure = plt.figure(figsize=(8, 8))
pcaAxes = pcaFigure.add_subplot(1, 1, 1)
```

```
pcaAxes.scatter(x1, pcaComponents[:,0], s=50, c='r',
marker="s", label='PC1')

pcaAxes.scatter(x2, pcaComponents[:,1], s=50, c='g',
marker="p", label='PC2')

pcaAxes.scatter(x3, pcaComponents[:,2], s=50, c='b',
marker="x", label='PC3')

plt.legend(loc='upper right')
```

The output is shown in *Figure 3.6*:

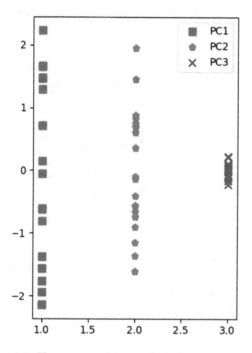

Figure 3.6 – The generated three principal components plot

This figure suggests that **PC1** captures the most variation, followed by **PC2** and **PC3**. But how can we quantify that the principle components have considered enough of the variance? How many components should be chosen in a particular problem? The answer is shown in the following code fragment:

```
# Show the variance ratio per principal component.
pca.explained_variance_ratio_
>> array([0.69943775, 0.29606821, 0.00449403])
```

We observe that the first component contains 69.9% of the variance, the second 29.6%, and the third 0.004%. A rule of thumb is that the first and second principal components should capture at least 85% of the variance for us to expect some useful insight into the data. Using these two components, we expect to recover most of the essential characteristics of the initial dataset. Fortunately, this threshold is reached in the previous example.

We are now ready to draw the plot of the data points in *Figure 3.4* on the new coordinate system using the following code:

```
# Create a data frame out of the principal components.
pcaFrame = pd.DataFrame(data = pcaComponents, columns =
['principal component 1', 'principal component 2', 'principal
component 3'])

# Generate the scatter plot.
pcaFigure = plt.figure(figsize=(15, 8))
pcaAxes = pcaFigure.add_subplot(1, 1, 1)
pcaAxes.set_xlabel('First principal component', fontsize=15)
pcaAxes.set_ylabel('Second principal component', fontsize=15)

pcaAxes.scatter(pcaFrame.loc[:, 'principal component 1'],
                pcaFrame.loc[:, 'principal component 2'],
                c='black', s=50)
```

Next, we add the index of each point to the plot and draw it:

```
index = [1, 2, 3, 4, 5, 6, 7, 8, 9, 10,
         11, 12, 13, 14, 15, 16, 17, 18, 19, 20]

for i, txt in enumerate(index):
    pcaAxes.annotate(txt, (pcaFrame.loc[i, 'principal component
1'], pcaFrame.loc[i, 'principal component 2']), fontsize=15)

pcaAxes.grid()
pcaFigure.show()
```

Figure 3.7 illustrates the output:

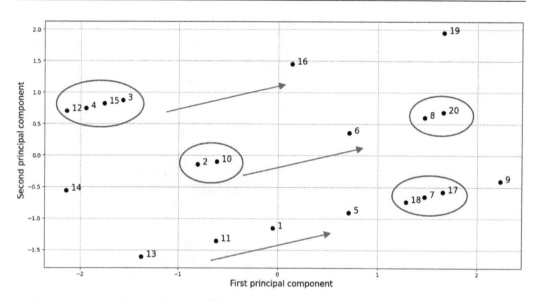

Figure 3.7 – A plot of the data points clusters in the new space

Each axis in *Figure 3.7* corresponds to one of the principal components. Moreover, a label with a number from **1** to **20** depicts a sample from *Figure 3.4*. The points now occupy a new position, with similar ones being closer than others. For example, look at the cluster with samples **3**, **4**, **12**, and **15**. Another interesting observation comes from the three trend lines. The samples that follow each line have the same *y* coordinate in *Figure 3.4*, such as points **2**, **6**, **8**, **10**, **14**, and **20**. Thus, a representation with a lower resolution (two dimensions) seems to include enough information from the initial dataset.

Now, it is logical to think that if a few principal components capture enough data variation, they can also be used as features for a given problem. For example, instead of using the *xyz* coordinates to classify the points, we can incorporate their PC1 and PC2 values. This assumption is precisely the idea behind feature extraction under dimensionality reduction: the new feature values (or components) express the data samples as a weighted sum of the original variables. Consider this example: an apartment's price can be reasonably predicted from its size in square meters, the number of rooms, its distance from public transportation, and the availability of shops nearby. PCA can weigh these features and reduce them to only two: *size* for the surface area and the number of rooms, and *location* for the proximity to essential facilities. In practice, PCA reduces the initial number of features in ML problems and can lead to simpler and more accurate classification models. While three principal components are needed for creating the three-dimensional plots of the data, a more significant number of components is typically required for feature extraction.

Hopefully, this basic analysis has provided you with a better understanding of the utility of PCA and how it can be incorporated to visualize higher-order spaces or to perform feature extraction. Keep in mind this discussion as we revisit the subject of visualizing multidimensional spaces in *Chapter 5, Recommending Music Titles*. Let's now discuss another typical method for dimensionality reduction.

Understanding linear discriminant analysis

Linear discriminant analysis (LDA) is the second dimensionality reduction technique discussed in this chapter. While PCA aims to identify the combination of principal components that maximize the variance in a dataset, LDA maximizes the separability between different classes by projecting the points onto a lower-dimensional space. It aims to find the linear projection of the data in this subspace that optimizes some measure of class separation. In contrast to the PCA algorithm, LDA is a supervised method. The plots in *Figure 3.8* can help us decipher their differences schematically:

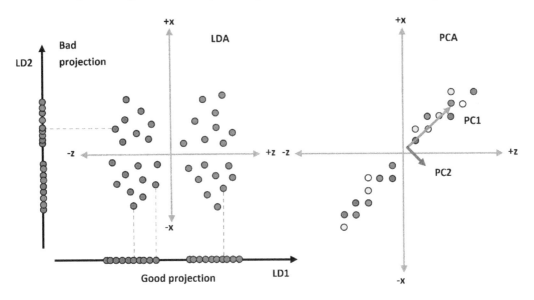

Figure 3.8 – The schematic difference between LDA and PCA

The plot on the left includes samples that belong to one of two classes. For example, suppose we want to reduce the number of dimensions in this plot from two to one. To accomplish this transformation, we project all points to **LD1** or **LD2**. Based on *Figure 3.8*, the first option is preferable because it separates the two classes perfectly. In reality, LDA considers all possible projections, not only those across the two axes. For the PCA case on the right plot, the labels of each class are irrelevant, and only the principal components for the highest variance are considered (**PC1** and **PC2**). The main difference between the two methods is that PCA can utilize unlabeled data, which is impossible for LDA.

It's about time to implement both methods to perform data visualization.

Putting PCA and LDA into action

Let's apply our knowledge about PCA and LDA to the 20 newsgroups dataset. In the following code, we extract a subset of the data for three specific news categories – comp.sys.ibm.pc.hardware, comp.sys.mac.hardware, and talk.politics.misc:

```
import matplotlib.pyplot as plt
import numpy as np
from sklearn import metrics
from sklearn.decomposition import PCA
from sklearn.feature_extraction.text import TfidfVectorizer


# Select one of the following three categories.
categories = ['comp.sys.ibm.pc.hardware', 'comp.sys.mac.
hardware', 'talk.politics.misc']
#categories = ['alt.atheism', 'comp.windows.x', 'talk.religion.
misc']
#categories = ['rec.sport.baseball', 'rec.sport.hockey', 'sci.
space']
#categories = ['rec.autos', 'rec.motorcycles', 'talk.politics.
guns']


# Load the news data only for the specific categories.
news = fetch_20newsgroups(categories=categories)
```

Notice the three other combinations of topics in the categories variable. We use them all to produce the plots that follow. Next, we limit the number of samples to 2000 and apply tf-idf vectorization:

```
# Keep a smaller portion of the data.
data_samples = news.data[:2000]
data_target = news.target[:2000]


# Create the tf-idf vectorizer.
vectorizer = TfidfVectorizer(max_df=0.95, min_df=2, max_
features=100, stop_words='english')


# Generate the tf-idf matrix for the dataset.
tfidf = vectorizer.fit_transform(data_samples)
```

Finally, we apply PCA using two principal components and show the visualization:

```
# Calculate 2 principal components.
pca = PCA(n_components=2)
pcaComponents = pca.fit_transform(tfidf.toarray())

# Create and show the plot.
plt.figure(figsize=(10, 10))
scatter = plt.scatter(pcaComponents[:,0], pcaComponents[:,1],
c=data_target)
labels = np.unique(data_target)
handles = [plt.Line2D([],[], marker="o", ls="", color=scatter.
cmap(scatter.norm(i))) for i in labels]
plt.legend(handles, categories)
```

We execute the same code three more times while uncommenting one of the categories variables. In this way, we can contrast four different combinations of news categories in the dataset. In the end, the merged output is shown in *Figure 3.9*:

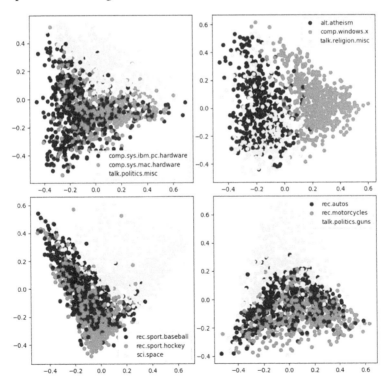

Figure 3.9 – Two-component PCA visualizations for different news categories

The immediate observation in all four plots is that the points of two topics appear to cluster closer together. Consider, for example, rec.autos and rec.motorcycles against talk.politics. guns in the bottom-right plot. As the first two refer to a similar topic, their samples overlap more than either one overlaps with the latter. Interestingly, we encounter a similar pattern for hardware versus politics (top left), religion versus computers (top right), and sports versus science (bottom left). This is an amazing result, as we applied PCA with only two principal components. Since these components did such good work for visualization, it is logical to use them as features. We explore this idea later in the chapter.

Let's now incorporate LDA for the same task using two components again in the code that follows:

```
from sklearn.discriminant_analysis import
LinearDiscriminantAnalysis

# Calculate 2 principal components.
lda = LinearDiscriminantAnalysis(n_components=2)
ldaComponents = lda.fit(tfidf.toarray(), data_target)
ldaComponents = lda.transform(tfidf.toarray())

# Create and show the plot.
plt.figure(figsize=(10, 10))
scatter = plt.scatter(ldaComponents[:,0], ldaComponents[:,1],
c=data_target)
labels = np.unique(data_target)
handles = [plt.Line2D([], [], marker="o", ls="", color=scatter.
cmap(scatter.norm(i))) for i in labels]
plt.legend(handles, categories)
```

The output is presented in *Figure 3.10*:

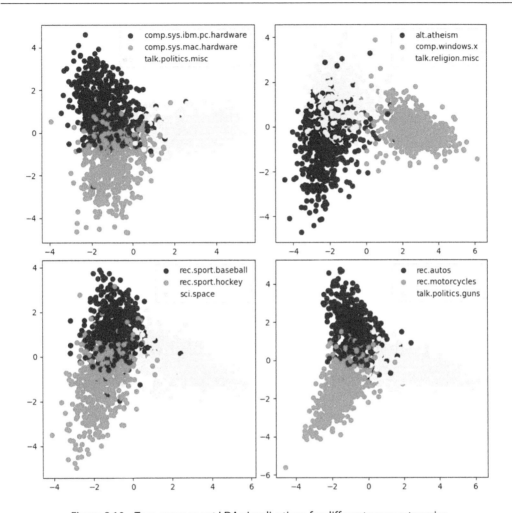

Figure 3.10 – Two-component LDA visualizations for different news categories

This time, the separation of the topics is much better, and the overlap is minimal. For this example, LDA did a great job compared to PCA!

Besides the visualization capabilities of LDA, we can extract other information from the dataset. For example, the code that follows shows how to obtain the top ten words in each topic:

```
# Print the 10 top words per news category.
feature_names = np.asarray(vectorizer.get_feature_names())
for i, category in enumerate(categories):
    top = np.argsort(lda.coef_[i])[-10:]
    print("%s: %s" % (category, " ".join(feature_names[top])))
```

```
>> comp.sys.ibm.pc.hardware: os program card help ide bus pc
dos windows host
comp.sys.mac.hardware: monitor ram work speed got software
thanks apple mac nntp
talk.politics.misc: said say did people cramer writes
stephanopoulos government clinton nntp
```

Observe output words such as `card`, `ide`, and `bus` for `comp.sys.ibm.pc.hardware`, `apple` and `mac` for `comp.sys.mac.hardware`, and `government` and `clinton` for `talk.politics.misc`. Each of these words fits well with the corresponding category; for example, we often encounter the words *card*, *IDE*, and *bus* in texts about hardware.

The discussion in this section focused on dimensionality reduction techniques and why they are important in ML problems. You can think of it as lossy data compression, reducing its size without losing much information. In this way, we can attack the curse of dimensionality while economizing in terms of computer memory. After finishing the exploratory analysis and getting more intuition about the dataset, we can move to the next analysis step and create models for classifying news posts using two fundamental ML algorithms.

Introducing the k-nearest neighbors algorithm

This section deals with a classification algorithm that is very easy to understand intuitively through an example. Consider the cloud in *Figure 3.11* that contains three types of smiley faces – happy, sad, and neutral. There is also a hidden face depicted by a question mark. If you had to guess what its actual type was, what would that be?

Figure 3.11 – A cloud with happy, sad, and neutral smiley faces

Most probably, it's a happy face. Right? The implicit assumption is that one needs to examine the neighborhood to identify the hidden type. As more happy faces are nearby, we can reasonably argue that the face shows a happy one.

This line of thought is precisely the intuition behind the **k-nearest neighbors** (**KNN**) algorithm. KNN is a non-parametric and lazy learning method that stores the position of all data samples and classifies new cases based on some similarity measure. *Lazy learning* means that the algorithm takes almost zero time to learn in this case. For KNN, the training samples are stored and used to classify new observations based on a majority vote. K is the only hyperparameter of KNN and specifies the number of closest neighbors to be considered. So, for example, when $K = 1$, the nearest neighbor class is assigned to the new sample; when $K = 3$, the three closest neighbors are examined, and so on. In practice, we tend to choose odd values for K to avoid a tie in the majority vote.

> **Note**
>
> ML models can be **parametric** or **non-parametric**. Parametric models know the number of parameters to be approximated regardless of the number of training instances. Conversely, in non-parametric models, the number of parameters is not fixed and depends on the amount of the training data.

But how can we identify the closest neighbors of a given data point? First, we need a distance measure to quantify the proximity between two points. The most straightforward metric of this kind is the **Euclidean distance** we encountered in *Chapter 2, Detecting Spam Emails*. Consequently, the nearest neighbors to the new sample should be the ones with the smallest Euclidean distance. Notice that a distance equal to zero implies that the points are identical.

Suppose that the features of two samples in the dataset are represented with two vectors. Let $P = (p_1, p_2, ..., p_m)$ and $Q = (q_1, q_2, ..., q_m)$ signify the two feature vectors in m-dimensional space. Their Euclidean distance is defined as the following:

$$d(P, Q) = \sqrt{\sum_{i=1}^{m} (q_i - p_i)^2}$$

To make the discussion easier, we consider each sample to have only two features. For the two-dimensional space, the equation is simplified to the **Pythagorean theorem** we all know from high school. *Figure 3.12* shows the distance between points **A** and **B** schematically and algebraically. An easy mnemonic is that surface of **III** is equal to the surface of **I** plus the one of **II**:

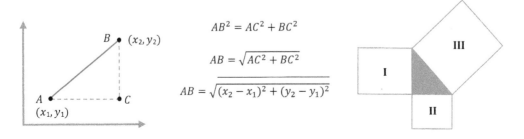

Figure 3.12 – The Pythagorean theorem

Let us now formalize the whole process through an example. Suppose we have the data points shown in *Figure 3.13* that belong to one of two classes, tagged with the symbols **x** and **o**:

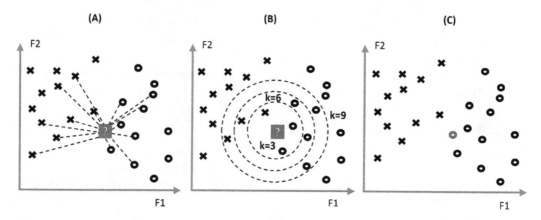

Figure 3.13 – KNN classification for two classes (x and o) and two features (F1 and F2)

When a new data point arrives (shown with a question mark in **A** of *Figure 3.13*), we must calculate the distance between the sample and every other data point in the training set. First, we narrow the search using different values for *K*, as shown in **B** of *Figure 3.13*. Specifically, we use *K* = 3, 6, 9 and examine the closest neighbors in each case. Finally, we assign the neighborhood's most frequent class (**C** in *Figure 3.13*), which is why the new sample receives the label **o**. It is not uncommon to obtain different classifications for each value of *K* and experimentation is the only way to know which works better.

Note that Euclidean distance is just one of the candidate distance measures in KNN. Other popular options are the **Manhattan distance** and the **Minkowski distance**, defined respectively as the following:

$$\sum_{i=1}^{m} |x_i - y_i| \qquad and \qquad \left(\sum_{i=1}^{m} (|x_i - y_i|)^q \right)^{\frac{1}{q}}$$

The Minkowski distance is a generalization of the other two. When *q=1*, it becomes the Manhattan distance, and for *q=2*, it becomes the Euclidean one. We can now proceed and use KNN to classify the newsgroup corpus.

Performing feature extraction

After boosting our knowledge of the theoretical aspects behind KNN, we can apply the algorithm to our topic classification problem. We already saw that the `fetch_20newsgroups` corpus consists of 20 different categories during the exploratory analysis. To make the example more concrete, we restrict the analysis to five categories, as shown in the following code, using `alt.atheism`, `comp.graphics`, `misc.forsale`, `rec.autos`, and `sci.crypt`:

```
# Select the following five categories.
categories = ['alt.atheism', 'comp.graphics', 'misc.forsale',
'rec.autos', 'sci.crypt']

# Load data only for the specific categories.
train_data = fetch_20newsgroups(subset='train',
categories=categories, random_state=123)
test_data = fetch_20newsgroups(subset='test',
categories=categories, random_state=123)

# Create the tf-idf vectorizer.
vectorizer = TfidfVectorizer(stop_words='english')

# Generate the tf-idf matrix for the two sets.
tfidf_train = vectorizer.fit_transform(train_data.data)
tfidf_test = vectorizer.transform(test_data.data)
```

Let's now print the shape of the sets:

```
print(tfidf_train.shape)
>> (2838, 39828)
print(tfidf_test.shape)
>> (1890, 39828)
```

The training and test sets consist of 2838 and 1890 samples, respectively, which yields a 60:40 proportion between the two groups. Moreover, notice the usage of English stop words in the tf-idf vectorizer and that no stemming or lemmatization occurs. The samples contain both the body and the metadata of the news posts. Finally, we pass `random_state` (*seed*) in the `fetch_20newsgroups` function to make all subsequent results reproducible. This step ensures that the same samples are read during data shuffling for the training and test sets.

> **Important note**
> The **seed** is a common technique in programming when some pseudo-random number sequences must be generated. It ensures that the exact numbers are created in every code run.

Before incorporating the classifier, we need to perform another critical step.

Performing cross-validation

We already mentioned that different values of the hyperparameter K yield different results. So while choosing a value for K, the question is what it should be. One option is to manually set a range of values and repetitively test the algorithm on the dataset. However, this approach can be time-consuming, especially when we need to test an extensive range of values. Hopefully, a more elegant technique can assist in fine-tuning the hyperparameters, called **cross-validation**. The method assumes the burden of the calculation by following three basic steps:

1. Partitioning the data into several subsets (folds)

2. Holding out one of the subsets each time and training the model with the rest

3. Evaluating the model with the holdout test

There are different types of cross-validation, and **k-fold** is one of them. *Figure 3.14* shows an example of a five-fold cross-validation case:

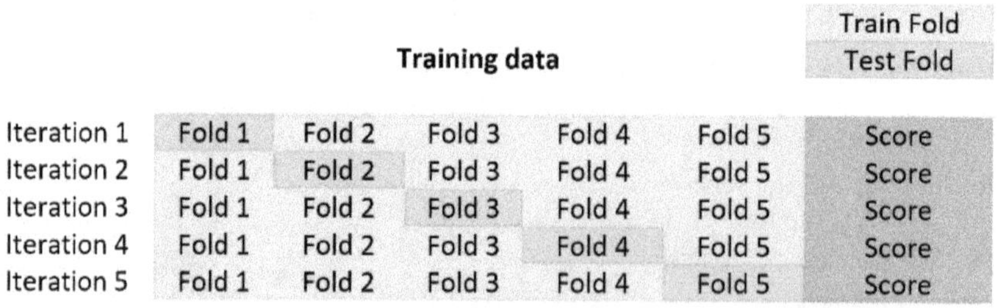

	Training data					Train Fold
						Test Fold
Iteration 1	Fold 1	Fold 2	Fold 3	Fold 4	Fold 5	Score
Iteration 2	Fold 1	Fold 2	Fold 3	Fold 4	Fold 5	Score
Iteration 3	Fold 1	Fold 2	Fold 3	Fold 4	Fold 5	Score
Iteration 4	Fold 1	Fold 2	Fold 3	Fold 4	Fold 5	Score
Iteration 5	Fold 1	Fold 2	Fold 3	Fold 4	Fold 5	Score

Figure 3.14 – A five-fold cross-validation example

We train the model using four folds during each iteration and evaluate it using the test fold. After the fifth iteration, we average the values of all the evaluation scores and report the result. By alternating the algorithm parameters and repeating the same procedure, we can find their appropriate values (in our case, the value of K).

Let's see the actual implementation of this process in the following code snippet. We investigate values of K between 1 and 100 using the training set:

```
from sklearn.model_selection import cross_val_score
from sklearn.neighbors import KNeighborsClassifier
```

```
import scipy.sparse as sp


# List of possible number of neighbors.
neighbors_values = list(range(1, 100))


# List of the mean scores.
mean_scores = []
```

Next, we perform the cross-validation:

```
# Perform 10-fold cross-validation.
for n in neighbors_values:


    # Create the classifier.
    classifier = KNeighborsClassifier(n_neighbors=n)


    # Obtain the cross-validation scores.
    scores = cross_val_score(classifier, tfidf_train, train_
data.target, cv=10, scoring='accuracy')
    # Store the mean value of the scores.
    mean_scores.append(scores.mean())


    # Calculate the errors.
    errors = [1 - x for x in mean_scores]


    # Obtain the best value for the hyperparameter.
    best_value = neighbors_values[errors.index(min(errors))]
```

Using 10 folds is very common in practical problems. Finally, we print the best value for *K*:

```
print(best_value)
>> 94
```

The output suggests a *K* equal to 94. Although it is an even number, there is a very low probability of producing any ties during inference. We can now proceed in the next section, train the KNN model on the training set, and evaluate it on test one.

Performing classification

Creating, training, and testing the KNN involves the typical steps we executed in *Chapter 2, Detecting Spam Emails*, for the SVM and the Naïve Bayes classifiers. The following code shows how to implement the same steps for the KNN:

```
import seaborn as sns
from sklearn.metrics import confusion_matrix

# Create the classifier.
knn_classifier = KNeighborsClassifier(n_neighbors=94)

# Fit the classifier with the train data.
knn_classifier.fit(tfidf_train, train_data.target)

# Get the predicted classes.
test_class_pred = knn_classifier.predict(tfidf_test)

# Calculate the accuracy on the test set.
metrics.accuracy_score(test_data.target, test_class_pred)
>> 0.9052910052910053
```

The accuracy is around 90.5%, which is quite a decent result. Next, we create and print the confusion matrix:

```
# Create the confusion matrix.
cm = confusion_matrix(test_data.target, test_class_pred)

# Plot confusion_matrix.
fig, ax = plt.subplots(figsize=(15, 5))

sns.heatmap(cm, annot=True, cmap="Set3", fmt="d",
xticklabels=categories, yticklabels=categories)
ax.set_yticklabels(categories, rotation=0)
plt.ylabel('Actual')
plt.xlabel('Predicted')
```

Figure 3.15 shows the output:

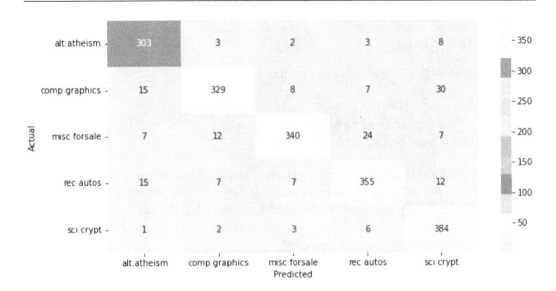

Figure 3.15 – A confusion matrix of the KNN classification

The confusion matrix provides a better analysis of the strengths and weaknesses of the model. Specifically, each row (or column) represents the instances in the actual class, while each column (or row) represents the instances in the predicted one. In the main diagonal, we quantify the number of samples for which the predicted label equals the actual one. The higher the diagonal values, the better it is – ideally, all the other elements should be zero. Confusion matrixes are a helpful visualization to identify the types of error, such as which of the classes are most often confused by the model. For example, in our case, **24** of the `misc.forsale` posts are mistakenly classified as `rec.autos` posts. The previous result is not particularly surprising, as we expect that a few sale posts can also refer to automobiles. We can experiment with other algorithms to attack these errors, fine-tune their hyperparameters, get more training data, or even merge the confused classes.

Next, we test the performance of KNN after removing any metadata from the samples in the dataset. The reason is to verify whether headers such as `From` and `Subject` impact the classification task. Moreover, we want to prevent KNN from overfitting metadata that includes `headers` (newsgroup headers), `footers` (blocks at the ends of posts that seem to be signatures), and `quotes` (lines that appear to be quoting another post). During the load of the newsgroup dataset, it is feasible to perform this action using the `remove` parameter, as shown in the following code:

```
# Load data only for the specific categories.
train_data = fetch_20newsgroups(subset='train',
categories=categories, random_state=123, remove=('headers',
'footers', 'quotes'))
test_data = fetch_20newsgroups(subset='test',
```

```
categories=categories, random_state=123, remove=('headers',
'footers', 'quotes'))
```

Rerunning the code of this section gives a new result:

```
# Calculate the accuracy on the test set.
metrics.accuracy_score(test_data.target, test_class_pred)
>> 0.20952380952380953
```

21% accuracy indicates a significant drop, and metadata eventually proves to be a valuable knowledge source for KNN. Perhaps specific keywords in the subject or the presence or absence of certain headers are critical factors for the efficiency of the KNN model. Let's conclude this section with a discussion.

Comparison to the baseline model

Obtaining an accuracy of 21% is a terrible result, but compared to what? To answer this question, we perform the following thought experiment. First, suppose that we are presented with a new sample and asked to label it with one of the five classes from *Figure 3.15*. Making an arbitrary decision yields a correct label one out of five times (20%). We simply chose one of the five categories randomly. Any ML algorithm to offer utility for a specific problem must achieve accuracy better than this value.

Another strategy is to check the training data and always pick the category with the most training samples. The assumption is that more frequent categories in the training set should also have more samples in the test one. Although our dataset is balanced, there are categories with a few more instances than the others (see *Figure 3.1*). The following code shows the number of samples for the categories used in this section:

```
samples_per_category
>> ... 'sci.crypt': 991, ... 'alt.atheism': 799, ... 'rec.
autos': 990, ... 'comp.graphics': 973, ... 'misc.forsale': 975,
...}
```

In this case, the sci.crypt category has the most samples, and we can get their number from the training and test sets respectively:

```
len(fetch_20newsgroups(subset='train', categories=['sci.
crypt']).data)
>> 595
len(fetch_20newsgroups(subset='test', categories=['sci.
crypt']).data)
>> 396
```

Based on the previous calculations, we decipher that $\frac{595}{2838} = 21\%$ of the samples in the training set are from `sci.crypt`. If we assign this category to every sample in the test set, we are correct $\frac{396}{1890} = 20.9\%$ of the time. The classifier that always predicts the majority category is called **ZeroR**, the simplest possible classifier.

Both strategies presented in this section help determine a baseline performance to benchmark more sophisticated ML algorithms. This performance is a reference point and creating a baseline is essential before resorting to a better solution. In our case study, an accuracy of 21% (KNN without metadata) equals the two baseline values, which is why the corresponding model doesn't offer any utility.

The following section introduces another typical ML algorithm and contrasts its performance with KNN.

Introducing the random forest algorithm

The method discussed in this section is based on the concept of **ensemble learning**, where multiple models (in our case, classifiers) are generated and combined to solve a particular problem. You can think of ensemble learning as having diverse people who bring different perspectives to the table for a decision. Ultimately, you want to harness those different perspectives and ensure a joint decision is reached.

A real-world example should shed some light on this type of learning. Suppose that you visit a city for the first time. After an exhausting day, there is finally some free time for dinner. One possible strategy in front of many dining choices is to walk around the city to find a good restaurant, a bistro, or a takeaway. Wandering around, the aim is to make the best possible choice for dinner based on several criteria (as in features), such as the quality of service, the ambience, and menu prices. Essentially, your brain runs a classification algorithm based on these features to assign a label to each place, for example, *good*, *neutral*, and *bad*.

A more efficient strategy is to exploit one of the numerous online services that provide suggestions, comments, or reviews and rely on many other classifiers (as in platform users). Based on their feedback, you can safely choose the right place, considering the one with the highest number of positive votes. Why is this strategy better? First, you cannot possibly check every option except in a tiny geographical area. Even if you made the best choice compared to all the ones you have seen, there might be a better option lurking elsewhere. In ML terminology, this situation is referred to as being stuck in a **local minimum** (we will revisit this topic in *Chapter 4, Extracting Sentiments from Product Reviews*).

A second impediment is that every individual judgment has biases. By taking the average over a larger population, we can cancel, to some extent, this idiosyncratic noise. For instance, one's eating habits or cultural background can make specific choices irrelevant, as in the case of vegetarian restaurants. Consequently, the wisdom of the crowd proves to be beneficial.

Finally, splitting the problem into multiple sub-problems can reduce the risk of a wrong decision. For example, some people prioritize the quality of the food, others prioritize the quality of service, and others focus on the price. As a result, restaurants that don't do well in many criteria (sub-problems) are less likely to be chosen.

The **random forest** method exploits the benefits of ensemble learning by constructing a multitude of **decision trees** on randomly selected data samples. Each decision tree produces its own prediction and the method is responsible for choosing the best result by voting. Decision trees are one of the most popular supervised ML algorithms because their models are intuitive and easy to explain. As the name suggests, the data is represented in a tree hierarchy where each internal (non-leaf) node is labeled with an input feature. In addition, the arcs in the internal nodes signify possible values for a specific feature. Finally, each leaf represents a class.

The created model can be used to visually and explicitly represent decisions. Consider the example in *Figure 3.16* used by a bank to determine the eligibility for a loan:

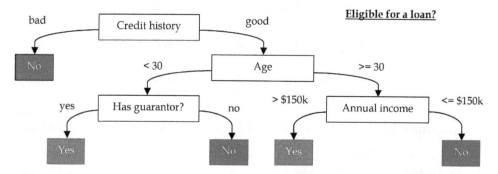

Figure 3.16 – A decision tree for determining the eligibility for a loan

Four features are scrutinized in the tree: **Credit history**, **Age**, **Has guarantor?**, and **Annual income**, which also determine its depth. Usually, decision trees have more nodes and a greater depth than the one illustrated in the figure. The prediction starts from the first (root) node, and after examining the values in the arcs, we follow the corresponding branch to the next node. For instance, a person with good credit history under 30 that lacks a guarantor is not eligible for a loan.

But how is the tree constructed in the first place? Which feature should appear higher in the hierarchy? Is it obligatory to use all features? We deal with these questions in the subsequent section.

Contracting a decision tree

There is no universal technique for contracting a decision tree; through the years, different methods have been proposed in the literature. Here, we examine one alternative referred to as **Iterative Dichotomiser 3 (ID3)**. The method utilizes two well-known metrics, named **entropy** and **information gain**. Entropy is a measure of uncertainty or disorder; the more certain or deterministic an event is, the less entropy it presents, and it's defined as follows:

$$E(S) = \sum_{i=1}^{c} -p_i log_2 p_i$$

Where:

- $S =$ *The current dataset for which we calculate the entropy*
- $C =$ *The set of classes in S*
- $p_i =$ *The percentage of class i to the number of elements in set S*

> **Interesting fact**
> We encounter **entropy** in diverse scientific fields. It refers to the notion that everything in the universe eventually moves from order to disorder, and entropy quantifies that change.

Suppose we want to calculate the entropy of a fair and a biased coin. Flipping the first coin has a 0.5 probability for a head and 0.5 for a tail. For the second case, the probabilities are 0.9 and 0.1, respectively. Therefore, the entropy in both scenarios is the following:

$$E(\text{"fair coin"}) = -0.5 \cdot log_2 0.5 - 0.5 \cdot log_2 0.5 = 1$$

and

$$E(\text{"biased coin"}) = -0.9 \cdot log_2 0.9 - 0.1 \cdot log_2 0.1 = 0.47$$

Essentially, the smaller entropy value for the biased coin indicates that we are more certain of the outcome. Of course, this makes sense since we get a head for 9 out of 10 throws. How about throwing a fair die? In this case, we are even more uncertain about the outcome compared to the fair coin, as the entropy is the following:

$$E(\text{"fair die"}) = -\frac{1}{6} \cdot log_2 \frac{1}{6} - \frac{1}{6} \cdot log_2 \frac{1}{6} - \frac{1}{6} \cdot log_2 \frac{1}{6} - \frac{1}{6} \cdot log_2 \frac{1}{6}$$
$$-\frac{1}{6} \cdot log_2 \frac{1}{6} - \frac{1}{6} \cdot log_2 \frac{1}{6} = 2.5849$$

But how does entropy assist in the construction of a decision tree? The answer is that we begin from the root node and construct the tree in steps. Thus, looking again at *Figure 3.16*, we determine to put the attribute **Age** after the attribute **Credit history** because this choice reduces the uncertainty (entropy) more than all the other candidate features. In the same way, we perform many iterations to position all attributes in the right place of the decision tree. The role of the **information gain** metric is to quantify the uncertainty reduction after splitting S on an attribute A. Specifically, it computes the difference between the entropy before and the average entropy after the split. The metric is defined as follows:

$$Information\ Gain(S, A) = E(S) - \sum_{t=1}^{K} p_t E_t$$

Where:

- $K = $ *The subsets created from splitting S on attribute A*
- $p_t = $ *The percentage of the number of elements in t to the number of elements in set S*
- $E_t = $ *The entropy of the subset t*

A practical example using ID3 should clarify the tree construction process. We will focus on the problem presented earlier for determining the eligibility for a loan based on a contrived dataset. *Table 3.1* shows 14 instances from previous decisions that can be utilized to create a decision tree classifier:

client	income	history	age	guarantor	loan
1	high	good	old	no	yes
2	moderate	good	old	yes	yes
3	moderate	bad	old	no	no
4	low	adequate	old	no	no
5	low	bad	old	no	no
6	low	bad	young	yes	no
7	moderate	bad	young	no	no
8	low	adequate	young	yes	no
9	low	good	young	no	no
10	moderate	good	old	no	yes
11	moderate	bad	old	yes	no
12	moderate	adequate	old	yes	yes
13	high	adequate	young	no	yes
14	moderate	good	young	yes	yes

Table 3.1 – Instances for determining the eligibility for a loan based on four attributes

The first step is identifying the tree's root node among the four attributes: **income**, **history**, **age**, and **guarantor**. Which one should that be? Based on the previous discussion, the answer is to select the attribute that exhibits the highest information gain. Let's see how.

The entropy using all 14 instances in *Table 3.1* is based solely on the number of positive (**yes**) and negative (**no**) answers. Therefore, we calculate the following:

$$Entropy(S) = -p(yes) \cdot log_2(yes) - p(no) \cdot log_2(no) = -\left(\frac{6}{14}\right) \cdot log_2\left(\frac{6}{14}\right) - \left(\frac{8}{14}\right) \cdot log_2\left(\frac{8}{14}\right)$$
$$= 0.985$$

Now, we consider the **income** attribute and regroup the instances in *Table 3.2* based on its three possible values (**high**, **moderate**, and **low**):

client	income	loan	client	income	loan	client	income	loan
1	high	yes	2	moderate	yes	4	low	no
13	high	yes	3	moderate	no	5	low	no
			7	moderate	no	6	low	no
			10	moderate	yes	8	low	no
			11	moderate	no	9	low	no
			12	moderate	yes			
			14	moderate	yes			

$$p(yes) = \frac{2}{2}, \quad p(no) = \frac{0}{2} \quad \Big| \quad p(yes) = \frac{4}{7}, \quad p(no) = \frac{3}{7} \quad \Big| \quad p(yes) = \frac{0}{5}, \quad p(no) = \frac{5}{5}$$

Table 3.2 – Instances grouped by the annual income attribute

We can now calculate the entropy in each case:

$$Entropy(income = high) = -\left(\frac{2}{2}\right) \cdot log_2\left(\frac{2}{2}\right) - \left(\frac{0}{2}\right) \cdot log_2\left(\frac{0}{2}\right) = 0$$

$$Entropy(income = moderate) = -\left(\frac{4}{7}\right) \cdot log_2\left(\frac{4}{7}\right) - \left(\frac{3}{7}\right) \cdot log_2\left(\frac{3}{7}\right) = 0.985$$

$$Entropy(income = low) = -\left(\frac{0}{5}\right) \cdot log_2\left(\frac{0}{5}\right) - \left(\frac{5}{5}\right) \cdot log_2\left(\frac{5}{5}\right) = 0$$

The information gain is as follows:

$$Information\ Gain(income) = 0.985 - \frac{2}{14} \cdot 0 - \frac{7}{14} \cdot 0.985 - \frac{5}{14} \cdot 0 = 0.493$$

Similarly, the gain for the other attributes is the following:

$$Information\ Gain(history) = 0.441$$

$$Information\ Gain(age) = 0.02$$

$$Information\ Gain(guarantor) = 0.011$$

Based on the previous results, the **income** attribute has the highest information gain, so we select it as the first node of the tree. Next, we move to the second iteration of the algorithm and construct *Table 3.3* for **income = moderate**:

income = moderate		
client	history	loan
2	good	yes
3	bad	no
7	bad	no
10	good	yes
11	bad	no
12	adequate	yes
14	good	yes

$$p(yes|good) = \frac{3}{3}, \quad p(no|good) = \frac{0}{3}$$

$$p(yes|adequate) = \frac{1}{1}, \quad p(no|adequate) = \frac{0}{1}$$

$$p(yes|bad) = \frac{0}{3}, \quad p(no|bad) = \frac{3}{3}$$

Table 3.3 – Instances and conditional probabilities when income = moderate

The entropy in each case is now as follows:

$$Entropy(income = mod.|history = good) = -\left(\frac{3}{3}\right) \cdot log_2\left(\frac{3}{3}\right) - \left(\frac{0}{3}\right) \cdot log_2\left(\frac{0}{3}\right) = 0$$

$$Entropy(income = mod.|history = adeq.) = -\left(\frac{1}{1}\right) \cdot log_2\left(\frac{1}{1}\right) - \left(\frac{0}{1}\right) \cdot log_2\left(\frac{0}{1}\right) = 0$$

$$Entropy(income = mod.|history = bad) = -\left(\frac{0}{3}\right) \cdot log_2\left(\frac{0}{3}\right) - \left(\frac{3}{3}\right) \cdot log_2\left(\frac{3}{3}\right) = 0$$

Using *Table 3.2*, we can extract the following quantity:

$$Entropy(income = moderate) = -\left(\frac{4}{7}\right) \cdot log_2\left(\frac{4}{7}\right) - \left(\frac{3}{7}\right) \cdot log_2\left(\frac{3}{7}\right) = 0.985$$

So, we can now proceed and calculate the gain:

$$Information\ Gain(income = moderate, history) = 0.985 - \frac{3}{7} \cdot 0 - \frac{1}{7} \cdot 0 - \frac{3}{7} \cdot 0 = 0.985$$

After performing the same steps for the **age** and **guarantor** attributes, we can extract the information gain in all cases:

$$Information\ Gain(income = moderate, age) = 0$$

$$Information\ Gain(income = moderate, guarantor) = 0$$

This time we select **history** as the next node in the tree. According to *Table 3.1*, when **income = high**, the decision to give a loan is always **yes**. Conversely, when **income = low**, the decision is **no**. These two constitute the leaf nodes under **income**. There is no need to present the other algorithm iterations, but hopefully, you get the basic idea. The output of the steps taken in this section is the incomplete decision tree shown in *Figure 3.17*:

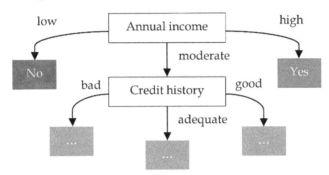

Figure 3.17 – An incomplete decision tree for the eligibility of a loan task

In practical problems, we can stop the expansion of the tree before using all features. This strategy is called the **pruning** of branches in ML terminology, which reduces the depth of the decision tree and prevents overfitting. Before concluding this section, let's make a final remark.

We already mentioned that random forest algorithms utilize many trees to make a decision. But how is it ensured that these trees are different? If we feed the same training data to the algorithm, it is logical to think that the same model is created in all iterations. The solution, in this case, is to allow each tree to randomly sample from the dataset with replacement. By sampling with replacement, each randomly selected sample is put back into the pool of samples and theoretically can be selected multiple times. The difference in the samples yields different trees, a process known as **bagging**. Another technique allows each tree to pick only from a random subset of features instead of using all of them. The result in both cases is a lower correlation among trees and more diversification.

But enough with the theory. Let's apply the method to our dataset.

Performing classification

In the code that follows, we create a random forests classifier and train it using the dataset without including the headers in each sample:

```
from sklearn.ensemble import RandomForestClassifier

# Create the classifier.
rf_classifier = RandomForestClassifier(n_estimators=100,
```

```
            random_state=123)


# Fit the classifier with the train data.
rf_classifier.fit(tfidf_train, train_data.target)


# Get the predicted classes.
test_class_pred = rf_classifier.predict(tfidf_test)


# Calculate the accuracy on the test set.
metrics.accuracy_score(test_data.target, test_class_pred)
>> 0.8
```

The accuracy reaches 80%, which is astonishingly better than the result obtained with the KNN classifier (21%). This significant difference is more evidence of the need to apply different classifiers to a given problem.

In the *Executing dimensionality reduction* section, we saw how PCA and LDA help to visualize high-dimensional data. Techniques of this kind can also be applied during classification to reduce the feature space of the problem. Too many features can degrade the performance of ML algorithms while increasing computation and memory requirements. Therefore, we incorporate a suitable method for dimensionality reduction called **Singular Value Decomposition (SVD)**. SVD works well with sparse matrices frequently encountered in text classification. We won't delve into the details of this method in this chapter, but the idea as before is to express the feature space in a new components system. In *Chapter 5, Recommending Music Titles*, we revisit SVD and provide more information on its mechanics. In the following code snippet, we apply SVD to the training and test sets:

```
from sklearn.decomposition import TruncatedSVD


# Load data only for the specific categories.
train_data = fetch_20newsgroups(subset='train',
categories=categories, random_state=123)
test_data = fetch_20newsgroups(subset='test',
categories=categories, random_state=123)


# Generate the tf-idf matrix for the two sets.
tfidf_train = vectorizer.fit_transform(train_data.data)
tfidf_test = vectorizer.transform(test_data.data)


# Calculate 200 components for the train and test sets.
```

```
svd = TruncatedSVD(n_components=200, algorithm='randomized',
n_iter=5, random_state=123, tol=0.0)

svdComponents_train = svd.fit_transform(tfidf_train.toarray())
svdComponents_test = svd.transform(tfidf_test.toarray())

print(svdComponents_train.shape)
>> (2838, 200)
```

Each of the 2838 samples in the training set is encoded with an array of 200 elements (the components of SVD). These elements constitute the features for the random forest classifier. We can also plot the percentage of the cumulative variance in a range of 1 to 200 components of SVD using the following code:

```
# Plot the cumulative variance percentage.
explained = svd.explained_variance_ratio_.cumsum()
plt.figure(figsize=(8, 8))
plt.plot(explained, '.-', ms=6, color='b')
plt.xlabel('#Num of components', fontsize= 14)
plt.ylabel('Cumulative variance percentage', fontsize=14)
plt.xticks(fontsize=14)
plt.yticks(fontsize=14)
```

Figure 3.18 shows the output:

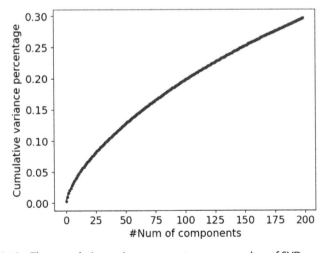

Figure 3.18 – The cumulative variance percentage per number of SVD components

According to *Figure 3.18*, the 200 components capture around 30% of the variance in the dataset. Next, we create, train, and test the classifier:

```
# Fit the classifier with the train data.
rf_classifier.fit(svdComponents_train, train_data.target)

# Get the predicted classes.
test_class_pred = rf_classifier.predict(svdComponents_test)

# Calculate the accuracy on the test set.
metrics.accuracy_score(test_data.target, test_class_pred)
>> 0.9047619047619048
```

The random forest classifier improves its performance and outputs an accuracy equal to 90% on the test set. If we rerun the same code, using KNN and 10 components for SVD (n_components=10), the accuracy is again 90%. This result is quite intriguing for two reasons. First, when we fed the same dataset (with no metadata), KNN failed to create an efficient model, as the accuracy was 21%. On the other hand, a much smaller representation with ten features provided the same performance as a model with 200 features. In general, there might be several possible and more complex alternatives for solving a particular problem. The rule of thumb is that precedence should be given to simplicity; the simpler explanation of the problem must be preferred between two competing theories. This principle is called **Occam's razor** and finds application when choosing a ML model and in many everyday situations.

Simpler can be better!

Here is a question for you: find the next number in the sequence: 1, 3, 5, 7, _.

Logically, anyone's answer would be 9. Right?

Wrong! The correct answer is 217,341 based on the following function:

$f(x) = 9055.5 \cdot x^4 - 90555 \cdot x^3 + 316942.5 \cdot x^2 - 452773 \cdot x + 217331$

$f(1) = 1, f(2) = 3, f(3) = 5, f(4) = 7$ *and* $f(5) = 217341$

This example shows that complex functions can sometimes output counterintuitive results. Therefore, according to **Occam's razor** principle, a simpler function is preferable in this case:

$f(x) = f(x-1) + 2,$ *where* $f(1) = 1$ *and x is positive natural number*

This section introduced the random forest classifier and provided a more profound look into its mechanics. We also had the opportunity to apply dimensionality reduction to the feature set and perform classification. Contrasting the performance of the models provided a better insight into the different issues. The subsequent section introduces a state-of-the-art representation of text data employed for the same task.

Extracting word embedding representation

We will start this section with an example to facilitate understanding. Suppose you are assigned to create the matching algorithm for a new dating service. This algorithm must identify people with similar characteristics and propose candidate profiles. Upon registering to the system, each user is asked a series of questions crafted to assess the five personality *traits*. The Big Five is a taxonomy for human personality and psyche. It includes extraversion, agreeableness, openness, conscientiousness, and neuroticism. Based on their answer, each user receives a score (percentage) for each trait according to the grayscale values of *Figure 3.19*:

Figure 3.19 – Grayscale values that signify the intensity of a characteristic

Figure 3.20 illustrates how we can visualize the users of the platform with a personalized grayscale vector that consists of five elements:

Profiles	Traits				
	E	A	O	C	N
User					
Candidate 1					
Candidate 2					
Candidate 3					
Candidate 4					
Candidate 5					

Figure 3.20 – Grayscale vectors of personality traits

Having these personality configurations at our disposal, we can suggest possible matches – vectors that look alike indicate similarity. By observing the profile of five candidates, what do you think the best match for **User** is? Most likely **Candidate 4**, right? The corresponding grayscale vectors seem to be visually similar.

In the following code, we translate grayscale percentages into actual numerical values and calculate the cosine similarity between the vectors:

```
import numpy as np
from sklearn.metrics.pairwise import cosine_similarity
```

```
# Create the data for our user and the candidate profiles.
user = np.array([[0.41, 0.22, 0.85, 0.08, 0.98]])
candidates = np.matrix([[0.2, 0.93, 0.83, 0.39, 0.19],
                        [0.89, 0.87, 0.7, 0.18, 0.25],
                        [0.72, 0.03, 0.05, 0.82, 0.06],
                        [0.43, 0.78, 0.79, 0.02, 0.86],
                        [0.02, 0.03, 0.71, 0.39, 0.42]])

# Calculate and print the cosine similarity.
for candidate in candidates:
    print(cosine_similarity(user, candidate))
>> [[0.65631656]]
[[0.69953423]]
[[0.31021596]]
[[0.91916887]]
[[0.84170647]]
```

The output of this process proves us correct. The fourth candidate has the highest cosine similarity with the reference user. Therefore, our dating application can now suggest their profile to **User**. Of course, one can argue that finding somebody too similar to you is not the best match, but that's another story!

Understanding word embedding

Now that you have grasped the reasoning behind the previous example, it should be straightforward to understand **word embedding**. Just as the five traits represent each person as a unique point in a five-dimensional space, word embedding represent words in a multidimensional space, typically in the order of hundreds. Following the same approach as before, we show in *Figure 3.21* the embedding vector of different English words:

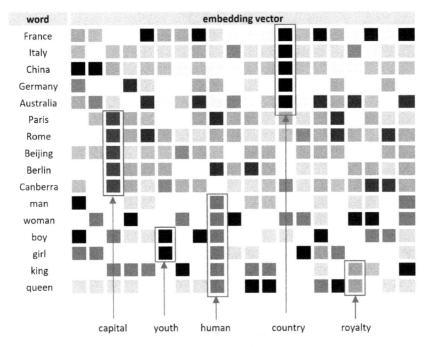

Figure 3.21 – The embedding vector of various English words

Each vector consists of 20 grayscale values, artificially constructed to facilitate the discussion. Take a look, for example, at the words for countries. They differ in all dimensions except for the 13th one. In the same manner, capital names match on the 3rd dimension, humans on the 9th (the dimension of humanity), boys and girls on the 9th and 6th (presumably the dimension of youth), and king and queen on the 9th and 17th (perhaps the dimension of royalty).

So, word embedding are a way to represent textual data numerically and also identify relationships between words. For this reason, they can lead to more powerful ML models by encapsulating the linguistic meaning of words. That is why they have gained a predominant role during the last few years.

In *Figure 3.22*, we *embed* the points of a set of English words into a three-dimensional space:

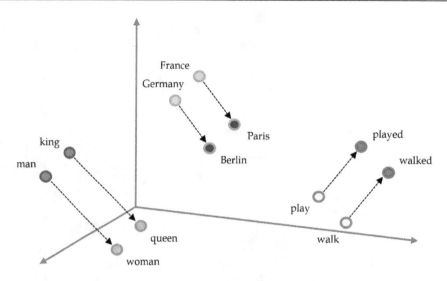

Figure 3.22 – Word embedding in a three-dimensional space

As expected, similar words appear to be closer – for example, verbs in the present tense, such as **play** and **walk**. However, there is another interesting phenomenon. The direction and distance (signified with the arrow) from **France** to **Paris** are the same as from **Germany** to **Berlin**. This unique characteristic allows building word analogies, using statements such as "*a is to b as c is to d.*" For example, "*Paris is to France as Berlin is to Germany,*" or "*King is to man as queen is to woman.*" This property is particularly intriguing since the embeddings were not initially created to perform this task. Let's now discuss a related functionality behind this text representation.

Performing vector arithmetic

We have seen that word embedding permit the capture of different semantic and syntactic similarity levels between words. For instance, the *country-capital* relation in *Figure 3.22* is an example of a semantic pattern, whereas the *verb in present-verb in past* signifies a syntactic pattern. So, consider the following equation and try to think what the correct answer is:

$$king - man + woman = ?$$

Did you guess the right response? We should get the word **queen** by subtracting the *man-ness* from the **king** and adding *woman-ness* to the result. Based on *Figure 3.22*, we can also extract similar relations:

$$germany - berlin = france - paris$$

and

$$walked - walk = played - play$$

We essentially subtract embedding vectors in all these equations, a process called **vector arithmetic**. With the gensim module, we can perform vector arithmetic using the pre-trained vectors model GoogleNews-vectors-negative300.bin.gz, which contains 3 million words and phrases. In the following code example, we perform several operations using the words from *Figure 3.22*. Notice that according to your system configuration, it might take several minutes to load and execute the code:

```
from gensim.models import KeyedVectors


# Load the Word2Vec model.
model = KeyedVectors.load_word2vec_format('./data/GoogleNews-
vectors-negative300.bin.gz', binary=True)


# Perform various word vector arithmetics.
model.most_similar(positive=['woman', 'king'],
negative=['man'], topn=1)
>> [('queen', 0.7118192911148071)]
```

Let's see another example:

```
model.most_similar(positive=['germany', 'paris'],
negative=['france'], topn=1)
>> [('berlin', 0.48413652181625366)]
```

Next, we use verbs in the present and past tense:

```
model.most_similar(positive=['play', 'walked'],
negative=['walk'], topn=1)
>> [('played', 0.6983103156089783)]
```

Another interesting fact is the gender biases often found in word embedding. As they are built using large text corpora, it is no surprise that they can mirror stereotypes often found in those texts. This situation is an unintended side effect and active research tries to remove these biases that can adversely affect software systems. For example, *man is to schoolteacher as woman is to housewife*. Similarly, we have:

$$man - psychiatrist = woman - psychologist$$

The following code snippet verifies this result:

```
model.most_similar(positive=['man', 'psychologist'],
negative=['woman'], topn=1)
>> [('psychiatrist', 0.639894962310791)]
```

Equipped with a good understanding of word embedding, it's about time to use them for classification. The sole change in the Python implementation concerns the word representation part, where instead of tf-idf, we incorporate word embedding.

Performing classification

Using the same pre-trained vectors of the previous section, we calculate the embedding vector of each word in `sample`:

```python
import re


def get_word_vector(sample):


    wv = np.zeros(300) # Word vector.
    n = 0 # Number of words that have a word vector.


    # Iterate over all words in the sample.
    for word in re.sub('\\(|\\)|\n|\t|   |,|\.|\?|/|=|\"', "",
sample).split(" "):


        # The word might not be present in the model.
        if word.lower() in model:
            wv = np.add(wv, model[word.lower()])
            n += 1


    if n == 0: # Use a dummy word.
        wv = np.add(wv, model["empty"])
    else: # Get an average value by dividing with n.
        wv = np.divide(wv, n)


    return wv
```

Something crucial to note is that the word embedding for each sample is an average value of the embedding for each word in it. Next, we iterate over all samples in `input`:

```python
def get_word_vect_from_data(input):


    # Word vectors of the samples.
```

```
    wv_vect = []

    # Iterate through the data.
    for sample in input:

        # Get the word vector.
        wv = get_word_vector(sample)

        # Store the result for the sample.
        wv_vect.append(wv)

    return wv_vect
```

Finally, we extract the word embedding for both the training and test sets:

```
# Get the word vectors for the training and test data.
wv_train = get_word_vect_from_data(train_data.data)
wv_test = get_word_vect_from_data(test_data.data)
```

As before, we train and evaluate the random forest classifier:

```
# Fit the classifier with the train data.
rf_classifier.fit(wv_train, train_data.target)

# Get the predicted classes.
test_class_pred = rf_classifier.predict(wv_test)

# Calculate the accuracy on the test set.
metrics.accuracy_score(test_data.target, test_class_pred)
>> 0.822222222222222
```

This time, the performance is around 82%, less than we initially anticipated. Presenting such a well-advertised text representation elevated the expectation barrier for the model's performance. Most probably, averaging the word embedding of all the words in a sample deteriorated performance.

There are a plethora of resources for word embedding in many languages; an alternative way to incorporate them into your code is using third-party tools. The following section provides an example.

Using the fastText tool

Before we finish the chapter, let's examine a popular tool that offers pre-trained word embedding models. **fastText** (`https://fasttext.cc/`) is an open source tool created by Facebook for text representation and classification. The following code utilizes the same training and test set as before, which we restructure in the appropriate form:

```
import fasttext


# Read and clean the data.
fasttext_train_data = [re.sub('\\(|\\)|\n|\
t|  |,|\.|\?|/|=|\"', "", sample) for sample in train_data.
data]
fasttext_test_data = [re.sub('\\(|\\)|\n|\t|  |,|\.|\?|/|=|\"',
"", sample) for sample in test_data.data]


# Read and change the class labels.
fasttext_train_target = [("__label__" + str(sample) + " ") for
sample in train_data.target]
fasttext_test_target = [("__label__" + str(sample) + " ") for
sample in test_data.target]


# Element wise concatenation of the two lists.
fasttext_train = [i + j for i, j in zip(fasttext_train_target,
fasttext_train_data)]
```

Let's see an example from the training set:

```
# Print a sample.
fasttext_train[0]
>> '__label__2 From: AGRGB@ASUACADBITNETSubject:
Re: CDs priced for immediate saleArticle-ID:
ASUACAD93096004253AGRGBOrganization: Arizona State
UniversityLines: 10Hey nowThe following cds are still available
Offerstrades consideredGowan - Lost BrotherhoodKatrina & the
Waves - Break of HeartsJoe Cocker - LiveCharles Neville -
DiversityThanksRich'
```

Now, we store the data and train the model:

```
# Write the data into a file.
with open('./data/fasttext.train', 'w') as f:
    for item in fasttext_train:
        f.write("%s\n" % item)


# Train the model.
fs_model = fasttext.train_supervised(input="./data/fasttext.
train", lr=1.0, epoch=100)
```

Using the test set, we can extract the accuracy of the model:

```
# Get the predictions using the test data.
predictions = fs_model.predict(fasttext_test_data)


# Assess the model.
fasttext_test_target_pred = [(label[0] + " ") for label in
predictions[:][0]]
metrics.accuracy_score(fasttext_test_target, fasttext_test_
target_pred)
>> 0.8952380952380953
```

The fastText-supervised classifier yields an accuracy of around 90%, which is the same as the best model so far. Unfortunately, we cannot surpass this threshold, but you are strongly urged to test different configurations of all the algorithms presented in this chapter. Then, perhaps you can discover a better model!

This section concludes our discussion on word embedding using a popular open source tool. First, we investigated the rather peculiar characteristics of word embedding that comprise implicit relationships between words on a semantic and syntactic level. These features are beneficial when training on data that relies on contextual information, such as human text. In this way, we enhanced our arsenal with one more text representation technique along with label, one-hot, and token count encoding, as well as tf-idf.

Summary

This chapter followed the path established in the previous chapter, further focusing on more advanced techniques for solving the topic classification problem.

Specifically, we saw how to extend the exploratory data analysis phase using different plot types to help make informed decisions. In this context, we had the opportunity to learn algorithms for dimensionality reduction, either for visualization or feature selection.

Then, we incorporated two supervised ML algorithms and introduced a novel representation of the text data based on word embedding. This representation was put into operation using our custom classifiers and an open source tool. The next chapter deals with another typical problem in NLP: how to perform *sentiment analysis* on a text corpus.

4

Extracting Sentiments from Product Reviews

Deciphering the emotional tone behind a sequence of words finds extensive utility in analyzing survey responses, customer feedback, or product reviews. In particular, the advent of social networks offered new possibilities for people to instantly express their opinions on various issues. Therefore, it is not surprising that many shareholders—such as companies, academia, or government—aim to exploit public opinion on various topics and acquire valuable insight.

This chapter focuses on another typical problem in **natural language processing** (**NLP**): the extraction of sentiment from a piece of text. For this reason, we incorporate an open source dataset with customer reviews from the Amazon online store. **Exploratory Data Analysis** (**EDA**) is again the first task in the pipeline, which helps us discuss important findings on the input data. During this phase, we create different visualizations and enhance our plot construction skills with Python. Next, the journey in **machine learning** (**ML**) continues with a deeper look at how the model's parameters are estimated using both an intuitive approach and numerical examples. Then, we introduce a state-of-the-art architecture that is nature-inspired. Finally, as in the previous chapter, we implement and contrast two classifiers for the same task while discussing different implications.

By the end of the chapter, you will feel more confident in your theoretical and programmatic skills and develop the proper mindset for solving pertinent problems.

In this chapter, we will go through the following topics:

- Creating models for predicting continuous values
- Acquiring a better understanding of how algorithms learn from data
- Examining optimization techniques
- Learning how to avoid overfitting
- Introducing state-of-the-art ML architectures
- Creating different classification models

Technical requirements

The chapter's code has been truncated in certain parts to facilitate reading the content. However, the whole code base is available as a Jupyter notebook in the book's GitHub repository: `https://github.com/PacktPublishing/Machine-Learning-Techniques-for-Text/tree/main/chapter-04`.

Understanding sentiment analysis

You are running for public office, and to increase the chances of being elected, you must perform a substantial effort to persuade the voters. This undertaking becomes even more challenging for non-sympathizers and ambivalent citizens. Hence, a possible strategy is to focus on less favorable regions to your candidacy, which can be identified from the sentiment expressed in social media posts in this area. Similarly, suppose you are the CEO of a company that recently deployed a new product. This time, you are interested in knowing how your customers perceive it and in understanding their opinions. In both scenarios, you should also be concerned about the competition and the sentiment against your opponents' political campaigns or competitor products. All these issues can be addressed by performing **sentiment analysis**: assigning a sentiment label to a piece of text. This task is the current chapter's theme.

Recall the discussion in the *Explaining feature engineering* section of *Chapter 2, Detecting Spam Emails*, about selecting the appropriate features to perform sentiment analysis on movie reviews. The idea was to enumerate high-valence words as either positive or negative and provide a crude sentiment categorization of the text. In real-world problems, however, this strategy cannot possibly work. One of the reasons is the inherent quirkiness of human languages, where the mix of positive and negative words can produce a different valence than initially expected. For instance, the phrase *pretty good* is less positive than *good*, although it contains the same word plus another positive one. Or, the phrase *perfect, I missed the meeting* has both a positive (*perfect*) and a negative (*missed*) word, but the emotional tone is evidently sarcastic.

The overarching goal of this chapter is to perform sentiment analysis using a dataset with product reviews from Amazon (`https://snap.stanford.edu/data/web-Amazon-links.html`). The dataset's content is around 35 million reviews gathered over 18 years. As there are many categories to work with, we use the data about software products. Unfortunately, the corpus does not include any explicit sentiment score, thus we incorporate a review rating to assign each sample a positive or negative sentiment label. The models created throughout the chapter use labeled samples from two categories, focusing on **supervised learning** and **binary classification**.

We begin with EDA.

Performing exploratory data analysis

After browsing the online dataset, we observe different files corresponding to various product categories. But before we focus on any particular group, we can explore the data found in the `categories.txt.gz` file (https://snap.stanford.edu/data/amazon/categories.txt.gz). Looking at its extension, we deduce that it is a compressed archive to occupy less storage space. Furthermore, each product is specified by a **unique identifier** and can be part of multiple categories. *Figure 4.1* shows two examples from the dataset:

B0027DQHA0

   Movies & TV, TV

   Music, Classical

0756400120

   Books, Literature & Fiction, Anthologies & Literary Collections, General

   Books, Literature & Fiction, United States

   Books, Science Fiction & Fantasy, Science Fiction, Anthologies

   Books, Science Fiction & Fantasy, Science Fiction, Short Stories

   ...

Figure 4.1 – Sample product IDs along with their categories

Python offers the `gzip` module to read data from a compressed file. So, first, we need to parse `categories.txt.gz` and read both the ID and the categories for each product. In the following code snippet, we define a method that does exactly that: iterates over all lines in the file, checks whether it refers to a product ID or category, and stores the corresponding value. Let's see each step one by one:

1. First, we create a method to obtain the product categories from a file, define a few variables, and open the file for reading:

    ```
    def readCategories(filename):
        i, productId, d = 0, '', {}
        f = gzip.open(filename, 'rb')
    ```

2. Next, we iterate over all lines in the file:

```
for l in f:
    spacesPos = l.find(b' ')
    l = l.strip().decode("latin-1")
```

3. Let's check whether the input is a product ID or a product category. In the second case, the line starts with a space:

```
if spacesPos != -1:
    # The categories are separated by a comma.
    for c in l.split(','):
        # Store the category for a specific product.
        d[i] = {'product/productId':productId,
'category':c}
        i += 1
    else:
        productId = l # Store the product id.
```

4. Finally, a *dataframe* with the requested information is returned by the method:

```
return pd.DataFrame.from_dict(d, columns=['product/
productId', 'category'],  orient='index')
```

We can now call the readCategories method for the categories.txt.gz file and obtain its data:

```
df = readCategories('./data/categories.txt.gz')

# Remove duplicate categories for each product.
df = df.drop_duplicates(subset=['product/productId',
    'category'], keep='first')

df.head()
>> product/productId  category
0  B0027DQHA0    Movies & TV
1  B0027DQHA0    TV
2  B0027DQHA0    Music
3  B0027DQHA0    Classical
4  0756400120    Books
```

Observe the output for B0027DQHA0, which consists of several product categories. Next, we merge the categories for each product into a new *dataframe* so that we can utilize this information later in the chapter:

```
# Merge the categories for each product.
df_merged = pd.DataFrame(df.groupby('product/productId', as_
index=False)['category'].apply(lambda x: "%s" % ' '.join(x)))


df_merged.head()
>>  product/productId  category
0   0000000868      Books New Used & Rental Textbooks...
1   0000020214      Books
2   0000024341      Books
3   0000025240      Books New Used & Rental Textbooks...
4   0000038504      Books
```

We can now extract the top five categories based on the number of reviews:

```
import matplotlib.pyplot as plt
import re
import seaborn as sns


sns.set(font_scale=1.5)


# Get the categories distribution and keep the top 5.
x = df.category.value_counts()
x = x.sort_values(ascending=False)
x = x.iloc[0:5]
```

Finally, we create a plot for the most popular categories:

```
# Create the plot.
ax = sns.barplot(x=x.index, y=x.values, alpha=0.8)
```

The output is the bar plot shown in *Figure 4.2*:

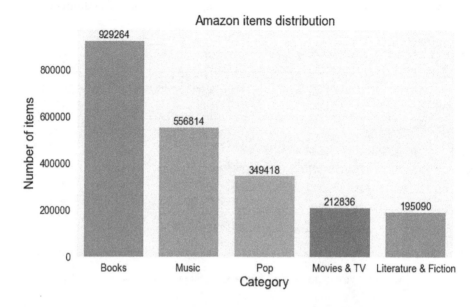

Figure 4.2 – Distribution of the top five categories

The bar plot suggests that the most popular category in the dataset is **Books**, followed by **Music**. Note that an item can be simultaneously part of the **Books** and **Literature & Fiction** categories. To reduce the computational requirements in this exercise, we focus solely on the **Software** category (not shown in the screenshot). However, the subsequent analysis can be equally applied to the other categories. Let's start!

Using the Software dataset

The samples for the **Software** items are available in the `Software.txt.gz` file (`https://snap.stanford.edu/data/amazon/Software.txt.gz`), which is also a compressed archive. The file includes information about each sample in the dataset with 10 key-value pairs. We use a few of these pairs in the exploratory phase and the subsequent sentiment analysis. *Figure 4.3* shows an example:

product/productId: B000068VBQ

product/title: Fisher-Price Rescue Heroes: Lava Landslide

product/price: 8.88

review/userId: unknown

review/profileName: unknown

review/helpfulness: 11/11

review/score: 2.0

review/time: 1042070400

review/summary: Requires too much coordination

review/text: I bought this software for my 5 year old. He has a couple of the other...

Figure 4.3 – Information about a sample in the Software category

Based on the information included in *Figure 4.3*, we implement the parseKeysValues method, which sequentially reads the keys and stores their value. Here are the steps:

1. First, we create this method, define a variable, and open the file for reading:

```
def parseKeysValues(filename):
  entry = {}
  f = gzip.open(filename, 'rb')
```

2. Next, we iterate over all lines in the file:

```
for l in f:
  l = l.strip()
```

3. Let's obtain the key-value pairs, which are separated by a colon:

```
colonPos = l.find(b':')
if colonPos == -1:
  yield entry
  entry = {}
  continue
key = l[:colonPos].decode("latin-1")
value = l[colonPos+2:].decode("latin-1")
```

```
        entry[key] = value
    yield entry
```

Now, we can create a method to read the review data, so let's do the following:

1. We define the method and a few variables (num specifies the number of samples to be read):

    ```
    def readReviews(path, num=-1):
      i = 0
      df = {}
    ```

2. Next, we iterate over all key/value pairs:

    ```
    for d in parseKeysValues(path):
      df[i] = d
      i += 1
      if i == num:
        break
    ```

3. Finally, we return a *dataframe* with the data:

    ```
    return pd.DataFrame.from_dict(df, orient='index')
    ```

We can now call the readReviews method and construct the complete *dataframe* to be used in the analysis that follows:

```
df_reviews = readReviews('./data/Software.txt.gz')


# Make the scores as float values.
df_reviews['review/score'] = df_reviews['review/score'].
astype(float)


df_reviews[['product/productId', 'review/score', 'review/
text']].tail()
>> product/productId  review/score    review/text
95079  B000068VAN        3.0          I purchased ...
95080  B000068VAN        3.0          my four year...
95081  B000068VAX        1.0          Got this for...
95082  B000068VAX        5.0          Clifford Mus...
95083  B000063W5A        5.0          STATVIEW is ...
```

We also need to include the product category in the data. Here's how we can do this:

```
df_reviews = pd.merge(df_reviews, df_merged, on='product/
productId', how='left')


df_reviews[['product/productId', 'review/score', 'review/text',
'category']].tail()


>> product/productId review/score review/text  category
95079  B000068VAN     3.0     I purch...    Softwar...
95080  B000068VAN     3.0     my four...    Softwar...
95081  B000068VAX     1.0     Got thi...    Softwar...
95082  B000068VAX     5.0     Cliffor...    Softwar...
95083  B000063W5A     5.0     STATVIE...    Softwar...
```

Let's get the total number of samples:

```
df_reviews.shape
>> (95084, 11)
```

The previous output informs us that there are 95084 reviews in the corpus. Moreover, we know that the dataset in the online repository contains duplicates, which we remove with the code snippet that follows:

```
# The dataset is known to contain duplicates.
df_reviews = df_reviews.drop_duplicates(subset=['review/
userId','product/productId'], keep='first', inplace=False)


df_reviews.shape
>> (84991, 11)
```

This time, the total number of samples becomes 84991. If necessary, we can reduce its size by filtering the set with a specific sub-category. The following code fragment shows the way:

```
# Keep only the reviews for the Software category (in practice
all).
df_software = df_reviews.loc[[i for i in df_
reviews['category'].index if re.search('Software', df_
reviews['category'][i])]]
df_reviews.shape
>> (84991, 11)
```

Notice that the `Software` category is ubiquitous in all samples. That is why the code outputs the same number of samples. Nevertheless, keep this step in mind if you need to filter the dataset in your tests.

Exploiting the ratings of products

Another helpful piece of information is `review/score`, a rating measure for a product. Next, we explore the scores and calculate their frequency:

```
# Get the rating distribution.
x = df_software['review/score'].value_counts()
x = x.sort_index()
```

Based on the previous calculations, we create a plot:

```
# Create the plot.
ax = sns.barplot(x=x.index, y=x.values, alpha=0.8)
```

The result is the bar plot shown in *Figure 4.4*:

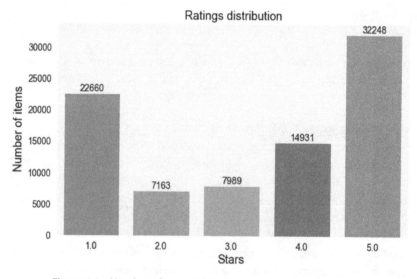

Figure 4.4 – Number of items having a rating between one to five

According to the screenshot, there are more ratings in the two extremes (**1.0** and **5.0**). This observation indicates that people tend to score a product when they are particularly satisfied or unsatisfied with the item.

Next, we extract the scores for six random products:

```
# Get the data for specific software.
df_software_sub = df_software.loc[
    (df_software['product/title'].str.match(r'Documents To Go
Premium Edition')) |
    (df_software['product/title'].str.match(r'TOPO! National
Geographic.* York')) |
    (df_software['product/title'].str.match(r'Pajama Sam 2
Thunder and Lightning')) |
    (df_software['product/title'].str.match(r'Instant Immersion
French: "New')) |
    (df_software['product/title'].str.match(r'Encyclopedia
Britannica 2000 Deluxe')) |
    (df_software['product/title'].str.match(r'Logos Bible
Atlas')) |
    (df_software['product/title'].str.match(r'Instant Immersion
German Platinum')) ]


# Reduce the name of the title.
df_software_sub['product/shorttitle'] = df_software_
sub['product/title'].str[0:12]
```

Creating a **boxplot**—also known as a **box and whisker** plot—is an elegant way to present condensed information about the data. It provides a visual five-number summary of the underlying data and is frequently encountered in EDA. For example, we can check whether the product scores are symmetric (roughly the same on each median side). In *Figure 4.5*, **Q1** is the median value of the first half of the dataset, whereas **Q3** is the median value of the second half:

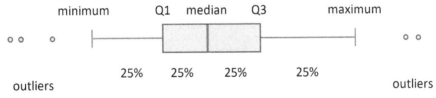

Figure 4.5 – Analysis of a boxplot

We use the relevant data and create a plot, as follows:

```
# Create the plot.
ax = sns.boxplot(x='product/shorttitle', y='review/score',
data=df_software_sub)
```

The generated boxplot is presented in *Figure 4.6*:

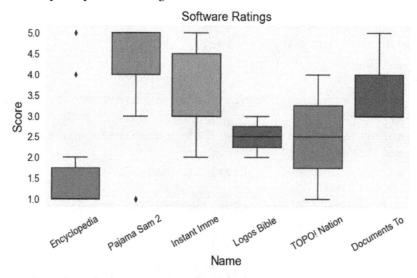

Figure 4.6 – Review score for six software products

Based on *Figure 4.6*, only the **Logos Bible** and **TOPO! Nation** products have symmetric scores. Additionally, there are outliers for the **Encyclopedia** and **Pajama Sam 2** cases. **Outliers** are data points significantly different from the other samples and may indicate some sort of abnormality. For example, an age field with a negative value is a sign of bad data and can distort the analysis. On the other hand, outliers can help detect anomalies in the data and find patterns that do not conform to the expected behavior. Examples are the detection of fraud, faults in safety-critical systems, or intrusion.

In the following section, the focus is on the actual review text.

Extracting the word count of reviews

The first statistic extracted from the text data is the number of words per review. The utility of such a calculation is to provide a general overview of the distribution of the reviews based on their word count. It can also help us define a cutoff threshold for the samples to be excluded from the subsequent analysis. The following code snippet shows the specific step and how to create a plot out of this data:

```
review_length = df_reviews['review/text'].apply(lambda col:
len(col.split(' ')))
df_reviews['review_length'] = review_length


# Create the plot.
ax = sns.histplot(data=review_length)
plt.xlim(0, 400)
```

The output is the histogram shown in *Figure 4.7*:

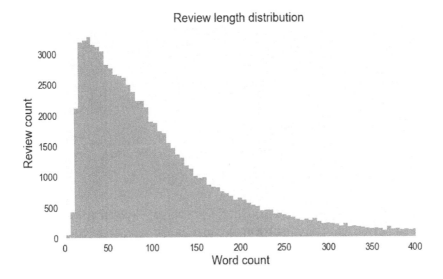

Figure 4.7 – Number of reviews with a specific word count

As we can observe from the screenshot, most reviews have fewer than 100 words. Notice that we purposely limit the *x* axis to 400 words (`plt.xlim(0, 400)`), as the dataset contains instances with many more words. Let's obtain some more insight into the data.

Exploiting the helpfulness score

The helpfulness score is the fraction of users who found one specific review helpful. There are many possibilities to exploit this score and other information during data exploration. For instance, it would be interesting to contrast the rating scores or helpfulness with the length of the reviews. Do users tend to write extensive reviews for products they like or those they don't? Do customers find lengthy reviews more helpful than short ones? Is the feedback from the most active reviewers somehow helpful to other customers? This section tries to answer the last question, defining the most active (top) reviewers in terms of their review count (more than 50 items).

First, we extract the IDs of the specific users, like so:

```
# Get the number of reviews per user.
reviewers = df_reviews.groupby(by=['review/userId'], as_
index=False).count().sort_values(by=['product/productId'],
ascending=False)
reviewers = reviewers[['review/userId', 'product/productId']]
```

```
reviewers.columns = ['review/userId', 'review/count']

# Store the top reviewers.
top_reviewers = reviewers[reviewers['review/count'] >= 50]
top_reviewers = top_reviewers[['review/userId']]

print(top_reviewers)
>>      review/userId
68463    unknown
2896     A15S4XW3CRISZ5
53129    A5JLAU2ARJOBO
```

Only three users adhere to the count criterion. The top one appears with an unknown ID, as it was impossible to associate certain reviews with a unique user. In this case, the relevant data cannot tell us much during the analysis of the top reviewers and should be removed. Next, we apply a second restriction and keep reviews with fewer than 400 words:

```
# Extract the data for top reviewers.
top_rev_help = pd.merge(top_reviewers, df_reviews, on='review/
userId', how='left')
top_rev_help = top_rev_help[top_rev_help['review/userId'] !=
'unknown']
top_rev_help = top_rev_help[top_rev_help['review_length'] <
400]
top_rev_help = top_rev_help.sort_values(by=['review/score' ],
ascending=False)
```

We also need to transform the `review/helpscore` field into a numerical value. Here's how we can do this:

```
# Calculate helpfulness score.
top_rev_help['review/helpfulness'] = top_rev_help['review/
helpfulness'].str.replace('/0', '/1')
top_rev_help['review/helpscore'] = top_rev_help['review/
helpscore'].fillna(1000).apply(pd.eval)

# Format the data.
top_rev_help['reviewers'] = 'top'
top_rev_help = top_rev_help.sort_values(by=['review/score' ],
```

```
    ascending=False)
top_rev_help = top_rev_help.reset_index(drop=True)
```

Finally, we generate a relational plot that shows the helpfulness score for each product for the top reviewers:

```
# Create the plot.
ax = sns.relplot(x=top_rev_help.index, y="review/helpscore",
hue="reviewers", size="review/score",
            sizes=(40, 400), alpha=.5, palette="muted",
            height=6, aspect=8/6, data=top_rev_help)
```

Figure 4.8 shows the output:

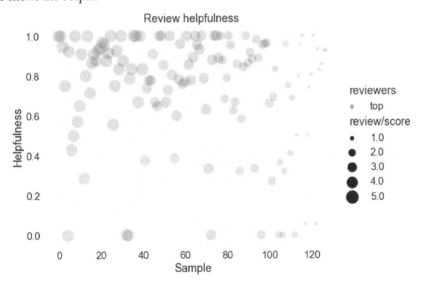

Figure 4.8 – Helpfulness score for the products of the top reviewers

A general remark from the plot is that the top reviewers' feedback seems, in the end, helpful to other customers. Most bubbles lie on the upper part of the plot, where helpfulness has high values. Moreover, there are more positive review scores than negative ones, as fewer bubbles have a size equal to **1.0** or **2.0**. But how do these outcomes contrast with those of users with minimal reviews?

In the following code snippet, we repeat a similar procedure for users that have only one review:

```
# Store the bottom reviewers.
bottom_reviewers = reviewers[reviewers['review/count'] == 1]
```

```
bottom_reviewers = bottom_reviewers[['review/userId']]


# Keep 1000 random bottom reviewers.
bottom_reviewers = bottom_reviewers.sample(130, random_
state=123)
```

Again, the results are restricted according to the 400 words threshold:

```
# Extract the data for bottom reviewers.
bottom_rev_help = pd.merge(bottom_reviewers, df_reviews,
on='review/userId', how='left')
bottom_rev_help = bottom_rev_help[bottom_rev_help['review_
length'] < 400]
bottom_rev_help = bottom_rev_help.sort_values(by=['review/
score'], ascending=False)
```

As before, we transform the `review/helpscore` field into a numerical value:

```
# Calculate helpfulness score.
bottom_rev_help['review/helpscore'] = bottom_rev_help['review/
helpfulness'].str.replace('/0', '/1')
bottom_rev_help['review/helpscore'] = bottom_rev_help['review/
helpscore'].fillna(1000).apply(pd.eval)


# Format the data.
bottom_rev_help['reviewers'] = 'bottom'
bottom_rev_help = bottom_rev_help.sort_values(by=['review/
score'], ascending=False)
bottom_rev_help = bottom_rev_help.reset_index(drop=True)
```

Next, we create a similar bubble plot:

```
# Create the plot.
ax = sns.relplot(x=bottom_rev_help.index, y="review/helpscore",
hue="reviewers", size="review/score",
              sizes=(40, 400), alpha=.5, palette="hls",
              height=6, aspect=8/6, data=bottom_rev_help)
```

The output is presented in *Figure 4.9*:

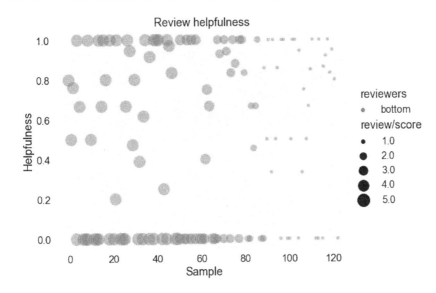

Figure 4.9 – Helpfulness score for the products of the bottom reviewers

Contrasting the two bubble plots, we observe more reviews with low helpfulness in *Figure 4.9*. A large proportion exhibits a score equal to **0.0**. Additionally, there are more negative reviews (bubbles with a size of either **1.0** or **2.0**). Both results suggest that evaluations from top reviewers with positive scores increase the review helpfulness for a given product. Notice, however, that comparing two quantities and finding an association doesn't necessarily imply a cause-and-effect relation. We will discuss this topic extensively in the next chapter.

Next, we create elaborate graphs and examine the two top reviewers individually based on their helpfulness scores. But first, we need to restructure the data in a suitable format:

```
# Unpivot the dataframe from wide to long format.
stripplot_df = pd.melt(top_rev_help[['review/userId', 'review/
helpscore']], "review/userId", var_name="m")
```

Afterward, we create a plot with the scores:

```
# Create the plots.
f, ax = plt.subplots()

# Create a plot to show the helpfulness score per reviewer.
sns.stripplot(x="value", y="m", hue="review/userId",
              data=stripplot_df, dodge=True,
              alpha=.6, zorder=1)
```

We also include the mean values of helpfulness:

```
# Show the conditional means of the scores.
sns.pointplot(x="value", y="m", hue="review/userId",
              data= stripplot_df, dodge=.8 - .8 / 3,
              join=False, palette="dark",
              markers="d", scale=1, ci=None)
```

The output is shown in *Figure 4.10*:

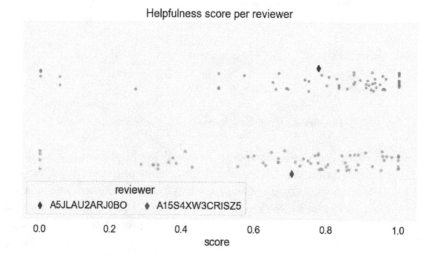

Figure 4.10 – Helpfulness score for the two top reviewers

Both reviewers receive high scores for their product evaluations. We often balance cumulative and individual statistics during the exploratory phase to better understand the data.

This section provided a deeper understanding of the Amazon reviews dataset for software products. This task permits using the data efficiently later in the chapter. You also reinforced your arsenal in analyzing and visualizing the input data, and you are now better equipped to perform a similar task for other datasets.

In the subsequent sections, we introduce the techniques to perform sentiment analysis.

Introducing linear regression

Before we delve into solving the main problem of this chapter, we need to provide the necessary theoretical framework. This section presents an ML technique purposely chosen to unfold the discussion and facilitate understanding of the methods that follow.

Let's consider the three plots in *Figure 4.11* that show the relationship between two variables: **x** and **y**. In this example, the opaque and transparent points correspond in one of two independent datasets:

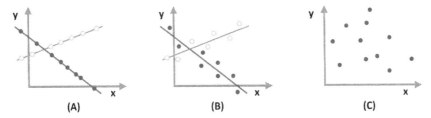

Figure 4.11 – Variables with deterministic (A), statistical (B), and random relationship (C)

In *Figure 4.11 (A)*, the points of both datasets reside on their line, which defines a clear deterministic relationship between the two variables. As **x** changes its value, we can precisely calculate the value of **y** using one of the line equations. In the middle plot, we cannot predict the exact value of **y**, but we can obtain a good approximation based again on the line equations. Finally, in *Figure 4.11 (C)*, the relationship is random, and we cannot find any function to infer **y** based on the values of **x**. In ML problems, we are often interested in identifying relationships such as in the left and middle plots to predict unseen observations. Conversely, the situation in the right plot is undesirable.

One of the most well-known algorithms to elicit the best relationship between an independent variable **x** and a dependent variable **y** is **linear regression**. In the case of a single independent variable, the method is referred to as **simple linear regression**, and for multiple ones, it is called **multiple linear regression**. The core idea is to obtain a regression line that best fits the data, exhibiting the lowest prediction error for all data points. The slope β_1 and the point of intercept β_0 with the y axis are the two coefficients that uniquely define the line. For a given dataset, the aim is to estimate these two coefficients to extract the line of best fit. The most popular method for this task is **ordinary least squares (OLS)**, which we explain with an example.

Look at *Figure 4.12*, which includes a series of data points and their distance from a candidate regression line:

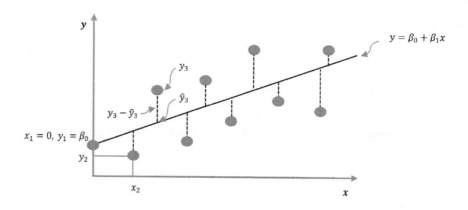

Figure 4.12 – Principal of least squares

As the line cannot pass through all the points simultaneously, we require that it predicts the **y** value with the minimum error. We can quantify this error by examining the difference between the observed value y_i and the predicted value $\hat{y}_i$. Consequently, the error for each point i (also called **residuals**) is defined as follows:

$$e_i = y_i - \hat{y}_i$$

We seek to minimize this quantity for all data points, and the OLS method helps in this direction. Summing all the residuals should tell us which line yields the minimum prediction error. But there is a caveat. We use their squared version to avoid positive and negative prediction errors canceling each other out when summed. The following equation formalizes the **loss function** (where $n = number$ *of data points*):

$$Loss = \sum_{i}^{n} (y_i - \hat{y}_i)^2 = \sum_{i}^{n} \left(y_i - (\beta_0 + \beta_1 x_i)\right)^2$$

Loss functions intuitively inform us about some *cost* associated with a decision. For example, the cost increases when the regression line doesn't fit the data well. Different functions can be incorporated to represent loss, and the one introduced previously is known as the **principle of least squares**. A numerical example helps us understand how it works.

Table 4.1 includes 10 observations for which we want to find the line of best fit. The data comes from a survey that reports the state of global happiness for 155 countries, named the *World Happiness Report* (https://www.kaggle.com/unsdsn/world-happiness). The independent variable represents the **GDP per capita** value for each country, and the dependent variable is the corresponding **Happiness score** value:

GDP per capita	Happiness score	Option A $y = 1.6715 + 3.8141x$			Option B $y = 1.7638 + 3.7829x$		
x_i	y_i	$\hat{y}_i$	$y_i - \hat{y}_i$	$(y_i - \hat{y}_i)^2$	$\hat{y}_i$	$y_i - \hat{y}_i$	$(y_i - \hat{y}_i)^2$
1.34	7.769	6.782	0.987	0.974169	6.832	0.937	0.877969
1.376	7.246	6.919	0.327	0.106929	6.969	0.277	0.076729
1.269	6.852	6.511	0.341	0.116281	6.564	0.288	0.082944
1.286	6.354	6.576	-0.222	0.049284	6.628	-0.274	0.075076
1.206	6.182	6.271	-0.089	0.007921	6.325	-0.143	0.020449
0.912	6.028	5.149	0.879	0.772641	5.213	0.815	0.664225
1.173	5.809	6.145	-0.336	0.112896	6.201	-0.392	0.153664
1.004	5.603	5.501	0.102	0.010404	5.561	0.042	0.001764
1.221	5.339	6.328	-0.989	0.978121	6.382	-1.043	1.087849
1.043	5.208	5.649	-0.441	0.194481	5.706	-0.498	0.248004
		Mean	0.559	3.323127	Mean	0.009	3.288673

Table 4.1 – Comparing two candidate regression lines for the happiness versus GDP dataset

Suppose that the two equations in the table define two candidate regression lines. Which one would you trust more for making future predictions about a country's happiness level? Based on the previous discussion, the answer is the one that yields the minimum sum of the squares. This requirement corresponds to option **B** with a sum equal to **3.288673**; we choose it as the best regression line for this minuscule dataset. Finally, notice that the sum of positive and negative prediction errors cancels each other when summed (**0.009**). The specific outcome clarifies why we need to square these quantities before their summation.

According to the equation of the principle of least squares, we need to estimate the values of the β_0 and β_1 coefficients that make the sum of the squared prediction errors the smallest possible. In practice, we cannot test an infinite number of pairs to extract this information, and even if we examine a large number, it is not sure that we can elicit the best combination of the coefficients. Problems of this kind are typical in mathematics and are called **optimization problems**; we seek the best solution from all feasible solutions. A common way to attack this situation is to use calculus to obtain the coefficients that minimize the value of the loss function. Let's see how.

The left plot of *Figure 4.13* shows the tangent lines at the three points **A**, **B**, and **C** of function **f**. It is a no-brainer to decipher that the minimum point of the function is **B**. There is also something interesting happening there; the slope **a** of the tangent line is equal to zero. At point **C**, the slope increases, whereas at point **A**, it decreases:

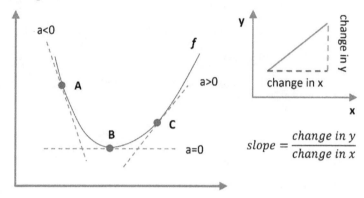

Figure 4.13 – Derivative of a function in three points A, B, and C

How can we exploit the changes in the slope of the tangent lines? Hopefully, calculus can assist us! The **derivative** of a function at a given point informs us about the rate of change of one variable with respect to another variable. For that reason, the derivative is equal to the slope of the tangent at this specific point. Finding the minimum value of a function translates into detecting where its derivative becomes zero.

Applying the same reasoning for the loss function, we have to zero its derivative and estimate the values of β_0 and β_1. We also use partial derivatives as two coefficients must be considered. Initially, we focus on the partial derivative of the *Loss* function with respect to β_1:

$$\frac{\partial Loss}{\partial \beta_1} = \frac{\partial \sum_i^n (y_i - \beta_0 - \beta_1 x_i)^2}{\partial \beta_1} = \sum_1^n [2(y_i - \beta_0 - \beta_1 x_i)(-x_i)]$$

Setting this equal to *0* and dividing both sides with the number *-2*, we get the following:

$$\sum_1^n y_i x_i - \sum_1^n \beta_0 x_i - \sum_1^n \beta_1 x_i^2 = 0 \Rightarrow \sum_1^n y_i x_i - \beta_0 \sum_1^n x_i - \beta_1 \sum_1^n x_i^2 = 0$$

We now repeat the same process for the partial derivative with respect to β_0:

$$\frac{\partial Loss}{\partial \beta_0} = \frac{\partial \sum_i^n (y_i - \beta_0 - \beta_1 x_i)^2}{\partial \beta_0} = \sum_1^n [2(y_i - \beta_0 - \beta_1 x_i)(-1)]$$

Setting again this equal to *0* and dividing both sides with the number *-2* gives us this:

$$\sum_1^n y_i - \sum_1^n \beta_0 - \sum_1^n \beta_1 x_i = 0 \Rightarrow \sum_1^n y_i - \beta_0 n - \beta_1 \sum_1^n x_i = 0$$

After executing a few algebraic steps, we end up with the two equations that allow the calculation of the two parameters:

$$\beta_0 = \frac{\sum_1^n y_i - \beta_1 \sum_1^n x_i}{n} \quad and \quad \beta_1 = \frac{n \sum_1^n x_i y_i - \sum_1^n y_i \sum_1^n x_i}{n \sum_1^n x_i^2 - (\sum_1^n x_i)^2}$$

In any dataset, the values of x_i and y_i are known in advance, so it is straightforward to calculate both coefficients and extract the line of best fit. In the next section, we implement linear regression in Python.

Putting linear regression into action

We use all 155 observations from the *World Happiness Report* dataset and implement the code to load and format the samples:

```
from sklearn.linear_model import LinearRegression

# Read the data from the csv file.
data = pd.read_csv('./data/2019.csv')

# Keep these two categories.
x = data['GDP per capita']
y = data['Score']

# Reshape the data.
x = x.values.reshape(-1,1)
y = y.values.reshape(-1,1)
```

Next, we create a model and acquire the predictions:

```
# Create and fit the linear regression model.
lmodel = LinearRegression()
lmodel.fit(x, y)
```

```
# Get the predictions.
predictions = lmodel.predict(x)
```

Finally, we reformat the data to generate a regression line plot:

```
# Create a dataframe with the data.
linear_df = pd.DataFrame(data, columns=['GDP per capita',
'Score'])
linear_df['Predictions'] = predictions


# Create the plot.
sns.scatterplot(data=linear_df, x='GDP per capita', y='Score')
sns.lineplot(data=linear_df, x="GDP per capita",
y="Predictions", color='red', linewidth=4)
```

The output is presented in *Figure 4.14*:

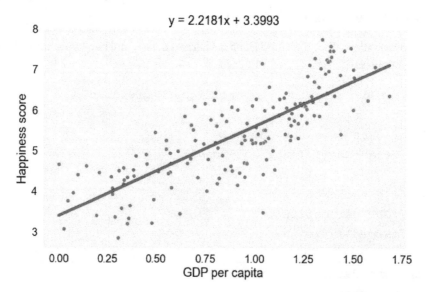

Figure 4.14 – Regression line for the happiness versus GDP dataset

The regression line with a slope of **2.2181** and point of intercept with the y axis equal to **3.3993** can help us predict the future. It mainly suggests that the more GDP per capita available, the higher the happiness score of a country. What a result!

The discussion in this section focused on one of the most frequently used techniques in ML. Even though it was not incorporated into the main problem of this chapter, it offers valuable insight into the content that follows. In particular, the utility of loss functions is a recurring topic in ML, and hopefully, the discussion in this section helped in enhancing your theoretical skillset. The following section introduces another method that, due to its close name with linear regression, often causes confusion.

Introducing logistic regression

Linear regression is well suited when predicting the value of a continuous numerical variable. Based on the assumption that there is a linear relationship between the dependent and the independent variable, the method aims to find the line of best fit and use it for prediction. In this chapter, however, we are dealing with a classification problem, as we need to assign a sentiment label (positive or negative) to a piece of text. Consequently, this is a different problem because the dependent variable is categorical and not numerical.

This section applies a supervised learning algorithm called **logistic regression**, which is suitable for binary classification problems. Notice that there is also the **multinomial logistic regression** algorithm option for multiclass problems. Logistic regression is a parametric learning algorithm that outputs a probability that an input belongs to a particular class. Instead of fitting a straight line to the data, the effort is to fit an *S-shaped* curve called the **sigmoid function**, defined as follows:

$$S(x) = \frac{1}{1 + e^{-x}}$$

Factor e is a numerical constant called Euler's number, and x is the sum of independent variables weighted by their coefficients (β_i). For example, when there are two predictors (independent) variables, we can write the sum as this:

$$\beta_0 + \beta_1 x_1 + \beta_2 x_2$$

The sigmoid function squeezes any real number in the interval (0, 1) that is essentially a range for probabilities. An input equal to *0* yields a probability equal to *0.5*. Conversely, a value above or below *0.5* classifies the sample in each of the two classes accordingly. *Figure 4.15* presents a classification task using a sigmoid function:

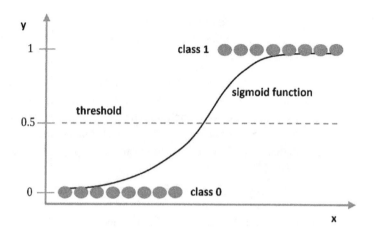

Figure 4.15 – Logistic regression model

As in the case of linear regression, the aim is to estimate the coefficients that reduce the difference between the observed and the predicted value. Formally, this difference can be expressed with a loss function such as the OLS we have seen before. However, this method is not suitable for logistic regression. This is because the form of the OLS loss function for logistic regression typically contains many local minima. Therefore, minimizing the loss based on zeroing the partial derivatives often fails to find the optimal solution. In the next section, we introduce an alternative technique to alleviate this restriction and examine it in detail.

Understanding gradient descent

ML algorithms aim to approximate the function that best fits the data. This task involves minimizing the error, cost, or loss function using optimization techniques that extract the minimum of this function. In this section, we introduce a relevant technique commonly encountered in many practical problems called **gradient descent** (*gradient = slope* and *descent = move downward*). The pseudocode of the algorithm is presented here:

```
REPEAT until we reach convergence
    FOR every coefficient b_i
        new_b_i ← previous_b_i - α ∂Loss/∂β_i
```

The basic idea behind the algorithm is the iterative update of the coefficients to be estimated until we reach convergence (ideally reaching a global optimum). At every iteration, we calculate the partial derivative of the loss multiplied by the factor α, known as the **learning rate**. Then, the product is subtracted from the coefficients to adjust its value. When a single training sample is used in each iteration, the variant is called **stochastic gradient descent** (**SGD**). With SGD, we calculate the error and update the model for each sample in the training set, which is computationally expensive. Therefore, using a smaller random subset of the training set in each iteration is preferable. This version is called **mini-batch gradient descent** (**MGD**) and splits the training dataset into small batches that consist of m out of N training samples. In a typical MGD technique, we must run through all the samples in the training set before updating the coefficients.

To intuitively comprehend this process, let us consider the example illustrated in *Figure 4.16*:

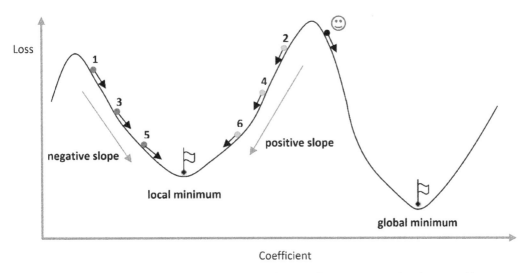

Figure 4.16 – Gradient descent finds the value of the coefficient associated with minimal loss

Suppose we are at either position **1** or **2** and want to reach the bottom of the specific curve (point with the left flag). How can we be sure that we are moving in the correct direction? This task is straightforward when one can see and plan ahead. Conversely, it is very challenging when blindfolded, and we do not *see* where this minimum exists. In this case, we need some guidance to perform each small step in the correct direction. Gradient descent can identify the slope of the *terrain* in our immediate vicinity and inform us how to perform the next step downward in the curve. This analogy helps understand optimization problems such as finding the logistic regression model's coefficients that minimize prediction error.

Figure 4.17 provides a numerical example for clarifying the mechanics behind gradient descent:

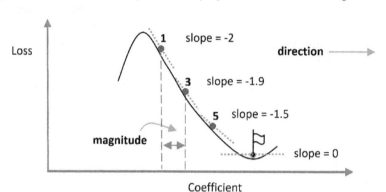

Figure 4.17 – Step calculation during gradient descent

Let's assume that the tangent slope to the curve at point **1** equals *-2*. By multiplying this number with the learning rate $\alpha = 0.2$, we obtain *-0.4*. This number contains two crucial pieces of information: the next step's *direction* and *magnitude*. To understand direction, look again at the pseudocode presented earlier. When subtracting a negative number from the previous coefficient, it is equivalent to adding a positive number; this is the direction. The absolute value of *0.4* signifies the magnitude of the step. The step size at point **3** decreases as the slope is smaller compared to point **1**. At point **5**, the magnitude of the step is even smaller. Moving toward the bottom of the curve, it is sensible to take small steps to avoid overshooting the minimum. The process terminates when we reach convergence (**slope = 0**). Notice that descending the curve from the left side gives coefficients that increase their value at every step. The opposite reasoning applies if we descend the curve from the right side, starting at point **2**.

Unfortunately, the previous solution is not ideal as we failed to find the global minimum (right flag). Depending on where we settle at the initial descent point, we may get stuck in a local valley. Gradient descent finds a minimum value (local or global) by taking steps from an initial random position. The way we initialize the model coefficients (starting points) may or may not lead to rest in the optimal position. It would have been better to start at the *smiley face* position in this example. Ideal problems are those where there is only one place where the slope is exactly zero, and the loss function converges—these problems are called **convex**. However, it is more common for high-dimensional loss surfaces to settle in one of the many local minima.

Another tricky situation concerns the choice of the learning rate, which dictates how small or big the steps we take in every iteration. For example, consider the left plot of *Figure 4.18*:

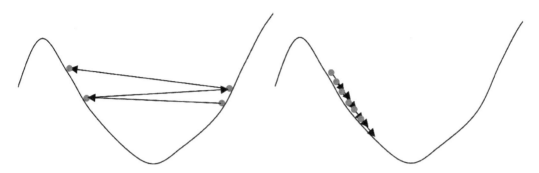

Figure 4.18 – Big (left) versus small (right) learning rate

Too large steps may inhibit the algorithm from reaching the minimum and bounce between the two sides of the curve. Conversely, small steps might take too long for the algorithm to converge (see the right plot of *Figure 4.18*). As a rule of thumb, we begin with values of about 0.01 or 0.001, and based on the performance during training (accuracy and time), we adapt the learning rate accordingly.

After providing an intuitive explanation behind gradient descent, we examine how to calculate the logistic regression coefficients in more detail. In the example that follows, we seek to extract the slope for a single example and a single coefficient β_i, using the chain rule (https://en.wikipedia.org/wiki/Chain_rule):

$$\frac{\partial Loss}{\partial \beta_i} = \frac{\partial (y - \hat{y})^2}{\partial \beta_i} = \frac{\partial (y - S(x))^2}{\partial \beta_i} = 2(y - S(x)) \frac{\partial (y - S(x))}{\partial \beta_i}$$

$$= -2(y - S(x)) \frac{\partial S(x)}{\partial x} \frac{\partial x}{\partial \beta_i} = -2(y - S(x)) \frac{\partial S(x)}{\partial x} x_i$$

The derivative of the sigmoid function is this:

$$\frac{\partial S(x)}{\partial x} = \frac{-(1 + e^{-x})'}{(1 + e^{-x})^2} = \frac{e^{-x}}{(1 + e^{-x})^2} = \frac{1 - 1 + e^{-x}}{(1 + e^{-x})^2} = -\frac{1}{(1 + e^{-x})^2} + \frac{1 + e^{-x}}{(1 + e^{-x})^2}$$

$$= -\frac{1}{(1 + e^{-x})^2} + \frac{1}{1 + e^{-x}} = \frac{1}{1 + e^{-x}} \left(1 - \frac{1}{1 + e^{-x}}\right) = S(x)(1 - S(x))$$

So, the loss equation can now be written as follows:

$$\frac{\partial Loss}{\partial \beta_i} = -2(y - S(x))S(x)(1 - S(x))x_i$$

Based on the previous analysis, the update rule becomes this:

$$new_{b_i} \leftarrow previous_{b_i} + \alpha\big(y - S(x)\big)S(x)\big(1 - S(x)\big)x_i$$

The number *2* just says that we have a learning rate twice as big and can be omitted. Let's now apply the presented theory to a contrived numerical example.

Using logistic regression

Physicians use specific criteria to determine whether a breast tumor is benign or malignant. For example, *Table 4.2* shows data for ten patients and three criteria: the tumor's radius, texture, and compactness. Based on the values of these features, the tumor can be categorized accordingly:

Mean radius	Mean texture	Mean compactness	Malignant (0=no, 1=yes)
x_1	x_2	x_3	y
2.362	3.421	1.181	0
1.042	2.552	1.275	0
6.229	1.773	1.563	1
0.843	2.033	1.012	0
7.535	2.088	1.851	1
5.244	0.462	1.456	1
7.864	0.541	1.791	1
1.124	2.362	1.198	0
8.377	3.549	1.562	1
2.996	5.077	1.231	0

Table 4.2 – Tumor categorization based on three features

We can now proceed with the estimation of the model's coefficients. We start with the first sample in the dataset (**y=0**) and initialize the coefficients to *0*. The logistic regression predicts the following value:

$$S(x) = \frac{1}{1 + e^{-x}} = \frac{1}{1 + e^{-(0 + 0 \cdot 2.362 + 0 \cdot 3.421 + 0 \cdot 1.181)}} = 0.5$$

We can now incorporate the update rule for estimating each coefficient using a learning rate equal to 0.2. Notice that for b_0, we can assume that it always has 1 as the input value (x_0):

$$b_0 = 0 + 0.2 \cdot (0 - 0.5) \cdot 0.5 \cdot (1 - 0.5) \cdot 1 = -0.025$$

$$b_1 = 0 + 0.2 \cdot (0 - 0.5) \cdot 0.5 \cdot (1 - 0.5) \cdot 2.362 = -0.059$$

$$b_2 = 0 + 0.2 \cdot (0 - 0.5) \cdot 0.5 \cdot (1 - 0.5) \cdot 3.421 = -0.086$$

$$b_3 = 0 + 0.2 \cdot (0 - 0.5) \cdot 0.5 \cdot (1 - 0.5) \cdot 1.181 = -0.03$$

In the next iteration, we use the second sample and obtain the following results:

$$S(x) = \frac{1}{1 + e^{-(-0.025 - 0.059 \cdot 1.042 - 0.086 \cdot 2.552 - 0.03 \cdot 1.275)}} = 0.415$$

$$b_0 = -0.025 + 0.2 \cdot (0 - 0.415) \cdot 0.415 \cdot (1 - 0.415) \cdot 1 = -0.045$$

$$b_1 = -0.059 + 0.2 \cdot (0 - 0.415) \cdot 0.415 \cdot (1 - 0.415) \cdot 1.042 = -0.08$$

$$b_2 = -0.086 + 0.2 \cdot (0 - 0.415) \cdot 0.415 \cdot (1 - 0.415) \cdot 2.552 = -0.137$$

$$b_3 = -0.03 + 0.2 \cdot (0 - 0.415) \cdot 0.415 \cdot (1 - 0.415) \cdot 1.275 = -0.055$$

Similarly, we proceed with all the other samples in the dataset. Every iteration over the same data is called an **epoch**; in our simplistic example, we use 10 epochs in total. Using MGD, yield to the model update after each epoch. After the last iteration, the output of the training process is the model shown here:

$$S(x) = \frac{1}{1 + e^{-(-0.241 - 0.716 \cdot x_1 - 0.901 \cdot x_2 - 0.188 \cdot x_3)}}$$

Interestingly, the model correctly classifies all the input samples. So, for example, considering the last row of *Table 4.2*, we get the following outcome:

$$S(x) = \frac{1}{1 + e^{-(-0.241 - 0.716 \cdot 2.996 - 0.901 \cdot 5.077 - 0.188 \cdot 1.231)}} = 0.053 \approx 0$$

It's about time to incorporate the method for the sentiment analysis dataset and perform classification. The first step in this process is to create training and test sets.

Creating training and test sets

Extracting a binary sentiment label for each sample in the dataset is based on the score assigned by the reviewer. Thus, in the following code snippet, we set all ratings with a score equal to or less than 3 to signify a negative review. A value above 3 denotes the opposite:

```
# Keep only the review text and score.
df = df_software[['review/text', 'review/score']]


# Every rating below or equal to 3 is considered negative (0)
and above 3 positive (1).
df['label'] = df['review/score'].apply(lambda x: 0 if x <=
3  else 1)


df.head()
>>    review/text    review/score  label
0  I bought this so...     2.0      0
2  It clearly says ...     1.0      0
5  I gave this game...     5.0      1
7  I think this on ...     4.0      1
8  It is great, my ...     5.0      1
```

We also check the number of positive and negative samples:

```
# Count the number of samples for each label.
df.label.value_counts()
>>   1    47179
     0    37812
```

The output suggests that the chosen threshold provides a relatively balanced dataset, which was expected according to *Figure 4.4*. We can now proceed and vectorize the text of the reviews:

```
from sklearn.feature_extraction.text import CountVectorizer
from sklearn.model_selection import train_test_split


# Get the training and test sets.
df_train, df_test = train_test_split(df, test_size=0.3,
stratify=df['label'], random_state=123)


# Create the count vectorizer.
```

```
vectorizer = CountVectorizer(binary=True)

# Fit on the training data and get the count vectors.
vectorizer.fit_transform(df_train['review/text'].values)
countvect_train = vectorizer.transform(df_train['review/text'].
values)
countvect_test = vectorizer.transform(df_test['review/text'].
values)
```

Next, we store the label for each training and test sample in two arrays:

```
# Get the class arrays.
train_class = df_train['label'].values
test_class = df_test['label'].values
```

As all datasets are now in place, we can proceed to the classification step.

Performing classification

The baseline performance allows us to benchmark the logistic regression model. We pick the category with the most training samples, corresponding to label 1:

```
from sklearn import metrics
from sklearn.linear_model import LogisticRegression

print("The baseline accuracy is: " + str(df[df.label ==
1].shape[0]/df.shape[0]))
>> The baseline accuracy is: 0.5551058347354426
```

Assigning label 1 to every sample from the dataset yields a baseline model that is correct 56% of the time. Next, we create, train, and evaluate the classifier:

```
# Create the classifier.
classifier = LogisticRegression(penalty='none', solver='lbfgs',
max_iter=10000, random_state=123)

# Fit the classifier with the train data.
classifier.fit(countvect_train, train_class)

# Get the predicted classes.
```

```
test_class_pred = classifier.predict(countvect_test)


# Calculate the accuracy on the test set.
metrics.accuracy_score(test_class, test_class_pred)
>> 0.7882971213428505
```

The obtained accuracy is around 79%, better than the baseline but still mediocre. We can try to calibrate the hyperparameter of the algorithm; for example, use another `solver` or increase `max_iter`. First, however, we put into action a more effective technique and take the opportunity to discuss a major topic in ML that adversely affects the performance of the algorithms. This is the theme of the next section.

Applying regularization

In *Chapter 3, Classifying Topics of Newsgroup Posts*, we introduced the Occam's razor concept: between two competing explanations (models), the simplest one should be preferred. The reason is that complex models tend to overfit the data and do not generalize well. On the other hand, aiming for too simple models engenders the opposite outcome and may result in solutions that underfit the data. Let's provide the theoretical context to understand this concept in more depth.

Suppose we perform an experiment acquiring 99% accuracy for the training set and 86% for the test one. What does this tell us? We created a model that learned the training data perfectly but didn't do that well on unseen data. The 1% error on the training set is the model's **bias**, whereas the difference with the error on the test set (14% - 1%) is the model's **variance**. In this specific experiment, the classifier has high variance; consequently, the model is overfitting. Performing a second experiment yields an accuracy of 87% for the training set and 83% for the test set. This time, the classifier exhibits high bias, and we can say that the model is underfitting.

There are different strategies for addressing both situations. For instance, we can add more features or try alternative ML algorithms for underfitting. On the other hand, one possible remedy for overfitting is adding more data to alleviate a possible mismatch between the training and test instances. The population of the training observations is not representative enough, and the model struggles to make good inferences from unseen data.

So, let's first check the performance on the training set:

```
# Get the predicted classes.
test_class_pred = classifier.predict(countvect_train)


# Calculate the accuracy on the test set.
metrics.accuracy_score(train_class, test_class_pred)
>> 0.9999663825996336
```

The accuracy, in this case, is excellent, but its difference from the test set implies high variance (99% - 78% = 21%). To attack the problem of overfitting, we use **regularization**, which penalizes the complexity of a model. We already encountered this technique in the *Adjusting the hyperparameters* section of *Chapter 2, Detecting Spam Emails*. The C hyperparameter of the **support vector machine (SVM)** algorithm is actually a parameter for regularization.

So far, the minimization of the loss function has been the primary way of eliciting the best model on a given dataset. Using regularization, however, we also need to minimize a second factor: the complexity of the model. Thus, the minimization task becomes twofold:

$$minimize(Loss + model\_complexity)$$

Loss functions should already be familiar from the discussion in this chapter, so we need to define the second term. How can we quantify complexity in this case? A common approach is to penalize models with high-weight values. The assumption is that smaller values result in simpler models. The model overfits as the weights grow in size to handle the specifics of the training observations. One method of this kind is **L2 regularization**, which considers the sum of the squared weights of each model:

$$w_1^2 + w_2^2 + \cdots + w_n^2$$

The larger the values of the weights, the higher the regularization penalty is. So, we can rewrite the minimization task as follows:

$$minimize\left(Loss + \lambda(w_1^2 + w_2^2 + \cdots + w_n^2)\right)$$

The loss and regularization terms are balanced by the λ hyperparameter that determines the severity of the penalty. Lower values of λ lead to more value fitting the data against the model's simplicity. Applying L2 regularization (`penalty='l2'`) is shown in the following code fragment:

```
# Create the classifier.
classifier = LogisticRegression(penalty='l2', C=1.0,
solver='lbfgs', max_iter=10000, random_state=123)


# Fit the classifier with the train data.
classifier.fit(countvect_train, train_class)


# Get the predicted classes.
test_class_pred = classifier.predict(countvect_test)
```

```
# Calculate the accuracy on the test set.
metrics.accuracy_score(test_class, test_class_pred)
>> 0.8524197976311868
```

Regularization worked favorably for the classification task, and the performance improved significantly. We can also adjust the C hyperparameter, which is the inverse of the regularization penalty. The value 1.0 was chosen randomly, but we can calibrate C with the technique presented in the *Performing cross-validation* section of *Chapter 3, Classifying Topics of Newsgroup Posts*. Consider extending the code with this step!

This section dealt with one of the most known ML algorithms. As a result, we acquired a more profound understanding of how algorithms learn from data. After presenting the necessary theoretical framework, we applied the method for sentiment analysis. We also discussed the L2 regularization technique that combats overfitting by penalizing models that have large weights. The following section focuses on state-of-the-art architecture encompassing many of the ideas presented so far.

Introducing deep neural networks

Nature has always inspired mathematicians and engineers to devise appropriate algorithms, designs, and artifacts for any given problem. So incorporating solutions that have proven themselves over millennia seems like a good idea. We can refer to numerous examples such as bats' echolocation that inspired human-made sonars, the high-speed trains that have a shape that resembles the elongated beak of kingfisher birds to prevent sonic booms, the flight of drones as a flock of birds to avoid collisions, and many more.

Throughout this chapter, we discussed many times how algorithms learn from data. What is more natural than to think that emulating the human brain and its functionalities can enhance artificial cognition? Exploiting the mode of operation of this astonishingly complex organ of the human nervous system might permit the creation of sophisticated algorithms in any domain. This section provides a gentle introduction to the topic and presents a bio-inspired architecture based on the fundamental functions of the human brain.

The elementary unit of the brain is known as a **neuron**, schematically illustrated in *Figure 4.19*:

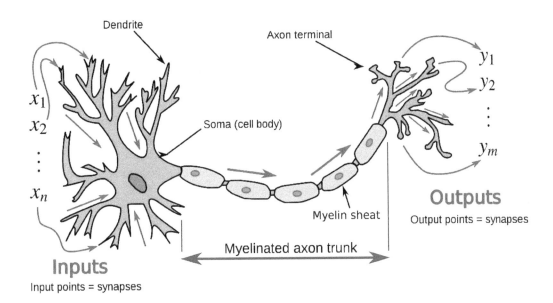

Figure 4.19 – Diagram of the components of a neuron (Source: https://en.wikipedia. org/wiki/Biological_neuron_model#/media/File:Neuron3.png)

We can identify three main components inside a neuron: the *dendrites*, the *soma*, and the *axon*. Dendrites act as inputs to the neuron (see $x_1 - x_n$), which come from other interconnected neurons. Then, they transfer each input (with a specific weight) to the soma, which works as a summation function. The axon receives the result, and once it reaches a specific electrical potential, it emits a signal pulse. Finally, the pulse is transferred to the terminals (see $y_1 - y_m$) that are connected to other neurons. Nature creates complex meshes of interconnected nodes by stacking many of these fundamental components. A typical human brain has around 86 billion neurons connected on average to 7,000 other neurons. Compare this to the number of stars in our Milky Way galaxy, which astronomers estimate somewhere between 200 and 400 billion. It's like everybody hosts a small galaxy inside their head!

While this knowledge is fascinating, it does beg the question: how can we apply it to create intelligent machines? Is it possible to replicate the functions of a biological neuron to construct an artificial brain? Unfortunately, no, for the moment. In practice, very few times are nature-inspired solutions applied unmodified. For example, the flying machines we use today hardly replicate the function of bird wings or digital cameras on how human eyes perceive optical stimuli. In the same sense, we use biological neurons as an inspiration to create artificial ones. The following section presents the steps to design an elementary unit to mimic aspects of a biological neuron.

Understanding logic gates

One of the first courses in any computer science program involves understanding how computer circuits work. Recall from the *Extracting word representations* section from *Chapter 2, Detecting Spam Emails*, that computers can only process signals containing two voltage levels or states. Then, the binary system expresses every quantity as a sequence of 1s (high voltage) and 0s (low voltage). But how can we create more demanding calculations besides identifying the two voltage levels? The answer is by stacking elementary electronic components called **logic gates**. The different types of gates receive one or two inputs, while their output results from a rule. Every logic gate has its **truth table** that dictates the exact output for a given input. Let us examine the example of *Figure 4.20*, which includes two of the most fundamental logic gates named **AND** and **OR**:

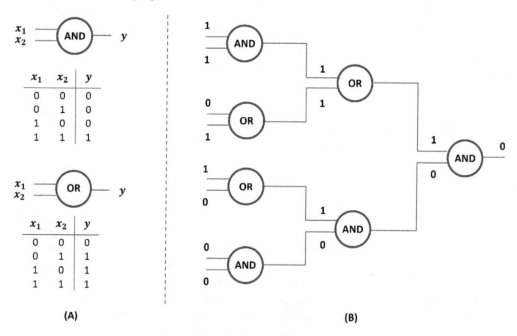

Figure 4.20 – Understanding logic gates

In *Figure 4.20 (A)*, the two gates receive two binary inputs and output a single binary value according to their truth tables. For example, when $x_1 = 1$ and $x_2 = 0$, the **AND** gate gives $y = 0$, while the **OR** gate outputs $y = 1$. The right-side plot shows a network with multiple gates, a possible input stream $(1, 1, 0, 1, 1, 0, 0, 0)$, and the corresponding output (0). Take a moment to go through each node and verify the operation using the truth tables. By connecting different numbers and types of gates, we can create complex networks and perform sophisticated calculations. Astonishingly, such a fundamental element is the building block of most modern computing devices.

For decades, engineers' main task has been to include more of these elements into a single processor or chip and devise novel architectures to utilize their function efficiently. How does this topology relate to the theme of the current chapter? The following section provides the answer, where we discuss a fundamental unit suitable for ML.

Understanding perceptrons

Building electronic circuits with logic gates yield the high-performing computers we use daily. However, using the same elementary blocks to construct an artificial brain seems insurmountable. We would need far more complex building units, and this section performs a small step in this direction. So, we present a fundamental element called a **perceptron** that has been available since the 1950s but started to get significant hype in recent years. As with the gates discussed earlier, a perceptron takes several binary inputs and emits a single binary output. There are a few subtle differences, however. Each input is multiplied by a weight coefficient and then added all together. The result is examined against a certain threshold, determining whether the preceptor emits *0* or *1*. The plots of *Figure 4.21* reveal several of the characteristics of this unit:

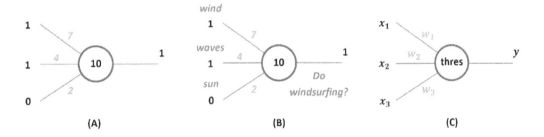

Figure 4.21 – A perceptron with three binary inputs

Specifically, in *Figure 4.21 (A)*, the perceptron receives the three inputs **1**, **1**, and **0** multiplied with the weights **7**, **4**, and **2**, respectively. Their sum is more than **10** (threshold), and that is why we get **1** at the output of the perceptron:

$$1 \cdot 7 + 1 \cdot 4 + 0 \cdot 2 = 11 > 10$$

Figure 4.21 (B) provides a practical example of how to incorporate this building block. The decision to go surfing on one specific day depends on three criteria: **wind**, **waves**, and **sun**. These exhibit different importance, and for that reason, they are assigned different weights. Finally, the weighted sum is compared against the same threshold (**10**).

We formalize this process in *Figure 4.21 (C)* and delineate it with the following formula:

$$Calculate \sum_{i=1}^{n} w_i x_i, \ and \ if \begin{cases} > threshold \rightarrow 1 \\ \leq threshold \rightarrow 0 \end{cases}$$

Note that a perceptron can receive more than three inputs in the general case. Next, we introduce a new term called **bias (b)**, which is defined as the negative of the threshold:

$$b \equiv -threshold$$

You can think of the bias of how easy it is to get output **1** from the perceptron. Notice that the term refers to something different from the same in the *Applying regularization* section. In general, biases are systematic errors in ML models due to incorrect assumptions in the ML process. For example, using data that is not sufficiently large or representative enough to teach algorithms is a case of sampling bias. In the perceptron case, the bias refers to the algorithm's assumption for the trigger threshold of this unit. So, the previous formula now becomes this:

$$Calculate \sum_{i=1}^{n} w_i x_i + b, \ and \ if \begin{cases} > 0 \rightarrow 1 \\ \leq 0 \rightarrow 0 \end{cases}$$

Contrary to the logic gates where nothing has to be learned—all decisions are based on the truth tables—for the perceptron case, we need to estimate (learn) the weights and the bias. As you might suspect, this optimization problem can be solved with *gradient descent*. First, we must define a loss function and then iteratively adjust the weights and the bias to minimize it. For the second step, we calculate the perceptron's delta function that determines the change to be added or subtracted from the weights and the bias and adjust their values using the gradient descent update rule. As a result, the error is usually reduced in every iteration until an acceptable performance is reached.

> **Two sampling biases**
>
> There is an inherent problem when TV or radio shows solicit their audience to participate in online polls, especially on controversial issues. Responses are given by self-selected people who often have a firm opinion on the issue (**voluntary response bias**).
>
> Bill Gates, Steve Jobs, and Mark Zuckerberg are famous university dropouts that became multi-billionaires. So, it's logical to think dropping out of university is a prerequisite to phenomenal success. However, this ignores the far more significant set of dropouts who never got anywhere (**survivorship bias**).

This section continued the discussion on the elementary blocks that assist in creating intelligent systems. A perceptron is an elegant conceptual abstraction to facilitate the discussion about artificial neurons, which is the topic of the next section.

Understanding artificial neurons

An important limitation of a perceptron is that it receives and offers only binary values. In many kinds of problems, however, we would like to make predictions from inputs of continuous value, and for that reason, perceptrons experience limited practical utility. This section introduces another fundamental block called an **artificial neuron**, and its basic components are illustrated in *Figure 4.22*:

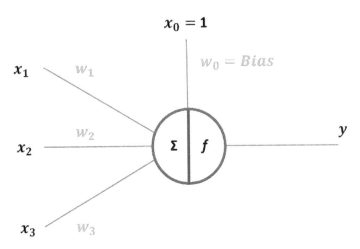

Figure 4.22 – Artificial neuron

The structure of an artificial neuron seems quite similar to one of the perceptron. The summation (Σ) of the weighted input is the same as before, but instead of comparing it with a fixed threshold, we pass it through the function **f**, like so:

$$f(\sum_{i=1}^{n} w_i x_i + w_0)$$

Its output is a range of values that shows how much the artificial neuron is activated. In this way, the neurons enhance their expressive power and cease to work as on/off switches. Contrast this with the binary outcome of the perceptron that indicates whether it is triggered or not. Furthermore, artificial neurons can be activated at different levels, making them more similar to their biological counterparts. For this reason, **f** is known as the neuron's **activation function**. *Figure 4.23* shows four different options for these functions:

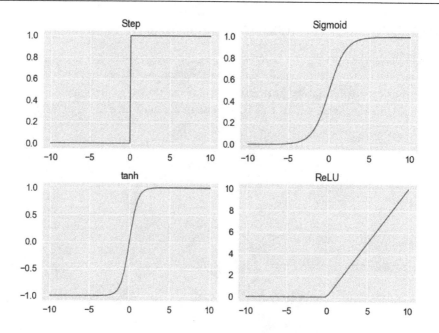

Figure 4.23 – Different activation functions

Observe that all functions are non-linear, which, according to the theory, is beneficial for approximating arbitrarily complex functions such as the decision boundaries of an ML model. Adding non-linearities into a network of artificial neurons is one of the main advantages of the activation functions.

Let's first consider the **Step** activation, which consists of two distinct levels. In this case, the neuron is not triggered if the weighted sum of the inputs is less than or equal to zero. Conversely, a sum greater than zero triggers the neuron. Notice that using the **Step** activation function yields a perceptron unit. On the other hand, the **Sigmoid** activation produces gradual changes in the output for inputs around zero. Contrast this to the **Step** function, where the change between the two levels is abrupt. The **tanh** option outputs both positive and negative values in a range between **-1.0** to **1.0**. Finally, the **ReLU** (**Rectified Linear Units**) presents a special non-linearity compared to the **Sigmoid** and **tanh** options. Specifically, it emits the input directly if it is positive; otherwise, the output is zero. There are many other options for an activation function; in practice, we need to experiment to find the most suitable choice.

Next, we discuss how to create networks of artificial neurons that can solve challenging ML problems.

Creating artificial neural networks

The real power of artificial neurons emerges when they are networked together to learn features from the data and inference from unseen instances. An **artificial neural network** (**ANN**) is a collection of connected nodes (artificial neurons) stacked in layers. For instance, looking at *Figure 4.24*, we can identify three types of layers—namely, the **Input**, **Hidden**, and **Output** layers:

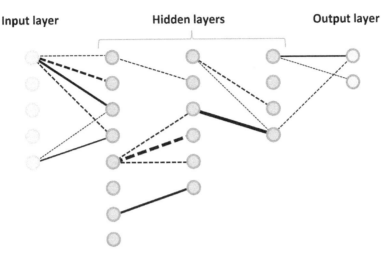

Figure 4.24 – A dense network of artificial neurons

The input layer receives data for the ANN, and its size is restricted by the number of features in each input sample. For example, if the network needs to learn from an embedding vector with 256 elements, the size of the input layer is 256.

The network includes a series of hidden layers, where the *true* values of their nodes are unknown and consequently *hidden* from the input data. They are the secret sauce of an ANN and provide its special power. Networks with many hidden layers are called **deep neural networks** (**DNNs**). In *Figure 4.24*, we omitted many of the connection lines for clarity. However, each neuron receives input from all neurons of the layer that precedes it. In this case, the fully connected layer is called a **dense layer**. The width of the lines signifies the strength of the connection, and it's related to the weight coefficient of the neuron. The thicker the line, the higher the absolute value of the weight. The dotted lines signify a negative weight in the specific visualization, whereas the straight lines are associated with a positive weight. Beware that the number of layers, neurons, and the type of activation functions is a design choice.

Hidden layers implicitly capture information from the input data and extract relationships between the features. Intuitively, hidden layers at the beginning of the network capture low-level relationships, whereas the layers to the end elicit high-level ones. A typical example is an ANN for classifying a human face. The first hidden layer detects light and dark pixels, the second extracts simple forms from the image (such as lines), and the third identifies more complex shapes (such as an eye or nose, and so on). We return to this cascading architecture in *Chapter 8, Detecting Hateful and Offensive Language*.

The output layer is the final layer of the network and determines the result of the ANN processing. The number of neurons in the output is related to the problem under study. For example, classifying an observation into two categories requires two output nodes. One node positively identifies the sample in one category and the other negatively in the second category. An educative interactive demonstration to create and train your own ANN can be found at the following link: `https://playground.tensorflow.org/`.

Training artificial neural networks

Before concluding this section, we need to address the learning aspect of an ANN. As you probably guessed, this is yet another optimization problem where we must define and minimize a loss function. One possible option for this task is to use the gradient descent technique we learned previously. However, due to the special nature of an ANN, we need to go through multiple layers to adjust the parameters. For this reason, gradient descent is paired with another technique called **backpropagation**.

The training process consists of a *forward* and a *backward* pass. We feed an input sample to the ANN and calculate the error in the first pass. In the backward one, we carry the information about the error in the reverse order and adjust the weights and biases of the network. The forward-backward steps are repeated multiple times until the error becomes sufficiently small. Let's consider the minimal **neural network (NN)** shown in *Figure 4.25* and a numerical example to clarify things:

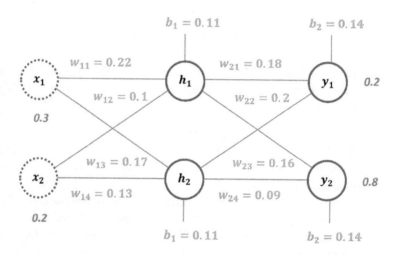

Figure 4.25 – A snapshot of a simplistic NN

The network consists of an input layer, a hidden layer, and an output layer, with two nodes each. The chosen activation function is the sigmoid one, and the values of the parameters are initialized according to the screenshot. The **0.3** and **0.2** inputs should produce **0.2** and **0.8** outputs.

We begin with the forward pass and calculate the input to the neurons of the hidden layer, like so:

$$in_{h1} = w_{11}x_1 + w_{12}x_2 + b_1 = 0.22 \cdot 0.3 + 0.1 \cdot 0.2 + 0.11 = 0.196$$

$$in_{h2} = w_{13}x_1 + w_{14}x_2 + b_1 = 0.17 \cdot 0.3 + 0.13 \cdot 0.2 + 0.11 = 0.187$$

The output of the neurons is this:

$$out_{h1} = \frac{1}{1 + e^{-in_{h1}}} = \frac{1}{1 + e^{-0.196}} = 0.549$$

$$out_{h2} = \frac{1}{1 + e^{-in_{h2}}} = \frac{1}{1 + e^{-0.187}} = 0.547$$

We repeat the same step with the output layer:

$$in_{y1} = w_{21}out_{h1} + w_{22}out_{h2} + b_2 = 0.18 \cdot 0.549 + 0.2 \cdot 0.547 + 0.14 = 0.348$$

$$in_{y2} = w_{23}out_{h1} + w_{24}out_{h2} + b_2 = 0.16 \cdot 0.549 + 0.09 \cdot 0.547 + 0.14 = 0.277$$

$$out_{y1} = \frac{1}{1 + e^{-in_{y1}}} = \frac{1}{1 + e^{-0.348}} = 0.586$$

$$out_{y2} = \frac{1}{1 + e^{-in_{y2}}} = \frac{1}{1 + e^{-0.277}} = 0.569$$

Next, we calculate the errors for the two output nodes:

$$error_{y1} = \frac{1}{2} \cdot \left(y_1 - out_{y1}\right)^2 = \frac{1}{2} \cdot (0.2 - 0.586)^2 = 0.074$$

$$error_{y2} = \frac{1}{2} \cdot \left(y_2 - out_{y2}\right)^2 = \frac{1}{2} \cdot (0.8 - 0.569)^2 = 0.027$$

The total *error* of the forward pass is, therefore, this:

$$error = error_{y1} + error_{y2} = 0.101$$

Let's now perform a backward pass and see how to update the model's parameters. We focus on the weights and examine how their change affects the total error using the following partial derivatives and the chain rule:

$$\frac{\partial error}{\partial w_{21}} = \frac{\partial error}{\partial out_{y1}} \cdot \frac{\partial out_{y1}}{\partial in_{y1}} \cdot \frac{\partial in_{y1}}{\partial w_{21}}$$

$$\frac{\partial error}{\partial w_{22}} = \frac{\partial error}{\partial out_{y1}} \cdot \frac{\partial out_{y1}}{\partial in_{y1}} \cdot \frac{\partial in_{y1}}{\partial w_{22}}$$

$$\frac{\partial error}{\partial w_{23}} = \frac{\partial error}{\partial out_{y2}} \cdot \frac{\partial out_{y2}}{\partial in_{y2}} \cdot \frac{\partial in_{y2}}{\partial w_{23}}$$

$$\frac{\partial error}{\partial w_{24}} = \frac{\partial error}{\partial out_{y4}} \cdot \frac{\partial out_{y2}}{\partial in_{y2}} \cdot \frac{\partial in_{y2}}{\partial w_{24}}$$

Specifically, for w_{21}, we have to calculate the different partial derivatives of the relevant equation. So, the formula should look like this:

$$\frac{\partial error}{\partial out_{y1}} = 2 \cdot \frac{1}{2}(y_1 - out_{y1})^{2-1} \cdot (-1) + 0 = -(0.2 - 0.586) = 0.386$$

$$\frac{\partial out_{y1}}{\partial in_{y1}} = out_{y1} \cdot (1 - out_{y1}) = 0.586 \cdot (1 - 0.586) = 0.243$$

$$\frac{\partial in_{y1}}{\partial w_{21}} = 1 \cdot out_{h1} \cdot w_{21}^{1-1} + 0 + 0 = out_{h1} = 0.549$$

We already learned how to calculate the derivative of the sigmoid function in the *Understanding gradient descent* section. Plugging the partial derivatives of the *error* with respect to W_{21} gives us this:

$$\frac{\partial error}{\partial w_{21}} = 0.386 \cdot 0.243 \cdot 0.549 = 0.051$$

We can now adjust the value of W_{21} to minimize the error using the gradient descent update rule:

$$new_{w21} = previous_{w21} - \alpha \cdot \frac{\partial error}{\partial w_{21}} = 0.18 - 0.05 \cdot 0.051 = 0.177$$

Notice that we used a learning rate equal to *0.05*. In the same way, we can calculate the other weights, which differ slightly from their previous version:

$$new_{w22} = 0.197$$

$$new_{w23} = 0.158$$

$$new_{w24} = 0.088$$

We then move on to the next step of the backward pass for the hidden layer. For example, to update w_{11}, we must now calculate the following quantity:

$$\frac{\partial error}{\partial w_{11}} = \frac{\partial error}{\partial out_{h1}} \cdot \frac{\partial out_{h1}}{\partial in_{h1}} \cdot \frac{\partial in_{h1}}{\partial w_{11}}$$

We do not present any further calculations here. Hopefully, you understood how the parameters are updated with backpropagation. At each epoch, the training set is fed to the forward pass. Then, a better estimation is obtained for the weights and biases in the backward one.

It is now time to apply the theory presented so far to the sentiment analysis problem of this chapter.

Performing classification

This exercise incorporates **TensorFlow**, an end-to-end open source platform for ML. We also use **Keras**, which is a high-level **application programming interface (API)** for TensorFlow. The created model consists of four hidden layers that include 256 neurons each. The following code snippet shows the specific configuration:

```
import tensorflow
tensorflow.random.set_seed(2)
from numpy.random import seed
seed(1)
from keras.layers import Dropout, Dense
from keras.models import Sequential


node_num = 256
layers_num = 4
dropout = 0.5
```

There is also another hyperparameter that defines the `dropout` rate. **Dropout** is a regularization method that prevents the model from overfitting. During training time, it randomly sets the output edges of the hidden neuron to zero at each step. In our example, we use a `dropout` rate equal to `0.5`, suggesting that half of the output edges must be dropped randomly.

We can now proceed in the construction of the NNs following these steps:

1. First, we define the type of the model:

    ```
    model = Sequential()
    ```

2. Next, we create an input layer:

    ```
    model.add(Dense(node_num, input_dim=countvect_train.
    shape[1], activation='relu'))
    model.add(Dropout(dropout))
    ```

3. We can now create hidden layers:

    ```
    for i in range(0, layers_num):
        model.add(Dense(node_num, input_dim=node_num,
    activation='relu'))
        model.add(Dropout(dropout))
    ```

4. Finally, we construct the output layer of the network:

    ```
    model.add(Dense(1, activation='sigmoid'))
    model.compile(loss='binary_crossentropy',
                optimizer='adam', metrics=['accuracy'])
    ```

One important remark concerns the size of the input layer, which is controlled by the size of the input samples. This constraint is specified with the `countvect_train.shape[1]` statement. Take a look also at the activation functions for the different layers. For example, the `relu` option is used for the input and hidden layers. Conversely, we use the `sigmoid` function for the output. During the inference phase, the `sigmoid` activation provides a score that helps decipher whether the sample includes a positive or negative sentiment.

Before training the model, let's print summary information about the network:

```
model.summary()
>> Model: "sequential"
```

```
Layer (type)                Output Shape              Param #
=================================================================
dense (Dense)               (None, 256)               19297024

dropout (Dropout)           (None, 256)               0

...
=================================================================
Total params: 19,560,449
Trainable params: 19,560,449
Non-trainable params: 0
```

An interesting observation concerns the number of parameters that need to be estimated, around 20 million. It is not uncommon to have many parameters in a DNN, and most commercial applications we use today have billions. We can also visualize the model as a graph using the following code:

```
from keras.utils.vis_utils import plot_model


# Plot the model.
plot_model(model, to_file='./images/model_plot.png', show_
shapes=True, show_layer_names=True, dpi=100)
```

Figure 4.26 shows the output:

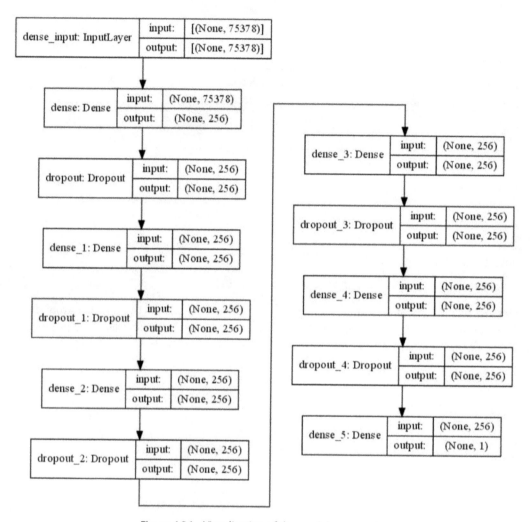

Figure 4.26 – Visualization of the model as a graph

Last, we can train the model for 10 epochs and use a `batch_size` value of `128` samples:

```
# Fit the classifier with the train data.
model.fit(countvect_train, train_class,
        validation_data=(countvect_train, train_class),
        epochs=10, batch_size=128, verbose=2)
```

```
>> Epoch 1/10
465/465 - 25s - loss: 0.4078 - accuracy: 0.8135 - val_loss:
0.2476 - val_accuracy: 0.9094

...

Epoch 10/10
465/465 - 36s - loss: 0.0500 - accuracy: 0.9839 - val_loss:
0.0068 - val_accuracy: 0.9988
```

The accuracy quickly reaches 98%, and we can now perform the real benchmark using the test data. As the predictions stem from a sigmoid function, we normalize them into two distinctive levels using the value 0.5 as a threshold:

```
# Get the predicted classes.
test_class_pred = model.predict(countvect_test)

# Normalize the predicted values to either 0 or 1.
test_class_pred = [(1 if i>0.5 else 0) for i in test_class_
pred]

# Calculate the accuracy on the test set.
metrics.accuracy_score(test_class, test_class_pred)
>> 0.8575574554867048
```

The model offers an accuracy of around 86%, close to the result obtained for the logistic regression case with regularization. However, as mentioned multiple times throughout the book, the solutions presented in the examples are indicative, and you are strongly urged to adjust the hyperparameters to obtain better performance.

This section concludes the discussion of the basics of DNNs. The content unfolded by presenting the different building blocks that perform elementary decisions. We started with logic gates and continued with perceptrons and artificial neurons. Finally, we saw how these units are combined to create complex networks. The real power of artificial neurons emerges when they are networked together. This topic is recurring in the subsequent chapters, as a vast number of state-of-art systems used today incorporate some architecture of this kind.

Summary

We covered a lot of ground in this chapter. Focusing on the sentiment analysis problem using real-world reviews from the Amazon online store, we became better acquainted with different algorithms and methods for supervised learning. Simultaneously, we broadened our coverage on how algorithms learn from data and how to incorporate optimization techniques for this task.

We worked on more advanced plots, starting with the EDA phase, and provided both cumulative and individual statistics for the reviewers. Additionally, we found an indirect way to assign a sentiment label to the data samples utilizing the reviewers' ratings.

The discussion around logistic regression facilitated the introduction of avoiding overfitting using regularization. Then, we detailed how artificial neurons are networked together to form complex networks. Finally, both algorithms were used to classify the samples in the dataset and provided good performance. Up next, we have another problem to deal with: implementing *recommender systems*.

5

Recommending Music Titles

Consumer choices and how they can be influenced are critical factors for every business. For instance, most people are interested in specific music genres, have favorite authors, or engage in particular hobbies. This information can be extracted from their purchase history or product reviews, and when utilized correctly, it can drastically increase the company's profit. A frequently cited case is the one million dollar prize awarded by Netflix in 2009 to a team that developed an algorithm that increased the accuracy of the company's recommendation engine by 10%. In the end, as more user interactions occur on any online platform, more data is available for analysis, leading to superior customized recommendations.

This chapter seeks to exploit product and user data to create recommender systems for music titles. We will base the discussion on a corpus of customer reviews from the Amazon online store. First, we will perform exploratory data analysis to identify possible shortcomings in the samples and carry out an extensive data cleaning task. Next, we will introduce two flavors of recommenders that rely either on product reviews or user ratings. We will discuss their strengths and weaknesses and implement different variants to suggest music titles. The implementations will utilize dimensionality reduction techniques, and as the chapter unfolds, we will have the opportunity to introduce a new method for this task. Finally, we will revisit the topic of hyperparameter tuning and discuss a related technique.

By the end of the chapter, you will be able to adapt the described pipeline to your own projects and inclinations.

In this chapter, we will go through the following topics:

- Understanding essential concepts in statistics
- Examining more advanced dimensionality reduction techniques
- Identifying hidden relations between products and customers
- Learning methods to compute optimal values of hyperparameters
- Creating models using autoencoders

Technical requirements

The chapter's code has been truncated in certain parts to facilitate reading the content. However, the whole code is available as a Jupyter notebook in the book's GitHub repository:

```
https://github.com/PacktPublishing/Machine-Learning-Techniques-for-
Text/tree/main/chapter-05
```

Understanding recommender systems

In an ever-growing digital world, customers are often overwhelmed by the choices available and need assistance finding what they want. It comes as no surprise that their habits and preferences are valuable assets to overcome this hurdle. Both assist in identifying user needs and permit companies to promote new products and services at the right time and place. Nonetheless, with most of the services being predominately online, having direct access to your customers is challenging. So, what is the solution?

Let's consider a few standard user inputs to answer this question, such as the number of stars awarded in an Amazon book review. Ratings provide a quality measure for the items in any online store. Similarly, the view count of a YouTube video is an engagement metric that can be used to recommend the same video to others. The number of views is an implicit indicator while rating scores are explicit. In both cases, however, an automatic system can exploit this information and expose users to content they may not know or keep them engaged with a service for a prolonged time. We have all encountered similar functionality on different online platforms that suggest products to buy, news to watch, friends to connect with, jobs to apply to, or restaurants to eat at. These systems fall under the general category of **recommender systems**, which is the current chapter's focus.

In general, recommender systems can be categorized into **content-based** and **collaborative filtering** types. The idea behind the first category is simple: create a model with the properties of the items already purchased by a customer and run this model on new items to identify those they are likely to buy. Generally, content-based systems become more accurate the more input a user provides. Let's consider the example of *Figure 5.1* and suppose that a customer purchases apples frequently:

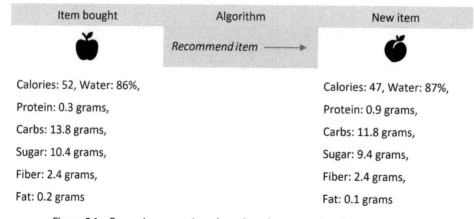

Figure 5.1 – Proposing a new item based on the properties of a purchased one

The recommender algorithm suggests oranges to purchase based on the apple's properties: **Calories**, **Water** percentage, **Protein**, **Carbs**, **Sugar**, **Fiber**, and **Fat** content. In the same way, a movie recommender can exploit certain information about a film, such as the actors, director, genre, and language, and, founded on these properties, provide suggestions.

A significant drawback of content-based recommenders is that they base their decision on items belonging to categories people already know they want. Referring solely to past purchase history creates a self-referential loop in which clients are informed about items in their range of interest. Consequently, there is a lack of any element of surprise, such as *I have never thought of this, but I think I like it!* Providing serendipitous recommendations allows the exploration of new options; this is where collaborative filtering comes into play. Systems of this kind try to identify similarities between customers based on past behaviors and people with similar purchase habits can recommend products to each other. The benefit, in this case, is that customers are exposed to items in which they have never expressed any explicit interest. The task becomes even more interesting when there is a rating metric for each product, a feature commonly encountered in most e-commerce and similar online services. *Figure 5.2* shows an example where an apple is suggested based on the individual and community item ratings:

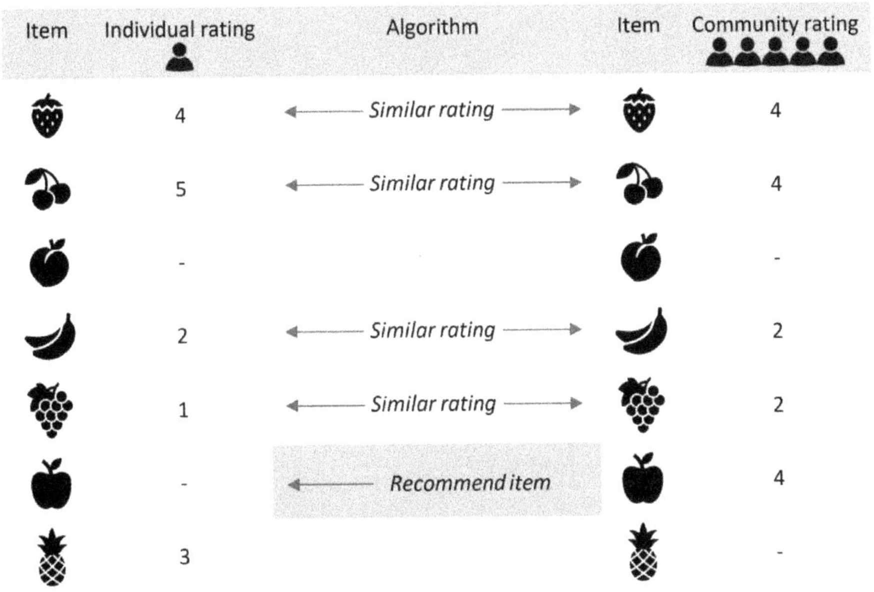

Figure 5.2 – Proposing a new item based on individual and community ratings

This chapter will deal with how to implement different recommendation systems for music products. As in *Chapter 4, Extracting Sentiments from Product Reviews*, we will incorporate a reviews corpus from Amazon (`https://snap.stanford.edu/data/web-Amazon-links.html`) comprising around 6.4 million five-star product ratings for relevant items. However, we have narrowed the subsequent analysis down into a smaller subset to make it less resource-intensive. Still, you are more than welcome to experiment by applying the pipeline presented to the whole corpus.

To comprehend a large amount of data, we need a way to contextualize it. So, once more, we will begin with the exploratory data analysis. This time, however, a more intensive data cleaning phase will be performed by identifying possible restrictions in the data.

Let's start!

Performing exploratory data analysis

The analysis begins by loading the data from the corpus. For this task, we will utilize the steps already presented in the *Performing exploratory data analysis* section of *Chapter 4, Extracting Sentiments from Product Reviews*. Therefore, refer to this same section to inspect the Python code for the readCategories, parseKeysValues, and readReviews methods that we will omit in this chapter. So, calling the first method, we extract 250000 samples from the dataset:

```
# Read the reviews from the data.
reviews = readReviews('./data/Music.txt.gz', 250000)
reviews.shape
>> (250000, 10)
```

Next, we will perform a couple of transformations on the data to facilitate the analysis:

```
# Rename the columns for convenience.
reviews.columns = ['productId', 'title', 'price', 'userId',
'profileName', 'helpfulness', 'score', 'time', 'summary',
'text']


# Make the scores float values.
reviews['score'] = reviews['score'].astype(float)
```

Let's now examine the first five lines in the dataset:

```
reviews[['productId', 'userId', 'score', 'text']].head(5)
>>    productId  userId          score  text
0     B000020661  unknown          5.0    I hope a lot of pe...
1     B000020661  A2KLYVAS0MIBMQ   5.0    My lovely Pat has ...
2     B000058A81  A18C9SNLZWVBIE   5.0    We've come a long ...
3     B000058A81  A38QSOKE2DD8JD   5.0    Final fantasy fans...
4     B000058A81  AKZLIIH3AP4RU    5.0    This has got to be...
```

The first observation is that one `userId` includes the `unknown` generic value assigned when the user cannot be identified. It's therefore advisable to exclude instances with this value from the dataset to avoid skewing the results. If not, reviews from different customers will be grouped under the same `userId`. Next, we will dedicate a separate section to performing the necessary data cleaning, as there are a few other situations to contemplate.

Cleaning the data

The cleaning phase starts with the removal of samples, including the `unknown` identifier, according to the following code:

```
# Remove reviews for unknown profiles.
reviews = reviews[reviews['userId'] != 'unknown']
reviews.shape
>> (202111, 10)
```

The result suggests that a large portion of the samples included this generic identifier. However, this is not the only problem in the dataset. A small subset of the samples do not include a title for the product:

```
# Remove reviews with empty titles.
reviews = reviews[reviews['title'] != '']
reviews.shape
>> (202066, 10)
```

Next, we decide to keep only one review for a specific product and user:

```
reviews = reviews.drop_duplicates(subset=['productId',
'userId'], keep='first')
reviews.shape
>> (197596, 10)
```

In the same sense, we will keep one review for a specific title and user:

```
reviews = reviews.drop_duplicates(subset=['title', 'userId'],
keep='first')
reviews.shape
>> (188837, 10)
```

Another annoying situation is when a product appears with more than one identifier. In this case, we will keep just one `productId` per item:

```
unique_ids = reviews[~reviews.duplicated(['productId',
'title'])]
unique_ids = unique_ids.drop_duplicates(subset=['title'],
keep='first')
reviews = reviews[reviews['productId'].isin(unique_
ids['productId'])]


reviews.shape
>> (178058, 10)
```

The filtering process reduced the initial set to 178058 instances, but our work is not finished yet. The names of several titles appear as slightly different versions, as the following example demonstrates:

```
reviews[reviews['title'].str.contains('Lonely Heart')].drop_
duplicates(subset=['title'], keep='first')
>>       productId  title
84481    B000I26XF6  Sgt. Pepper's Lonely Hearts Club Band
198901   B000MU2LJG  Sgt. Peppers Lonely Hearts Club Band
```

Including both titles in our dataset wouldn't make sense – one option is to merge the reviews under a common name. Still, the most straightforward workaround is to only keep one of the multiple versions. For this task, we incorporate the **Levenshtein distance** to extract the similarity between the two titles. This is the topic of the following section.

Applying the Levenshtein distance

First, let's discuss a few things about this important metric in **natural language processing** (NLP) for measuring text similarity. To get a basic understanding of the calculations, consider the example of *Figure 5.3*, which shows comparisons for three sets of homophones (words with the same pronunciation but different meanings):

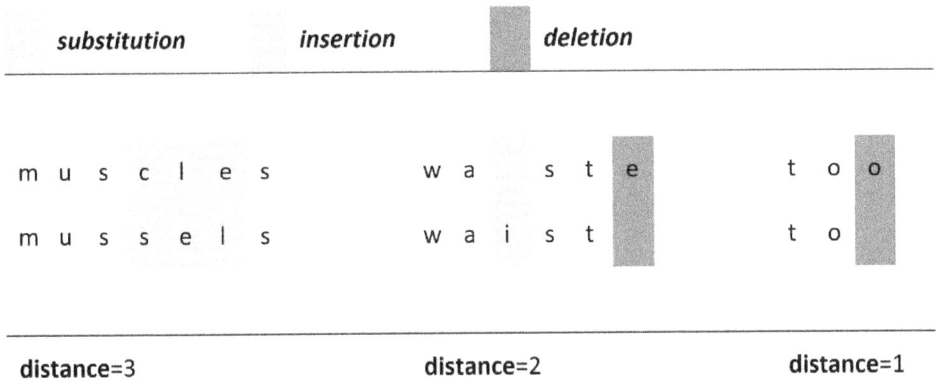

Figure 5.3 – The Levenshtein distance for different pairs of homophones

To calculate the distance, we need to count the minimum number of character edits to change one word to the other. For example, **muscles** can be transformed into **mussels** with a minimum of **3** substitutions. For the **waste** and **waist** pair, we have to make one insertion and one deletion; thus, the distance equals **2**. For the third pair, **1** deletion suffices. Mathematically, the Levenshtein distance between two strings, a and b, is given by the following equation:

$$lev(a,b) = \begin{cases} |a| & if\ |b| = 0 \\ |b| & if\ |a| = 0 \\ lev(tail(a), tail(b)) & if\ a[0] = b[0] \\ 1 + min \begin{cases} lev(tail(a), b) \\ lev(a, tail(b)) \\ lev(tail(a), tail(b)) \end{cases} & otherwise \end{cases}$$

Here, the following applies:

- $|x|$ = length of the string x
- $tail(x)$ = string x except for its first character
- $x[0]$ = first character of string x

The first element in the *min* part of the equation corresponds to deletion, the second to insertion, and the third to substitution (all in string a).

Next, we apply the metric to the problem under study and construct the d_score method, which returns a similarity score:

```
import nltk


# Method for calculating the distance between two strings.
```

```
def d_score(s1, s2):
    score = nltk.edit_distance(s1, s2)
    if score == 0.0:
        score = 1.0
    else:
        score = 1 - (score / len(s1))
    return score
```

We can now extract the unique titles and create a `dataframe` to host similar ones:

```
# Extract the unique titles.
unique_titles = reviews['title'].unique()


similar_titles = pd.DataFrame(columns=['title1', 'title2',
'distance'])
```

Then, we calculate the distance scores for all titles, keeping the most similar items:

```
# Iterate over all titles and calculate their distance from the
other ones.
for idx, x in enumerate(unique_titles):
    for y in range(idx, len(unique_titles)):
        distance = d_score(x, unique_titles[y])
        if distance < 1 and distance > 0.8:
            similar_titles = similar_titles.append({'title1':x,
'title2':unique_titles[y], 'distance': distance}, ignore_index
= True)
```

Notice that we used an abstract threshold equal to 0.8 to determine whether any two samples are similar. Consequently, the process performs a good approximation for the similarity extraction task, but it's less than perfect. It can filter out samples that are indeed unique and do not relate to any other title, but there's a price that we have to pay. You are welcome to experiment with the specified threshold and find a better trade-off if you can.

Finally, we will store the output in a file to avoid repeating the same process:

```
# Save the result in a csv file.
similar_titles.to_csv("./data/similar_titles.csv", sep='\t')
```

Based on the previous steps, we can now filter the titles in the dataset:

```
# Load music items with similar titles.
similar_titles = pd.read_csv("./data/similar_titles.csv",
sep='\t')


# Remove similar titles from the dataset.
reviews = reviews[~reviews['title'].isin(similar_
titles['title2'])]


reviews.shape
>> (172160, 10)
```

So far, the cleaning phase yields `172160` observations, but there is still a final step to take.

Adding the genres

The dataset needs to be augmented with a `category` column using the `merged` variable extracted in the same way as in the *Performing exploratory data analysis* section of *Chapter 4, Extracting Sentiments from Product Reviews*:

```
# Add the category for each item.
reviews = pd.merge(reviews, merged, on='productId', how='left')


reviews[['productId', 'userId', 'score', 'text', 'category']].
head()
>>  productId  userId    score  text       category
0   B000020... A2KLYV... 5.0    My love... Music| Pop| Rock
1   B000058... A18C9S... 5.0    We've c... Music| Pop| S...
2   B000058... A38QSO... 5.0    Final f... Music| Pop| S...
3   B000058... AKZLII... 5.0    This ha... Music| Pop| S...
4   B000058... A1FELZ... 5.0    I used ... Music| Pop| S...
```

Notice that each item is labeled with multiple genre categories. This outcome is not surprising, as it's not uncommon for music albums or songs to be tagged using more than one genre. However, there is a portion of the products that are not strictly music-oriented, as we can identify with the following code snippet:

```
# Check for non-specific music-oriented items.
reviews[~reviews['category'].str.startswith("Music")].head(1)
```

```
>>...title        ...              category
196  Perfect Gentlemen [VHS]   Movies & TV| TV| Music| R&B
```

We decide to exclude these less relevant products:

```
# Keep the items that are specifically music-oriented.
reviews = reviews[reviews['category'].str.startswith("Music")]


reviews.shape
>> (162989, 11)
```

The data cleaning phase yields 162989 samples to work with. Unfortunately, most of the subsequent analysis would have been based on false assumptions if we had skipped the previous cleaning steps. Therefore, we will proceed to the next section with a cleaned-up dataset and can extract some insightful information from the samples.

Extracting information from the data

The first step is to obtain the number of unique products in the dataset, using their productId:

```
print("Number of music ids in the corpus: " +
str(len(reviews['productId'].unique())))
>> Number of product ids in the corpus: 19453
```

A quick calculation reveals that each product is reviewed 32 times on average (162989/19453). Let's now obtain the different product categories:

```
import re


# Extract the categories of the music items.
cat = ';'.join(reviews['category'])
cat = [item.lstrip() for item in re.split(';|\|', cat)]
categories = pd.DataFrame(cat, columns=['category'])


categories['category'].unique()
>> array(['Music', 'Pop', 'Rock', 'Soundtracks', 'Classical',
'World Music', 'Dance & Electronic', 'New Age', 'Jazz',
'Broadway & Vocalists', 'Country', 'Folk', 'Blues', 'Classic
Rock', 'R&B', 'Alternative Rock', 'Latin Music', 'Rap & Hip-
Hop', 'Miscellaneous', 'Hard Rock & Metal', "Children's Music",
'Christian', 'Gospel', 'Musical Instruments', 'Instrument
```

Accessories', 'General Accessories', 'Patio', 'Lawn &
Garden', 'Pest Control', 'Tools & Home Improvement', 'Building
Supplies', 'Building Materials', 'Doors', 'Garage Doors',
'Openers & Parts', 'Hardware', 'Keyboard Accessories', 'Player
Piano Accessories'], dtype=object)

Next, we remove `Music` from the categories and only keep the genres of the products:

```
# Keep only the genres of the items.
categories = categories[categories['category'] != "Music"]
```

We can now plot the number of products per genre category:

```
# Get the genres distribution and keep the top 8.
x = categories['category'].value_counts()
x = x.sort_values(ascending=False)
x = x.iloc[0:8]

# Plot the distribution.
pd.DataFrame(x).T.plot.barh(stacked=True,colormap='Paired',
figsize=(10,2)).legend(bbox_to_anchor=(1.05, 1),
fontsize='large')
```

The output is the horizontal bar plot in *Figure 5.4*:

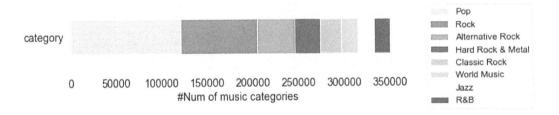

Figure 5.4 – Number of products per genre category

A large quantity of the items is labeled `Pop`, followed by `Rock` and `Alternative Rock`. Plots like the one here help us identify underrepresented categories in the dataset. If this is the case, we can balance the categories by randomly removing samples from dominant categories or excluding those with too few instances.

Another interesting piece of information is the distribution of the rating reviews:

```
# Create the distribution plot including kernel density
estimation.
sns.displot(data=reviews['score'], kde=True, bins=45, height=4,
aspect=2)
```

Figure 5.5 shows the distribution plot:

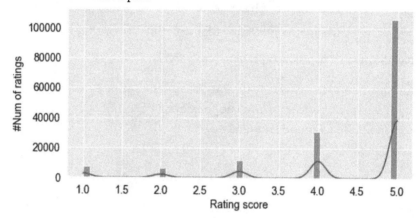

Figure 5.5 – Distribution of the rating values

Based on a five-scale rating (1.0 – 5.0), the largest proportion of the scores falls on the right-hand side of the *x*-axis – in this example, above or equal to the value of 3.0. Thus, there is a clear imbalance in the ratings toward positive scores, suggesting that users who decided to review an item most probably liked it.

Next, we extract rating scores for two random products:

```
# Calculate the count of reviews per each rating for the two
items.
r_count_1 = reviews[reviews['productId']=="B0007NFL1I"
].groupby('score')['score'].count()
r_count_2 = reviews[reviews['productId']=="B000I26XF6"
].groupby('score')['score'].count()
```

Let's combine the previous counts into a single dataframe:

```
# Create a dataframe from the data.
r_count = pd.concat([r_count_1.rename('The Massacre [Vinyl]'),
r_count_2.rename('Sgt. Pepper\'s Lonely Hearts Club Band')],
axis=1)
```

```
r_count['rating'] = r_count.index
r_count = pd.melt(r_count, id_vars="rating")
```

The obtained statistics can assist in the visualization of the ratings and comparison of the two products:

```
# Create and show the plot.
g = sns.catplot(data=r_count, kind="bar", x="rating",
y="value", hue="variable", ci="sd", palette="dark", alpha=.6,
height=5, aspect=2)
```

The output is the categorical plot in *Figure 5.6*:

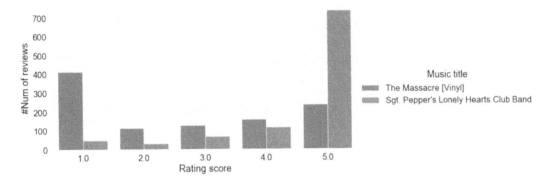

Figure 5.6 – Ratings of The Massacre versus Sgt. Pepper's Lonely Hearts Club Band

Contrasting the two products reveals an asymmetry in their rating scores, as Sgt. Pepper's Lonely Hearts Club Band is perceived more positively than The Massacre [Vinyl]. The simplest recommendation algorithm can exploit this information and propose products with the most positive ratings; in this case, the Sgt. Pepper's Lonely Hearts Club Band album.

Descriptive statistics complement data visualizations and provide simple summaries of the observations and their measures. The analysis that follows focuses on the ratings of the products:

```
import numpy as np


# Calculate the number of ratings per product along with their
mean value.
product_stats = reviews.groupby('productId').agg({'score': [np.
size, np.mean]})


# Half of the products (50%) have 2 ratings at most.
product_stats['score']['size'].describe()
```

```
>>
count      19453.000000
mean           8.378605
std           34.877318
min            1.000000
25%            1.000000
50%            2.000000
75%            5.000000
max         1836.000000
Name: size, dtype: float64
```

According to the printed statistics, half of the items have less than two ratings. The specific result amends the calculation at the beginning of the section that each product is rated on average 32 times. The next step is to obtain the most highly rated products:

```
# Keep the unique product titles.
unique_titles = reviews[['productId', 'title', 'category']].
drop_duplicates(subset='title', keep='first')
```

Let's keep those with more than 100 ratings and sort them in descending order:

```
# Focus on products with at least 100 ratings.
product_subset = product_stats['score']['size'] >= 100

# Filter and sort the products based on their rating size.
m = product_stats[product_subset].sort_values([('score',
'size')], ascending=False)
product_ext_1 = unique_titles.set_index('productId').join(m).
sort_values(('score', 'size'), ascending=False).dropna()
```

We can now plot the 15 most popular items in terms of rating size:

```
# Plot the product titles with the most ratings.
sns.barplot(x=product_ext_1[:15][('score', 'size')], y =
product_ext_1[:15]['title'], alpha=0.8)
```

The bar plot in *Figure 5.7* presents this information:

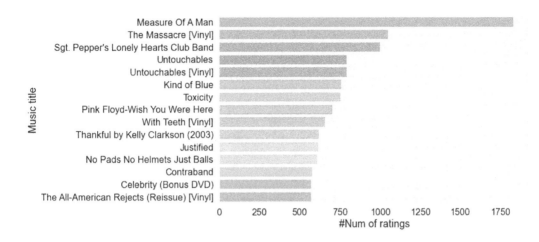

Figure 5.7 – Most popular products in terms of rating size

The term *popular* is somehow misleading, as the rating size doesn't always imply high rating scores. For example, recall `The Massacre [Vinyl]`'s results in *Figure 5.6* and compare them to its position in *Figure 5.7*. Let's examine this relationship in more depth and investigate whether there is any mathematical basis for the most-rated movies having higher rating values. The focus is on two variables; namely, the number of ratings (`m['size']`) and the mean rating score (`m['mean']`) defined in the following code:

```
# Filter and sort the products based on their mean rating.
m_rating = product_stats[product_subset].sort_values([('score',
'mean')], ascending=False)
product_ext_2 = unique_titles.set_index('productId').join(m_
rating).sort_values(('score', 'mean'), ascending=False).
dropna()


# Create a new dataframe with the two variables.
m = pd.DataFrame()
m['size'] = product_ext_1[('score', 'size')]
m['mean'] = product_ext_2[('score', 'mean')]
```

We are interested in examining the extent to which these two variables correlate using the **Pearson correlation** metric:

```
# Calculate the correlation between the two variables.
m.corr(method='pearson')
>>  size    mean
```

```
size   1.000000   -0.067582
mean   -0.067582   1.000000
```

The calculated value equal to -0.067582 signifies that there is no linear correlation between the two variables, which we can also visualize using the following code:

```
# Show the joint plot for rating size and mean.
g = sns.jointplot(x='size', y='mean', kind='reg', data=m)
```

The output is the joint plot illustrated in *Figure 5.8*:

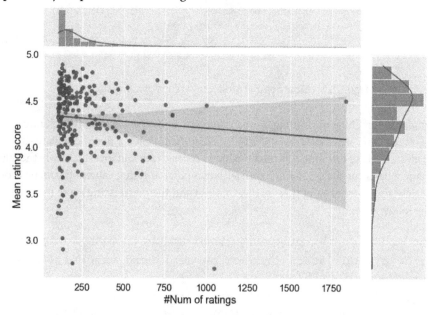

Figure 5.8 – Visualizing the correlation between product rating size and mean score

According to the plot, items with around **750** ratings have a mean score in the area of **4.5** points. The regression line shows the relationship between the two variables and its slope indicates how changes in the variable on the *x*-axis affect the variable on the *y*-axis. A slope further from zero suggests rapid changes, whereas a slope close to zero indicates the opposite. In our case, the slope is negative and not steep. A correlation of *+1* or *-1* means that all data points are included on the regression line. Otherwise, they are spread out, as in our example. Correlation is a measure of variation away from the regression line.

In conclusion, the slope and correlation are used for different reasons – they do not have the same value, but they share the same sign (in our case, both are negative). In this example, we do not encounter a correlation between the most-rated music items and high scores, as previously suggested. However, before we continue the analysis, let's decipher the term *correlation* between two variables, as it's a universal theme in data analytics.

Understanding the Pearson correlation

The correlation between two changing portions (or variables) indicates how the change of the first variable affects the direction of change for the second one. A typical example is a correlation between height and weight. As height increases, weight tends to increase too, and we can say that these variables are positively correlated. A correlation coefficient, p, indicates both the direction and strength of this relation in statistics. A typical variant is the Pearson correlation, which receives values between $+1$ and -1. A value of $+1$ indicates a total positive linear correlation, whereas a value equal to -1 signifies a total negative linear correlation. Finally, when $p = 0$, there is no linear correlation between the variables. Values between 0 and 0.3 (or -0.3 and 0) indicate a weak positive (or a weak negative) linear relationship, between 0.3 and 0.7 (or -0.7 and -0.3) indicate a moderately positive (or moderately negative) linear relationship, and values between 0.7 and 1.0 (or -1.0 and -0.7) indicate a strong positive (or strong negative) linear relationship. Notice that these values are guidelines and whether an association is strong or not also depends on the use case. *Figure 5.9* shows a few examples:

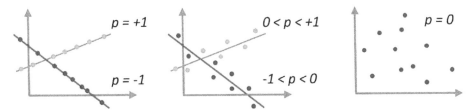

Figure 5.9 – Examples of the correlation coefficient p between two variables

> **Important note**
>
> A common fallacy is that **correlation** implies **causation**. Although it might be accurate in certain situations, it is not always the case. For example, the geographical distribution of Covid-19 cases in the US strongly correlates with 5G coverage, focusing on major cities and metropolitan areas. Conspiracy theories suggest that 5G may be causing the pandemic despite the apparent explanation that extended 5G coverage and Covid-19 cases appear in areas of overpopulation, which are cities.

This discussion concludes the exploratory data analysis section of this chapter. We have seen once more how this process helps us understand the *Music* dataset and how to filter out incomplete or unrelated samples. Additionally, it has been a good exercise for implementing different plot types and using them to visualize the information from the dataset. We can now proceed to the core methods for creating various recommender systems.

Introducing content-based filtering

Systems based on content-based filtering exploit the properties of items to recommend new products with similar features. The statement that drives the central paradigm behind these recommenders is *show me items similar to the ones I liked in the past*. What can be considered properties of an item is an open issue and it is up to the system developer to define a proper set. Sometimes, it is evident from the samples; otherwise, we have to improvise and experiment to elicit the proper features. A poorly chosen set can negatively impact the outcome; this is where an experienced data scientist can make a difference.

This book's focus on text data drives our decision on the properties to implement in the recommender system. Thus, we create a bag of words for each music item containing its review text and genres. We call it `metadata`:

```python
# Group all tags per product id.
product_tags = pd.DataFrame(reviews.groupby('productId')
['summary'].apply(lambda x: "%s" % ' '.join(x)))


# Include the tags in the product dataframe.
products = pd.merge(unique_titles, product_tags,
on='productId', how='left')


# Create product metadata that consists of tags and genres.
products['genres'] = products['category'].str.replace('|',' ')
products['metadata'] = products[['summary', 'genres']].
apply(lambda x: ' '.join(x), axis = 1)
```

Let's print a few samples:

```
products[['title', 'metadata']][50:55]
>>   title                   metadata
50   Hard Hard Traveling Man  Fantastic!! The Best !! ...
51   Memorial Album 7          A Great Cd filled with R...
52   Accesories- Rarities...  The Gathering hands out ...
53   Sweet Nothing             Australia's best-kept se...
54   The Formula               80's synth-rock for.......
```

Finally, the data is appropriately formatted to proceed to the next step. Exploiting the metadata to identify item similarity is the simplest way to implement a content-based recommendation system. You are more than welcome to experiment with different mixtures of metadata – for example, adding the titles part. Other similar datasets include columns with information about the performing artists, release date, or record label, which can also be part of the metadata.

Let us now start the fun part and produce recommendations!

Extracting music recommendations

To represent the text in metadata, we use **tf-idf**, as discussed in *Chapter 2, Detecting Spam Emails*, and reduce its dimensionality with the **Singular Value Decomposition (SVD)** method presented in *Chapter 3, Classifying Topics of Newsgroup Posts*. The latter reduces the size of the tf-idf matrix while preserving a similar structure among its columns. The output of SVD is latent vectors that try to capture the most variance within the original data frame. The word *latent* has a Latin root that means *lay hidden*. Latent representations encode the information in the data that we can later decode in the processing pipeline. Applying SVD on the count or tf-idf matrices is known as **Latent Semantic Analysis (LSA)**. The vectorizer and dimensionality reduction algorithms are incorporated with specific values for their hyperparameters. These should not be chosen randomly and we will discuss a more systematic way of tuning their values in the *Performing parameter tuning* section later in this chapter.

For the time being, let's begin with tf-idf vectorization:

```
from sklearn.decomposition import TruncatedSVD
from sklearn.feature_extraction.text import TfidfVectorizer


# Create the tf-idf vectorizer.
vectorizer = TfidfVectorizer(max_df=0.95, min_df=2, stop_
words='english')


# Generate the tf-idf matrix for the dataset.
tfidf = vectorizer.fit_transform(products['metadata'])


# Create a dataframe from the matrix.
tfidf_data = pd.DataFrame(tfidf.toarray(), index=products.
index.tolist())


tfidf_data.shape
>> (19453, 14896)
```

Each of the 19453 unique products is represented with an array of 14896 values. Next, we apply SVD to reduce the column size using 200 components:

```
# Calculate 200 components for the tfidf dataframe.
svd = TruncatedSVD(n_components=200, algorithm='randomized',
n_iter=5, random_state=123, tol=0.0)


# Calculate the latent matrix.
```

```
latent = svd.fit_transform(tfidf_data)


# Create the latent dataframe.
latent_data = pd.DataFrame(latent, index=products['title'].
tolist())


latent_data.shape
>> (19453, 200)
```

A vector with 200 components now describes each of the 19453 products, all included in latent_
data. Then, we can recommend similar items for a music title based on the Euclidean distance, the
Pearson correlation, or the cosine similarity between two vectors in the dataframe. As an example,
we choose the Led Zeppelin [Vinyl] title from the famous group and incorporate the cosine
similarity method discussed in the *Using tf-idf encoding* section of *Chapter 2, Detecting Spam Emails*:

```
from sklearn.metrics.pairwise import cosine_similarity


# Obtain the latent vector for a product.
led_zeppelin = np.array(latent_data.loc['Led Zeppelin
[Vinyl]']).reshape(1, -1)


# Calculate the similarity of the product with the other ones.
similarity = cosine_similarity(latent_data, led_zeppelin).
reshape(-1)


# Create the dataframe from the array.
similarity_data = pd.DataFrame(similarity, index=latent_data.
index, columns=['measure'])
```

Using similarity_data, we obtain ten recommendations for the reference title:

```
# Obtain the 10 top recommendations.
recommend = similarity_data.sort_values('measure',
ascending=False).head(11)
# Get the title and genre for the recommendations.
tg = products[products['title'].isin(recommend.index.tolist())]
[['title', 'category']]


# Join the information from the two dataframes.
```

```
recommend = tg.set_index('title').join(recommend, how='left',
lsuffix='_left', rsuffix='_right')
```

Finally, we will print the list of recommendations in descending order in terms of cosine similarity:

```
# Recommend 10 products.
recommend = recommend.sort_values('measure', ascending=False)
recommend[~recommend.index.duplicated(keep='first')]
>>
```

title	category	measure
Led Zeppeli..	Classic Rock|Hard Rock&Metal|Rock	1.000000
In the Heat..	Classic Rock|Hard Rock&Metal|Po..	0.852006
Definitely...	Alternative Rock|Hard Rock&Meta..	0.851303
Tuesday Night	Rock	0.840619
Garth Brooks	Country|Pop	0.809610
Innoncence...	Rock	0.808551
Ritchie Bla..	Rock	0.806990
When Dream ..	Hard Rock&Metal|Pop|Rock	0.798694
Bon Jovi	Classic Rock|Hard Rock&Metal|Pop	0.781751
Legalize It	Pop|World Music	0.775196
Iron Maiden	Alternative Rock|Hard Rock&...	0.760014

It's reassuring that the most similar result (the first element in the output) is the Led Zeppelin [Vinyl] title. The system seems to work quite well, as many products are related to the reference item, whether in the Rock genre or another relevant variation. Then, we will repeat the previous process using the Mozart: Fantasias & Sonatas title as input:

```
# Obtain the latent vector for a product.
mozart = np.array(latent_data.loc['Mozart: Fantasias &
Sonatas']).reshape(1, -1)
...
>>
```

title	category	measure
Mozart: Fantasias & Sonatas	Classical	1.000000
Mozart- Harnoncourt: The Late ..	Classical	0.987406
Symphonies 1-15 / Philharmonic..	Classical	0.987111
Schnabel Plays Mozart	Classical	0.984056
Romantic Moments Vol. 1: Mozart	Classical	0.981416
Zukerman Conducts Mozart	Classical	0.979731

Mozart: Le Nozze di Figaro (..	Classical	0.979172
Mozart: Symphony No, 40 K 550..	Classical	0.974895
Mozart: Bastien und Bastienne	Classical|Pop	0.961341
Mozart: Flute Concertos Nos. ..	Classical	0.921402
Mozart: Violin Con. No. 1 in ..	Classical	0.920338

This time, the recommendation list only contains titles from the same composer, while the measure values are higher than in the previous example. The more products from the same artist appear in the dataset, the more candidate recommendations there are. In this example, it's rather myopic to suggest the complete list of Mozart's titles. In an actual application, we could skip a few titles containing the composer's name to benefit elements with a lower measure score in the list.

This section dealt with implementing our first recommender using the techniques discussed in previous chapters. The analysis was item-oriented, utilizing different information about the music products. Still, it can also become user-oriented by considering metadata such as gender, age, and so on if such a piece of information is available in the dataset. We will continue in the next section with the presentation of the second family of recommender applications.

Introducing collaborative filtering

Collaborative filtering relies on mutual preferences, as it identifies items that a user might like based on how other similar users rated them. The central paradigm behind this approach is driven by the statement *Show me the items people like me have chosen. I might find them interesting*. There are two methods for implementing collaborative filtering systems: **memory-based** and **model-based**. In the first case, we utilize user rating data to compute the similarity between users or items. In the second case, models are developed incorporating **machine learning** (ML) algorithms to predict user ratings for unrated items. Let's see both in more detail, starting with the memory-based approach.

Using memory-based collaborative recommenders

Before implementing the recommender, we need to sort out the data. One design choice is to utilize instances from reviewers who have made at least five evaluations. The reason is to exploit the most active users in the dataset, who are typically more trustworthy than occasional users. The following code shows this step:

```
# Keep reviewers with more than 5 reviews.
v = reviews['userId'].value_counts()
reviews = reviews[reviews['userId'].isin(v.index[v.gt(5)])]

reviews.shape
>> (29687, 11)
```

With 29687 reviews at our disposal, we can extract the unique product IDs:

```
unique_products = reviews.drop_duplicates(subset=['productId'],
keep='first')
```

The pivot table calculated in the following code snippet summarizes the rating of each product (row) and each user (column):

```
# Keep the ratings for the products of interest.
ratings = reviews[reviews['productId'].isin(unique_
products['productId'].tolist())]
ratings = ratings[['productId', 'userId', 'score']]


# Reshape data based on column values.
ratings_pivot = ratings.pivot(index=['productId'],
columns='userId', values='score').fillna(0)


ratings_pivot
>> userId     A1020L7BWW9RAX   A103KNDW8GN92L   A103W7ZPKGOCC9..
productId
1889212032    0.0              0.0              0.0
9051861079    0.0              0.0              0.0
B000000305    0.0              0.0              0.0

...

8684 rows × 2191 columns
```

We observe that the pivot table has many zero values in it and is therefore sparse. Moreover, it contains ratings for 8684 products and 2191 reviewers.

Next, we will use the Pearson correlation to measure similarity among the 8684 products. Notice that the main diagonal of the table includes only ones, as it relates each product with itself:

```
# Calculate the correlation coefficients.
corr_coef = np.corrcoef(ratings_pivot)
pd.DataFrame(corr_coef)
>> 0          1           2           3           4...
0  1.000000   -0.000457   -0.000457   -0.000457   -0.000457
1  -0.000457  1.000000    -0.000457   -0.000457   -0.000457
2  -0.000457  -0.000457   1.000000    -0.000457   -0.000457
3  -0.000457  -0.000457   -0.000457   1.000000    -0.000457
```

```
4    -0.000457   -0.000457   -0.000457   -0.000457   1.000000

...
```

We can now extract the correlation of the `Led Zeppelin [Vinyl]` title with the other ones and sort the output in descending order:

```
# Obtain the coefficients for a product.
led_zeppelin = corr_coef[list(unique_products['title']).
index('Led Zeppelin [Vinyl]')]


# Obtain the recommendations.
recommend = pd.DataFrame({'title': unique_products['title'].
tolist(),'category': unique_products['category'].tolist(),
'measure': led_zeppelin})


recommend = recommend.sort_values(by=['measure'], ascending =
False)
recommend.set_index('title')
```

Finally, let's print ten recommendations:

```
recommend.head(11)
>>  title                   category                  measure
Led Zeppelin [Vinyl]    Classic Rock|Hard Rock&..  1.000000
Symphony 0              Classical                  0.615228
Slaughter of the Soul  Pop|Rock                   0.615228
Native Sons            Alternative Rock|Pop|Rock  0.615228
Whammy! [Vinyl]        Alternative Rock|Pop|Rock  0.615228
Living Proof: Mgm..    Classic Rock|Country|Har.. 0.615228
Island [Vinyl]         New Age|Pop|Rock|World ..  0.615228
Structures             Alternative Rock|Dance&..  0.527255
Raisin Cain            Blues|Classic Rock|Hard..  0.492025
La bella dormente..    Classical                  0.480028
Sacred Arias           Classical|Miscellaneous... 0.434575
```

The list contains related Rock music products but lower measure scores than those in the *Introducing content-based filtering* section, so let's see whether we can increase the scores by reducing the feature space's size. It should be no surprise that we need to incorporate a dimensionality reduction technique once more. Working with sparse matrixes such as the previous pivot table poses unnecessary computation and memory waste. In the *Introducing the random forest algorithm* section of *Chapter 3, Classifying*

Topics of Newsgroup Posts, we mentioned that SVD works well with sparse matrices. So, in the next section, we will exploit this feature for the problem under study.

Applying SVD

Throughout the book, we often saw the value of reducing the parameters in ML problems using **principal component analysis (PCA)** or SVD. Specifically, a simplified model that works as well as a more complex one is always preferable. Continuing this line of discussion, let us apply SVD to the rating pivot table and obtain the latent vectors of the products:

```
# Calculate 200 components for the pivot table.
svd = TruncatedSVD(n_components=200, algorithm='randomized',
n_iter=5, random_state=123, tol=0.0)


# Calculate the latent matrix.
latent = svd.fit_transform(ratings_pivot)


# Create the latent dataframe.
latent_data = pd.DataFrame(latent, index=unique_
products['title'].tolist())


latent_data.shape
>> (8684, 200)
```

Each of the 8684 unique products is now represented by a vector with 200 elements. Next, we calculate the distance between the reference product and all the others using cosine similarity to obtain candidate recommendations:

```
# Obtain the latent vector for a product.
led_zeppelin = np.array(latent_data.loc['Led Zeppelin
[Vinyl]']).reshape(1, -1)


# Calculate the similarity of the product with the other ones.
similarity = cosine_similarity(latent_data, led_zeppelin).
reshape(-1)


# Create the dataframe from the array.
similarity_df = pd.DataFrame(similarity, index=latent_data.
index, columns=['measure'])
```

```
# Obtain the 10 top recommendations.
recommend = similarity_df.sort_values('measure',
ascending=False).head(11)
```

We also need to include the necessary metadata for the products:

```
# Get the title and genre for the recommendations.
tg = unique_products[unique_products['title'].isin(recommend.
index.tolist())][['title', 'category']]


# Join the information from the two dataframes.
recommend = tg.set_index('title').join(recommend, how='left',
lsuffix='_left', rsuffix='_right')
```

Let's now proceed to the recommendation of 10 music products:

```
# Recommend 10 products.
recommend.sort_values('measure', ascending=False)
>>
```

title	category	measure
Led Zeppelin [Vinyl]	Classic Rock|Hard Rock&..	1.000000
Symphony 0	Classical	0.907534
Native Sons	Alternative Rock|Pop|Rock	0.907534
Slaughter of the Soul	Pop|Rock	0.907534
Structures	Alternative Rock|Dance&..	0.907495
Joy of Christmas	Music	0.891911
La bella dormente..	Classical	0.885290
Tao of Mad Phat ..	Jazz|Pop|R&B	0.866656
Lotusland/Sleeping..	Classical	0.863544
Genesis	Classic Rock|Pop|Rock	0.844771
Squirt Pt.1	Dance&Electronic|Pop..	0.843914

Again, the list of results seems to be along the right lines. Notice, however, that the values for the measure scores are now much higher. Once more, reducing the dimensions of the problem is beneficial to the outcome. Hence, it's prime time to learn about another dimensionality reduction technique in the next section.

Clustering handwritten text

Suppose you work at a regional post office and are assigned to sorting incoming and outgoing daily mail. In your job, it's sufficient to examine the postal code of each piece of post and put it in the right bag that will be sent to the corresponding local post office. However, this task is laborious and error-prone, and an automatic procedure would be more than welcome. In this section, we will briefly detour from the chapter's main problem and present how to automate this task. In addition, the discussion facilitates the presentation of another dimensionality reduction technique used later in the chapter.

The optical recognition of the handwritten digits dataset (https://archive.ics.uci.edu/ml/datasets/Optical+Recognition+of+Handwritten+Digits) contains different images for 10 classes of digits (0 to 9). The samples have been size-normalized, centered in a fixed-size image, and made available through the scikit-learn library. We will use this dataset to learn about a model for clustering digits.

So, first, let's load the samples:

```
from sklearn.datasets import load_digits

# Load the digits dataset.
digits = load_digits()
digits.data.shape
>> (1797, 64)
```

The dataset consisted of 1797 instances with 64 features each. The features are the pixel values of each sample 8 x 8 (= 64) image. Then, we organize this information in a convenient dataframe structure along with the target classes to facilitate the processing that follows in this section:

```
# Create unique ids for the 64 pixels of each image.
pixel_ids = [str(i) for i in range(digits.data.shape[1])]

# Create a dataframe from the data.
df = pd.DataFrame(digits.data, columns=pixel_ids)
df['target'] = digits.target
df['digit'] = df['target'].apply(lambda i: str(i))
```

We plot a few sample digits for each category to see what they look like:

```
# Plot 10 sample digit images.
plt.gray()
fig = plt.figure(figsize=(10, 10))
for i in range(0, 10):
```

```
    ax = fig.add_subplot(3, 5, i+1,
title="digit:"+str(df.loc[i, 'digit']) )
    ax.matshow(df.loc[i, pixel_ids].values.reshape((8, 8)).
astype(float))
```

The output is illustrated in *Figure 5.10*:

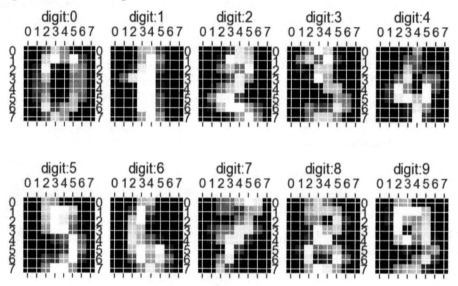

Figure 5.10 – 10 image samples of handwritten digits

A few images are challenging even for the human eye to decipher, so in the following two sections, we will discuss how dimensionality reduction can assist with this task.

Using PCA

We saw how PCA is used on linearly separable data in the *Understanding principal component analysis* section of *Chapter 3, Classifying Topics of Newsgroup Posts*. This technique reduces the dimensionality of highly correlated data, which is achieved by constructing a linear transformation to represent the original dataset with a new one (principal components). In simple terms, PCA is primarily geometric, looking for axes that explain as much data variance as possible. Of course, during the transformation, PCA is concerned with preserving the global structure of the data.

First, let us incorporate the familiar PCA method using three components:

```
from sklearn.decomposition import PCA


# Calculate 3 principal components.
```

```
pca = PCA(n_components=3)
pcaComponents = pca.fit_transform(df[pixel_ids].values)
df['PC1'] = pcaComponents[:, 0]
df['PC2'] = pcaComponents[:, 1]
df['PC3'] = pcaComponents[:, 2]


# Keep only 100 examples for demonstration.
df_sub = df[:100]
```

Visualizing the samples is done with the following code:

```
# Create the plot.
plt.figure(figsize=(14, 8))
p = sns.scatterplot(x="PC1", y="PC2", hue="target",
    palette=sns.color_palette("hls", 10),
    data=df_sub, legend="full")


# Include the digit label for each datapoint.
for i in range(0, len(df_sub.index)-1):
    p.text(df_sub['PC1'].iloc[i]+1.0, df_sub['PC2'].iloc[i],
df_sub['digit'].iloc[i], horizontalalignment='left',
size='medium', color='black', weight='normal')
```

The output is the scatter plot in *Figure 5.11*:

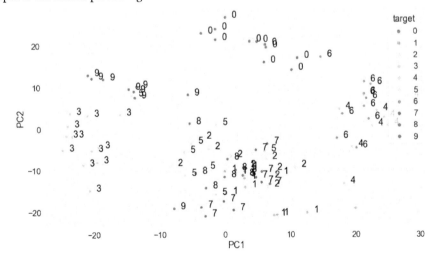

Figure 5.11 – Digit clusters in the 2D PCA plot

According to the plot, certain digit classes are separated quite well – for example, **0, 3,** and **9** – but others are entirely mixed – for instance, **2, 5,** and **7.** Can another method do a better job for this task? The answer is given in the following section.

Using t-distributed Stochastic Neighbor Embedding

It's about time to introduce another dimensionality reduction technique called **t-distributed Stochastic Neighbor Embedding (t-SNE)**, which embeds data points from a higher dimensional space into a lower one. In technical terms, the method starts by converting the high-dimensional Euclidean distances between data points into conditional probabilities that represent similarities. Contrary to PCA, the aim is to preserve the neighborhood of each point as closely as possible – namely, its local structure. Presenting the actual mechanics of t-SNE is beyond the book's scope and we will only refer to a couple of typical examples. Hopefully, they should provide some insight into this method.

Consider the data points in *Figure 5.12* that create the spiral structure known as the *Swiss roll* (inspired by the rolled sponge cake filled with whipped cream, jam, or icing):

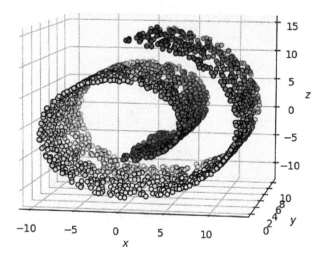

Figure 5.12 – Swiss roll data points

Each point belongs to a specific class (depicted with a different color) that can be clustered in a lower-dimension space using PCA or t-SNE. Let's examine the first option using either one or two principal components. The plots in *Figure 5.13* illustrate the output in both cases:

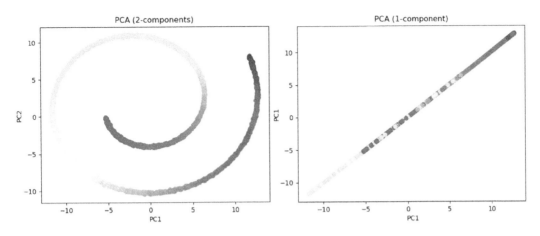

Figure 5.13 – PCA with two or one principal component

PCA is supposed to preserve the global structure of the data and the plot on the left verifies this expectation; the spiral form and each color's position in the roll are well-preserved. However, applying PCA didn't make us any wiser, and the method fails to identify the fact that a Swiss roll is essentially a band of data points that has been curved. Squashing the roll (as though you were stepping on it from above) causes the colored points to mix and produces the plot on the right. Technically, applying one-component PCA to the data brings the distant points closer (especially in the middle of the line). The Swiss roll is an example of the deficiency of PCA for *non-linear manifold structures* that have a geometric shape or surface, such as a sphere.

> **Note**
>
> A **manifold** is a mathematical object with a curved shape that appears flat locally. So, for example, walking on the surface of a manifold in 3D looks like walking on a flat plane. Likewise, the Earth's surface can be considered a manifold for a person walking on it (locally). Conversely, shapes with spikes or edges do not strictly constitute a manifold; a cube is one example.

t-SNE, on the other hand, zooms in on each individual data point along with its neighborhood, aiming to find a lower-dimension manifold where the data lives. The method extracts clustered local groups of samples so that a dataset that comprises several manifolds at once becomes visually disentangled. *Figure 5.14* shows the separation of the Swiss roll into multiple manifolds:

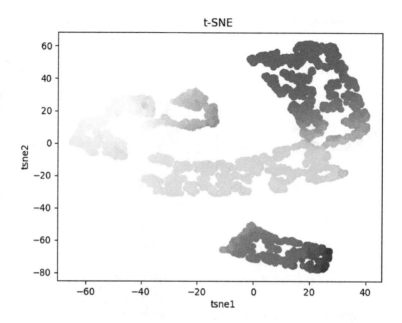

Figure 5.14 – Manifold of the Swiss roll data points as a 2D representation with t-SNE

Why is the output in the previous plot better than that of the two-component PCA? For instance, suppose we want to implement a classifier that labels an example in one of the categories of the Swiss roll. Due to the spiral form of the output in the left-hand plot of *Figure 5.13*, it's more challenging to find a linear classifier that generalizes well for this task. Conversely, for the t-SNE case, it's straightforward to define an efficient linear classifier.

Coming back to the digit classification problem, we can apply t-SNE to the dataset using two components:

```
from sklearn.manifold import TSNE

# Calculate 2 tsne components.
tsne = TSNE(n_components=2, perplexity=40, n_iter=300, random_
state=123)
tsneEmbedded = tsne.fit_transform(df[pixel_ids].values)
df['tsne1'] = tsneEmbedded [:, 0]
df['tsne2'] = tsneEmbedded [:, 1]
```

Next, we will visualize the result of the method:

```
# Create the plot.
plt.figure(figsize=(12,8))
```

```
sns.scatterplot(x="tsne1", y="tsne2", hue="target",
    palette=sns.color_palette("hls", 10),
    data=df, legend="full", alpha=0.8)
```

The output is the scatter plot shown in *Figure 5.15*:

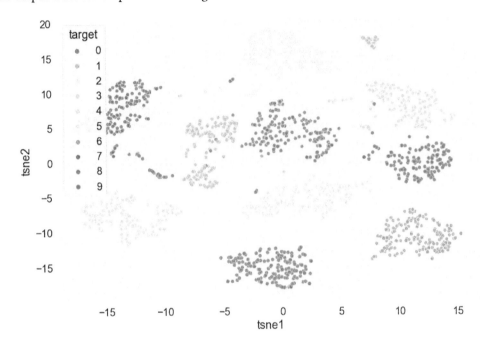

Figure 5.15 – Manifold of handwritten digits as a 2D representation with t-SNE

Again, t-SNE does a better job, and the digit clusters are separated clearly. The drawback of t-SNE is that it is computationally expensive and we are limited to two or three components. To combine the benefits of reserving both the global and local data structure, it is not uncommon to apply PCA first and then t-SNE.

The following section will examine the effect of t-SNE on implementing a recommender.

Applying t-SNE

We will conclude our discussion of t-SNE by applying it to the problem of study for this chapter, as we did with SVD:

```
# Calculate 3 components for the pivot table.
tsne = TSNE(n_components=3, perplexity=5, random_state=123)
```

```
# Calculate the latent matrix.
tsneEmbedded = tsne.fit_transform(ratings_pivot)

# Create the latent dataframe.
latent_data = pd.DataFrame(tsneEmbedded, index=unique_
products['title'].tolist())

latent_data.shape
>> (8684, 3)
```

Contrary to the digits example, the method incorporates three components (n_components=3). First, notice that the `perplexity` argument relates to the number of nearest neighbors (=5) used for manifold learning. As our dataset is relatively small, the chosen value for `perplexity` is also small. The code for obtaining the latent vectors, calculating the cosine similarity, and including the metadata, is the same as before and thus omitted.

We can now output a recommendation with 10 products:

```
# Recommend 10 products.
recommend.sort_values('measure', ascending=False)
>>
title                  category                      measure
Led Zeppelin [Vinyl]   Classic Rock|Hard Rock&..     1.000000
Island [Vinyl]         New Age|Pop|Rock|World M..     0.999456
Whammy! [Vinyl]        Alternative Rock|Pop|Rock      0.999456
Living Proof: Mgm..     Classic Rock|Country|Har..    0.999455
Sacred Arias           Classical|Miscellaneous|..     0.998777
Shriner's Convention   Country|Miscellaneous          0.998502
20th Century Maste..    Christian|Classic Rock|C..    0.998453
Killer In The Crow..    Alternative Rock|Pop|Rock     0.998453
I See Good Spirits..    Alternative Rock|Dance..      0.998453
Live at the Quick      Country|Jazz|Pop|Rock          0.998378
Sgt. Pepper's Lone..    Pop                           0.998377
```

The results are more Rock-oriented than those we have encountered before and with very high measure scores. This is great!

In our discussion on collaborative filtering recommenders, we worked on the memory-based variant using the pivot table, which summarizes each product's rating and user. We also incorporated dimensionality reduction techniques to extract better recommendations in this process. If you have followed the discussion, it shouldn't be difficult to guess the next topic of this chapter. We need to delve into model-based collaborative systems and focus more on user preferences for making recommendations.

Using model-based collaborative systems

After our short detour on t-SNE, we can now steer to the main path of the chapter. The focus this time is on providing recommendations for specific users instead of specific items. This section will demonstrate model-based collaborative filtering, which aims to develop the necessary models to predict how a specific user would rate an item they have never encountered before. Consequently, items with a high predicted rating are candidate recommendations for the specific person.

We utilize the rating table from the previous sections and a technique known as **matrix factorization** that allows us to discover the latent features underlying the interactions between users and items. In the *Using memory-based collaborative recommenders* section, we already saw that the rating table is a sparse matrix, as a single user can't possibly rate all the available products. For this reason, we imputed the missing data with zero and used truncated SVD to reduce its dimensionality. Next, we will revisit the SVD algorithm and decompose the original sparse matrix into two low-dimensional matrices with latent features and less sparsity. The specific implementation employs gradient descent to minimize the squared error of the predicted and actual ratings. The output of this process is a model that we can poll to recommend music items to a particular user.

The idea behind factorization is quite simple; express a quantity as a product of smaller ones, called *factors*. Consider, for example, the following quantities and their corresponding factors: $6 = 2 \times 3$, $588 = 2^2 \times 3 \times 7^2$, $x^2 + 4x + 3 = (x + 3)(x + 1)$. The process can be extended so that an input matrix is expressed as a product of two rectangular matrices with smaller dimensions. Factorization is also used in cryptographic algorithms, such as **Rivest-Shamir-Adleman (RSA)**, which predominately uses it to create ciphers.

> **Interesting fact**
>
> RSA is a public-key cryptosystem widely used for secure data transmission. It's based on the multiplication of two large prime numbers and its security relies on the practical difficulty of factoring the product of these two numbers.

We apply the method to the user or item rating matrix, hereafter called R. To formalize this process, let's define U and I as the two factors so that their dot product yields the matrix R, namely $R = U \cdot I$. The first matrix U can be considered the user matrix, where rows represent users and columns are latent factors. Similarly, the matrix I can be seen as the item matrix, where rows represent latent factors and columns are the items.

Notice that to perform the dot product, the number of columns in U should be the same as the number of rows in I. To calculate U and I, we employ ML over SVD to find the values of the hyperparameters that capture the most variance within the original matrix R. The benefit of SVD is that it can approximate R with a much smaller latent space and generalize for the missing ratings. By the end of this process, the dot product of U and I should be a good approximation of R – namely, R' and its element provide a rating for a specific user or item combination.

For example, the rating r of user m for product I is equal to the following:

$$r_{m1} = [u_{m1}, \cdots, u_{mk}] \cdot [i_{11}, \cdots, i_{k1}]^T$$

Here, m is the number of users, n is the number of items, and k is the number of latent factors – see *Figure 5.16*:

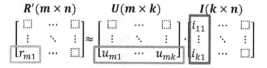

Figure 5.16 – Decomposition of the rating matrix

Let's consider a numerical example that sheds light on the calculations. In *Table 5.1*, three users (**U1** to **U3**) have rated three movies (**M1** to **M3**), and there is one missing rating depicted with the question mark:

	M1: Taxi Driver (psychological thriller)	M2: Insomnia (psychological thriller)	M3: Donnie Brasco (crime drama)
U1	2	1	0
U2	5	4	1
U3	5	3	?

Table 5.1 – Movie ratings by three users

It should be evident that **U3** is more similar to **U2** than **U1** regarding their preferences. What should **U3**'s rating of **M3** be, then? Suppose that the latent space, in this case, consists of two latent factors, namely **F1** and **F2**. The first could refer to whether *Robert De Niro* appears in the specific film and the second as to whether the movie is a **psychological thriller** or not. Notice that latent factors do not have such clear associations with people, objects, or concepts in practice. Based on these assumptions, we obtain the factorization shown in *Figure 5.17* using the values from *Table 5.1*:

$$
\underset{U(3 \times 2)}{\begin{bmatrix} 1 & 1 \\ 4 & 1 \\ 3 & 2 \end{bmatrix}} \cdot \underset{I(2 \times 3)}{\begin{bmatrix} 1 & 1 & 0 \\ 1 & 0 & 0 \end{bmatrix}} = \underset{R'(3 \times 3)}{\begin{bmatrix} 2 & 1 & 0 \\ 5 & 4 & 0 \\ 5 & 3 & 0 \end{bmatrix}}
$$

Figure 5.17 – Predicting U3's rating for M3

For **U3**, a score equal to **3** points is assigned to **F1**, while a score of **2** points is assigned to **F2**. As none of these factors apply to **M3**, the corresponding values in the matrix are both equal to zero. We can finally calculate the missing rating using the formula $3 \times 0 + 2 \times 0 = 0$.

Hopefully, you understood the reasoning behind the matrix factorization technique well. Still, before proceeding to its practical implementation, we must introduce one more important technique for automatically tuning ML algorithms.

Performing parameter tuning

We have seen in previous chapters that any ML algorithm can be tuned by adjusting the values of its hyperparameters. However, knowing beforehand which combination provides the best performance is hard until you test them all. For example, a matrix might have different factorizations and we need to experiment to find the right one. During the discussion in the *Introducing the k-nearest neighbors algorithm* section of *Chapter 3, Classifying Topics of Newsgroup Posts*, we saw how to find the best value of the *k* hyperparameter using cross-validation. Consider now the example of *Figure 5.18 (A)*, which consists of a grid of points for two parameters:

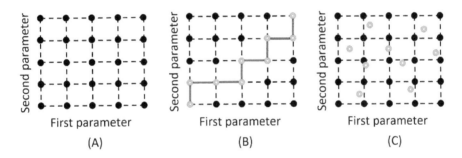

Figure 5.18 – Grid of two parameters (A), manual search (B), and random search (C)

Each point contains a particular combination of the hyperparameter values for training the ML algorithm. However, as the grid grows, training with all possible combinations becomes non-trivial. Furthermore, ML algorithms typically utilize several hyperparameters. For instance, 5 hyperparameters with 3 possible values each require $3 \times 3 \times 3 \times 3 \times 3 = 243$ different tests. Another option is to traverse the grid following a specific path and examine a subset of the points, as in *Figure 5.18 (B)*. A better option, in this case, is choosing random points in the grid, which has been experimentally proven to be a good practice (*Figure 5.18 (C)*).

Fortunately, the `surprise` module (`https://surprise.readthedocs.io/en/stable/index.html`) provides a technique that alleviates the burden of creating the grid manually. The technique is known as **grid search** and helps us quickly tune the SVD algorithm and calculate its latent factors. Next, we will narrow the analysis to a subset of the data, as the process is resource-intensive, and define the `grid` Python `dictionary` with four hyperparameters, `n_factors`, `n_epochs`, `lr_all`, and `reg_all`:

```
from surprise import accuracy, Dataset, Reader, SVD
from surprise.model_selection import cross_validate
from surprise.model_selection import GridSearchCV, KFold


# Define a Reader for our custom dataset and load the data from
the ratings.
reader = Reader(rating_scale=(1, 5))


# For efficiency load part of the dataset.
data = Dataset.load_from_df(ratings[['userId', 'productId',
'score']][0:100000], reader)


# Create the grid with the hyperparameter values to test.
grid = {'n_factors':[180,200], 'n_epochs':[5,10], 'lr_
all':[0.002,0.005], 'reg_all':[0.4,0.6], 'random_state':[2]}
```

After creating a grid of possible values for the hyperparameters, we will perform an exhaustive search ($2 \times 2 \times 2 \times 2 = 16$ combinations). Then, we will evaluate the average `rmse` and `mae` over a three-fold cross-validation procedure (`cv`):

```
# Perform the grid search for SVD.
grid_search = GridSearchCV(SVD, grid, measures=['rmse', 'mae'],
cv=KFold(3, random_state=2))
grid_search.fit(data)
algo = grid_search.best_estimator['rmse']
```

Notice that the `measures` argument in the `GridSearchCV` class corresponds to the cost function to minimize so that we can elicit the best combinations for the hyperparameters. In the example, we choose two options. First, the **Root Mean Squared Error** (**RMSE**), which is defined as the square root of the mean of the square of all of the errors given by the following equation:

$$RMSE = \sqrt{\frac{1}{n}\sum_{i=1}^{n}(S_i - O_i)^2}$$

Here, S_i is the predicted i^{th} value and O_i is the ith observation. Ideally, this error should be equal to zero.

Second, the **Mean Absolute Error** (**MAE**), which measures the average magnitude of the errors without considering their direction, given as follows:

$$MAE = \frac{1}{n}\sum_{i=1}^{n}|S_i - O_i|$$

One crucial difference between the RMSE and MAE is that the first penalizes large errors since they are squared before being averaged.

Once `fit` has been applied to the data, the `best_estimator` attribute returns an algorithm instance with the optimal set of parameters. These steps entail the matrix factorization part and the minimization of the RMSE for every product rating in the rating matrix. We can now print the best `rmse` score extracted by the grid search:

```
print("The best RMSE score: " + str(grid_search.best_
score['rmse']))
>> The best RMSE score: 0.9216964630324304
```

In this case, the optimal values of the hyperparameters are the following:

```
print("Hyperparameter values for the best RMSE score: " +
str(grid_search.best_params['rmse']))
>> Parameters for the best RMSE score: {'n_factors': 180, 'n_
epochs': 10, 'lr_all': 0.005, 'reg_all': 0.4, 'random_state':
2}
```

According to the output, the model with the lowest error for SVD has `180` latent factors. Next, we use this best model to calculate its accuracy using five-fold cross-validation:

```
# Report accuracy of the best algorithm using cross-validation.
cross_validate(algo, data, measures=['RMSE', 'MAE'],
cv=KFold(5, random_state=2), verbose=True)
>> Evaluating RMSE, MAE of algorithm SVD on 5 split(s).
```

	Fold 1	...	Fold 5	Mean	Std
RMSE (testset)	0.9152	...	0.9087	0.9139	0.0069
MAE (testset)	0.7024	...	0.7032	0.7046	0.0052
Fit time	0.79	...	0.77	0.77	0.01
Test time	0.03	...	0.03	0.03	0.00

It's now time to proceed with the implementation of the recommender.

Training the recommendation model

After extracting the configuration of the best model, we can use the whole dataset and train a new one:

```
from surprise.model_selection import train_test_split


# Load the whole dataset.
data = Dataset.load_from_df(ratings[['userId', 'productId',
'score']], reader)


# Sample random trainset and testset (30% of the data is used
for testing).
trainset, testset = train_test_split(data, test_size=0.3,
random_state=123)


# Use the SVD algorithm.
algo = SVD(n_factors=180, n_epochs=10, lr_all=0.005, reg_
all=0.4, random_state=123)


# Train the algorithm on the trainset, and predict ratings for
the testset.
algo.fit(trainset)
predictions = algo.test(testset)
```

The process outputs a similar RMSE to that of the previous section:

```
# Compute the Root Mean Square Error.
accuracy.rmse(predictions)
>> RMSE: 0.9099
0.9098979396765616
```

With best model at our disposal, we can move to the next section and propose music titles to a reference user.

Extracting music recommendations

Let us randomly choose AJYSM99XWVT4O as our user, who, according to the following code snippet, has performed 33 reviews:

```
uid = "AJYSM99XWVT4O"
```

```
# Find the products that the specific user has not rated.
rated = ratings[ratings['userId'] == uid]['productId'].tolist()
not_rated = unique_products[~unique_products['productId'].
isin(rated)]

len(rated)
>> 33
```

Using the best model from the previous section, we iterate over all available music titles and predict whether they should be suggested to this specific person. Notice that the `predict` method takes the user and the product IDs as arguments:

```
pred = []

# Iterate over all not rated products and predict whether they
should be recommended.
for index, row in not_rated.iterrows():
    p = algo.predict(uid, row['productId'])
    pred.append((row['title'], p[3]))

# Create a dataframe from the predictions.
predictions = pd.DataFrame(pred, columns=['products',
'measure'])
predictions.sort_values('measure', ascending=False,
inplace=True)
predictions.set_index('products', inplace=True)
```

Next, we obtain 10 recommendations for the reference user:

```
# Obtain the 10 top recommendations.
recommend = predictions.head(10)

# Get the title and genre for the recommendations.
tg = unique_products[unique_products['title'].isin(recommend.
index.tolist())][['title', 'category']]

# Join the information from the two dataframes.
recommend = tg.set_index('title').join(recommend, how='left',
lsuffix='_left', rsuffix='_right')
```

As in all previous examples, we will print a list of the recommendations:

```
# Recommend 10 products.
recommend.sort_values('measure', ascending=False)
>>
title                 category                        measure
Jackie Wilson - 20..  Blues|Pop|R&B                   4.931706
Shaft: Music From ..  Blues|Pop|R&B|Soundtracks       4.929420
Aja                   Rock                            4.918036
Velvet Underground    Alternative Rock|Pop Rock       4.905956
Me Against the World  Rap&Hip-Hop                     4.897946
A Love Supreme        Jazz|Pop                        4.892095
Made in Japan [Vinyl] Classic Rock|Hard Rock&..       4.881098
Fulfillingness        Classic Rock|Pop|R&B|Rock       4.865284
Kind of Blue          Music|Jazz                      4.862929
Pleasure to Kill      Hard Rock&Metal|Rock            4.859903
```

Hopefully, the output should persuade AJYSM99XWVT4O to buy one of the suggested titles! In the following section, we will continue our discussion by presenting another type of artificial neural network suitable for building model-based collaborative filtering systems.

Introducing autoencoders

In *Chapter 4, Extracting Sentiments from Product Reviews*, we encountered neural network architectures for the first time. This section will continue along this path and focus on learning about techniques that leverage neural networks. Specifically, we will present a family of feature extractor methods that are designed to identify inherent patterns in data. These fall under the family of **autoencoders**, which are neural networks that try to shape their structure so that a given input and output are the same. An autoencoder network consists of two connected networks, an **Encoder** and a **Decoder** part, as shown in *Figure 5.19*:

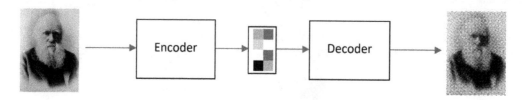

Figure 5.19 – The typical autoencoder architecture

The encoder takes in the input and converts it into a smaller, more dense representation. The aim is to preserve as much pertinent information as possible and discard any irrelevant parts. Next, the decoder network uses the compressed encoding from the previous step to reconstruct the original input as accurately as possible. Autoencoders are used for dimensionality reduction and information retrieval. Newer, more sophisticated versions are incorporated for advanced tasks, such as image generation.

In its simplest form, an autoencoder architecture consists of a feed-forward neural network such as the one shown in *Figure 5.20*:

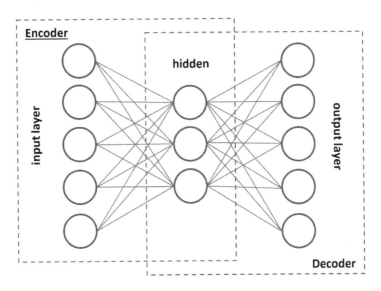

Figure 5.20 – A simple autoencoder architecture

The input and output layers have the same number of nodes connected through a hidden layer with fewer nodes. During training, the aim is to minimize the difference (reconstruction error) between the input X and the output X' using backpropagation.

You might wonder about the need to use fewer nodes for the hidden layer. To reconstruct the original input in the previous example, it seems more logical to use five nodes instead of three. However, doing so creates an excellent memorizer of the input but lacks generalization capability. As a result, the autoencoder becomes overfitted to the training data and works less well with an unseen input. Conversely, a hidden layer with fewer nodes acts as an information filter that only stores the gist of the training data. This architecture can provide a reasonable reconstruction of both the training and unseen data.

Now, please take a moment to think about why this approach helps us create product recommenders. The answer is given in the following section.

Understanding Restricted Boltzmann Machines

Restricted Boltzmann Machines (**RBMs**) are similar to autoencoders but are implemented differently. An autoencoder consists of three layers where the output nodes are connected back to the input ones. On the other hand, an RBM is shallow and uses a two-layer neural architecture. The first input layer is *visible* and the second is *hidden*. Additionally, its nodes make stochastic decisions based on some probability distribution to determine whether to transmit the input signal or not. *Figure 5.21* shows the architecture of an RBM:

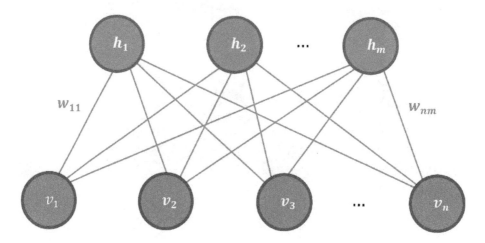

Figure 5.21 – The architecture of an RBM

However, what is probability distribution? Consider this question: *if you had to bet on the sum of rolling two dice, what would that be ?* Without too much thinking, the magic number is **7** simply because there are more combinations that get this sum than **12**, for example. *Figure 5.22* shows the probability distribution of this experiment:

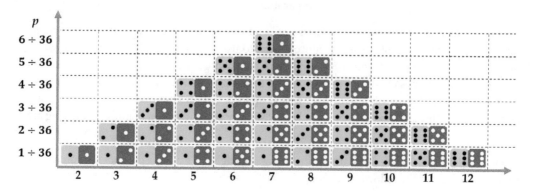

Figure 5.22 – Distribution of the outcomes after rolling two dice

The data creates a bell-shaped curve, known as the **Gaussian** or **normal distribution**, which is encountered in infinite everyday situations. For example, the height of a population, grades of students, and IQ scores follow the normal distribution. Note, of course, that there are many other probability distributions in statistics.

In the same sense, different versions of the RBM use different distributions to perform their stochastic decision, either for the visible or hidden units. The two most well-known types are the **Bernoulli-Bernoulli RBM** and the **Gaussian-Bernoulli RBM**, which, as the names suggest, differ in terms of their visible units. In the first case, they are binary, whereas the visible units are continuous in the second case. For both types, the hidden units are binary. Notice that the **Bernoulli distribution** models a random experiment with only two outcomes: *yes* or *no*, *success* or *failure*, or *true/false*.

When working with a specific dataset, it assumes that its samples adequately represent the general population. If this is not the case, we can hardly make any predictions for unseen data. In technical terms, the probability distribution of the dataset should be very close to the one of the whole population that we want to model.

Equipped with a good understanding of the RMB, we will move on to the next section and put a Bernoulli RBM into action.

Putting a Bernoulli RBM into action

The scikit-learn module provides an easy way to train an RBM from the rating pivot table, as shown in the following code:

```
from sklearn.neural_network import BernoulliRBM


# Normalize the ratings and get the transpose dataframe.
rp = ratings_pivot.div(5.0)
rp = rp.reset_index(drop=True).T


# Create the Bernoulli RBM and fit it with data.
rbm = BernoulliRBM(n_components=100, learning_rate=0.01, n_
iter=20, random_state=123, batch_size=200, verbose=True)
rbm.fit(rp)


# Perform one Gibbs sampling step.
res = rbm.gibbs(np.array(rp))
>>

. . .

[BernoulliRBM] Iteration 19, pseudo-likelihood = -2793.37, time
= 1.85s
```

```
[BernoulliRBM] Iteration 20, pseudo-likelihood = -2713.01, time
= 1.95s
```

The model is trained after 20 iterations, so let's use it to determine whether a product should be recommended to a user (the same as before, AJYSM99XWVT4O):

```
# Keep track of whether a product should be recommended for a
specific user.
unique_products['recommend'] = res[rp.index.get_loc(uid)]
unique_products[['title', 'category', 'recommend']].head()
>>  title                    category            recommend
3   Chrono Cross: Original.. Pop|Soundtracks     False
57  Vagrant Story: Origina.. Pop|Soundtracks     False
65  Roy Orbison: Authorize.. Pop|Rock            False
86  Bird Lives               Jazz                False
97  Hardest Pit in the Lit.. Pop|Rap&Hip-Hop     True
```

Next, we will filter out non-relevant recommendations:

```
# Keep the product to recommend.
recommend_products = unique_products[unique_products.
recommend==True]
print("Number of recommendations: {:d}".format(len(recommend_
products)))
>> Number of recommendations: 2240
```

In the end, we have 2240 possible results to output at our disposal. However, before doing so, we need to check how many of the 33 user-rated products appear in the filtered list:

```
# Keep their product id.
m_ids = (recommend_products.productId).tolist()


# Percentage of recommended products already rated.
print("{:.2f}".format(100*len(list(set(rated).intersection(m_
ids)))/len(rated)) + "%")
>> 27.27%
```

The user has already rated almost one-third of the music items, so we need to exclude them from the possible recommendations:

```
# Recommend 10 products.
recommend_products[~recommend_products.productId.isin(rated)]
[['title', 'category']].head(10)
>>   title                            category
97   Hardest Pit in the Litter        Pop|Rap&Hip-Hop
137  Letters From Home                Country|Pop
149  Fanfare for the Warriors [Vinyl] Jazz|Pop
181  Songs of Courage                 Jazz
194  Hard Hard Traveling Man          Country
209  Chocolate                        Dance&Electronic|Po..
262  Ferenc Fricsay: A Life in Mus..  Classical|Dance&Ele..
267  Guerrilla Warfare                Pop|Rap&Hip-Hop
370  Return Journey                   Country|Folk
476  Catch Without Arms               Alternative Rock|Ha..
```

The recommendations list is not comparable to those in the *Extracting music recommendations* section. Those items were sorted in descending order in terms of their measure score, with the most highly ranked appearing first. In the case of the RBM, the decision to recommend a product is binary, so we do not get any score in the output list.

After presenting and using an RBM, we can conclude our discussion of model-based collaborative filtering recommender systems. The aim was to create models that predict user ratings for unrated items. We can also hypothesize that the recommendations would have been more accurate if the dataset had been much larger. Notice that the only requirement is to change the code in the *Performing exploratory data analysis* section to read more samples during data loading, but this is an exercise for you to verify and test!

Summary

This chapter dealt with the topic of the recommender systems that are ubiquitous on our daily journeys online. Compared to the previous chapters, we didn't perform any classification tasks; instead, we focused on the most noteworthy techniques in ML for implementing recommender systems. Utilizing a corpus of Amazon reviews, we tried to elicit customized suggestions for music titles.

To wrap up, in the first part of the chapter, we performed the necessary data cleaning to eliminate corrupted data that would affect the quality of the developed systems. Then, we manipulated the dataset to make it suitable for the analysis that followed. We also enhanced our arsenal of data visualization methods with new types of plots.

In the second part, we attacked the problem by focusing on the properties of products or customer ratings. We then detailed the suitable methods for both cases and implemented various recommenders. Simultaneously, we broadened our coverage of dimensionality reduction techniques and learned how to tune the values of the hyperparameters efficiently. In the next chapter, we will present one of the hottest topics in NLP: *machine translation*.

6
Teaching Machines to Translate

The universal translator is a prominent yet imaginary device commonly encountered in many science fiction novels, films, and TV series. Star Trek, for example, long ago included the device in its screenplay to accommodate the unhindered translation of alien languages into the native language of the user. But unfortunately, a Star Trek-like device doesn't exist yet, and the vision of a universal translator has not been realized. This shortcoming comes as no surprise, given human languages' fluidity, inherent ambiguity, and flexibility. Nevertheless, the effort to teach machines to work as efficient translators is constant, with fascinating results in recent years.

This chapter seeks to present the different methods for machine translation and, at the same time, enhance your skillset with many standard techniques for NLP. The differences in the methods presented are an excellent opportunity to contrast the design philosophy of top-down and bottom-up approaches. In the first case, domain experts are required to create models replicating the data, whereas in the second, the data is derived from the model. This chapter's content focuses on the evolution of machine translation systems over the years in terms of four main category types. Besides the many practical hints, there is a special focus on understanding complex architectures for sequence-to-sequence learning. Finally, we will present specific evaluation methods and metrics to assess the performance of relevant systems.

By the end of this chapter, you will be able to use many of the described generic techniques in similar or completely diverse projects and implement machine translation systems from scratch.

In this chapter, we will go through the following topics:

- Understanding machine translation
- Introducing rule-based machine translation
- Introducing statistical machine translation
- Introducing sequence-to-sequence learning
- Measuring translation performance

Technical requirements

This chapter's code has been truncated in certain parts for ease of reading. However, the entire code is available as different Jupyter notebooks in this book's GitHub repository: `https://github.com/PacktPublishing/Machine-Learning-Techniques-for-Text/tree/main/chapter-06`.

Understanding machine translation

A serious impediment to spreading new information, ideas, and knowledge is the language barriers imposed by the different languages spoken worldwide. Despite the cultural richness brought to our global heritage, they can pose significant hurdles to efficient human communication. This chapter focuses on **machine translation** (**MT**), which aims to alleviate these barriers. MT is the process of automatically converting a piece of text from a source into a target language without human intervention. This task is more than a modest goal and demands the synergy of various emerging fields to address the peculiarities of human language. For instance, with their inherent ambiguity and flexibility, you can expect multiple situations where more than one best translation exists. Despite many prominent MT systems appearing in recent years, the technology is not new. In the 50s, it was part of the first computing applications. Nevertheless, significant progress has been made lately with systems that achieve state-of-the-art results. *Figure 6.1* presents the major milestones in the evolution of MT that we are going to explore throughout this chapter:

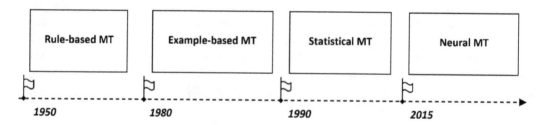

Figure 6.1 – Evolution of MT technologies

Before we start discussing these methods, let's consider a useful representation that helps in identifying the basic steps of any MT system, called the **Vauquois triangle** (see *Figure 6.2*):

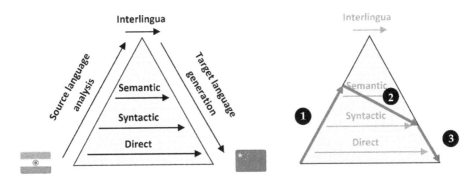

Figure 6.2 – The Vauquois triangle

This specific representation, introduced by French researcher B. Vauquois in 1968, acts as a roadmap for translating a source sentence into the correct target. At a high level, the MT algorithm needs to perform three distinct steps, shown schematically in the plots:

1. First, ascend the left-hand side of the triangle and create an internal representation of the source sentence (**Source language analysis**).

2. Then, traverse the triangle and transfer the source representation to the target one. The different levels inside the triangle signify different levels of analysis. For example, **Syntactic** analysis determines whether a sentence is *well formed*, while **Semantic** analysis analyzes its meaning and whether it *makes sense*.

3. Finally, descend to the right-hand side and generate the target sentence (**Target language generation**).

There is no single way to perform the previous steps, and we can follow multiple paths to reach a translation. Ascending too high means that the algorithm dedicates more effort to create a better source representation and, consequently, deeper transfer rules are required. On the other hand, moving directly from the source to the target sentence (bottom of the triangle) demands shallow transfer rules and little effort in constructing internal representations. Finally, at the extreme, reaching the peak of the triangle allows the representation of the source sentence in a universal language (**Interlingua**). In this case, we can proceed to the third step, bypassing the second one completely. If all these sound a little bit vague, don't worry. Let's build our own MT systems to demystify this process!

Introducing rule-based machine translation

We will begin our journey of MT with the classical approach, known as **rule-based machine translation** (**RBMT**), which aims to exploit linguistic information about the source and target languages. RBMT techniques fall under the broad category of **knowledge-based systems**, which mainly aim to capture the knowledge of human experts to solve complex problems. For example, try to recall your first efforts in learning a foreign language. First, we had to find the correct translation of a sentence, which involved searching for it in a dictionary and mapping each word of the source sentence to a word in the target. Then, we had to make a few adjustments, such as finding the correct verb conjugation. *Figure 6.3* illustrates this approach with an English sentence translated into French:

Source sentence (EN)		Target sentence (FR)
The sky is blue		*Le ciel est bleu*
The	⟶	Le
sky	⟶	ciel
is	⟶	est
blue	⟶	bleu

Figure 6.3 – A word-for-word mapping from the source (EN) to the target (FR) language

We can follow a similar approach and create word-for-word mapping rules for any other translation pair. A complete bilingual English-to-French dictionary would suffice for this task. However, basic knowledge of a second language suggests that a word-for-word translation rarely works in practice. Words can appear or disappear in the target language; they can be highly context-dependent, while word morphology (the components inside a word, such as its stem, suffix, and so on) is extremely important. For example, consider the word *up*, the 42nd most popular English word (`https://en.wikipedia.org/wiki/Most_common_words_in_English`), which has 50 different meanings (`https://en.wiktionary.org/wiki/up`). The chances are 1 out of 50 (2%) of getting the correct translation of this polysemous word without its *collocations* (series of words or terms that co-occur – for example, *came up*). Therefore, it is necessary to analyze the complete sentence before proceeding to its translation. Also, the general context of the source text must be considered since different conditions apply, for example, when translating literature versus a technical document. For these reasons, the translation rules must be more sophisticated than simply mapping between dictionaries. Over several decades, the effort has been to craft rules that can achieve good translation quality in a particular domain. All rules are handwritten, thus we can immediately identify the source of a mistranslation. Rules offer the competitive advantage of total control and don't require much data, making RBMT relevant even today.

The following sections explore the three main categories of RBMT systems. Their differences lie in the level at which they aim for a language-independent representation and the source language's depth of analysis.

Using direct machine translation

Let's consider a more complex translation pair: *Life is good* (English) → *La vie est belle* (French). In this case, the number of words differs, so following a word-for-word approach won't work. Instead, more complex rules are required while considering the source and target languages' lexical, syntactic, and semantic levels. Here is where **direct machine translation** (**DMT**) comes into the scene. The rules are usually developed by linguists with the necessary knowledge of the languages involved. In their simplest form, the rules need to do a mapping between source and target words, as we saw in *Figure 6.3*. In the more general case, the source sentence is split into lexical units, and the effort is to find the correct units in the target language. These can be a single word, a part of a word, or a chain of words. Creating the internal representation of the source sentence is minimal, with or without morphological analysis or lemmatization, and the transfer rules are shallow. Next, we will discuss a more sophisticated type of RBMT method.

Using transfer-based machine translation

The first task in the Vauquois triangle focuses on analyzing the source sentence. Again, a relevant analogy is a task we all had to endure during our early language courses at school. One of the primary assignments was grammatically analyzing a sentence and locating the basic sentence units – for example, the subject, verb, and object. Similarly, **transfer-based machine translation** (**TBMT**) systems parse the source sentences to extract richer internal representations. In the following subsections, we will explore different methods to identify how words are combined to form constituents (linguistic parts of a larger sentence, phrase, or clause), how words relate to other words, and more.

Executing part-of-speech tagging

We will begin with a method that categorizes words in a piece of text with a particular tag, based on their definition and context, called **part-of-speech** (**POS**) tagging. *Figure 6.4* shows the outcome of this process using a sample input phrase:

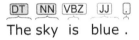

Figure 6.4 – Part-of-speech tagging example

The source sentence, *The sky is blue*, is analyzed and placed in four POS tags, codified as determiner (**DT**), noun (**NN**), third-person singular present (**VBZ**), and adjective (**JJ**). Various software toolkits are available for this type of parsing, such as Stanford's CoreNLP (https://corenlp.run/) and spaCy (https://spacy.io/). In this section, we will incorporate nltk to perform POS tagging while using the following code from the machine-translation.ipynb notebook:

```
import nltk

# Tokenize the input text.
text = nltk.word_tokenize("The sky is blue")

# Parse the input.
nltk.pos_tag(text)
>> [('The', 'DT'), ('sky', 'NN'), ('is', 'VBZ'), ('blue', 'JJ')]
```

Notice that the output is the same as the one in *Figure 6.4*. POS tagging provides useful information about each word and facilitates translation. For example, the word *damage* can be either a *verb* or a *noun*. Identifying its POS tag in a sentence provides the correct context for its translation.

Creating context-free grammar

A more insightful representation is the **parse tree**, which provides information on how a word joins with the other words of the sentence. We can quickly build our parse tree in Python using nltk and **context-free grammar** (**CFG**). A CFG is a set of recursive rules used to parse or generate patterns of strings. For example, the following code creates a CFG (named analysis_grammar) that consists of six rules signified with the -> symbol:

```
# Create the grammar that consists of six rules.
# S:sentence, NP:noun phrase, DT:determiner, NN:noun,
# VBZ:verb in the third person singular, JJ:adjective.
analysis_grammar = nltk.CFG.fromstring("""
    S -> NP VBZ JJ
    NP -> DT NN
    DT -> 'The'
    NN -> 'sky'
    VBZ -> 'is'
    JJ -> 'blue'
    """)
```

S and NP are non-terminal rules (can be expanded further), while DT, NN, VBZ, and JJ are terminal. Next, we must parse the input phrase using the analysis grammar:

```
# Create the input.
input = ['The', 'sky', 'is', 'blue']

# Parse the input.
parser = nltk.ChartParser(analysis_grammar)

# Print the parse trees.
for tree in parser.parse(input):
    print(tree)
>> (S (NP (DT The) (NN sky)) (VBZ is) (JJ blue))
```

In this example, the output is a single parse tree, but when the CFG becomes sufficiently large, it can output multiple parses for the same input.

We can also visualize the tree:

```
        ...
    tree.draw()
```

The output is shown in *Figure 6.5*:

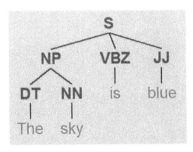

Figure 6.5 – Parse tree example

A *determiner* (**DT**) and a *noun* (**NN**) are combined to form a *noun phrase* (**NP**), which, along with the *verb* (**VBZ**) and the *adjective* (**JJ**), form the *sentence* (**S**).

Creating the previous analysis grammar was not particularly challenging. On the other hand, it can only parse one sentence! What about extending the rules so that they support sentences such as *The sky is blue*, *The sky is red*, *The sea is blue*, and *The sea is red*? The solution, in this case, is to use the notational shorthand, |, which can be read as *or*. This operator allows multiple rules within a single line to be included. For example, NN can either be `sky` or `sea` while JJ can either be `blue` or `red`. The following code shows the extended grammar:

```
# The grammar consists of six but more powerful rules.
analysis_grammar = nltk.CFG.fromstring("""
    S -> NP VBZ JJ
    NP -> DT NN
    DT -> 'The' | 'the'
    NN -> 'sky' | 'sea'
    VBZ -> 'is'
    JJ -> 'blue' | 'red'
    """)
```

To verify that it supports all the necessary phrases, let's generate 10 (n=10) possible expansions:

```
from nltk.parse.generate import generate


# Generate ten examples at most.
for sentence in generate(analysis_grammar, n=10):
    print(' '.join(sentence))
>> The sky is blue
The sky is red
The sea is blue
The sea is red
the sky is blue
the sky is red
the sea is blue
the sea is red
```

The output consists of eight sentences that include the total coverage initially planned. Let's continue this discussion with another type of analysis for the source sentence.

Creating dependency grammars

While CFG is concerned with how words and sequences of words combine to form constituents, other types of grammar focus on how words relate to other words; specifically, **dependency grammar** keeps track of the relation between a *head* word and its *dependents*. More often, the head of the sentence is the verb. Every other word depends on the head or connects to it through other dependencies. Using a dependency parser, we can analyze the grammatical structure of a sentence and obtain the relationships between head words and those that modify the heads. For example, in *Figure 6.6*, the arrow from the word **blue** to the word **sky** indicates that the latter modifies **blue**, and the label **nsubj** assigned to the arrow describes the dependency – in this case, *nominal subject*:

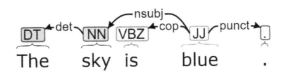

Figure 6.6 – Dependency parsing example

To clarify these concepts, let's create a grammar that consists of three rules for word-to-word dependency relations and incorporate it through a dependency parser:

```
# Create the dependency grammar that includes three rules.
dependency_grammar = nltk.DependencyGrammar.fromstring("""
    'is' -> 'sky' | 'sea' | 'blue' | 'red'
    'sky' -> 'The' | 'the'
    'sea' -> 'The' | 'the'
    """)


# Create the dependency parser.
pdp = nltk.ProjectiveDependencyParser(dependency_grammar)
```

Based on the previous grammar, the verb `is` constitutes the head of the sentence. Next, we must feed the parser with an input phrase:

```
# Create the input.
input = ['The', 'sky', 'is', 'blue']


# Parse the input.
trees = pdp.parse(input)


# Print the parse trees.
```

```
for tree in trees:
    print(tree)
>> (is (sky The) blue)
```

For this simplistic grammar, only one parse tree is generated, which we can visualize in *Figure 6.7*:

Figure 6.7 – Dependency tree example

This tree helps us identify semantic relations between words in the sentence, contrary to the trees from CFGs, which only tell us how words join with the other words of the sentence. In this example, the words `sky` and `blue` are related through the verb `is`. Note that we capture bare dependency information in this example without specifying its type. The following section presents another important analysis technique.

Executing name entity resolution

During any translation task, we can encounter words in the source language that should not be translated into the target. For instance, names of people, organizations, expressions of times, locations, and so on can be transferred without any alternation (especially when the language pair shares a common alphabet). But how can we know this? The solution is an information extraction technique known as **named-entity resolution (NER)**. NER seeks to locate and classify named entities in text into predefined categories. In *Figure 6.8*, we are performing NER using some sample text from Wikipedia (https://en.wikipedia.org/wiki/Apollo_11):

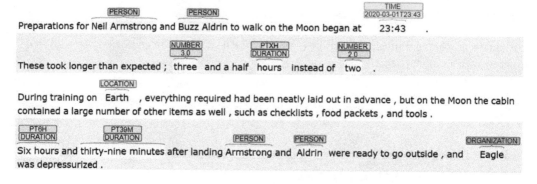

Figure 6.8 – NER of a sample phrase

Different tags have been identified correctly, such as **PERSON, LOCATION, TIME, NUMBER,** and **DURATION**. However, the lunar module, **Eagle**, has been falsely tagged as **ORGANIZATION**.

Now, let's learn how to perform NER in `nltk` while using the phrase `The Aston Martin is blue` as input:

```
# Download nltk models/corpora.
nltk.download('maxent_ne_chunker')
nltk.download('words')

# Tokenize the input text.
text = nltk.word_tokenize("The Aston Martin is blue")

# Parse the input.
tags = nltk.pos_tag(text)

# Find the name entities.
tree = nltk.ne_chunk(tags)
```

After tokenizing the input, we execute POS tagging. The tagging output constitutes the input to the `ne_chunk` method, which acts as a chunker. *Chunking* is a type of shallow parsing that follows POS tagging (grammatical information) and adds more structure to the sentence (semantic information). While a deep parse tree has many levels between the root and the leaves, there are only a few in shallow parsing. The benefits, in this case, are that it is quicker and generally more accurate. You can consider chunking a lightweight alternative to NER, as the latter is computationally more extensive.

Next, we must draw the tree:

```
tree.draw()
```

The output is shown in *Figure 6.9*:

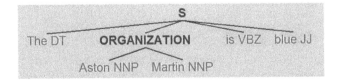

Figure 6.9 – NER tree sample

Compared to *Figure 6.4*, there is a new tag for **Aston** and **Martin** called **NNP**, which signifies a proper noun in singular form. The semantic value of the phrase **Aston Martin** refers to an organization, so if we were to translate it into French, we could simply copy it from the English text.

Next, we must extract the tagging tokens using the **IOB format** (short for inside, outside, beginning), which is used for tagging tokens in a chunking task:

```
# Get the IOB tags.
iob_tags = nltk.tree2conlltags(tree)


# Print the IOB tags.
print(iob_tags)
>> [('The', 'DT', 'O'), ('Aston', 'NNP', 'B-ORGANIZATION'),
('Martin', 'NNP', 'I-ORGANIZATION'), ('is', 'VBZ', 'O'),
('blue', 'JJ', 'O')]
```

IOB provides three tags to refer to parts of a chunk (group of words). These are similar to POS tags but can denote the inside, outside, and beginning of a chunk:

- The I- prefix before a tag indicates that the tag is inside a chunk

- The B- prefix before a tag indicates that the tag is the beginning of a chunk

- The O tag indicates that a token belongs to no chunk (outside)

In our example, most words do not belong to any particular chunk; that is why they are noted with **O**. **Aston** is at the beginning of the ORGANIZATION chunk, so it's labeled as **B-ORGANIZATION**. Similarly, **Martin**, inside the same chunk, is labeled as **I-ORGANIZATION**.

In summary, all the different steps for analyzing a source sentence let us create the representations for the two examples phrases shown in *Figure 6.10*:

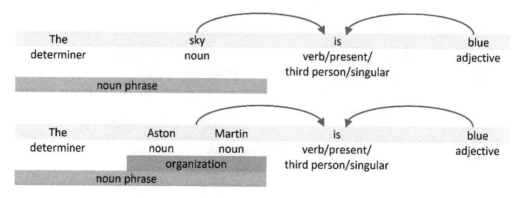

Figure 6.10 – Two source sentence representations

Even with these simple phrases, we can observe multiple levels of analysis. For example, each word is assigned a grammatical category (POS tag), while the verb's morphology is identified correctly (**is** = third-person singular). Furthermore, some words are grouped into constituents to form noun phrases (such as **The sky**), and the words **sky** and **blue** relate to each other through the verb **is**. Finally, **Aston Martin** should remain untranslated to the target language.

Recall that we are still in the ascending phase of the Vauquois triangle, where the aim is to elicit useful representations of the source sentences. We can now proceed to the second step and learn how to create rules that can transfer the source representation to the target one.

Creating transfer and generation grammar

A **feature-based grammar** in nltk is a convenient way to create transfer rules for MT. The reason is that it offers feature structures in the form of attribute-value pairs, which can be used to encode the grammatical categories of the words. So far, we have tried to extract useful information about the source sentences that can facilitate their translation into the target language. For the sake of simplicity, however, the transfer rules created in this section only exploit the CFG presented earlier and omit any information coming from the dependency grammar or the NER task.

In the following code, we start with the definition of our feature grammar:

```
# Create the grammar string.
g = """

# S expansion productions.
S[AGR1=?np, ARG2=?vbz, ARG3=?jj] -> NP[AGR=?np] VBZ[AGR=?vbz]
JJ[AGR=?jj]

# NP expansion productions.
NP[AGR=[DT=?dt, NN=?nn]] -> DT[AGR=?dt] NN[AGR=?nn]

# Lexical productions.
DT[AGR=[TEXT='Le', SEM='determiner']] -> 'The'
DT[AGR=[TEXT='le', SEM='determiner']] -> 'the'
NN[AGR=[TEXT='ciel', SEM='noun']] -> 'sky'
NN[AGR=[TEXT='mer', SEM='noun']] -> 'sea'
VBZ[AGR=[TEXT='être', SEM='verb', TENSE='present',
NUM='singular']] -> 'is'
JJ[AGR=[TEXT='bleu', SEM='adjective']] -> 'blue'
JJ[AGR=[TEXT='rouge', SEM='adjective']] -> 'red'
"""
```

The grammar includes several attribute-value pairs; for example, the SEM attribute can have noun as its value. With the aid of the transfer rules, we can parse a source representation (in English) and return a sequence of attributes named TEXT with the target language representations (in French). Observe the hierarchical expansion of the rules as the sentence, S, consists of noun phrases, NP, which consists of nouns, NN, and determiners, DT. Now, we can use this grammar to parse an input phrase:

```
# Create the input, transfer grammar, and parser.
input = ['The', 'sky', 'is', 'blue']
transfer_grammar = nltk.grammar.FeatureGrammar.fromstring(g)
parser = nltk.parse.FeatureEarleyChartParser(transfer_grammar)

# Parse the input and print the result.
trees = parser.parse(input)
for tree in trees: print(tree)
>> (S[AGR1=[DT=[SEM='determiner', TEXT='Le'], NN=[SEM='noun',
TEXT='ciel']], ARG2=[NUM='singular', SEM='verb',
TENSE='present', TEXT='être'], ARG3=[SEM='adjective',
TEXT='bleu']]
  (NP[AGR=[DT=[SEM='determiner', TEXT='Le'], NN=[SEM='noun',
TEXT='ciel']]]
    (DT[AGR=[SEM='determiner', TEXT='Le']] The)
    (NN[AGR=[SEM='noun', TEXT='ciel']] sky))
  (VBZ[AGR=[NUM='singular', SEM='verb', TENSE='present',
TEXT='être']]
    is)
  (JJ[AGR=[SEM='adjective', TEXT='bleu']] blue))
```

To demystify the previous output, let's summarize the most important information in *Figure 6.11*:

Le	ciel	être	bleu
determiner	noun	verb/present/ third person/singular	adjective
noun phrase			

Figure 6.11 – Internal representation in the target language

Based on the previous output, we managed to obtain an internal representation in the target language, but our work is not finished yet. The word **être** is the infinitive form of the verb *to be* in French and must agree with the subject in the sentence. Therefore, we need to transform it into the present tense, third-person singular form.

It's about time to introduce the third step in the Vauquois triangle and create a generation grammar. The latter transforms the internal representation in the target language into the translation emitted by the system. We must use a feature grammar again:

```
# Create the grammar string.
g = """

# S expansion productions.
S[AGR1=?np, ARG2=?vbz, ARG3=?jj] -> NP[AGR=?np] VBZ[AGR=?vbz]
JJ[AGR=?jj]

# NP expansion productions.
NP[AGR=[DT=?dt, NN=?nn]] -> DT[AGR=?dt] NN[AGR=?nn]

# Lexical productions.
DT[AGR=[TEXT='Le']] -> 'Le'
DT[AGR=[TEXT='le']] -> 'le'
NN[AGR=[TEXT='ciel']] -> 'ciel'
NN[AGR=[TEXT='mer']] -> 'mer'
VBZ[AGR=[TEXT='est', SEM='verb', TENSE='present',
NUM='singular']] -> 'être'
JJ[AGR=[TEXT='bleu']] -> 'bleu'
JJ[AGR=[TEXT='rouge']] -> 'rouge'
"""
```

Finally, we must create the parser using the generation grammar and test it with the representation we encountered earlier:

```
# Create the input, transfer grammar, and parser.
input = ['Le', 'ciel', 'être', 'bleu']
generation_grammar = nltk.grammar.FeatureGrammar.fromstring(g)
parser = nltk.parse.FeatureEarleyChartParser(generation_
grammar)

# Parse the input and print the result.
trees = parser.parse(input)
for tree in trees: print(tree)
>> (S[AGR1=[DT=[TEXT='Le'], NN=[TEXT='ciel']],
ARG2=[NUM='singular', SEM='verb', TENSE='present', TEXT='est'],
```

```
ARG3=[TEXT='bleu']]
   (NP[AGR=[DT=[TEXT='Le'], NN=[TEXT='ciel']]]
     (DT[AGR=[TEXT='Le']] Le)
     (NN[AGR=[TEXT='ciel']] ciel))
   (VBZ[AGR=[NUM='singular', SEM='verb', TENSE='present',
TEXT='est']]
      être)
   (JJ[AGR=[TEXT='bleu']] bleu))
```

The output is indeed the correct translation of the input phrase! A French speaker, however, should have spotted a problem with the generation rules. *The sea* in English should be translated into *La mer* in French, not *Le mer*, which is wrong. The articles *le* and *la* refer to masculine and feminine nouns, respectively. We must extend the rules to ensure the determiner agrees with the noun it modifies in terms of number and gender. As more sentences must be supported, more complex rules should be added to the grammar. The linguist's job becomes harder as they must try to include more and more cases and exceptions to these rules. Additionally, syntax parsing methods suffer from structural ambiguity, as there is often the possibility that more than one correct parse for a given sentence exists. So, TBMT approaches work well for limited domain applications (although the effort can still be very high), but for general-purpose MT systems, the task becomes insurmountable.

The following section concludes the discussion on RBMT systems with a technique that presents competitive advantages when we need to support multiple translation pairs in the same application.

Using interlingual machine translation

The third technique for RBMT allows us to reach the peak of the Vauquois triangle using analysis grammar and mapping the source sentence into a universal interlingua representation, hence the name **interlingual machine translation** (IMT). From this point, a generation grammar can be used to obtain the target sentence without the need to incorporate any transfer rules. The idea behind a universal representation of languages is not new. In 1629, Marin Mersenne (https://en.wikipedia. org/wiki/Marin_Mersenne) and René Descartes (https://en.wikipedia.org/ wiki/Ren%C3%A9_Descartes) proposed an artificial universal language with equivalent ideas in different tongues sharing one symbol. Essentially, they proposed cataloging all the elements of human imagination. If this were possible, the translation among languages would be effortless through the shared symbols.

While in TBMT, the linguistic rules are specific to each source-target pair, in IMT, they are specific to every single language and their interlingua. Generally, for *N* languages, we need to implement *Nx(N-1)* sets of linguistic rules in the TBMT and *2xN* sets for the IMT case. *Figure 6.12* illustrates an example with six languages (for brevity, only a subset of the combinations has been presented):

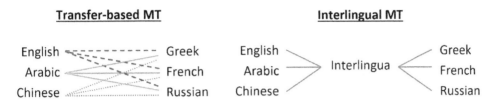

Figure 6.12 – Number of rule sets for TBMT (3x3) and IMT (3+3)

You are probably wondering what this interlingual representation looks like. An analogy is illustrated in *Figure 6.13*:

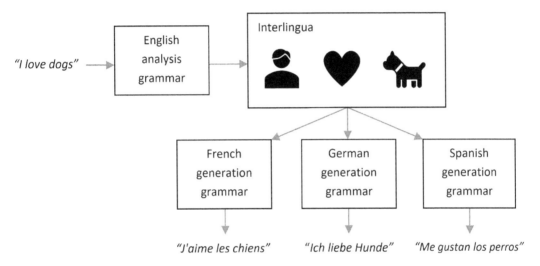

Figure 6.13 – Interlingua translation using pictograms

Suppose we are asked to translate the source phrase **I love dogs** into French, German, and Spanish. Based on *Figure 6.13*, the first step is extracting the semantic representation of the sentence using an English analysis grammar. Next, the representation is translated into an interlingua, which is depicted as a series of language-agnostic pictograms. Afterward, specific generation grammars translate the interlingua into one of the target languages.

It's hardly convincing that pictograms are the right way to create an interlingual representation. Images are notoriously ambiguous, and there is no agreement among cultures on universal designs. Moreover, there are not enough pictograms to represent all concepts, and it's cumbersome to design and sketch them in the first place. Similar issues arise for text-based interlingual representations, as they must be both abstract and independent of the source and target languages. Although RBMT techniques are still in use, they target a narrow set of applications.

The following section presents the next milestone in MT's evolution.

Introducing example-based machine translation

In the era of RBMT systems, it became apparent that a new paradigm in MT was necessary. The reliance on linguistic rules presents many shortcomings. As we saw previously, using a corpus of already-translated examples could serve as a model to base the translation task on. This is the basic idea behind **example-based machine translation** (**EBMT**) systems; keep track of well-translated fragments and use this information to facilitate the translation of new sentences. Humans often process short sentences this way; first, they split the source into smaller fragments, then translate the pieces by analogy into previous examples, and, finally, recombine those translations into the target sentence. Deep linguistic analysis is not necessary, and the more examples that are available, the more the translation accuracy improves. *Figure 6.14* shows an example:

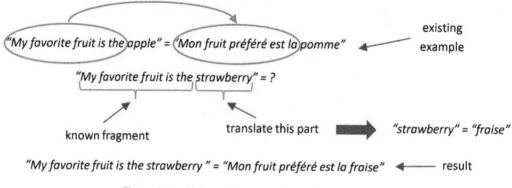

Figure 6.14 – Using existing translated fragments in MT

The primary resource of an EBMT system is parallel bilingual corpora created by professionals that are available either as proprietary or as a free resource. For instance, *CLARIN* (https://www.clarin.eu/resource-families/parallel-corpora) and *OPUS* (http://opus.nlpl.eu/) are well-known resources that contain pairs of source and target sentences. The effort of creating these corpora is significant as, besides acquiring the translation pairs, we need to perform text alignment at the sentence and word levels to identify the fragments. Manual alignment by experts is often performed for this task; most of the time, however, automatic methods are incorporated, though this has a price in terms of precision.

Let's learn how to use the alignments that have been defined for a bilingual pair programmatically. In the following code, we are considering two examples from the English-to-French pair:

```
from nltk.translate import AlignedSent, Alignment

# Hold the bi-lingual text.
bitext = []
```

```
# Create two examples from German to English, along with the
alignments.
bitext.append(AlignedSent(['blue', 'is', 'The', 'sky'],
                          ['Le', 'ciel', 'est', 'bleu'],
                          Alignment.fromstring('0-3 1-2 2-0 3-1')))
bitext.append(AlignedSent(['yellow', 'is', 'The', 'sun'],
                          ['Le', 'soleil', 'est', 'jaune'],
                          Alignment.fromstring('0-3 1-2 2-0 3-1')))


# Print the source words in the second example.
bitext[1].words
>> ['yellow', 'is', 'The', 'sun']
```

For example, the word yellow at position 0 is aligned with the word jaune at position 3. By the way, the color of the sun is white, as it emits all colors of the rainbow more or less evenly.

We can verify these alignments using the following code:

```
# Print the target words in the second example.
bitext[1].mots
>> ['Le', 'soleil', 'est', 'jaune']


# Print the alignments in the second example.
bitext[1].alignment
>> Alignment([(0, 3), (1, 2), (2, 0), (3, 1)])
```

As mentioned previously, creating the alignment by hand is cumbersome; another option is to use off-the-shelf parallel corpora with alignments. The nltk toolkit includes comtrans, a subset of *Europarl's* sentence-aligned parallel corpus (https://www.statmt.org/europarl/) for various languages. Let's load the module and pick the first example from the English-to-French dataset:

```
# Download nltk corpus.
nltk.download('comtrans')


from nltk.corpus import comtrans


# Get the first example from the english/french corpus.
fe = comtrans.aligned_sents('alignment-en-fr.txt')[0]
```

```
# Print the source words.
fe.words
>> ['Resumption', 'of', 'the', 'session']
```

The target words in this case are as follows:

```
# Print the target words.
fe.mots
>> ['Reprise', 'de', 'la', 'session']
```

Now, we can extract the alignments between the source and the target:

```
# Print the alignments.
fe.alignment
>> Alignment([(0, 0), (1, 1), (2, 2), (3, 3)])
```

In the previous example, the mapping of the words is one-to-one. Unfortunately, this is not the case in most MT tasks. Consider, for example, the following pair:

```
# Get the 52nd example from the English/French corpus.
fe = comtrans.aligned_sents('alignment-en-fr.txt')[52]

# Print the source words.
fe.words
>> 'We', 'do', 'not', 'know', 'what', 'is', 'happening', '.']

# Print the target words.
fe.mots
>> ['Nous', 'ne', 'savons', 'pas', 'ce', 'qui', 'se', 'passe',
'.']
```

The output in this case is as follows:

```
# Print the alignments.
fe.alignment
>> Alignment([(0, 0), (1, 1), (2, 3), (3, 2), (4, 4), (4, 5),
(5, 6), (6, 7), (7, 8)])
```

There is a mix of alignments here, so performing this task by hand is laborious. In this case, we can incorporate models that automatize this process. The *IBM Model 2* lexical translation model is such an option that's available from nltk. The following code demonstrates a few bilingual pairs from French to English that can be used to train a lexical translation model:

```
import nltk.translate.ibm2
from nltk.translate import AlignedSent, Alignment


# Hold the bi-lingual text.
bitext = []


# Create examples from French to English.
bitext.append(AlignedSent(
    ['petite', 'est', 'la', 'maison'],
    ['the', 'house', 'is', 'small']))
bitext.append(AlignedSent(
    ['la', 'maison', 'est', 'grande'],
    ['the', 'house', 'is', 'big']))
bitext.append(AlignedSent
    (['le', 'livre', 'est', 'petit'],
    ['the', 'book', 'is', 'small']))
bitext.append(AlignedSent(
    ['la', 'maison'], ['the', 'house']))
bitext.append(AlignedSent(['le', 'livre'], ['the', 'book']))
bitext.append(AlignedSent(['un', 'livre'], ['a', 'book']))
```

Based on the previous examples, we can create a model and examine the probability of the word livre being translated as book:

```
# Create the lexical translation model from the examples.
ibm2 = nltk.translate.ibm2.IBMModel2(bitext, 5)


# Get the translation probabilities from the model.
print(round(ibm2.translation_table['livre']['book'], 3))
>> 0.879
```

Don't be surprised that the output probability is not equal to 1.0. All models suffer from certain limitations such as biases, vagaries of data noise and sampling, and so forth. Comparing `livre` with any other word in the example gives a much smaller probability. Finally, we can obtain the alignments for one sample phrase:

```
test_sentence = bitext[2]
test_sentence.words
>> ['le', 'livre', 'est', 'petit']
test_sentence.mots
>> ['the', 'book', 'is', 'small']
test_sentence.alignment
>> Alignment([(0, 0), (1, 1), (2, 2), (3, 3)])
```

The output provides the correct result, but admittedly, our bilingual corpus was tiny and thus targeted the lowest end of complexity.

To summarize this section, the three main tasks in the EBMT approach are as follows:

1. Matching phrase fragments of the source sentence to existing examples.
2. Identifying the corresponding translation fragments.
3. Recombining the translation fragments to create the target sentence.

Among these three steps, the first is the most critical and challenging. In real-world applications, the search space is huge, as source sentences can be segmented in multiple ways. Each bilingual corpus can have many aligned fragments relevant to our source sentence; thus, there could be multiple translations for the same source in the reference table. Sentence aligning can be performed through sophisticated methods such as the **Gale-Church algorithm**, for which a description is outside the scope of this book. However, it works on the principle that equivalent sentences should roughly correspond in length and uses dynamic programming to find their proper alignment.

> **Note**
>
> **Dynamic programming** is a technique in computer programming that can simplify processes containing multiple subproblems. It finds the optimal solution to each subproblem and then makes an informed choice to combine the results for the global solution.

Another approach related to EBMT is translation memory, which is frequently encountered in **computer-assisted translation** (CAT) tools. Systems of this kind aim to assist professional translators in their work by providing ready-made translations of fragments from a database. While EBMT is a method of performing the MT task automatically, CAT tools are simply an aid for translators who are in charge of making the final decision.

Now, let's look at the next important milestone in the field of MT.

Introducing statistical machine translation

EBMT paved the way for data-driven approaches, where the primary source of knowledge is the observed data. As a result, less emphasis is given to the representation logic, such as creating hand-crafted rules. Instead, analyzing the data directly, especially when there's a large amount of it, can reveal information we couldn't easily identify otherwise. RBMT techniques follow a top-down approach, and domain experts are required to create models that can replicate the data. Conversely, data-driven approaches are bottom-up, and the data derives the model. This section focuses on **statistical machine translation** (**SMT**), which involves exploiting models whose parameters are learned from bilingual text corpora. Strictly speaking, SMT systems do not follow the Vauquois triangle as neither a source nor a target representation is incorporated. Intuitively, they work on the assumption that every sentence in one language can be translated into any sentence in the target one. The overarching goal is to find the most probable translation in each case. The SMT method starts from the source sentence, and different alternative paths are constructed to deduce the correct translation. As the process evolves, low-probability paths are pruned until we reach the most probable outcome, as shown in *Figure 6.15*:

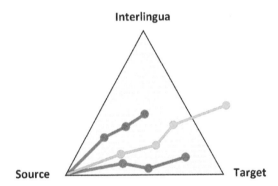

Figure 6.15 – Multiple paths to reach the most probable translation in an SMT system

The whole process is not deterministic; each SMT algorithm is judged on its ability to find the best path. We'll examine the details in the next section.

Modeling the translation problem

We have already mentioned that SMT aims to find the most probable translation, T, given a source sentence, S. So, we need to find the specific T that maximizes the probability, $P(T|S)$. This task is known as **maximum likelihood estimation** (MLE), written in mathematical formalism as $argmax_T P(T|S)$. Theoretically, we can perform an exhaustive search on all possible translations until we find the one that maximizes the previous conditional probability. In practice, however, this is not feasible, and Bayes' theorem, presented in *Chapter 2, Detecting Spam Emails*, provides a solution. Using this theorem, we can expand the previous expression, which now becomes $argmax_T P(S|T)P(T)/P(S)$. Even if we examine all possible translations against the source sentence, the portion, $P(S)$ (probability of the source sentence), remains constant. In maximization problems, we are interested in quantities that vary. Therefore, constants are irrelevant, and we can remove them from the subsequent calculations. Now, the expression is simplified as follows:

$$argmax_T P(S|T)P(T)$$

The initial problem is decomposed into two factors (subproblems), the first of which is the conditional probability, $P(S|T)$, known as the **translation model**. This model is estimated from bilingual parallel corpora; more about this in the next section. It expresses our confidence that the source sentence, S, had a particular translation, T.

Let's consider an example where S is the phrase *Life is beautiful* and has four candidate translations, T, in French: *Bon le ciel est*, *La fille est belle*, *Vie est belle*, and *La vie est belle*. Then, using a contrived translation model, we can perform the following calculations:

$$P(\text{``Life is beautiful''}|\text{''Bon le ciel est''}) = 0.0000004$$

$$P(\text{``Life is beautiful''}|\text{''La fille est belle''}) = 0.0000008$$

$$P(\text{``Life is beautiful''}|\text{''Vie est belle''}) = 0.000032 \checkmark$$

$$P(\text{``Life is beautiful''}|\text{''La vie est belle''}) = 0.000024$$

The third option has the highest probability out of the four candidate translations. However, the fourth candidate is the correct answer. What should we do? It's time to incorporate the second factor of MLE. The probability, $P(T)$, is known as the **language model** and expresses our confidence that the sentence is probable in the target language. Intuitively, it is like showing a sentence to a native French speaker and asking them whether it makes sense. The language model can be constructed in various ways, and in practice, we can use any corpus in the target language. In the next section, we will revisit this topic in more detail but for the time being, let's consider the following revised calculations:

$$P(\text{``Life is beautiful''}|\text{''Bon le ciel est''})P(\text{''Bon le ciel est''}) = 0.0000004 \cdot 0.000001$$

$$P(\text{“Life is beautiful”}|\text{”La fille est belle”})P(\text{“La fille est belle”}) = 0.0000008 \cdot 0.0003$$

$$P(\text{“Life is beautiful”}|\text{”Vie est belle”})P(\text{” Vie est belle”}) = 0.000032 \cdot 0.000002$$

$$P(\text{“Life is beautiful”}|\text{”La vie est belle”})P(\text{“La vie est belle”}) = 0.000024 \cdot 0.0002 \checkmark$$

This time, we obtain the correct translation for the input sentence, which is the fourth option. In summary, we search for the result that is highly probable (depicted with the + symbol in *Table 6.1*) in both the translation and language models:

	P(S/T)	P(T)
Bon le ciel est	-	-
La fille est belle	-	+
Vie est belle	+	-
La vie est belle	+	+

Table 6.1 – Looking for the most probable result in the translation and language models

It should be evident that splitting the translation problem into two subproblems is beneficial. But how are these created in the first place? We'll answer this question in the following section.

Creating the models

First, to create the translation model, we use a *phrase table* that includes sequences of words in the source and target languages, along with their probability:

```
from collections import defaultdict
from math import log
from nltk.translate import PhraseTable
from nltk.translate.stack_decoder import StackDecoder


# Create the phrase table.
phrase_table = PhraseTable()


# Populate the table with examples.
phrase_table.add(('das',), ('the', 'it'), log(0.4))
phrase_table.add(('das', 'ist'), ('this', 'is'), log(0.8))
phrase_table.add(('ein',), ('a',), log(0.8))
phrase_table.add(('haus',), ('house',), log(1.0))
phrase_table.add(('!',), ('!',), log(0.8))
```

The table is populated with five German-to-English pairs and their log probability quantifying how probable the specific translation is. If you are wondering why the `log` function is used, the reason is that it can turn multiplication into addition. And computers are much faster in performing addition! We must perform many multiplications to find the most probable translation in SMT, which can lead to underflow. The condition is that multiplying very small numbers outputs an even smaller result that a computer cannot represent. Therefore, using log probabilities is hugely beneficial.

Now, let's create the language model:

```
# Create the dictionary of probabilities for each n-gram.
language_prob = defaultdict(lambda: -999.0)


# Populate the dictionary uni-grams and bi-grams.
language_prob[('this',)] = log(0.8)
language_prob[('is',)] = log(0.6)
language_prob[('a', 'house')] = log(0.2)
language_prob[('!',)] = log(0.1)


# Create the language model.
language_model = type('', (object,), {'probability_change':
lambda self, context, phrase: language_prob[phrase],
'probability': lambda self, phrase: language_prob[phrase]})()
```

This model has been constructed using four n-grams, along with their log probability. In *Chapter 9, Generating Text in Chatbots*, we will perform this task more intensively.

A `stack decoder` utilizes the two models to extract the translation of the German phrase *das ist ein haus* (formally, nouns in German should be capitalized):

```
# Create the stack decoder and translate a sentence.
stack_decoder = StackDecoder(phrase_table, language_model)
stack_decoder.translate(['das', 'ist', 'ein', 'haus', '!'])
>> ['this', 'is', 'a', 'house', '!']
```

And voilà, the correct translation is emitted by the decoder!

Before finishing this section, let's say a few things about the decoding process. First, in phrase-based translation, the source sentence is segmented into phrases of one or more words, along with their translations. As the segmentation can be done differently, we might end up with multiple translations for the same source in the phrase table. Consequently, the decoder needs to keep parallel hypotheses, and the search space grows quickly. The decoder narrows the space using dynamic programming because hypotheses with a lower score are pruned.

The Jupyter notebook for this chapter contains code for creating the two models from files available by *Moses*, a statistical MT system used to train translation models for any language pair (`http://www.statmt.org/moses/download/sample-models.tgz`).

The methods presented so far provided the necessary context to understand the evolution of MT systems. The relevant discussion doesn't imply by any means that these are obsolete techniques or that they can't be applied to modern deployments. On the contrary! Hopefully, you have familiarized yourself with these methods, which are still used today and can be incorporated into other NLP applications in the future. In this respect, you have enhanced your toolbox! Of course, it would be a deficit if we don't present state-of-the-art MT architectures, which is the topic of the following section.

Introducing sequence-to-sequence learning

Many kinds of problems in machine learning involve transforming an input sequence into an output one. **Sequence-to-sequence** (**seq2seq**) learning has proven useful in applications that demand this transformation. For instance, free-form question answering (generating a natural language answer to a natural language question), text summarization, conversational interfaces such as chatbots, and so forth can benefit from seq2seq learning. It is not surprising that MT applications can also exploit this technique to convert a source sequence, such as an English phrase, into the corresponding target sequence, such as an Arabic translation. Seq2seq, pronounced as *seek-to-seek*, learning falls under the category of neural MT, and unlike solutions based on RBMT and SMT, no domain knowledge of the languages involved is necessary. You can treat the translation problem as the association between input and output tokens of words or characters. Moreover, the translation is end-to-end, which means that one model is required instead of many.

A common problem in seq2seq learning is context persistence, especially when the sequences become too lengthy. Why does this matter? Consider, for instance, the following sentences: *Tom and Jerry are playing outside. They like it a lot!* In this case, we must read the first sentence to make sense of the word *They*. While reading this book, you constantly do a similar task, keeping track of information far beyond adjacent sentences.

Similarly, context is crucial for choosing the correct translation in an MT system. For example, the word *back* can be either a noun, verb, adjective, or adverb, and it is hard to guess which form or meaning to choose without the proper context. We may also need to identify the gender of the present subject so that the correct pronoun is used later in the translation. **Recurrent neural networks (RNNs)** alleviate this problem as they are suitable for sequential data and have loops for persisting information. The main difference with a feed-forward neural network is the presence of a memory loop, thus the name *recurrent*. RNNs have a *memory* to register all information that has been extracted so far. A typical neural network uses its data once, generates an output, and compares its prediction with the reference one. Then, based on the calculated accuracy, the model's parameters are adjusted through backpropagation, and the process repeats until an acceptable performance is achieved. For an RNN, however, the loop feeds the context back to the model at every timestep. The left-hand side of *Figure 6.16* shows this process schematically:

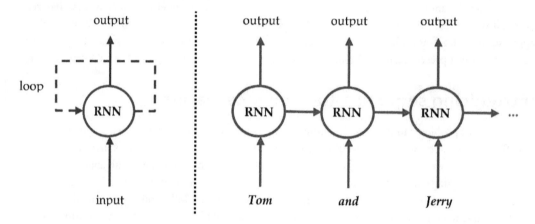

Figure 6.16 – High-level architecture of an RNN (left) and an unrolled RNN example (right)

To be more precise, let's unroll the RNN using an example phrase, as shown on the right-hand side of *Figure 6.16*. During the first timestep, the RNN receives the word **Tom** as input without any context. Then, the RNN produces some kind of output, depending on the task, and a context vector that is passed in the second timestep, along with the word **and**. This process repeats until the last word in the input sentence is consumed. Intuitively, it is like doing a copy-paste of the same network, passing a message to the successor at each timestep. By the end of this process, the propagated message should contain enough information to associate **Tom** and **Jerry** with the word **They**.

The following section shows how RNNs can be glued together to create robust models.

Deciphering the encoder/decoder architecture

If you grasped the basic concepts from the previous discussion, it is straightforward to deduce how RNN can be used to solve the main topic of this chapter. Initially, we model the source and target sequences with a separate recurrent network that can extract the necessary dependencies. The first network encodes the source sentence, hence the name **encoder**, while the second network decodes the input into the target language, hence the name **decoder**. Gluing these networks together creates an end-to-end translation pipeline for any pair of languages. A critical remark is that we must create two separate network topologies for inference or training the model. *Figure 6.17* shows a typical encoder-decoder seq2seq architecture for inference:

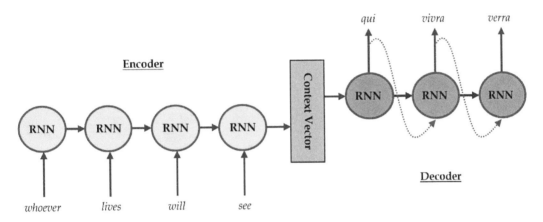

Figure 6.17 – Typical encoder-decoder seq2seq architecture for inference

The aim is to decode an unknown source sequence and predict its target output. The model consists of three main parts that work synergetically:

1. The encoder (left part) consumes words sequentially from the input sentence. The first RNN cell processes the first source word and emits a hidden state that is fed to the subsequent cell. The latter emits a new hidden state after consuming the second word. The encoding terminates when the end of the input is reached.

2. The context vector (middle part) is essentially the final hidden state of the encoder. It aims to encapsulate the information from all input elements.

3. The decoder (right part) predicts a word as output (translation) at each timestep. The first RNN cell utilizes the context vector to produce an output and a hidden state. Both are fed to the subsequent cell, which repeats similar processing. Every word in the translation is conditional to the entire source sentence and the translated word that preceded it. The decoding terminates when no more predictions are made or we reach a maximum threshold of iterations.

In this example, observe that the source and target sequences do not have the same length. This powerful feature of seq2seq models makes them germane for MT applications.

To train the model, we must use a slightly different topology, as illustrated in *Figure 6.18*:

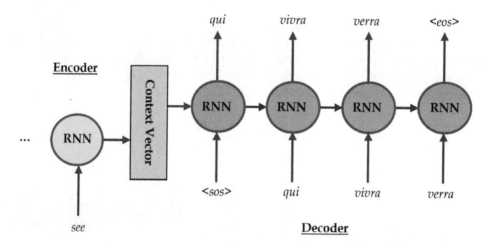

Figure 6.18 – Typical encoder-decoder seq2seq architecture for training

The critical change happens in the decoder part, which uses ground truth as input instead of the prior step output. The correct translation for every source sentence is known so that we can feed this information to the decoder at each timestep. Notice the usage of two special tokens, namely *start_of_ stream* (<**sos**>) and *end_of_stream* (<**eos**>). The first token signifies the start of the translation, which is why it's fed into the first cell of the decoder. The second token is the final output and signifies the end of the translation process. The encoder and the decoder consist of several cells of RNN that are trained simultaneously from the data. The model learns by the decoder's output errors being propagated to the encoder via backpropagation. Intuitively, it is like having a teacher at each timestep correcting the decoder. An analogy is illustrated in *Figure 6.19*:

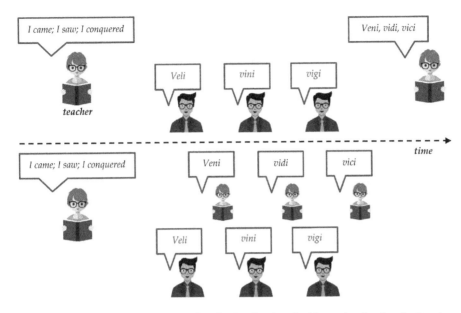

Figure 6.19 – Training without teacher forcing (top) and with teacher forcing (bottom)

While in the first scenario (top), the teacher corrects the student at the end, while in the second case (bottom), they intervene after every interaction. For this reason, the second strategy, known as **teacher forcing**, proves beneficial for training an encoder-decoder seq2seq model.

You might be wondering how the context vector is calculated in the first place. The next section sheds light on this.

Understanding long short-term memory units

We have often stressed the distinctive feature of RNN to *memorize* important information. But is there an upper bound on this ability? Human mental capacity is limited, and we have all found ourselves moving back and forth in a piece of text to spot crucial information that helps us decipher its meaning. Although, in theory, RNNs can handle *long-term dependencies*, they can effectively process sequences with a length of less than 10 in practice. The reason is an inherent problem in neural networks called the **vanishing gradient**. In our discussion in the *Training artificial neural networks* section of *Chapter 4, Extracting Sentiments from Product Reviews*, we saw how backpropagation uses gradient descent to update the parameters of a deep neural network during the training phase. At each iteration, the network's parameters receive an update proportional to the partial derivative of the cost function concerning the current parameter. According to the chain rule, the derivatives of each layer are multiplied from the final layer to the initial one. There are situations, however, where the derivatives become small, and their multiplication decreases the gradient very quickly. Due to the gradient becoming vanishingly small, the earlier layers of the network learn slower than the later ones. In extreme cases, the training process can stop completely. There are no vanishing gradient problems when a relatively small number of hidden layers are used. For long sequences, however, an RNN is unable to propagate useful gradient information to the layers near the input of the model, reducing its effectiveness.

One solution to this problem is to use another recurrent layer type called **long short-term memory** (**LSTM**) units. The basic principle behind these units is analogous to RNN: at each timestep, use a token from the data sequence, along with input from the previous timestep. The distinctive feature of LSTM, however, is its ability to remember information for long periods. For this reason, the structure of an LSTM is much more complex compared to the structure of an RNN. *Figure 6.20* shows a schematic diagram of an LSTM. As daunting as it might seem, we can identify a few basic functions:

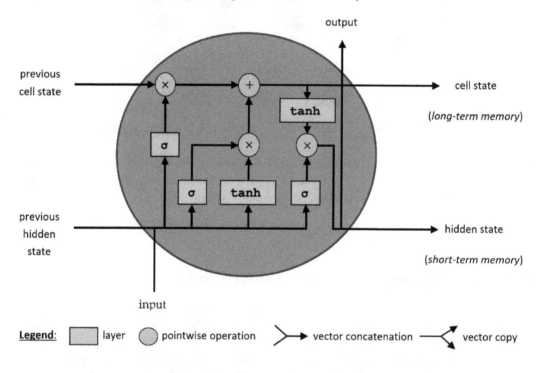

Figure 6.20 – Schematic diagram of LSTM

LSTM aims to keep track of both long and short-term dependencies in the input sequence. As the learning process evolves, the network needs to *memorize* important information and throw away information that is not relevant anymore. Recall the discussion in the *Understanding artificial neurons* section of *Chapter 4, Extracting Sentiments from Product Reviews*, about the role of an activation function. Essentially, it is a gate that allows or blocks information from passing through the next layer. The sigmoid layer (σ) outputs numbers between zero and one and, along with the pointwise multiplication operator, determines the amount of information to pass in the next step. An output of *0* from the sigmoid layer means that any input should be discarded entirely.

Conversely, an output of *1* lets everything pass through. An LSTM contains three gates (sigmoid layers) to control the flow of new information, which is the concatenation of the input in the current timestep and the hidden state from the preceding one. The whole process outputs a cell and a hidden state corresponding to long- and short-term memory. Depending on the application, we also get a third output, which results from the processing at each timestep. Notice that the new information has more than one chance to affect the cell and hidden states through the several sigmoid and **tanh** paths. At each timestep, the network decides on what information to keep for the local context (hidden state) and what for the global one (cell state). In all cases, however, every path has a sigmoid layer as a gatekeeper.

Let's examine LSTM in more detail, starting from the first step in the pipeline, as shown on the left-hand side of *Figure 6.21*:

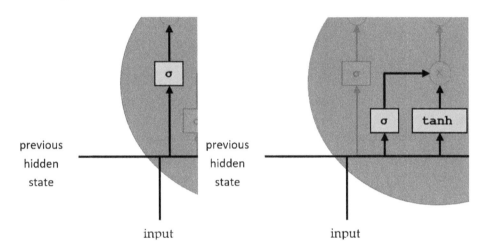

Figure 6.21 – LSTM forget gate (left) and input gate (right)

This step decides whether we should keep the information from the previous timestamp or forget it. For example, if the network encounters a feminine name such as Alice, and after a few sentences, a male name such as Bob appears, it makes sense to forget the first person. Memorizing information in this way allows the proper gender pronoun to be applied later in the process. For this reason, the structure shown in this figure is called a **forget gate**.

The next step is determining which information must be kept in the cell state (long-term memory). Again, the structure shown on the right-hand side of *Figure 6.21* does this. As before, the information passes through a sigmoid layer that transforms the values between *0* and *1*. However, this time, we also use a **tanh** layer to regulate the values flowing through the network. As the LSTM unrolls, many mathematical computations take place, such as a number being multiplied by a value multiple times. In this case, it can explode after several iterations, causing other values to seem insignificant.

Using the **tanh** layer is essential to transform all the possible values between *-1* and *1*. Based on the previous example, we would like the network to register Bob as the reference person. The structure shown here is called the **input gate**.

Then, we can update the cell state based on what we need to forget and what we wish to remember. As shown in *Figure 6.22*, we can apply the appropriate pointwise operations to the output of the two gates and update the previous cell state accordingly. After this step, the global context should have forgotten Alice and remember only Bob:

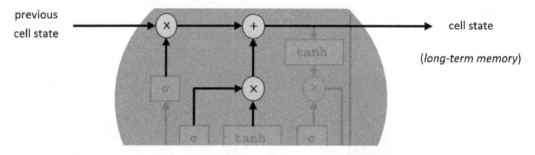

previous cell state

cell state

(*long-term memory*)

Figure 6.22 – Updating the cell state

Finally, the LSTM needs to emit the local context (new hidden state), as shown in *Figure 6.23*:

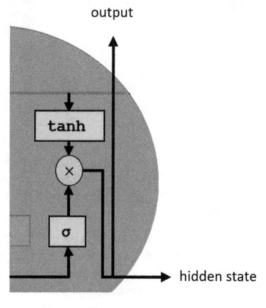

output

tanh

hidden state

(*short-term memory*)

Figure 6.23 – LSTM output gate

This step uses the newly modified cell state and passes it through a **tanh** layer. The result of this process is multiplied by the sigmoid output to determine what information the hidden state should carry. For example, we can register whether the subject is singular or plural in the local context and use this information to conjugate the verb in the next time step correctly. For obvious reasons, the structure in this figure is called the **output gate**. Note that although the process seems quite deterministic, like a perfectly regulated watch always working in the same way, it's not. Machine learning algorithms are, in general, non-deterministic, and depending on the random initialization of their weights, they produce outcomes that vary.

To summarize, the forget gate decides what is relevant to keep from the previous steps, while the input gate decides what information to add from the current step. Both gates update the cell state (known as the global context or long-term memory). The output gate determines the hidden state (known as the local context or short-term memory). The result of this processing is a new cell and hidden states that are used to analyze the next token of the input sequence. The process terminates when the final token is fed to the LSTM.

In practice, we can use LSTM or **Gated Recurrent Units** (**GRUs**) networks in an encoder/decoder architecture, as both are a type of RNN. GRUs can be considered variations of the LSTM, which also try to solve the vanishing gradient problem. However, they have fewer parameters, and for that reason, they are computationally more efficient.

Now, let's combine our accumulated knowledge and apply it to build an MT system.

Putting seq2seq in action

To create the seq2seq model, we will utilize an English-to-French bilingual corpus consisting of ~200K source-target pairs. Due to resource limitations, we will only keep 8000 of those pairs to build the model. The code that follows (included in the seq2seq-LSTM.ipynb notebook) shows the specific steps:

```
import pandas as pd
import re

# Read the first 8K pairs in the dataset.
data = pd.read_table('./data/fra.txt',  usecols=range(2),
names=['source', 'target'], nrows=8000)

# Replace no-break and thin spaces in the target sentences.
data.target = data.target.apply(lambda x: re.sub(u'\xa0|\
u202f|\u2009', u' ', x))
data.sample(5, random_state=123)
```

```
>>          source            target
5676        Tom is loyal.     Tom est fidèle.
617         I'm game.         J'en suis.
415         Back off!         Cassez-vous.
7687        Life is crazy.    La vie est dingue.
6708        I caused this.    J'ai causé ceci.
```

Next, the <sos> and <eos> tokens are added to the target sentences at the beginning and the end, respectively:

```
# Add two special tokens in the target sentences (start_of_
stream/end_of_stream).
data['target'] = '<sos> ' + data['target'] + ' <eos>'
data.target[100]
>> '<sos> Je payai. <eos>'
```

Let's extract the vocabulary size of the sentences in the source and target corpora:

```
# Extract the vocabulary of the source/target sentences.
src_voc = sorted(list(data['source'].str.split(' ',
expand=True).stack().unique()))
trg_voc = sorted(list(data['target'].str.split(' ',
expand=True).stack().unique()))

# Get the vocabulary size for the source/target sentences.
Increase by one for the padding token.
src_voc_size = len(src_voc) + 1
trg_voc_size = len(trg_voc) + 1

print("Vocabulary size of the source sentences:", src_voc_size)
print("Vocabulary size of the target sentences:", trg_voc_size)
>>
Vocabulary size of the source sentences: 2504
Vocabulary size of the target sentences: 4818
```

Next, we must obtain the maximum length of the sentences in each case:

```
# Extract the maximum sentence length in the source/target
sentences.
max_src_len = max([(len(s.split(' '))) for s in
```

```
data['source']])
max_trg_len = max([(len(s.split(' '))) for s in
data['target']])


print("Maximum length of the source sentences:", max_src_len)
print("Maximum length of the target sentences:", max_trg_len)
>>
Maximum length of the source sentences: 5
Maximum length of the target sentences: 12
```

The previous statistics are essential as they let us configure the dimensions of the different units of the model. Recall that the power of seq2seq models lies in their ability to handle input and output sequences of different lengths.

Another step to facilitate data processing is to build word-to-index and index-to-word dictionaries. The first allows the input words to be transformed into numerical values for the encoder. Similarly, we need a dictionary to map numerical values to the output words for the decoder. The following code shows how:

```
# Create the word-to-index dictionary for the source/target
tokens.
# Zero index reserved for the padding token.
src_word2idx = dict([(word, idx+1) for idx, word in
enumerate(src_voc)])
trg_word2idx = dict([(word, idx+1) for idx, word in
enumerate(trg_voc)])


print(trg_word2idx['Non'])
>> 675
```

And here is the code for the index-to-word dictionary:

```
# Create the index-to-word dictionary for the source/target
tokens.
src_idx2word = dict([(idx, word) for word, idx in src_word2idx.
items()])
trg_idx2word = dict([(idx, word) for word, idx in trg_word2idx.
items()])


print(trg_idx2word[675])
>> Non
```

The encoder receives as input an array whose size is 8000×5 (corpus samples multiplied by the maximum sentence length). For the decoder, the input is an 8000×12 array. The elements of the rows contain the numerical identifier of each word in the sentence using the word-to-index dictionary. For example, the numerical representation of the phrase *I play* is *[165, 1772, 0, 0, 0]* because the value *165* corresponds to the word *I* and the value *1772* to the word *play*. In general, the vectors of the sentences are sparse as they contain many zeros. Later, we will see that the model's output consists of a dense layer with softmax activations, so the decoder's output should be in the form of one-hot vectors. Specifically, each target word is represented by a one-hot vector whose size is 4818 (vocabulary size), which is why each target sentence requires 12 (maximum sentence length) of these vectors. In the end, an array of 8000×12×4818 can include the whole target sentence set.

Now, let's examine these steps by specifying the format of the input and output data:

```
import numpy as np


# The input/output data of the model.
enc_input_data = np.zeros((len(data['source']), max_src_len),
dtype='float32')
dec_input_data = np.zeros((len(data['source']), max_trg_len),
dtype='float32')
dec_output_data = np.zeros((len(data['source']), max_trg_len,
trg_voc_size), dtype='float32')
```

Observe how `max_src_len` and `max_trg_len` determine the size of the created arrays. Next, we iterate over the whole dataset, transforming words into numerical values for the encoder's and the decoder's input while creating the one-hot array for the decoder's output:

```
# Iterate over the whole dataset.
for i, (src_sentence, trg_sentence) in
enumerate(zip(data['source'], data['target'])):

    # Create the input for the encoder.
    for j, word in enumerate(src_sentence.split()):
        enc_input_data[i, j] = src_word2idx[word]

    # Create the input/output for the decoder.
    for j, word in enumerate(trg_sentence.split()):
        # Skip the '<eos>' word in the decoder input.
        if j < len(trg_sentence.split())-1:
            dec_input_data[i, j] = trg_word2idx[word]
```

```
    # Skip the '<sos>' word in the decoder output.
    if j > 0:
        dec_output_data[i, j-1, trg_word2idx[word]] = 1.0
```

Now, we can set up the architecture of the training model, which is a *graph of layers*. Let's examine each step:

1. First, the input layers of the encoder and the decoder are constructed:

    ```
    from keras.layers import Input, LSTM, Embedding, Dense
    from keras.models import Model

    # Create the input layers for the encoder/decoder.
    enc_input = Input(shape=(None,), dtype='float32',)
    dec_input = Input(shape=(None,), dtype='float32',)
    ```

2. Instead of feeding the input layers with the previously created sparse arrays, we incorporate word embedding. Recall the discussion in the *Extracting word embedding representation* section of *Chapter 3, Classifying Topics of Newsgroup Posts*, concerning the competitive benefits of this technique, such as its ability to retain the relationships among words. For this reason, we add an embedding layer after the input ones. Each of the 2504 words of the source language and the 4818 words of the target one is embedded in a 256-dimensional space:

    ```
    # Create the embedding layers for the encoder/decoder.
    embed_layer = Embedding(src_voc_size, 256, mask_
    zero=True)
    enc_embed = embed_layer(enc_input)
    embed_layer = Embedding(trg_voc_size, 256, mask_
    zero=True)
    dec_embed = embed_layer(dec_input)
    ```

3. The LSTM layers receive the embedding of each word and perform the seq2seq learning, as described earlier. Note that during the training phase, we are only interested in the states of the encoder and the output of the decoder. The output of the encoder and the states of the decoder are not used. In Python, the _ symbol signifies that specific values can be ignored:

    ```
    # Create the LSTM layers for the encoder/decoder.
    enc_LSTM = LSTM(256, return_state=True)
    _, state_h, state_c = enc_LSTM(enc_embed)
    dec_LSTM = LSTM(256, return_state=True, return_
    sequences=True)
    # The initial states of the decoder are the output from
    ```

```
the encoder.
dec_output, _, _ = dec_LSTM(dec_embed, initial_
state=[state_h, state_c])
```

4. Finally, the softmax layer in the output of the decoder provides probabilities for each of the 4818 words in the target language. In this way, the most probable word is emitted by the decoder at each timestep:

```
# Create the output layer for the decoder.
dec_dense = Dense(trg_voc_size, activation='softmax')
dec_output = dec_dense(dec_output)
```

Now that all the pieces are in place, we can start constructing and training the complete encoder/decoder model.

Training the model

As mentioned several times, the training model takes two inputs (enc_input and dec_input) and emits one output (dec_output):

```
# Create and compile the model.
model = Model([enc_input, dec_input], dec_output)
model.compile(optimizer='rmsprop', loss='categorical_
crossentropy', metrics=['accuracy'])
model_params = np.sum([np.prod(v.get_shape()) for v in model.
trainable_weights])
print("Number of trainable parameters:", model_params)
>> Number of trainable parameters: 4163282
```

As a measure of the complexity of the model, we print the number of its trainable parameters. In total, 4163282 parameters must be estimated. Quite a lot!

Now, let's visualize the different layers of the training model that we created in the previous section:

```
from keras.utils.vis_utils import plot_model


# Plot the model.
plot_model(model, to_file='./images/model_plot.png', show_
shapes=True, show_layer_names=True, dpi=100)
```

The output is illustrated in *Figure 6.24*:

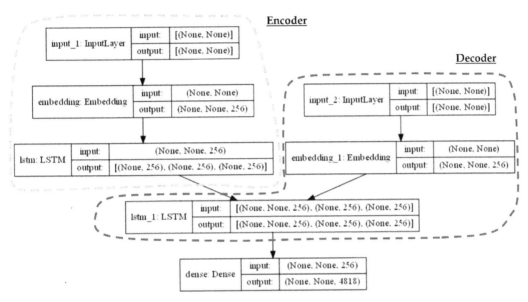

Figure 6.24 – The encoder/decoder model for training

The input, embedding, and LSTM layers appear in both the encoder and the decoder parts. The arrows signify the flow of data from each layer to the next, while the **None** elements represent dimensions where the shape is not explicitly set, and for that reason, it's unknown. For example, the only restriction for the input to the **lstm** layer is that it should consist of embeddings of size **256**. After the whole architecture is in place, we start the training process by fitting the data to the model:

```
# Fit the data to the model.
model.fit([enc_input_data, dec_input_data], dec_output_data,
batch_size=128, epochs=100, validation_split=0.2, shuffle=True)
>>
...
Epoch 99/100
50/50 [==============================] - 6s 115ms/step - loss:
0.0903 - accuracy: 0.8755 - val_loss: 2.1945 - val_accuracy:
0.3988
Epoch 100/100
50/50 [==============================] - 6s 115ms/step - loss:
0.0897 - accuracy: 0.8756 - val_loss: 2.2089 - val_accuracy:
0.3998
```

According to the `validation_split` parameter, 80% of the bilingual pairs are used for training, while the other 20% are used for testing. After `100` epochs, we achieve an accuracy of around 88%. Notice that we reached this rather good score without the need to annotate the training data in any way. No domain knowledge of the languages involved was necessary, and a simple bilingual corpus with pairs of sentences was enough to train the model. In the following section, we will test the implemented MT system.

Testing the model

Before using the trained model for inference, we must change its architecture so that the output of each decoder timestep becomes an input to the subsequent one. The encoder remains unchanged. Let's examine the appropriate steps:

1. First, we must create the encoder part and specify that the input of the decoder is the hidden (`dec_state_in_h`) and cell (`dec_state_in_c`) states. We must also define an embedding layer for the input word (`dec_embed_2`):

```
# Model to encode the input.
enc_model = Model(enc_input, [state_h, state_c])


# The hidden and cell states of the decoder at each step.
dec_state_in_h = Input(shape=(256,))
dec_state_in_c = Input(shape=(256,))


# Set the embedding layer.
dec_embed_2 = embed_layer(dec_input)
```

2. The LSTM unit (`dec_LSTM`) is configured based on the previous layers and reuses its weights from the training phase. To make predictions, the decoder's output is passed through a dense layer:

```
# Set the LSTM layer.
dec_output_2, dec_state_out_h, dec_state_out_c = dec_
LSTM(dec_embed_2, initial_state=[dec_state_in_h, dec_
state_in_c])


# Set the output layer for the decoder.
dec_output_2 = dec_dense(dec_output_2)
```

3. Now, let's create the decoder model:

```
decoder_model = Model([dec_input] + [dec_state_in_h,
dec_state_in_c], [dec_output_2] + [dec_state_out_h, dec_
state_out_c])
```

4. Next, we must visualize the architecture of the altered decoder:

```
plot_model(decoder_model, to_file='./images/inference_
model_plot.png', show_shapes=True, show_layer_names=True,
dpi=100)
```

We get the following output:

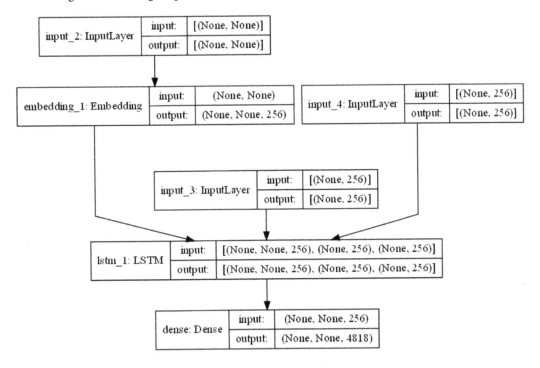

Figure 6.25 – The decoder model for inference

Now, it's time to extract a translation for a given sentence. Here, we must include the necessary steps in the getTranslation method and present them in detail. First, the method receives the index part of an example in the dataset:

```
# Translate an input sentence.
def getTranslation(index):
```

```
translation = word = ''

# Choose a sequence from the data set.
source_seq = enc_input_data[index:index+1]
```

Next, the encoder creates the context vector from the input:

```
# Get the initial input states for the decoder.
states_h_c = enc_model.predict(source_seq)

# The first input token to the decoder is start_of_stream.
token = np.zeros((1,1))
token[0, 0] = trg_word2idx['<sos>']
```

The decoding process is a loop that iterates until we hit <eos> or until a threshold has been reached. In this example, the decoding stops when the length of the target sentence exceeds 100 characters. At each timestep, the decoder outputs a one-hot encoded vector to which we apply np.argmax to get the maximum value:

```
# Start the decoding process.
while (word != '<eos>' and len(translation) <= 100):

    # Predict the next token and states.
    output, state_h, state_c = decoder_model.
predict([token] + states_h_c)

    # Store the emitted token and the states for the next
iteration.
    idx = np.argmax(output[0, -1, :])
    token[0, 0] = idx
    states_h_c = [state_h, state_c]
```

Let's extract the corresponding word from the dictionary using idx:

```
# Extract the emitted word.
word = trg_idx2word[idx]
translation += ' ' + word


return translation
```

Finally, it's time to call the method:

```
print("Input sentence:", data['source'][1308])
print("Reference translation:", data['target'][1308].
replace(""",""").replace(""","""))
print("Hypothesis:", getTranslation(1308)[:-6])

>>

Input sentence: Seriously?
Reference translation: C'est vrai ?
Prediction:   Vraiment ?
```

The model's prediction seems incorrect as it differs from the reference translation. In reality, however, the English input sentence can be translated equally into both versions in French. Thus, we should feel happy with the outcome of our model!

With this presentation of seq2seq models, we conclude our discussion of many important methods for MT; in *Chapter 7, Summarizing Wikipedia Articles*, we will encounter another appropriate method for MT. Starting from RBMT systems, where humans are responsible for crafting the proper rules for translation, we concluded by presenting neural architectures. The second approach aims to create translation models directly from the data without exploiting any particular knowledge of the languages involved.

Throughout this book, we will discuss the importance of assessing the quality of the developed systems and, more importantly, comparing competing implementations. MT cannot be an exception to this rule. The following section introduces the last topic of this chapter: the evaluation methodology and the relevant metrics for MT.

Measuring translation performance

The most straightforward way to evaluate an MT system is to ask humans (preferably, professional translators) to assign a score to each output. However, this leads to other problems, which include the subjectiveness of the evaluator, the number of sentences that can be assessed, potential costs, and so forth. As in every machine learning task, we can incorporate automatic metrics to assess the quality of the output. Accuracy, precision, recall, and F-score were encountered in *Chapter 2, Detecting Spam Emails*, so let's see how they can be incorporated to evaluate an MT system.

Consider the source phrase in English *and in the rain your letters flow in the rivers*, which has a reference translation in French of *et sous la pluie tes lettres coulent dans les rivières*. Let's assume that the system outputs the prediction *sous la pluie les lettres coulent dans la rivière*, as illustrated in *Figure 6.26*:

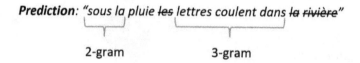

Reference: *"et sous la pluie tes lettres coulent dans les rivières"*

Prediction: *"sous la pluie ~~les~~ lettres coulent dans ~~la rivière~~"*

2-gram   3-gram

Figure 6.26 – Reference and predicted translation example

Here, we can make the following calculations:

$$Precision = \frac{correct\_words}{\#words\_prediction} = \frac{6}{9} = 67\%$$

$$Recall = \frac{correct\_words}{\#words\_reference} = \frac{6}{10} = 60\%$$

$$\textit{F-score} = 2 * \frac{precision * recall}{precision + recall} = 2 * \frac{0.67 * 0.6}{0.67 + 0.6} = 63\%$$

It is unclear, however, how to interpret these values under the prism of MT. In this case, a more appropriate metric for evaluating the quality of MT systems is the **BiLingual Evaluation Understudy** (**BLEU**) score. Using BLEU, we compare the generated prediction to a reference sentence by counting matching n-grams in both cases. Specifically, for each n-gram whose size is between 1 and 4 in the prediction, we count the number of times they appear in the reference. Notice that the order of the n-grams does not play any role. A brevity penalty is also added to the score to prevent very short candidates from receiving too high BLEU values. This way, predictions closer to the length of the reference translation get a higher score. The formula of BLEU is as follows:

$$BLEU = \min{(1, \frac{\#words\_prediction}{\#words\_reference})}(\prod_{i=1}^{4} precision_i)^{\frac{1}{4}}$$

A score of 1 indicates a perfect match, while a score of 0 indicates a perfect mismatch. The benefits of BLEU are that it is easy to apply and understand and correlates well with human evaluation. The more common patterns that are found in both the prediction and reference, the more confident we are about the translation. In *Table 6.2*, we are calculating BLEU step by step using two hypothetical predictions of an MT system:

Metric	Prediction 1 *"sous la pluie ~~les~~ lettres coulent dans ~~la rivière~~"*	Prediction 2 *"sous la pluie tes lettres coulent dans ~~la rivière~~"*
Precision 1-gram	6/9	7/9
Precision 2-gram	4/8	6/8
Precision 3-gram	2/7	5/7
Precision 4-gram	0/6	4/6
Brevity penalty	9/10	9/10
BLEU score	**0%**	**65%**

Table 6.2 – BLEU score for two possible predictions

According to the table, **Prediction 2** receives a higher score and is preferable compared to **Prediction 1**. Notice that the absence of one common 4-gram in the first case is sufficient to yield a score of **0%**. In practice, when we want to compare two different MT models, we calculate BLEU using a large corpus of annotated examples and pick the model with the highest overall score.

In the following code snippet, we are using Python to perform a similar calculation:

```
from nltk.translate.bleu_score import sentence_bleu

hypothesis = getTranslation(1006)[:-6].split()
reference = data['target'][1006].replace("<sos>","").
replace("<eos>","").split()

# Calculate the BLEU score.
bleu = sentence_bleu([reference], hypothesis, weights=(1, 1,
1))
```

The `weights` parameter determines which n-grams should be used to calculate BLEU. This example only includes uni-grams, bi-grams, and tri-grams:

```
print("Input sentence:", data['source'][1006])
print("Reference translation:", reference)
print("Hypothesis:", hypothesis)
print("BLEU score:", bleu)
>>
Input sentence: I relaxed.
Reference translation: ['Je', 'me', 'suis', 'détendue.']
Hypothesis: ['Je', 'me', 'suis', 'détendu.']
BLEU score: 0.25
```

According to the output, the prediction differs from the reference translation by one word (détendu), and the BLEU score is 0.25. Finally, we can verify the calculation by counting the corresponding n-grams and applying the formula:

$$BLEU = \frac{1}{1} \times (\frac{3}{4} \times \frac{2}{3} \times \frac{1}{2})^{\frac{1}{4}} = 0.25$$

In this section, we revisited different metrics from previous chapters to assess MT performance. Then, we introduced BLEU, a more pertinent score for these types of systems. Using specialized performance benchmarks is a good practice, as they allow you to assess the most relevant characteristics of any machine learning implementation. We will encounter a few other examples in the rest of this book.

Summary

In this chapter, we diverted from the standard presentation flow we adopted in the previous chapters, where we performed exploratory data analysis, created the machine learning models, and evaluated their performance. Instead, the content unfolded while following the historical evolution of MT systems so that you could become acquainted with basic NLP techniques that find applicability in a gamut of tasks. For example, POS tagging and NER are typical methods for categorizing words in a sentence. In the same way, different grammars can be used either for parsing an input phrase or generating an output sentence.

We contrasted two fundamental approaches for creating MT applications, the first of which relies on human knowledge to derive the translation rules. Conversely, data is the driving force for model creation in the second case. Finally, an in-depth presentation of seq2seq models revealed their power to efficiently convert a source sequence into a target.

In the final section, we focused on how specific metrics can be used to evaluate machine translation systems. Finding specialized scores such as BLEU provides a better way to compare different MT implementations. In the next chapter, we will deal with the topic of *text summarization*.

7
Summarizing Wikipedia Articles

There is a commonly referred-to analogy that data is to this century what oil was to the previous one. Human text is part of this valuable resource, which, contrary to oil, keeps increasing. Undoubtedly, the amount of textual data available from various sources has exploded. With the advent of Web 2.0, online users ceased to be merely consumers of this material and became content creators, further enhancing the abundance of online text data. But the more content that is available online, the less easy it is to discover and consume the most important information efficiently. Automatically extracting the gist of longer texts into an accurate summary and thus eliminating irrelevant content is urgently needed. Once more, machines can undertake this role.

This chapter introduces another challenging topic in **natural language processing** (**NLP**) and demystifies methods for text summarization. To implement pertinent systems, we exploit data coming from the web. In this respect, we examine techniques for accessing and automatically parsing web resources. Besides the standard text summarization methods, we delve into a state-of-the-art architecture that provides exceptional performance in many real-world applications. The specific topology extends the **sequence-to-sequence** (**seq2seq**) architectures we have already discussed and combines many concepts encountered throughout the book. Finally, as we did in previous chapters, we discuss the metrics to assess the performance of relevant systems.

By the end of the chapter, you will have the generic skill of gathering text data from any online resource, but more importantly, you will be able to apply more complex techniques for seq2seq learning.

In this chapter, we will go through the following topics:

- Discussing different techniques for text summarization
- Applying web crawling and data scraping
- Understanding related web technologies

- Implementing state-of-the-art architectures for text summarization
- Evaluating relevant systems using the appropriate metrics

Technical requirements

The chapter's code has been truncated in certain parts to facilitate reading the content. However, the whole code is available as different Jupyter notebooks in the book's GitHub repository: `https://github.com/PacktPublishing/Machine-Learning-Techniques-for-Text/tree/main/chapter-07`.

Understanding text summarization

With the burden of a busy daily schedule, we all seek to reduce the time spent reading text data. Take a moment to contemplate the number of emails, reports, news articles, tweets, blog posts, and so on you confront in 24 hours. The human brain employs different strategies to compensate for this challenge, such as skipping sentences in the text or searching for specific keywords before focusing on the content. Many studies have examined this phenomenon, and one of the most cited ones refers to how people in the west read the content of a web page. Using eye-tracking techniques, researchers from the Nielsen Norman Group (`https://www.nngroup.com/articles/f-shaped-pattern-reading-web-content-discovered/`) showed that humans follow a reading pattern resembling the letter *F*, as illustrated in *Figure 7.1*:

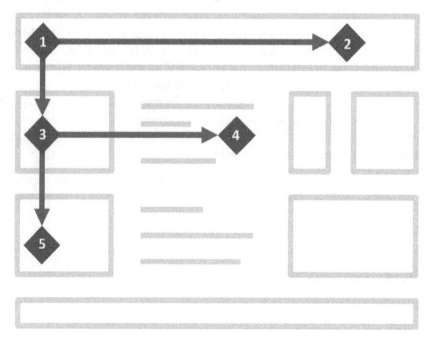

Figure 7.1 – F-shaped reading pattern of a web page

The reading usually starts at the upper part of the content area (point **1**). Then, it follows a horizontal path (until point **2**)—the top bar of the letter *F*. Next, the reader, moves down the page a bit, scanning for an interesting initial sentence. When this happens (point **3**), a typically shorter reading continues horizontally (until point **4**), creating the lower bar of the letter. Finally, a vertical scan on the left part of the page forms the letter *F*'s stem (point **5**). Why does this matter for a web designer? Simply because they can prioritize the content on a page according to the order most visitors scan it. For example, they can place the most important content at the top.

The previous finding is just one of the many examples demonstrating people's inherent tendency to reduce their information load by attending to specific parts of their visual stimuli. It is, therefore, not a surprise that companies seize the opportunity to offer products that alleviate this load. The current chapter focuses on **text summarization**, which is the process of condensing a piece of text into a shorter version while preserving critical information and the overall meaning of the original. Similar to machine translation, the task is not a simple text-to-text transformation because context is essential to fluently pass the intended message in the output summary.

The task becomes even more challenging as other constraints must be addressed. For instance, while summarizing a scientific publication about a new medical treatment, we need to consider the target audience for the summary. Should we include specialized terms in the output? Probably yes, to inform scientific peers of the publication's key points. Conversely, a summary for a news post targeting a general audience should present the most critical findings in casual language.

In school, we were often asked to summarize large documents and demonstrate our capacity to understand and extract the most valuable information from the text. Some students would highlight specific parts of the original document and include verbatim reproductions of these fragments in the output summary. Others aimed to comprehend the content more deeply and identify the most crucial information. Then, they had to formulate sentences from scratch that conveyed the original meaning. As you might expect, the second approach is the most challenging option.

Based on this analogy, there are two types of text summarization: **extractive** and **abstractive**. *Figure 7.2* shows an example for each case using the same input:

Input

The graphics processing unit, or GPU, is optimized hardware for training artificial intelligence and deep learning models. With a large number of cores, it allows the breaking down of complex tasks into smaller subtasks and sets them to run in parallel. Consider the central processing unit (CPU), a Ferrari, and the GPU, a big truck. This is because a CPU can quickly fetch a small amount of data from the RAM, whereas a GPU can fetch a large amount at once.

Extractive summary	Abstractive summary
The GPU is hardware for training models. It allows subtasks to run in parallel. A CPU can fetch a small amount of data whereas a GPU a large amount.	The GPU is hardware optimized for training machine learning models using concurrent subtasks. While a CPU can fetch a small amount of data, a GPU has more fetching capacity.

Figure 7.2 – An example of extractive and abstractive summarization

This contrived example shows that text summarization is a non-trivial task. The highlighted text in the input is used for the extractive summary, but it's unclear how we chose it in the first place. Moreover, creating the formulation in the abstractive summary is even more obscure. Besides the different techniques for text summarization, we discuss web scraping and how it can assist in accumulating online data. In this respect, we provide a very brief presentation of relevant web technologies to ensure that everybody is on the same page. So, let's begin with this exciting topic!

Introducing web scraping

Throughout the book, we repeatedly see data's value in creating intelligent systems. None of the discussions presented so far would make any sense without its presence. For instance, we incorporated publicly available corpora and built-in datasets from Python libraries in various case studies. In reality, however, suitable corpora are rarely available for free, and it's the data scientist's primary responsibility to harvest them. The **world wide web** (**WWW**) is a goldmine where we can resort to finding or augmenting our datasets using **web scraping**, the process of collecting and parsing raw data from the web. Afterward, the data is converted into the appropriate format to proceed with the subsequent analysis.

For this task to succeed, **web crawlers** are used to retrieve the requested content. These are also known as **spiders** because they crawl all over the web, just as real spiders crawl on their spiderwebs. The specific processing is performed in three steps:

1. Initially, the crawler is seeded with manually selected URLs in a list. Then, the list is iteratively grown as more pages need to be visited.

2. The crawler performs a fetch for each URL, and its content is scraped. Any new links are added to the list of URLs, and the specific page is marked as *crawled*.

3. The crawler ensures that there are no self-referential loops and that the same link is not visited twice.

Interesting note

The web crawlers used by search engines cannot possibly index every URL. This is because the web comprises well over a trillion distinct addresses, and repeatedly searching for visited sites would be a nightmare. So, instead, these crawlers incorporate a technique called **Bloom filter** to test whether an element is a member of the visited addresses.

The filter is an array of bits that are set to 0 initially. Then, we hash the URL and calculate the modulo of the result by the array's length. The outcome is the position of the array that we set to 1. It signifies that the specific URL has been visited. Although this technique is not perfect, as two different URLs can have the same hash, it saves significant time and space during the crawling process. In practice, more than one hash function is used, setting more bits to 1. Then, the lookup for a URL yields a 1%-2% error.

To understand these concepts, let's visualize the crawling process as an upside-down tree, shown in the left plot of *Figure 7.3*:

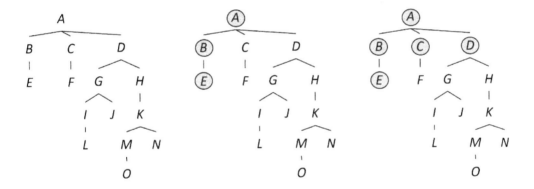

Figure 7.3 – Web traversal strategies: depth-first (middle) and breadth-first (right)

We begin the crawling from the tree's trunk—in this case, URL **A**, and move to each branch, extending out the URLs linked from the previous ones. However, from this visualization, the processing order of the different nodes remains unclear.

Implementing a web crawler typically dictates choosing a traversal strategy, and the two most prominent options are the **depth-first (DFS)** and **breadth-first (BFS)** algorithms. In the DFS case (middle plot), the strategy is first to retrieve all the URLs in the maximum depth before proceeding to the URL at the same level. So, in our example, the URLs are crawled in the following order: **ABECFDGILJHKMON**. Conversely, in the BFS case (right plot), we first retrieve all the URLs in the current depth before proceeding to the next level. The order now is **ABCDEFGHIJKLMNO**. These two algorithms are extensively used in many computer science applications, especially when a search problem is involved. Depending on where the best solution resides, it might take more or less time to discover it following either DFS or BFS. Consider, for example, the number of steps reaching **L** in both strategies. In this example, DFS finds the specific node in fewer steps than BFS. Finally, note that the tree is not static during web crawling but constantly updated with new pages to be visited.

Unfortunately, our problems do not finish in the crawling order of the different pages. The web scraping task is far from easy, as websites come in different shapes and forms. Moreover, it might be in the self-interest of the site to block the scraping process to protect its data and avoid overwhelming the server with requests. It is prevalent that a web server stops responding after multiple requests from the same source. Additionally, the **completely automated public turing test to tell computers and humans apart (CAPTCHA)**, despite being annoying for end users, helps verify that the request came from an actual human, not an internet bot. CAPTCHAs are one of the most popular anti-scraping techniques available. As a way to assist the scraping process, many websites include a file called `robots.txt` (for example, `https://edition.cnn.com/robots.txt`) that explicitly dictates which parts of the site cannot be crawled. The `robots.txt` plain text file follows the **robots exclusion standard** (`https://en.wikipedia.org/wiki/Robots_exclusion_standard`) and consists of one or more rules.

An example is the following rule that disallows access to the shown folder of the web server: `Disallow: /WEB-INF/`. The robots exclusion standard is purely advisory, and most of the time, no repercussions are applied by the website owner. Nevertheless, do not be surprised if the latter decides to block your crawler when disrespecting the standard. In the next section, we create a spider to implement a few of these concepts.

Scraping popular quotes

In this exercise, we use text data from `http://quotes.toscrape.com`, a website that includes popular quotes from famous people. The site was created explicitly for scraping purposes, so there are no concerns about violating any usage terms. The web page illustrated in *Figure 7.4* is well organized and includes groups of quotes, along with a link to the author's biography, and various tags:

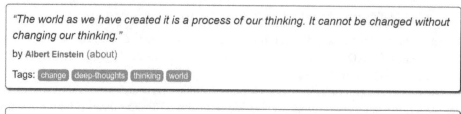

Figure 7.4 – A web page retrieved from quotes.toscrape.com

A web scraper requires access to the web page's content, and the **hypertext markup language** (HTML) is the standard markup language to provide this information. An HTML page contains elements that tell the browser how to display its contents on the screen. *Figure 7.5* shows part of the HTML code for the previous example:

```
<div class="quote" itemscope="" itemtype="http://schema.org/CreativeWork">

    <span class="text" itemprop="text">
        "The world as we have created it is a process of our thinking.
        It cannot be changed without changing our thinking."</span>

    <span>by <small class="author" itemprop="author">
        Albert Einstein</small>
        <a href="https://quotes.toscrape.com/author/Albert-Einstein">
            (about)</a></span>

    <div class="tags">
        Tags:
        <meta class="keywords" itemprop="keywords"
            content="change,deep-thoughts,thinking,world">

        <a class="tag"
            href="https://quotes.toscrape.com/tag/change/page/1/">
            change</a>

        <a class="tag"
            href="https://quotes.toscrape.com/tag/deep-thoughts/page/1/>
            deep-thoughts</a>

        <a class="tag"
            href="https://quotes.toscrape.com/tag/thinking/page/1/">
            thinking</a>

        <a class="tag"
            href="https://quotes.toscrape.com/tag/world/page/1/">
            world</a>

    </div>
</div>
```

Figure 7.5 – The HTML code behind the quotes.toscrape.com page

At first glance, the page's text seems chaotic, but it's actually very well structured. Looking at the different elements, we only need to scrape the parts that contain useful information. For example, to get the text of the quote, we need to find a `div` element of the `quote` class that includes a `span` element of the `text` class. Next, we see how to perform these steps programmatically.

The `scrapy` framework is an elegant way to implement spiders in Python for large-scale web scraping. In the code of the `quote-scraper.ipynb` notebook, we create a crawler and set the start URL, like so:

```
import scrapy

# Create a spider for scraping quotes.
class QuotesSpider(scrapy.Spider):
    name = 'quote_spider'
    start_urls = ['http://quotes.toscrape.com']
```

Inside the crawler's class, we define a method to be called every time a page needs to be parsed. Observe in the `for` loop how we scrape the relevant information for each quote—namely, `text`, `author`, and `tags`:

```
    # Define its parse method.
    def parse(self, response):
        print(f"Visiting: {response.url}")

        # Parse the info for each quote.
        for quote in response.css("div.quote"):
            text = quote.css("span.text::text").get()
            author = quote.css("small.author::text").get()
            tags = quote.css("div.tags a.tag::text").getall()

            print(dict(text=text, author=author, tags=tags))
```

We parse the information using *selectors*, which are patterns that match against elements in a document. These are a core component of **cascading style sheets** (**CSS**), a language describing the rendering of HTML documents on the screen. While HTML is responsible for the structure of a web page—for instance, using paragraphs, headings, sections, and so forth—CSS takes care of its look and feel, such as changing the background color or the font type.

An example of a selector is this one: `div.tags a.tag::text`. The pattern matches the `div` element of the `tag` class, including the `a` anchor of the `tag` class, and extracts the corresponding `text` value.

Let's create and start a crawler process using `QuotesSpider`:

```
from scrapy.crawler import CrawlerProcess
```

```
# Create a crawler process using the quote spider.
process = CrawlerProcess({
    'USER_AGENT': 'Mozilla/4.0 (compatible; MSIE 7.0; Windows
NT 5.1)'
})


# Start the crawling.
crawler = process.create_crawler(QuotesSpider)
process.crawl(crawler)
process.start()
>>
Visiting: http://quotes.toscrape.com
{'text': '"The world as we have created it is a process of
our thinking. It cannot be changed without changing our
thinking."', 'author': 'Albert Einstein', 'tags': ['change',
'deep-thoughts', 'thinking', 'world']}
...
```

The output is a JSON-formatted string with three key-value pairs. Compare this result with the browser's output in *Figure 7.4* to verify that they are the same.

Before we close out the section, here is a list of typical data formats that you need to know, along with an example:

- **JavaScript Object Notation (JSON)**:

  ```
  { "title": "ML4Text", "author": "NT"}
  ```

- **Extensible Markup Language (XML)**:

  ```
  <entry> <title>ML4Text</title> <author>NT</author></entry>
  ```

- **Comma-Separated Values (CSV)**:

  ```
  title, author
  ML4Text, NT
  ```

- **Tab-Separated Values (TSV)**:

  ```
  title          author
  ML4Text        NT
  ```

The example of this section demonstrated a spider that was used to download and scrape a single web page. But as we already know, web crawlers are crafted to extract links on the page and iteratively crawl them. This is the topic of the next section.

Scraping book reviews

As with the quotes example, we crawl a website with book reviews, including 152 book items split into 8 web pages (http://books.toscrape.com/). The created spider is seeded with a selected URL and is responsible for identifying and iteratively visiting all embedded links in the URL. A screenshot of the selected site is shown in *Figure 7.6*, which corresponds to the first of eight relevant pages. To move to the next page, we must click on the **next** button on the lower-right part of the screenshot. The spider must extract the relevant HTML code to perform the navigation step programmatically:

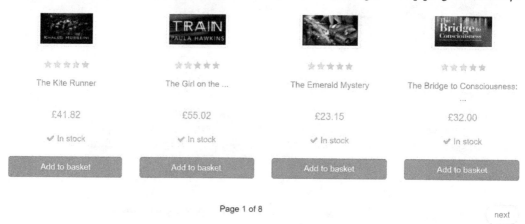

Figure 7.6 – One out of eight pages from the books.toscrape.com site

Item in scrapy is a logical grouping (container) of extracted data points from a website. In the code of the text-summarization.ipynb notebook, we define a BookItem class to read the title and the product description of a book:

```
import scrapy
from scrapy.loader.processors import MapCompose, TakeFirst

# Remove the double quotes from the input.
def remove_quotes(input):
    input = input.replace("\"", "")
    return input

# Create the book item for scraping.
class BookItem(scrapy.Item):

    # The item consists of a title and a description.
```

```
    title = scrapy.Field(output_processor=TakeFirst())
    product_description = scrapy.Field(input_
processor=MapCompose(remove_quotes), output_
processor=TakeFirst())
```

Observe the two fields—`title` and `product_description`—defined inside the `BookItem` class. `TakeFirst` and `MapCompose` are built-in processors that deal with the extracted data as soon as it's received. For example, the latter uses the `remove_quotes` method to remove quotes from the input. Let's now create a crawler and set the start URL:

```
from scrapy.loader import ItemLoader


# Create a spider for scraping book info.
class BookSpider(scrapy.Spider):
    name = 'book_spider'
    allowed_domains = ['books.toscrape.com']
    start_urls = ['https://books.toscrape.com/catalogue/
category/books/default_15/index.html']
    custom_settings = {
        "FEEDS" : { "books.json": { "format": "json",
"overwrite": True}}
    }
```

Notice that the output of the scraping process is stored in the `books.json` file. The `parse` method that follows iterates over all book items on a specific page and calls the `parse_book_info` method to handle each one of them:

```
    # Parse the info for each page with books.
    def parse(self, response):

        # Iterate over all products on the page.
        for article in response.css("article.product_pod"):

            # Get the url for one book.
            book_url = article.css("div > a::attr(href)").get()

            if book_url:
                # Parse the info for the specific book.
                yield response.follow(
```

```
                              url=book_url,
                              callback=self.parse_book_info,
                              dont_filter=True)

        # Go to the next books page.
        next_url = response.css("li.next > a::attr(href)").
get()
        if next_url:
            yield response.follow(url=next_url, callback=self.
parse)
```

Moving each time to the next book page, we need to extract the link and store it in the `next_url` variable. For this reason, we use the appropriate CSS selectors until the eight pages are consumed.

The `parse_book_info` method that follows provides a convenient mechanism for populating scraped items using `ItemLoader`. The latter can automatize common tasks such as parsing the raw data before assigning it. Conceptually, `Item` provides the container of scraped data, while `ItemLoader` provides the mechanism for populating that container:

```
    # Callback method for scraping a specific book's page.
    def parse_book_info(self, response):

        item_loader = ItemLoader(item=BookItem(),
response=response)
        item_loader.add_css('title', "div > h1::text")
        item_loader.add_css('product_description',
"div#product_description + p::text")

        return item_loader.load_item()
```

As in the previous section, we create and start a crawler process using `BookSpider`:

```
from scrapy.crawler import CrawlerProcess

# Create a crawler process using the book spider.
process = CrawlerProcess({
    'USER_AGENT': 'Mozilla/4.0 (compatible; MSIE 7.0; Windows
NT 5.1)'
})
```

```
# Start the crawling.
crawler = process.create_crawler(BookSpider)
process.crawl(crawler)
process.start()
```

Let's verify that everything worked as expected:

```
# Print statistics from the scraping process.
stats_dict = crawler.stats.get_stats()
stats_dict
>>
...
 'request_depth_max': 8,
 'item_scraped_count': 152,
...
```

Indeed, 8 pages are downloaded, 152 book items are scraped, and their data is stored in the books. json file. Beware that running the same code on your side might yield a different order of the book items inside the file. The reason is that the scrapy process is asynchronous, meaning that the crawler continues execution after initiating the request to the web server and processes the result whenever the latter makes it available. So, although the requests are made in a particular order, the responses can be received differently. We conclude the discussion on web crawling with one more technique.

Scraping Wikipedia articles

XML Path Language (**XPath**) is an expression language for selecting tags in XML documents and HTML. It is an alternative to the CSS selectors, and this section provides just a flavor of its usage. As before, we implement a spider in the wikipedia-scraper.ipynb notebook, set the start URL, and define a parse method:

```
import scrapy


# Create a spider for scraping Wikipedia articles.
class WikipediaSpider(scrapy.Spider):
    name = 'wikipedia_spider'
    allowed_domains = ['en.wikipedia.org']
    start_urls = ['https://en.wikipedia.org/wiki/Athens']


    # Parse the info for a specific page.
```

```
    def parse(self, response):

        print(response.xpath("//span[@class='mw-headline']/
text()").getall())
```

The `//span[@class='mw-headline']/text()` XPath is equivalent to the `span.mw-headline::text` CSS selector. Both extract the text of a `span` element with the `mw-headline` class. Inspecting the page's HTML code reveals that this element contains the titles of the headlines. Notice that CSS selectors are usually faster and easier to learn than XPath, which is more flexible in constructing scrape queries.

Then, starting the crawler yields all headlines for the city of `Athens` Wikipedia article specified in the `start_urls` variable:

```
. . .
# Start the crawling.
crawler = process.create_crawler(WikipediaSpider)
. . .
>> ['Etymology and names', 'History', 'Geography',
'Environment', 'Safety', 'Climate', 'Locations',
'Neighbourhoods of the center of Athens (Municipality
of Athens)', 'Parks and zoos', 'Urban and suburban
municipalities', ..., 'Museums', 'Tourism', 'Entertainment
and performing arts', 'Sports', 'Overview', 'Sports clubs',
'Olympic Games', '1896 Summer Olympics', '1906 Summer
Olympics', '2004 Summer Olympics', 'See also', 'References',
'External links']
```

This section concludes the discussion on web crawling and scraping. Both methods allow the acquisition of valuable data for our projects. The presented code is generic and can be applied whenever we need to augment our dataset from the web. However, some restrictions for accessing certain websites or using their resources may apply. Therefore, you must always read the site's terms of use to verify the usage rights and what you are entitled to do with the offered data. Moreover, you must consult the `robots.txt` file to identify which parts of the site cannot be crawled. Next, we move to the main topic of this chapter: introducing techniques for text summarization.

Performing extractive summarization

In the chapter's introduction, we mentioned that extractive summarization identifies important words or phrases and stitches them together to produce a condensed version of the original text. In this section, we use the previously created `books.json` file and employ different methods to extract summaries for an input document. Due to space limitations and the need to focus on state-of-the-art techniques, we do not present the theory behind the methods. However, there is a plethora of online resources that can be consulted. A good starting point is the following link: `https://miso-belica.github.io/sumy/summarizators.html`.

Let's begin by loading the data from the file and printing a few examples:

```
import pandas as pd


df = pd.read_json('books.json')
df.head()
>>  title                    product_description
0   Tracing Numbers on...    Start preparing children for ...
1   The Kite Runner          Khaled Hosseini's #1 New York...
2   The Psychopath Tes...    They say one out of every hun...

...

151 A Visit from the G...    Bennie is an aging former pun...
152 rows × 2 columns
```

Next, we ensure that there are no missing values:

```
# Remove missing values.
df = df.dropna()
df.shape
>> (151, 2)
```

The previous output indicates that one of the instances was removed. From 152 rows, we now have 151. Checking for missing or corrupted data is not only recommended but also requested. We can now print a sample description:

```
print(df['product_description'][136])
>> How can we make intelligent decisions about our increasingly
technology-driven lives if we don't understand the difference
between the myths of pseudoscience and the testable hypotheses
of science?...more
```

Then, we define a generic method that performs summarization:

```
stop_words = stopwords.words('english')


# Summarize the input given method and sentence number.
def summarize(input, method, sentence_num, language='english'):
```

```
summarizer = method(Stemmer(language))
summarizer.stop_words = get_stop_words(language)

# For this summarizer, we can define positive (bonus),
# negative (stigma), and stop words.
if isinstance(summarizer, EdmundsonSummarizer):
    # The bonus and stigma sets are empty.
    summarizer.bonus_words = ['']
    summarizer.stigma_words = ['']
    summarizer.null_words = stop_words


# Extract the summary.
summary = summarizer(PlaintextParser(input,
Tokenizer(language)).document, sentence_num)


return summary
```

EdmundsonSummarizer is a special case, as we need to set the bonus_words variable, which is for words we want to see in the summary and are significant. On the other hand, stigma_words are unimportant, while null_words are stop words. This summarizer is the only one having this kind of feature. Recall the discussion in the introduction related to the target audience of a summary. Having the ability to fine-tune the list of words helps in the creation of customized summaries.

It's time to extract summaries using seven methods:

```
for method in [EdmundsonSummarizer, KLSummarizer,
LexRankSummarizer, LsaSummarizer, LuhnSummarizer,
ReductionSummarizer, TextRankSummarizer]:

    print('>> ' + method.__name__ + ':')
    summary = summarize(df['product_description'][136], method,
1)
```

Let's print their output on the screen:

```
# Print the summary.
for sentence in summary:
    print(sentence)


print('')
```

```
>> EdmundsonSummarizer:
How can we make intelligent decisions about our increasingly
technology-driven lives if we don't understand the difference
between the myths of pseudoscience and the testable hypotheses
of science?
...
>> LexRankSummarizer:
Pulitzer Prize-winning author and distinguished astronomer Carl
Sagan argues that scientific thinking is critical not only to
the pursuit of truth but to the very well-being of How can we
make intelligent decisions about our increasingly technology-
driven lives if we don't understand the difference between the
myths of pseudoscience and the testable hypotheses of science?
...
```

The result for these two methods seems quite good, don't you agree? Even the implementation of the relevant code was straightforward.

In the following section, we proceed to the second category of summarization systems and introduce an advanced seq2seq architecture.

Performing abstractive summarization

Abstractive summarization generates novel sentences by rephrasing the reference and introducing new text. This task is quite challenging, and for this reason, more sophisticated methods are required. This section adopts a step-by-step approach to present pertinent concepts and techniques. Ultimately, we glue all the pieces together in a state-of-the-art model for abstractive summarization. Let's begin with the first concept.

Introducing the attention mechanism

In *Chapter 6, Teaching Machines to Translate*, we presented an encoder-decoder seq2seq architecture suitable for translating sentences from a source language to a target one. A key characteristic of the whole pipeline is that the complete input is encoded in a context vector used by the decoder to produce a translation. In actual human communications, we tend to listen to the whole sentence before responding. Intuitively, the context vector represents this process; it crams the whole input into a single vector. But as humans tend to forget important information, so can seq2seq models.

As we saw in the previous chapter, one possible solution is **Long Short-Term Memory** (**LSTM**) units and **Gated Recurrent Units** (**GRUs**), with their distinctive feature of remembering information for longer periods. However, when the input sequences become sufficiently large, even these networks cease to include all important information in their context vector. The words' influence at the beginning of the input becomes smaller and smaller after the consecutive updates in the intermediate hidden states of the encoder. In the example of *Figure 7.7*, the word **Tom** is fed to the encoder during the first timestep, but its influence fades after several steps:

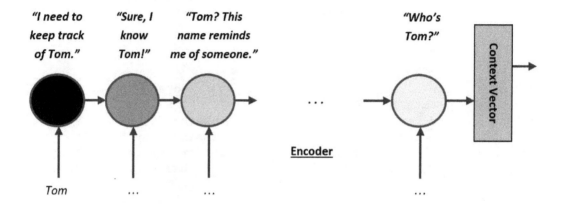

Figure 7.7 – Fading influence of the word Tom during encoding

A better approach is to use all hidden states and weigh individual words in the input sequence according to their impact on the target. This approach is the basic idea behind **attention** mechanisms, which intuitively resembles the visual attention shown earlier in *Figure 7.1*. During every timestep, the output is not dependent on a single fixed context vector but is a sum of hidden states multiplied by attention weights. In this way, the decoder ceases to have limited access to the information provided by the input but can selectively attend to the most useful words. Relating to the previous chapter, it's like reading a very long text that needs to be translated. We must be more systematic about the information stored in our mind (attend); otherwise, important contexts might be forgotten. *Figure 7.8* shows the output of the encoder that consists of all hidden states:

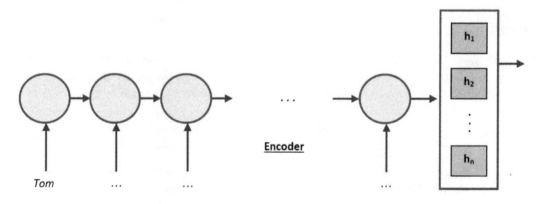

Figure 7.8 – The encoder passes all hidden states to the decoder

So far, we have seen which changes should happen on the encoder part for supporting attention. Similarly, the decoder needs to be slightly adapted. For instance, before emitting an output at each step, the decoder needs to pay attention to specific words in the input that are important for the output. For this reason, it creates a context vector particular to the current decoding step. *Figure 7.9* shows an example:

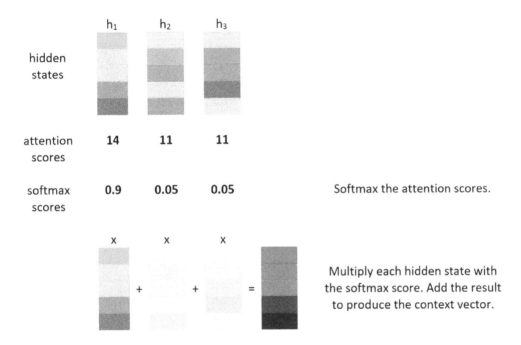

Figure 7.9 – Attention on the decoder part

In the previous example, the input consists of three words, so the encoder provides three hidden states (**h1**, **h2**, and **h3**). Each hidden state vector is multiplied by an attention score to which we have previously applied the softmax function. The **softmax function** converts the attention vector [**14, 11, 11**] into a probability distribution of three possible outcomes [**0.9, 0.05, 0.05**]. Finally, the output vectors are added to produce a context vector. Observe how vectors multiplied with a small softmax score have attenuated and fade out. In the current example, the model attends to the first word of the input sentence. The same process is repeated for all timesteps in the decoder with obviously different attention scores. The scores are trainable parameters of the model learned during the training phase. Notice that there are many types of attention, and this section shows the simplest one. In the next section, we stand on the knowledge accumulated so far to dive deeper.

Introducing transformers

The **transformer** model replaces the recurrent layers most commonly used in encoder-decoder architectures with multi-headed self-attention to boost the performance of **deep neural networks** (**DNNs**). If the previous sentence sounds cryptic, don't worry. We'll clarify all essential elements one by one.

The transformer model shown in *Figure 7.10* also consists of an encoder and a decoder part:

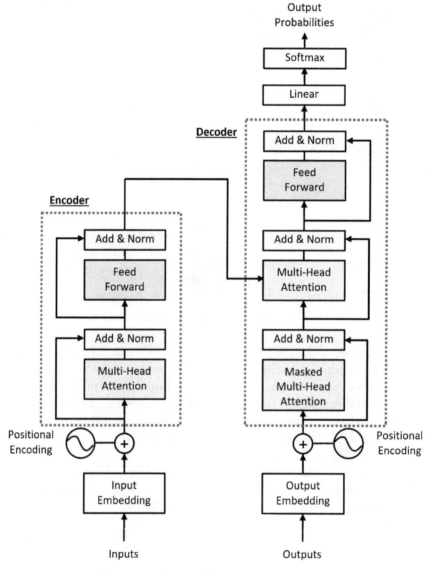

Figure 7.10 – The transformer model architecture

Each component consists of a few other sub-components with various connection paths. The architecture probably seems daunting, so let's try to demystify its functionality, starting with the input to the encoder.

Understanding positional encoding

Before examining the encoder part, we need to preprocess the input using word embedding. We already know the power behind this word representation, as each element in the embedding vector represents a linguistic feature of the word. Word embedding lack a critical element, however. They can represent words well but not their position in the sentence. In every language, word order is essential, as identical words placed in different positions can change the sentence's meaning entirely. For example, the following phrases include the same words but have completely different meanings: *Paul bit a dog* and *A dog bit Paul*. When using LSTM, this deficiency of word embedding is not a problem, as words are consumed sequentially by the model.

On the other hand, transformers receive all embeddings at once, speeding up the processing time but at the expense of losing word order. **Positional encoding**, the next step in the pipeline, comes as a rescue by adding the necessary spatial information about each word in a vector of the same size as the embeddings one. After calculating the positional encoding vector, we add it to the embedding vector, which now includes an *injected* pattern with spatial information for the words. *Figure 7.11* shows this process, where e_i and p_i are the ith embedding and positional vector, respectively, and e_p^i is the concatenated vectors emitted from the positional encoding step:

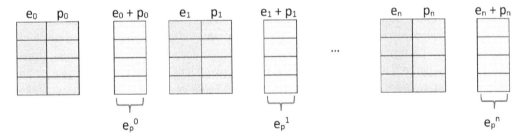

Figure 7.11 – The output of the positional encoding step

Two formulas are employed to identify each element in the positional encoding vector p_i:

$$PE_{(pos,2i)} = \sin\left(\frac{pos}{n^{\frac{2i}{d}}}\right) \quad and \quad PE_{(pos,2i+1)} = \cos\left(\frac{pos}{n^{\frac{2i}{d}}}\right)$$

Here, the following applies:

- pos = *Position of the word in the input sequence.*
- d = *Size of the output embedding space.*
- i = *Index to column indices* $0 \leq i < d/2$. *A single value of i maps to both sine and cosine functions.*
- n = *User-defined scalar.*

Let's see a numerical example to clarify the situation. Suppose that we would like to perform positional encoding for the phrase *deep learning*, using four-dimensional embedding vectors (d=4) and n=100. *Table 7.1* shows the calculations:

word	pos	i=0	i=0	i=1	i=1
deep	0	$\sin\left(\dfrac{0}{100^{\frac{2\cdot0}{4}}}\right)$	$\cos\left(\dfrac{0}{100^{\frac{2\cdot0}{4}}}\right)$	$\sin\left(\dfrac{0}{100^{\frac{2\cdot1}{4}}}\right)$	$\cos\left(\dfrac{0}{100^{\frac{2\cdot1}{4}}}\right)$
learning	1	$\sin\left(\dfrac{1}{100^{\frac{2\cdot0}{4}}}\right)$	$\cos\left(\dfrac{1}{100^{\frac{2\cdot0}{4}}}\right)$	$\sin\left(\dfrac{1}{100^{\frac{2\cdot1}{4}}}\right)$	$\cos\left(\dfrac{1}{100^{\frac{2\cdot1}{4}}}\right)$

Table 7.1 – Calculating positional encoding for a sample phrase

Each of the two words receives a positional vector with four elements that can be concatenated with the respected embeddings vector. Without delving into too many details, the previous discussion should be enough to understand the need for positional encoding and its implementation. Let's now move to the encoder part of the transformer.

Understanding multi-head attention

Having a rich representation of the input at our disposal, we need a component that can attend to the most critical information. We already discussed attention mechanisms before, but transformers incorporate a much more powerful type of attention that helps the model focus on the critical words of any input sentence. This type is called **self-attention** and differs from simple attention in various ways. The most crucial difference is that the latter allows the model to focus on the input while producing the output. In contrast, in self-attention, the inputs can interact with each other. Consider the example in *Figure 7.12* for both types of attention:

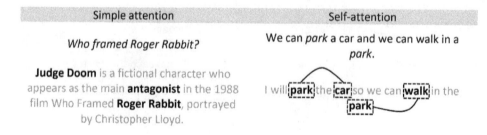

Figure 7.12 – Simple versus self-attention example

In simple attention, we focus on specific words with respect to some external query such as the question in *Figure 7.12*: **Who framed Roger Rabbit?** For example, attending to **Judge Doom**, the **antagonist**, and **Roger Rabbit** is sufficient to respond to the query. On the other hand, self-attention compares each word with all the others in the sentence, reweighing the word embedding (that also include positional information) to include contextual relevance. The intuition behind self-attention is similar to how humans judge the meaning of a word, simply by examining the context in which it appears. In the previous example, each of the two occurrences of the word **park** is compared to all the other words and reweighed to include the relevance of the word **car** (first occurrence) and the word **walk** (second occurrence).

We can now zoom in on the components in the transformer model for implementing the self-attention mechanism. This is where **dot-product attention** comes into the scene, schematically shown in *Figure 7.13*:

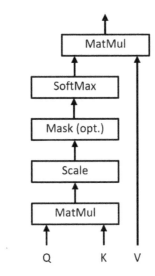

Figure 7.13 – Scaled dot-product attention

The role of this component is to implement self-attention using as inputs three matrices named **Query** (**Q**), **Key** (**K**), and **Value** (**V**). To get a better understanding of the utility of these matrices, consider the example in *Figure 7.14*, stemming from the information retrieval field:

Figure 7.14 – The Query, Key, and Value analogy

In the simplest scenario, when we type a **Query** in the Google search bar, the algorithm tries to find the **Key** from a database most similar to the search query. Then, we retrieve the corresponding **Value**—a web page, in our example. All search engines provide more than one key-value pair ranked on their similarity measure with the query. When the algorithm tries to provide the most relevant results, it essentially attends to the most important information in the web page's **Key** (for example, its title).

Let's observe how tree matrices are created using the visualization in *Figure 7.15*:

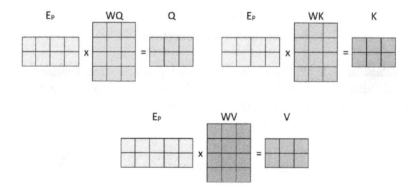

Figure 7.15 – Creation of Query (Q), Key (K), and Value (V) matrices

Interestingly, they all use the same input, $\mathbf{E}_p$—the word embedding with positional encoding, which are multiplied with different weights (**WQ**, **WK**, and **WV**). The latter are parts of three district linear layers and are learned through backpropagation. Linear layers use matrix multiplication to transform the input into output using a weight matrix. This step aims to map the input to the correct output for **Q**, **K**, and **V** and reduce their size for computational purposes.

The term *similarity* should be very familiar from our previous endeavors in solving **machine learning** (**ML**) problems throughout the book. We encounter the same concept in dot-product attention for calculating the similarity of the query and the key matrices. The **MatMul** operation in *Figure 7.13* performs the multiplication of **Q** and **K** matrices using the transpose version for the latter. Then, the **Scale** step divides each element of the multiplication matrix by the factor $\sqrt{d_k}$, where d_k is the dimensions of the key vector. We can summarize this calculation with the following formula:

$$\frac{QK^T}{\sqrt{d_k}}$$

The previous quantity resembles the cosine similarity formula discussed in the *Calculating vector similarity* section of *Chapter 2, Detecting Spam Emails*. The numerator is the dot product of two matrices. In contrast, the denominator is a scaling factor. Recall that for the cosine similarity case, the scaling factor is the product of the magnitudes of each vector.

The next step in the pipeline applies a softmax function to the previous output to convert all values from zero to one and produce the final attention filter. Notice that we deliberately skipped **Mask (opt.)** for later. When performing the second **MatMul** operation with the specific filter and the **Value** matrix, we drown out irrelevant words, as these are multiplied with very small numbers in the filter. Consider an intuitive example using various image filters in *Figure 7.16*:

Figure 7.16 – Attention filter (left), the original image (middle), and filtered image (right)

Multiplying the attention filter with the original image produces a filtered image that includes the information we are interested in. In the specific example, we focus on the weather conditions, the place, or the person's activity.

The whole process of dot-product attention is summarized in the following formula that provides a filtered value matrix:

$$Attention(Q, K, V) = softmax\left(\frac{QK^T}{\sqrt{d_k}}\right)V$$

Is applying a single attention filter enough to attend to all critical information? Unfortunately not, but stacking more than one dot-product attention component together allows us to focus on different parts of the input. *Figure 7.17* shows a technique called **multi-head attention** that exploits this idea:

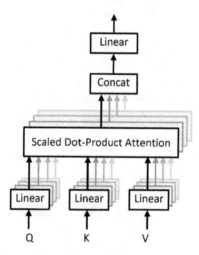

Figure 7.17 – Multi-head attention consists of several attention layers running in parallel

Transformers use multi-head attention to learn multiple attention filters that capture separate linguistic phenomena. After this point, we can perform the **Concat** step and, as the name suggests, concatenate all attention filters into one. The final **Linear** component reduces the size of the concatenated matrix to the size of each separate attention filter, which is the final output of the multi-head attention component.

Finalizing the encoder part

We need to cover a few more components to complete the discussion on the transformer architecture for the encoder. Looking back at *Figure 7.11*, we observe that the data flow can take different routes. We might skip certain pipeline nodes following the different paths (depicted with the arrows). For example, we can move directly from the positional encoding step to the **Add & Norm** component, skipping the **Multi-Head Attention** component. This **residual connection** provides alternative paths for data to reach the latter parts of the **neural network** (**NN**) by bypassing some layers. The specific functionality is counterintuitive, as NNs are meant to process data, and occasionally skipping computational steps sounds like a contradiction. There is a reason, however. The more processing that happens to the data, the more information is lost about its original form. There are situations where this is a drawback, and preserving possible previous versions of the data becomes a necessity. The residual connection plays this role and allows data preservation. There is also another reason.

One particular problem while training a NN is caused by exploding and vanishing gradients, as already discussed in the *Understanding long short-term memory units* section of *Chapter 6, Teaching Machines to Translate*. Residual connections are empirically shown to converge much more easily, even if the network is very deep. Instead of going through a single path of fixed length (number of layers), a feed-forward network with residual connections consists of many paths of varying lengths. This topology presents a competitive advantage because the network behaves as an *ensemble* of independent networks. Although the ensembles do not resolve the exploding or vanishing gradient problems, they circumvent those situations by producing shallow networks. In the *Introducing the random forest algorithm* section of *Chapter 3, Classifying Topics of Newsgroup Posts*, we have seen the power of ensemble learning, which relies on combining multiple models to increase classification performance. Perhaps this is the reason that residual connections lead to more accurate models.

Let's go a step further and see what happens in the **Add & Norm** component that adds the output of the positional encoding (through the residual connection) and the **Multi-Head Attention** component. Then, we normalize the values of the summed output through a process called **layer normalization**, which enables smoother gradients, faster training, and better generalization accuracy. Layer normalization means standardizing the neuron activation along the dimensions of the features. Specifically, each element of the matrix is standardized using the mean and the variance of all features. Again, you can refer to a relevant discussion in the *Understanding principal component analysis* section of *Chapter 3, Classifying Topics of Newsgroup Posts*.

The next step in the pipeline is to incorporate a fully connected **Feed Forward** network consisting of a couple of linear layers with a ReLU activation in between. The role of this network is to process the attention output further, capture more linguistic patterns, and provide richer representations. Finally, its output is fed to an **Add & Norm** component, as the one we discussed before. At this point, we conclude the presentation of the encoder part, and in the next section, we focus on the decoder.

Finalizing the decoder part

The decoder contains many components, also included in the encoder, and a few other slightly different ones. First, the two components differ in the number of their inputs. While the encoder receives just one input, the decoder receives the encoder's output and its own output from the previous timestep. In the first iteration of the decoder, there is no previous output to feedback, so it is fed with a special `<go>` token that signifies the start of the generated text. Conversely, the generation process ends when the decoder emits a `<stop>` token. The names of these tokens are arbitrary, and you can use whatever makes sense for your application.

Let's say a few things about the **Mask (opt.)** step that we skipped a few pages before, which is part of the masked multi-head attention of the decoder. First, during the training phase, we do not want the decoder's attention mechanism to access tokens (words) that are not yet predicted. Instead, attention should be applied to tokens up to the current position. That is the index until which prediction is done by the transformer. Otherwise, it would be like cheating, and we need a way to hide future tokens. A good analogy is the teacher forcing strategy discussed in the *Introducing sequence-to-sequence learning* section of *Chapter 6, Teaching Machines to Translate*. The teacher lets the student make their best effort to speak out the answer (token) and corrects them if needed. So, we incorporate a method to prevent computing attention scores for future words called **masking**. The method applies a look-ahead mask that is added before calculating the softmax (**SoftMax**) and after scaling the scores (**Scale**).

In this section, we had the opportunity to examine the demanding yet exciting transformer architecture that has proven to be very powerful in NLP tasks. The discussion focused on the various subcomponents of this **deep learning** (**DL**) model, and we tried to shed some light on their functionality. We will finally implement a transformer model for text summarization in the following section.

Putting the transformer into action

After the presentation of the transformer architecture, we can move to the fun part and put it into action! The Python code is based on the implementation taken from a relevant TensorFlow tutorial (`https://www.tensorflow.org/text/tutorials/transformer`), which, due to space limitations, cannot be included as a whole in the book. However, the relevant Jupyter notebook contains the necessary code and explanations to help you understand the different steps. In this section, we cherry-pick a few coding snippets and relate them to our earlier discussion. But first, we need data to implement this powerful DL model!

Loading the dataset

As a widely accessible and free encyclopedia, Wikipedia contains information on all branches of knowledge, so it's an excellent resource for data. In this respect, we extract Wikipedia pages and use them for training and evaluating the transformer model. Instead of implementing a crawler from scratch, we use a Python library that makes it easy to access and parse data from Wikipedia. Let's see how.

The code in the `text-summarization-transformer.ipynb` notebook requests the wiki page for `Athens`, the Greek capital, and prints the titles of the different sections:

```
import wikipedia

# Use the English language version.
wikipedia.set_lang("en")
```

```
# Get the wiki content for 'Athens'.
wikisearch = wikipedia.page("Athens")


# Print page sections.
wikisections = wikisearch.sections
print(wikisections)
>> ['Etymology and names', 'History', 'Geography',
'Environment', 'Safety', 'Climate', 'Locations',
'Neighbourhoods of the center of Athens (Municipality
of Athens)', 'Parks and zoos', 'Urban and suburban
municipalities', ..., 'Museums', 'Tourism', 'Entertainment
and performing arts', 'Sports', 'Overview', 'Sports clubs',
'Olympic Games', '1896 Summer Olympics', '1906 Summer
Olympics', '2004 Summer Olympics', 'See also', 'References',
'External links']
```

Comparing the output with the one in the *Scraping Wikipedia articles* section, we do not observe any differences, which is reassuring. Next, for our analysis, we download the wiki pages of 40 capitals:

```
import pandas as pd


# Get the wiki page for the following capitals.
capitals = [ 'Amsterdam', 'Ankara', 'Athens', 'Beijing',
'Canberra', 'Copenhagen', 'Dakar', 'Dhaka', 'Dublin',
'Guatemala City', 'Harare', 'Islamabad', 'Jakarta',
'Jerusalem', 'Khartoum', 'Kinshasa', 'Kyiv', 'Lisbon',
'London', 'Madrid', 'Manila', 'Mexico City', 'Montevideo',
'Moscow', 'Nairobi', 'New Delhi', 'Ottawa', 'Paris', 'Riyadh',
'Rome', 'San Salvador', 'Seoul', 'Stockholm', 'Tehran',
'Tirana', 'Tokio', 'Washington D.C.', 'Wellington', 'Yerevan',
'Zagreb']
```

The dataset consists of a summary and content part:

```
# Store specific information from each page.
df = pd.DataFrame(columns=['summary', 'content'])


# Iterate in the list of capitals and search for the
corresponding wiki page.
for capital in capitals:
```

```
    wikisearch = wikipedia.page(capital)
    # We need to remove the summary from the content.
    df = df.append({'summary' : wikisearch.summary.
replace("\n", " "), 'content' : wikisearch.content.
replace(wikisearch.summary, "").replace("\n", " ")}, ignore_
index=True)
```

Before dealing with the transformer, let's examine the data by creating a method to extract triplets with the subject, verb, and object from the text:

```
# Extract the subject, verb, and object from the text.
def extract_SVO(text):
    subjects, verbs, objects = [], [], []
    doc = nlp(text)

    # Get the tuples with the results.
    tuples = textacy.extract.subject_verb_object_triples(doc)

    # Iterate over all tuples.
    for x in tuples:

        subjects.append(str(x[0]).replace("[", "").replace("]",
""))
        verbs.append(str(x[1]).replace("[", "").replace("]",
""))
        objects.append(str(x[2]).replace("[", "").replace("]",
""))

    return subjects, verbs, objects
```

Next, we apply the method using Athens as a case study and store the triplets for visualization:

```
# Obtain the triples for 'Athens'.
subjects, verbs, objects = extract_SVO(df['content'][2])

# Create the dataframe used for visualization.
```

```
kg_df =  pd.DataFrame({"source": subjects, "edge": verbs,
"target": objects})
kg_df.sample(3, random_state=12)
>>    source              edge            target
191   neighbourhoods      include         Kypseli
20    Athens              had, become     rebellion
219   They                brought         Rebetiko, music
```

The *subject-verb-object* relation can be visualized with a data structure known as a **knowledge graph** (**KG**). A KG is a convenient way to show visually how two entities relate to each other. Instead of a lengthy text document, a KG can immediately demonstrate important relations, so it's a valuable tool for data scientists. In the following code snippet, we generate a KG using only 15 relations for clarity:

```
import networkx as nx


# Create a directed graph from a dataframe using 15 triples.
G = nx.from_pandas_edgelist(kg_df[kg_df['source'] == 'Athens']
[0:15], "source", "target", edge_attr=True, create_using=nx.
MultiDiGraph())


# Draw the graph.
plt.figure(figsize=(10, 10))


pos = nx.spring_layout(G)
nx.draw(G, with_labels=True, node_color='skyblue', edge_
cmap=plt.cm.Blues, font_size=16, edge_color='r', pos=pos)
nx.draw_networkx_edge_labels(G, font_size=14, pos=pos)
```

The output is presented in *Figure 7.18*:

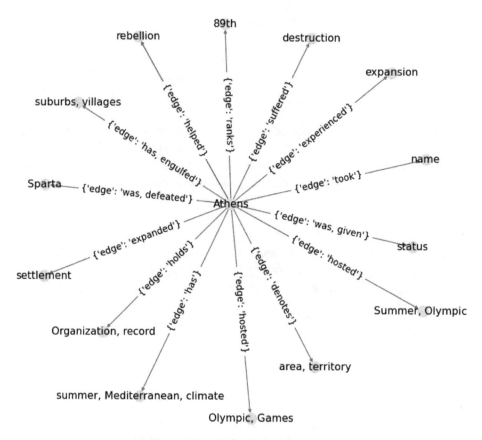

Figure 7.18 – KG for the word Athens

Athens is connected to all the other entities by an edge that represents the relationship between the two nodes. From *Figure 7.18*, we observe the following relations: **Athens – hosted – Olympic Games**, **Athens – has – summer Mediterranean climate**, and **Athens – was defeated – Sparta**. Having the Python library do a lot of the heavy lifting for us, we can proceed to the training of the transformer model in the next section.

Training the model

Before we start, remember that we only present part of the code and that a few lines are truncated to enhance clarity. Our training set consists of pairs of summaries and the full content for each capital city. First, let's examine the `Transformer` class shown in the following code snippet:

```
class Transformer(tf.keras.Model):
    def __init__(self, num_layers, d_model, num_heads, dff,
```

```
input_vocab_size, target_vocab_size, pe_input, pe_target,
rate=0.1):
        super(Transformer, self).__init__()


        self.encoder = Encoder(num_layers, d_model, num_heads,
dff, input_vocab_size, pe_input, rate)


        self.decoder = Decoder(num_layers, d_model, num_heads,
dff, target_vocab_size, pe_target, rate)


        self.final_layer = tf.keras.layers.Dense(target_vocab_
size)
```

The transformer includes an `Encoder` part, a `Decoder` part, and a final linear layer (Dense). Observe the different parameters used as input arguments to the layers. It's highly recommended to alter their values and experiment.

Next, we examine what happens inside the `Encoder` part:

```
class Encoder(tf.keras.layers.Layer):
    def __init__(self, num_layers, d_model, num_heads, dff,
input_vocab_size, maximum_position_encoding, rate=0.1):
        super(Encoder, self).__init__()


        self.d_model = d_model
        self.num_layers = num_layers


        self.embedding = tf.keras.layers.Embedding(input_vocab_
size, d_model)
        self.pos_encoding = positional_encoding(maximum_
position_encoding, self.d_model)


        self.enc_layers = [EncoderLayer(d_model, num_heads,
dff, rate) for _ in range(num_layers)]
```

The input goes through an embedding layer, which is summed with the positional encoding. The output of this summation is the input to the encoder layers shown in the following code snippet:

```
class EncoderLayer(tf.keras.layers.Layer):
    def __init__(self, d_model, num_heads, dff, rate=0.1):
```

```
        super(EncoderLayer, self).__init__()

        self.mha = MultiHeadAttention(d_model, num_heads)
        self.ffn = point_wise_feed_forward_network(d_model,
dff)

        self.layernorm1 = tf.keras.layers.
LayerNormalization(epsilon=1e-6)
        self.layernorm2 = tf.keras.layers.
LayerNormalization(epsilon=1e-6)

    def call(self, x, training, mask):
        attn_output, _ = self.mha(x, x, x, mask)
        out1 = self.layernorm1(x + attn_output)

        ffn_output = self.ffn(out1)
        out2 = self.layernorm2(out1 + ffn_output)

        return out2
```

We observe that the `EncoderLayer` class includes the components for multi-head attention, feed-forward network, and layer normalization. Moreover, notice how the residual connection is implemented. The `ffn` feed-forward network input is `out1`, which is the summation of X (word embedding and positional encoding) and the output of the attention module, `attn_output`. The decoder follows a similar architecture, so we don't present it explicitly.

Another topic that deserves special mention is how we can use an adaptive learning rate. We present this task in the section that follows.

Adapting the learning rate

Recall the discussion in the *Understanding gradient descent* section of *Chapter 4, Extracting Sentiments from Product Reviews*, about choosing the correct value for the learning rate. Too large steps may inhibit the algorithm from reaching the minimum, while small steps might take too long for the algorithm to converge. In our implementation, we use an adaptive learning rate to move fast at the beginning of the training process and slow down as we reach the minimum. The learning rate is based on the following formula:

$$lrate = d_{model}^{-0.5} * \min{(step\_num^{-0.5}, step\_num \cdot warmup\_steps^{-1.5})}$$

Here, d_{model} is the number of expected features in the encoder/decoder inputs, equal to 128 in our example. The formula suggests an increase of the learning rate linearly for the first `warmup_steps` (= 4000) training steps. Afterward, it is decreased proportionally to the inverse square root of the step number. The code that follows shows the calculations:

```
class CustomSchedule(tf.keras.optimizers.schedules.
LearningRateSchedule):
...

    def __call__(self, step):
        arg1 = tf.math.rsqrt(step)
        arg2 = step * (self.warmup_steps ** -1.5)


        return tf.math.rsqrt(self.d_model) * tf.math.
minimum(arg1, arg2)
```

Based on the previous formula, we create a `learning_rate` variable and the Adam optimizer that uses it:

```
learning_rate = CustomSchedule(d_model)


optimizer = tf.keras.optimizers.Adam(learning_rate, beta_1=0.9,
beta_2=0.98, epsilon=1e-9)
```

Recall that we already used the Adam optimizer in the *Performing classification* section of *Chapter 4, Extracting Sentiments from Product Reviews*, and the `rmsprop` optimizer in the *Training the model* section of *Chapter 6, Teaching Machines to Translate*.

For calculating loss, we incorporate `SparseCategoricalCrossentropy`, which computes the cross-entropy loss between the labels and predictions, suitable when the output labels are integer values:

```
loss_object = tf.keras.losses.
SparseCategoricalCrossentropy(from_logits=True,
reduction='none')
```

Cross-entropy builds upon the idea of entropy from the information theory, as discussed in the *Contracting a decision tree* section of *Chapter 3, Classifying Topics of Newsgroup Posts*. It calculates the number of bits required to represent an average event from one distribution compared to another.

Another impediment is that the training runs can take several hours or even days to finish. We need a way to keep track of the progress and resume the process in case of failure without starting from scratch. A useful feature, in this case, is the `Checkpoint` mechanism used in the following code snippet:

```
ckpt = tf.train.Checkpoint(transformer=transformer,
optimizer=optimizer)
```

The code creates a bunch of files in a predetermined folder, and we can specify the frequency of the checkpoints. For example, we can save a checkpoint every fifth epoch:

```
if (epoch + 1) % 5 == 0:
        ckpt_save_path = ckpt_manager.save()
        print ('Saving checkpoint for epoch {} at {}'.
format(epoch+1, ckpt_save_path))
```

This section aimed to provide the necessary hooks to start working with the Jupyter notebook. The following section introduces the last topic of this chapter concerning the evaluation methodology and the relevant metrics for text summarization.

Measuring summarization performance

As with the discussion in the *Measuring translation performance* section of *Chapter 6, Teaching Machines to Translate*, using the **BiLingual Evaluation Understudy** (BLEU) score, we present a metric for assessing the performance of text summarization systems. The **Recall-Oriented Understudy for Gisting Evaluation** (ROUGE) score is the subject of the current section, and although its name sounds complicated, it's incredibly easy to understand and implement. It works by comparing an automatically produced summary against a human reference summary using n-grams. In that sense, it is symmetrical to the BLEU score. Additionally, ROUGE is a set of metrics rather than a single one. They all assign a numerical score to a summary that tells us how good it is compared to a reference one. Let's examine the first variant.

ROUGE-N measures the overlap of unigrams, bigrams, trigrams, and higher-order n-grams, where *N* represents the n-gram order. Thus, for *ROUGE-1*, we would measure the match rate of unigrams between our prediction and the reference. The calculations are based on recall, precision, and F-score. In the *Measuring translation performance* section of *Chapter 6, Teaching Machines to Translate*, we saw an example based on *Figure 6.26*. Without explicitly mentioning this fact, we did calculate *ROUGE-1*. You can refer to the specific discussion for the step-by-step calculations.

We can also change the granularity of the comparison by using bigrams or trigrams. Then, *ROUGE-2* and *ROUGE-3* are the chosen metric, respectively. To facilitate our discussion, consider the example in *Figure 7.19*, contrasting a prediction with the reference summary:

Reference: "Trying is the first step towards your great success."

Prediction: "Trying is really the first step towards failure."

Figure 7.19 – Reference and predicted summarization example

Then, we can make the following calculations:

$$ROUGE2_{precision} = \frac{\#common\_bigrams}{\#bigrams\_prediction} = \frac{4}{7} = 57\%$$

$$ROUGE2_{recall} = \frac{\#common\_bigrams}{\#bigrams\_reference} = \frac{4}{8} = 0.5\%$$

$$F\text{-}score = 2 * \frac{ROUGE2_{precision} * ROUGE2_{recall}}{ROUGE2_{precision} + ROUGE2_{recall}} = 2 * \frac{0.57 * 0.5}{0.57 + 0.5} = 0.53\%$$

When the summaries become long, the *ROUGE-2* score becomes small because there are fewer possible bigrams to match. This situation is especially true for abstractive summarization, where the generated sentences are novel. For this reason, it is common to report both *ROUGE-1* and *ROUGE-2* in an evaluation.

Another variant that does not use n-grams is *ROUGE-L*, which measures the **longest common subsequence (LCS)** between our prediction and reference. A subsequence is a sequence that appears in the same relative order but is not necessarily contiguous. So, looking at the prediction, the longest common subsequence is *Trying is the first step towards*, and the relevant measurements are these:

$$ROUGEL_{precision} = \frac{LCS\_length}{\#words\_prediction} = \frac{6}{8} = 75\%$$

$$ROUGEL_{recall} = \frac{LCS\_length}{\#words\_reference} = \frac{6}{9} = 67\%$$

$$F\text{-}score = 2 * \frac{ROUGEL_{precision} * ROUGEL_{recall}}{ROUGEL_{precision} + ROUGEL_{recall}} = 2 * \frac{0.75 * 0.67}{0.75 + 0.67} = 71\%$$

The main benefit of *ROUGE-L* compared to *ROUGE-N* is that it doesn't depend on n-grams, so it tends to capture similarity patterns more accurately. Notice that there are a few more ROUGE variants that we don't cover in this section.

We can now proceed with the calculation of ROUGE in Python. In the following code snippet, we define a `summarize` method that returns the summary of an input document:

```
# Summarize an input document.
def summarize(input_document):

    summarized = evaluate(input_document=input_document)[0].
numpy()
```

```
    # Exclude <go> token.
    summarized = np.expand_dims(summarized[1:], 0)
    return summary_tokenizer.sequences_to_texts(summarized)[0]
```

Next, we call the method using one sample from the documents:

```
result = summarize(document[2])
print(result)
>> athens ath enz greek αθήνα romanized athína a'θina listen
ancient greek ἀθῆναι romanized athênai pl atʰɛ̂ːnai̯ is the capital
city of greece with a population close to 4 million it is the
largest city in greece and the...
```

The reference, in this case, is this:

```
reference = ' '.join(summary[2].split()[1:51]).lower()
print(reference)
>> athens ( ath-enz; greek: αθήνα, romanized: athína [a'θina]
(listen); ancient greek: ἀθῆναι, romanized: athênai (pl.)
[atʰɛ̂ːnai̯]) is the capital city of greece. with a population
close to 4 million it is the largest city in greece, and the...
```

Finally, the scores are calculated, as follows:

```
from rouge_score import rouge_scorer


# Calculate the Rouge scores.
scorer = rouge_scorer.RougeScorer(['rouge1', 'rouge2',
'rougeL'], use_stemmer=True)
scores = scorer.score(result, reference)
print(scores)
>> {'rouge1': Score(precision=0.9807692307692307,
recall=0.9807692307692307, fmeasure=0.9807692307692307),
'rouge2': Score(precision=0.9607843137254902,
recall=0.9607843137254902, fmeasure=0.9607843137254902),
'rougeL': Score(precision=0.9807692307692307,
recall=0.9807692307692307, fmeasure=0.9807692307692307)}
```

The output suggests high values for the scores, and as expected, *ROUGE-2* is slightly inferior. Of course, beware that we measured performance on a sample also used for training the model. In general, the dataset and the hyperparameters of the trained model are deliberately chosen to facilitate the discussion of the current chapter. Also, the code needs to be executed in a reasonable amount of time. In the chapter's Jupyter notebook, you can experiment with more data and demanding configurations. You are already equipped for this task!

So, this concludes the discussion on ROUGE and how it measures syntactical matches rather than semantics. As with BLEU, it does not cater to different words with the same meaning, which is an apparent deficiency of both metrics. Nevertheless, ROUGE offers a straightforward and concise way to assess the performance of any summarization system.

Summary

This chapter dealt with text summarization, yet another hot topic in NLP. Systems of this kind aim to reduce the information load imposed by the overabundance of online text data. We used various extractive and abstractive text summarization techniques to deliver accurate summaries.

The first part of the chapter focused on web crawling and scraping, where you became acquainted with the basic concepts, the relevant technologies, and how to implement web spiders in Python. The provided coding examples constitute a sufficient guide to implementing your web crawlers for different tasks.

Next, we discussed various topics that led to the comprehension of the transformer model. For example, we debated why having a single context vector between the encoder and the decoder is a bottleneck. We also discussed attention mechanisms that enhance some parts of the input data while diminishing others. Finally, utilizing a corpus of Wikipedia pages, we created a dataset and trained the transformer model.

In the last section, we focused on how specific metrics can be used to evaluate text summarization systems. Using specialized scores such as ROUGE provides a better way to compare different text summarization implementations.

The next chapter deals with another exciting theme: we exploit text data extracted from Twitter to perform *hateful and offensive language detection*.

8

Detecting Hateful and Offensive Language

Sparked by the alarming situation on social media platforms, where there is a dramatic increase in inflammatory language, companies have already implemented algorithms to regulate or even remove extreme posts. On the other hand, freedom of opinion and expression is a cornerstone of many societies, raising concerns that attempts to curb inappropriate language could also lead to the restraint of free speech. The current chapter aims to identify hateful and offensive language in tweets. Without delving into the particulars of this debate, we will address a few technical challenges and provide possible solutions in this setting. During this process, we also introduce many new concepts and techniques for machine learning.

A central theme of this chapter concerns the reuse and tuning of third-party models to minimize the effort of a new deployment. Using an open source dataset with hateful and offensive tweets, we will examine the steps to build a state-of-the-art language model and use it for classification. The presented algorithms have been in the spotlight recently due to their usage in winning prestigious competitions in the field. We will also utilize a validation test to adjust the model's parameters and avoid certain pitfalls. Finally, we will examine the strategies for dealing with imbalanced data.

By the end of the chapter, you will be capable of making an essential leap into more advanced machine-learning techniques and enhancing your programming toolbox.

In this chapter, we will go through the following topics:

- Implementing state-of-the-art language models
- Building more complex neural architectures
- Applying new algorithms for text classification
- Understanding the need for validation sets
- Treating imbalanced datasets

Technical requirements

The chapter's code has been truncated in certain parts to facilitate reading the content. However, the whole code is available as different Jupyter notebooks in the book's GitHub repository:

`https://github.com/PacktPublishing/Machine-Learning-Techniques-for-Text/tree/main/chapter-08`

Introducing social networks

In the late 1960s, the famous psychologist Stanley Milgram decided to investigate the *small-world concept*, which states that the entire world is connected through short chains of acquaintances. Performing an ingenious experiment, Milgram asked a few hundred people from various locations to get a letter to a stranger in Boston. The participants were given information about the target recipient and instructed to send the letter to someone they knew that would more likely know that individual. The following person in the chain had to repeat the same task and send the letter to someone even closer. When Milgram examined the letters that reached the target, he realized they had changed hands about six times on average. The result demonstrated that, on average, any two individuals in the US are separated by five connections, known by the phrase *six degrees of separation*.

Although this outcome can be debated for many reasons, it paved the way for similar experiments in social networks, such as a study about Facebook in 2016. The study showed that each platform user is connected to every other person by an average of three and a half other people. Similar numbers apply to Twitter, and on platforms such as LinkedIn, we are notified about the distance of potential connections (second-degree or third-degree ones). It's, therefore, a no-brainer that social networks have shortened the gap between any two people in the world. However, this has not come without a cost.

The spread of hate speech and fake news is a serious side effect of expanding social networks. Most of the time covered by anonymity, social network users feel more comfortable speaking hate or disseminating fabricated information as opposed to real life, where they have to confront the consequences of what they say. All major social networks make an enormous effort to deal with such a problem, and machine learning is a powerful tool in this arena.

The current chapter focuses on identifying hateful and offensive language in tweets using a state-of-the-art language model and other classification methods. To perform this task, we will use, for convenience, a publicly available corpus from `https://github.com/t-davidson/hate-speech-and-offensive-language`. If you are interested, you can also extract tweets directly from the platform using tools such as *Tweepy* (`https://www.tweepy.org/`).

The difference between hate and offensive speech can be subtle, with difficult-to-discern boundaries. The providers of this dataset define hate speech as language that expresses hatred toward a targeted group or is intended to be derogatory, and is used to humiliate, or insult the group's members. On the other hand, sexist tweets are generally classified as offensive. So, let's consider three examples:

- *Hate speech*: I hate the ghetto trash at the special school across the street from my building. All of them will grow up to be criminals.

- *Offensive speech*: God, my tweets are so ghetto.

- *Neither offensive nor non-offensive speech*: So many weird people in the ghetto at this time.

We should warn the reader of the sensitive and offensive content in the dataset, which is solely used for educational purposes. In this respect, this chapter aims to equip you on how to filter similar deleterious content from public exposure. So, without further ado, let's begin the discussion with a state-of-the-art language model.

Understanding BERT

Looking at the transformer's encoder/decoder architecture discussed in the *Introducing transformers* section of *Chapter 7, Summarizing Wikipedia Articles*, we can observe a clear separation of tasks. The encoder is responsible for extracting features from an input sentence, such as syntax, grammar, and context. At the same time, the decoder maps it to a target sequence – for example, translates it to another language. This separation makes the two components self-contained; therefore, they can be used independently.

This section introduces a state-of-the-art transformer-based technique to generate language representation models named **Bidirectional Encoder Representation from Transformers** (**BERT**). BERT incorporates a stack of transformer encoders to understand the language better.

Similarly to word embedding, the method belongs to the self-supervised learning family because it does not require human-annotated observation labels. Therefore, BERT can be utilized in various tasks, such as machine translation, sentiment analysis, text summarization, and so forth, which were the focus of previous chapters.

The power of BERT in different natural processing tasks is accessed using the **General Language Understanding Evaluation** (**GLUE**) benchmark (`https://gluebenchmark.com/`). The specific benchmark is a collection of resources for training, evaluating, and analyzing natural language understanding systems. GLUE is centered around nine English sentence understanding tasks – for example, determining whether a sentence is grammatically correct or not.

A typical step when incorporating BERT is to pre-train the model to understand the language and adjust it for specific applications. This way, the knowledge that is extracted during the pre-training phase, which takes place once, can be transferred to several applications without much effort. This feature is essentially the basic idea behind **transfer learning**, where we first pre-train a model using a large dataset and then fine-tune it for a specific task using a smaller one.

Consider, for example, applications for recognizing human faces. All these applications share a common step – extracting the human face's basic characteristics, such as the eyes, nose, and mouth, and their differences rely mainly on the setting. For example, a video surveillance system aims to identify a human face from a distance, while for an access control system, the person is usually close to the camera. A robust pre-trained model can be tuned with a smaller context-dependent dataset in both cases.

In the same sense, transfer learning is a frequently adopted strategy in natural language processing. We can resort to powerful language models that can be adapted to the peculiarities of a specific task. The benefit of this case is that we can reuse the large language model multiple times without starting from scratch, saving a lot of computational time. Even if we are willing to undertake this task, assembling sufficiently large and representative text corpora is notoriously difficult and costly.

To have an order of magnitude, BERT was trained on Wikipedia (2,500 million words) and Google's Books corpora (800 million words) using the specialized hardware **Tensor Processing Unit (TPU)**. The first implementations, *BERT-Base* and *BERT-Large*, had the following configurations: 12 layers, 768 hidden nodes, 12 attention heads, and 110 million parameters; and 24 layers, 1,024 hidden nodes, 16 attention heads, and 340 million parameters respectively. For many competitive reasons, applying transfer learning when possible is preferable. The coming two sections delve into more detail about BERT's pre-training and tuning phases.

Pre-training phase

Models such as **long short-term memory (LSTM)** present a fundamental deficiency, as the input words are treated sequentially. Therefore, they have difficulty identifying a sentence's true context. Bidirectional LSTMs also exist, where input is fed from both left to right and right to left, obtaining a better understanding of the words. However, this is a compromise, as the two input sequences are treated independently. The transformer architecture solved these problems by receiving the input sentence as a whole and not in chunks. This feature allowed the model to learn the context of both directions simultaneously. BERT architecture takes advantage of this capability and utilizes two custom models to increase its learning capacity.

The **masked language model** (**MLM**) enforces bidirectional learning by masking a word (or a percentage of words) in the input sentence and directing BERT to find a word that better predicts the masked one. You can relate this approach to a fill-in-the-blanks kind of problem. For example, in the following phrase, *A picture is worth a _____ words*, we can reasonably predict that the missing token is probably the word *thousand*. A particular configuration in BERT is that masking happens in 15% of the input tokens. More specifically, 80% of these tokens are replaced with the token *[MASK]*, 10% are replaced with a random word, and the rest, 10%, are left unchanged to introduce bias to the correct word. But before any processing takes place, the input needs to be adapted accordingly, as shown in *Figure 8.1*:

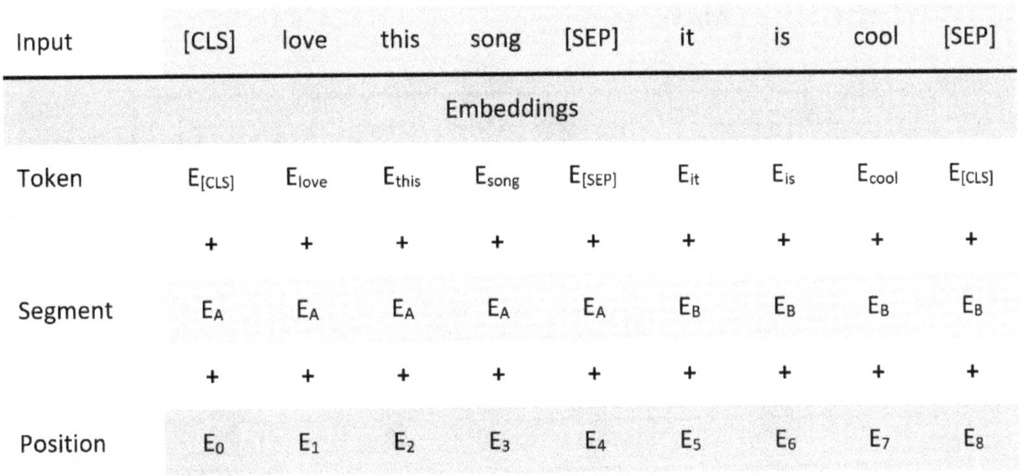

Input	[CLS]	love	this	song	[SEP]	it	is	cool	[SEP]
Embeddings									
Token	$E_{[CLS]}$	E_{love}	E_{this}	E_{song}	$E_{[SEP]}$	E_{it}	E_{is}	E_{cool}	$E_{[CLS]}$
	+	+	+	+	+	+	+	+	+
Segment	E_A	E_A	E_A	E_A	E_A	E_B	E_B	E_B	E_B
	+	+	+	+	+	+	+	+	+
Position	E_0	E_1	E_2	E_3	E_4	E_5	E_6	E_7	E_8

Figure 8.1 – BERT input representation

In this example, the input consists of two sentences, **love this song** (**A**), and **it is cool** (**B**). The input to the encoder is then the sum of three embeddings vectors:

- The **Token** embeddings include the special classification token, [**CLS**], as the first symbol and [**SEP**] as the last to separate two sentences.

- The **Segment** embeddings are used as markers to help the encoder distinguish between two sentences.

- The **Positional** embeddings indicate the position of each token in the input.

The second model used by BERT is the **next sentence prediction** (NSP), which, as the name suggests, predicts whether a given sentence follows the previous one. The specific step helps BERT understand the context across different sentences. For example, if we encounter the phrase *I am hungry* in a piece of text, there is a higher probability that the coming phrase is *Let's have dinner* rather than *The broader geopolitical context is fluid.*

The NSP process should give a higher probability for the first option than the second one. Combining MLM and NSP allows BERT to *understand* the language sufficiently.

To summarize all the steps during the pre-training phase, consider *Figure 8.2*:

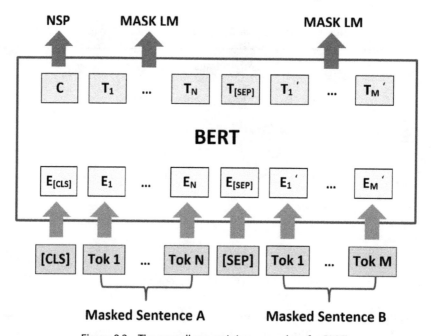

Figure 8.2 – The overall pre-training procedure for BERT

The input during the pre-training phase is pairs of sentences (**A** and **B**), with some of their words (**Tok**) being masked. Then, the words are converted to vectors using pre-trained embeddings (**E**). The binary output, **C**, corresponds to the NSP procedure and becomes 1 when sentence **B** follows sentence **A** and 0 in the opposite case. Each **T** in the output is a word vector created by the MLM procedure.

In the following section, we will discuss the fine-tuning phase in BERT.

Fine-tuning phase

After creating a generic language model, we can fine-tune it for any application under study. Using the self-attention mechanism in the transformer permits BERT to model many downstream tasks by simply fine-tuning all pre-trained parameters. For example, suppose that we are building a question-answering system. In this case, we need a dataset with questions and answers similar to sentences **A** and **B**. *Figure 8.3* illustrates the fine-tuning procedure, using pairs that include a question and a paragraph that contains the answer:

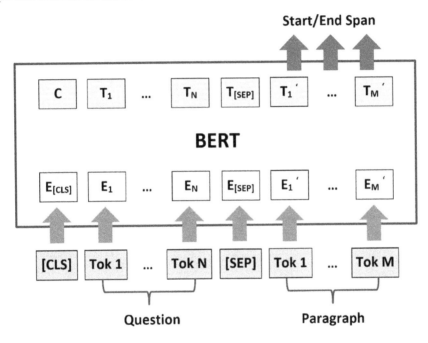

Figure 8.3 – The overall fine-tuning procedure for BERT

As before, the **[CLS]** token is added before every input example. The **[SEP]** symbol separates the question and the paragraph. The output is the start and the end token from the paragraph that most likely answers the question. Another example of using a sentence **A** and a sentence **B** combination is for sentence pair classification (see the top part of *Figure 8.4*):

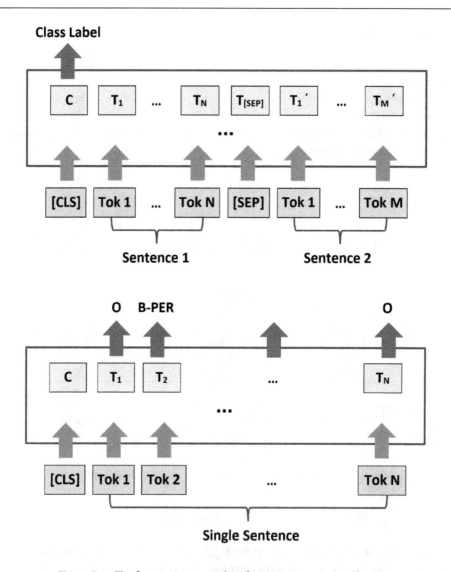

Figure 8.4 – The fine-tuning procedure for sentence pair classification
(the top part) and NER (the bottom part)

One example of sentence pair classification is the sentence entailment task, where, given two sentences, the aim is to decide whether the meaning of one can be entailed (inferred) from the other. Note that using a pair of sentences is one of the options to employ BERT. Instead of two sentences packed together, the input can also be a single sentence. An example, in this case, is the single sentence tagging task, such as named entity recognition, where a tag must be predicted for every word in the input (the bottom part of *Figure 8.4*).

Observe the NER output using the IOB format (**O** and **B-PER**) that we encountered in the *Executing name entity resolution* section of *Chapter 6, Teaching Machines to Translate*. In conclusion, we can use BERT for various tasks, and a great benefit of fine-tuning compared to pre-training is that it is relatively inexpensive. Equipped with a good understanding of the concepts behind the model, we can proceed to the next section and incorporate BERT for the hate classification problem of this chapter.

Putting BERT into action

To utilize BERT, we need to perform two distinct tasks. First, the proper dataset should be prepared, and then the model implemented. We will start with the first task.

Preparing the dataset

Let's load the instances from the tweets dataset:

```
import pandas as pd

# Read the data from the csv file.
data = pd.read_csv('./data/labeled_data.csv')

data.sample(random_state=4)
>>... hate_speech    offensive_language    neither    class
...      0                   3                 0         1
```

Each sample was annotated by three people who labeled each tweet as either `hate_speech=0`, `offensive_language=1`, or `neither=2`. It is not uncommon to encounter disagreement among the annotators, so `class` of the tweet is determined by a majority vote. In the previous example, all three annotators agreed, however. Next, we print an example for each class:

```
# Print an example for each class.
print("Hate speech:", data.iloc[10477].tweet)
print("Offensive speech:", data.iloc[9463].tweet)
print("Neither offensive nor non-offensive speech:", data.
iloc[20963].tweet)
>>
* Hate speech: I hate the ghetto trash at the special school
across the street from my building. All of them will grow up to
be criminals.
* Offensive speech: God my tweets are so ghetto
* Neither offensive nor non-offensive speech: So many weird
people in the ghetto at this time.
```

A significant reason for using BERT is the small size of our dataset (~25,000 tweets). It would be challenging to build a language model solely from this corpus. The code that follows shows the number of samples per each class:

```
# Print the number of examples per class.
data['category'] = data['class'].map({0: 'hate_speech', 1:
'offensive_language', 2: 'neither'})
data['category'].value_counts()
>>
offensive_language     19190
neither                 4163
hate_speech             1430
Name: category, dtype: int64
```

One crucial observation is that the dataset is imbalanced, as many more instances exist for the offensive_language class. Keep a note here because this is something that we need to deal with later.

Another important issue is that the tweets do not merely consist of human text, and they can frequently contain handles, emojis, and HTML links. These are also text elements, and using the following code, we can extract this information:

```
# Extract the number handles, emojis, and links in the tweets.
handles_count = data['tweet'].str.count("@[A-Za-z0-9]")
emojis_count = data['tweet'].str.count("[&#A-Za-z0-9];")
links_count = data['tweet'].str.count("http:|https:")

data['handles_count'] = handles_count
data['emoji_count'] = emojis_count
data['links_count'] = links_count
# Plot the distribution of handles per category.
sns.violinplot(data=data, x='handles_count', y='category',
orient='h')
```

We can identify patterns such as @ML4Text (handle) or 😌 (emoji) using regular expressions. The violin plots in *Figure 8.5* show the distribution of the handle elements in the three categories:

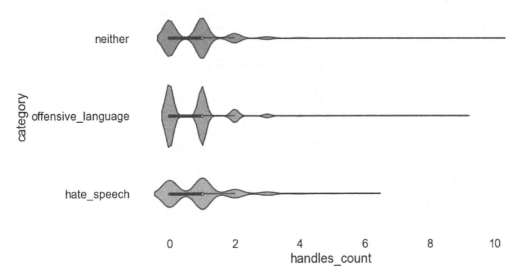

Figure 8.5 – Distribution of handles per category

Violin plots resemble boxplots in that they show summary statistics, such as the median and interquartile ranges, but they can also present the data distribution. For example, *Figure 8.6* contrasts the two types of plots for the same dataset:

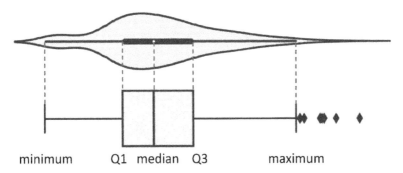

Figure 8.6 – Violin versus boxplot

The output suggests a similar distribution in the three classes, including a small number of handles. For this reason, we decide to remove these extra elements using the preprocess_text method:

```
import re


# Remove emojis, handles, HTML character references, and links.
```

```
def preprocess_text(text):
    regrex_pattern = re.compile(pattern = "&#[A-Za-z0-9]+;|@
[A-Za-z0-9]+|&[A-Za-z0-9]+;|(http|https)://[A-Za-z0-9./]+")
    return regrex_pattern.sub(r'', text)


data['tweet'] = data['tweet'].apply(lambda x: preprocess_
text(x))
```

At this point, we have available a cleaned dataset to proceed to the next phase.

Implementing the BERT model

The implementation of BERT is based on a TensorFlow tutorial: `https://www.tensorflow.org/text/tutorials/classify_text_with_bert`, using the **TensorFlow Hub**, an open repository and library for reusable machine learning. The `tensorflow_hub` module contains a gamut of BERT models, which are pre-trained with different datasets. In our case, the demand for smaller BERT models stems from the need to use them in less powerful computational environments – for instance, a home laptop:

```
# The name of the BERT model.
model_name = 'small_bert/bert_en_uncased_L-4_H-512_A-8'
name_handle_dict = {

...

    'small_bert/bert_en_uncased_L-4_H-512_A-8':
'https://tfhub.dev/tensorflow/small_bert/bert_en_uncased_L-4_H-
512_A-8/1',

...

name_preprocess_dict = {

...

'small_bert/bert_en_uncased_L-4_H-512_A-8': 'https://tfhub.dev/
tensorflow/bert_en_uncased_preprocess/3',

...
```

Note that the `model_name` choice also maps to a preprocessing model. Each BERT model has a matching preprocessing model from TensorFlow Hub to transform text inputs into numeric tokens and arrange them in several **tensors**. In TensorFlow, all the computations involve tensors, which are multi-dimensional arrays with uniform types. In the available Jupyter notebook, there are many models to use and experiment with:

```
encoder_handle = name_handle_dict[model_name]
preprocess_handle = name_preprocess_dict[model_name]

print("Using the BERT model: " + encoder_handle)
print("Using the preprocess model: " + preprocess_handle)
>>
Using the BERT model: https://tfhub.dev/tensorflow/small_bert/
bert_en_uncased_L-4_H-512_A-8/1
Using the preprocess model: https://tfhub.dev/tensorflow/bert_
en_uncased_preprocess/3
```

Let's now create the preprocess and BERT models:

```
import tensorflow_hub as hub

# Use the handle to create the preprocess model.
preprocess_model = hub.KerasLayer(preprocess_handle)

# Use the handle to create the BERT model.
bert_model = hub.KerasLayer(encoder_handle)
```

Then, we use the BERT model:

```
# Feed the text to the BERT model.
results = bert_model(text_preprocessed)

print("The shape of the pooled outputs:", results["pooled_
output"].shape)
print("The shape of the sequence outputs:", results["sequence_
output"].shape)
>>
The shape of the pooled outputs:(1, 512)
The shape of the sequence outputs:(1, 128, 512)
```

There are two keys in `results`. First, `pooled_output` is the embedding of each tweet, while `sequence_output` is the contextual embedding of every token in the tweet. We use the first to represent every tweet in the dataset:

```
# Represent each tweet as an embedding.
data['pooled'] = data['tweet'].apply(lambda x: (bert_
model(bert_preprocess_model(tf.constant([x])))) ["pooled_
output"].numpy())
```

After finishing this step, we have at our disposal an extended dataset with the embeddings of the tweets. Be aware that this outcome comes from the pre-trained BERT model, and no fine-tuning has taken place so far. From this point on, you can apply any classification algorithm from the previous chapters. However, in the next section, we will continue with another prominent family of relevant algorithms that have proven influential in recent years.

Introducing boosting algorithms

The term **boosting** refers to a family of algorithms that use ensemble learning to build a collectively robust classifier from several weak classifiers. The difference with other ensemble techniques is that in boosting, we build a series of trees, where every other tree tries to fix the mistakes made by its predecessor. Contrast this approach with how the random forest classifier performs decisions presented in the *Contracting a decision tree* section of *Chapter 3, Classifying Topics of Newsgroup Posts*. In that case, multiple trees are constructed in parallel using the bagging technique. Another distinctive characteristic of boosting algorithms is their ability to deal with the *bias-variance trade-off* discussed in the *Applying regularization* section of *Chapter 4, Extracting Sentiments from Product Reviews*. Let's present the major boosting algorithms in the following sections.

Understanding AdaBoost

Adaptive Boosting (**AdaBoost**) was the first successful boosting algorithm for classification and regression problems. It commences by training decision trees with a single split, called a **stump**. It also uses the notion of weighting misclassified observations so that the next decision tree in the sequence pays more attention to the errors. All observations are weighted equally during the creation of the first decision stump. The image in *Figure 8.7* visualizes the process of classifying data points using the AdaBoost algorithm:

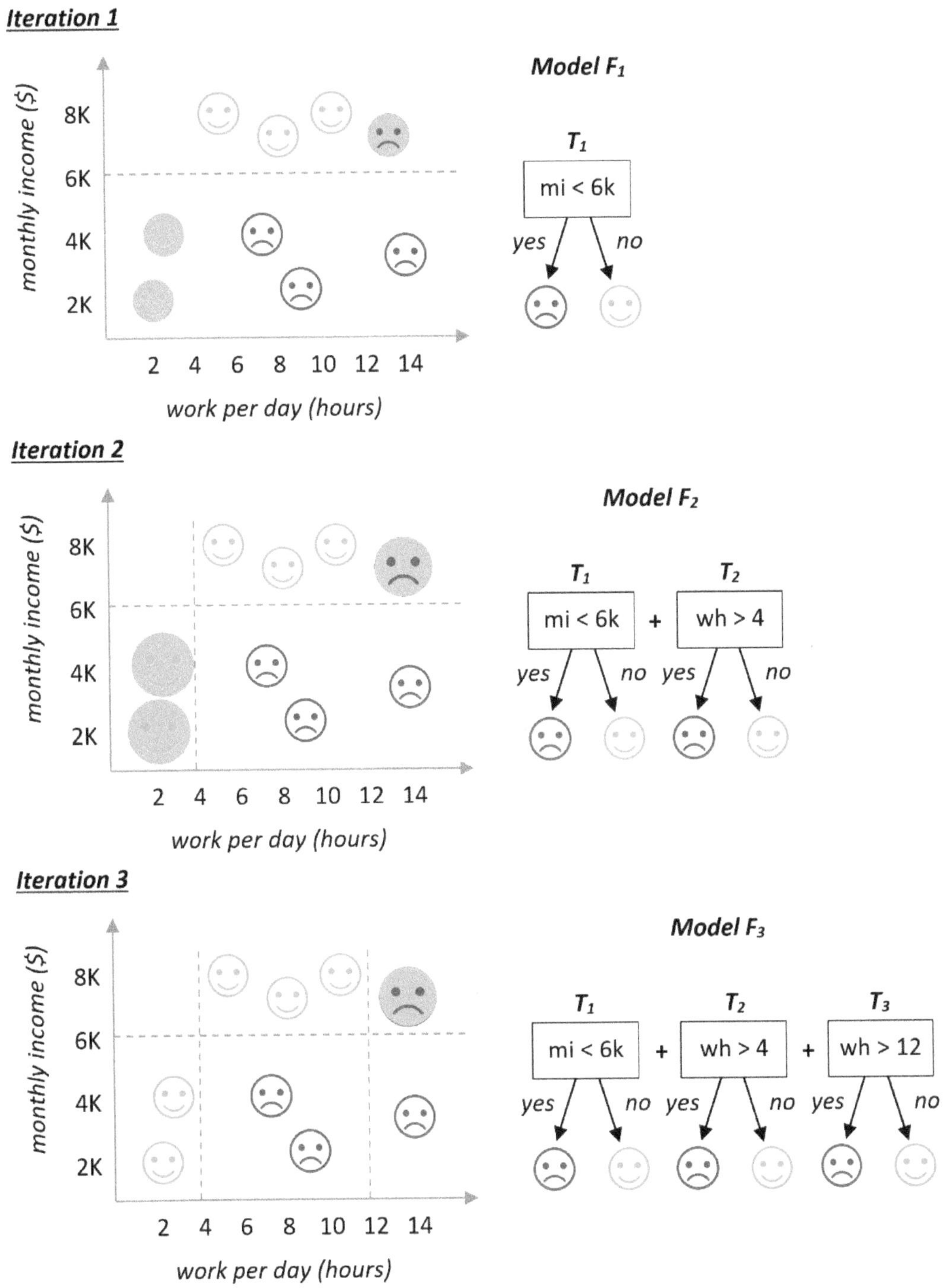

Figure 8.7 – AdaBoost visual example

Suppose that in the presented toy example, the samples are pairs of two numbers, working hours, and the monthly income for different individuals. Each pair is annotated either with a happy or a sad smiley face. The algorithm creates a very shallow tree (T_1) from the training data during the first iteration. The decision based on this stump is depicted with the horizontal line, $y=6$, so that a person receiving more than **$6K** per month is labeled with a happy face. The F_1 model consists only of the specific decision tree. Unfortunately, this decision stump misclassifies three samples that are shown with the opaque fill. In the second iteration, a new stump is created (T_2) that tries to rectify the previous errors. The incorrectly classified observations now carry more weight than the observations that were correctly classified. For this reason, the corresponding icons appear larger than the others. The vertical line, $x=4$, which is the stump's outcome, corrects two errors.

Note that the F_2 model is the sum of T_1 and T_2. Only one error remains unresolved during the third iteration, treated by the T_3 stump. Another vertical line, $x=12$, separates the sad smiley faces from the happy ones. Finally, the new F_3 model is the sum of T_1, T_2, and T_3 that correctly classifies all the data points. Observe the sequence of trees and how the output of one tree is the input of the next. In practical problems, we expect that the final classifier has higher accuracy than all the weak classifiers involved. Let's continue with another essential boosting algorithm.

Understanding gradient boosting

Gradient boosting is an extension of boosting, where gradient descent is used to boost weak models. A primary component of the algorithm is the loss function, such as the mean squared error for regression or the logarithmic loss function for classification. The only prerequisite is that the function is differentiable to apply gradient descent. Although many models can be used for weak learners, decision trees are almost always incorporated in practice. Compared to AdaBoost, which creates a stump of depth equal to 1, gradient boosting starts by making a single leaf, representing an initial guess of the model. Next, the first decision tree is created, usually larger than a stump. In practice, the method uses a maximum number of leaves between 8 and 32, and the tree construction happens sequentially, such as AdaBoost, which aims to rectify the errors of its predecessor. Therefore, an essential task during gradient boosting is to model specific errors appropriately.

Let's continue with a numerical example demonstrating the previous steps in more detail. We use the gradient boosting variant for regression to facilitate the calculations, but the steps are symmetrical for classification. The toy dataset in *Table 8.1* includes three attributes for predicting the price of a car:

car	year	km	cylinders	price ($)	$\widehat{y_1}$	residuals_1	$\widehat{y_2}$	residuals_2
1	2012	90000	4	11000	30000	-19000	28100	-17100
2	2017	21000	4	28000	30000	-2000	29800	-1800
3	2018	18000	4	33000	30000	3000	31650	1350
4	2015	45000	6	18000	30000	-12000	28800	-10800
5	2022	3000	6	60000	30000	30000	31650	28350

Table 8.1 – Instances for determining a car's price based on three attributes

Gradient boosting begins by creating an initial guess of the price for each car that is simply the average of the **price ($)** column. The mean value is equal to $30,000 and constitutes the base model. Thus, if the algorithm stops at this step, the predicted price of each car would be that number (the $\widehat{y_1}$ column). What is the residual (error) in this case? The **residuals_1** column provides the answer based on the *actual value – predicted value*. For example, the error of the first car is $11,000 - 30,000 = -19,000$. Next, we build the first decision tree to predict the residuals shown in the table, and not the actual values (**price ($)**).

This choice seems counterintuitive, but adding residual predictions by a weak model to an existing model's approximation nudges the model toward the correct target. The constructed tree is shown in *Figure 8.8*, where we restrict the number of leaves to four:

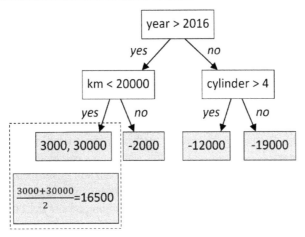

Figure 8.8 – The decision tree for gradient boosting

Note that we average their values when there is more than one residual element in a leaf. Next, we can perform new predictions based on the two components: the one-leaf (base) model and the newly created decision tree. For example, the new prediction for the fifth car in the dataset is the following:

$$base\_prediction + learning\_rate \cdot residual = 30,000 + 0.1 \cdot 16,500 = 31,650$$

The learning rate factor scales the tree and leads to a small step in the right direction. Empirically, the small steps prove to be beneficial for the model by reducing its variance. So, using the two models, we managed to get slightly better predictions for all observations (the $\widehat{y_2}$ column). The new errors shown in the **residuals_2** column reflect that we are heading in the correct direction. We contract a new tree based on these errors, and the same process repeats. There is no need to show all the steps, but hopefully, you got the basic idea. To summarize, constructing a chain of trees eventually leads to a model that can successfully predict the samples of the training set (low bias) and the unseen observations (low variance). *Figure 8.9* illustrates how the different models, **F0–F4**, are chained in gradient boosting:

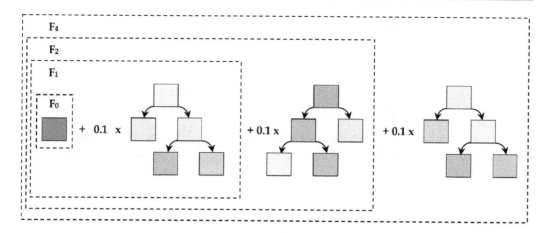

Figure 8.9 – Chained models in gradient boosting

In the specific example, a learning rate of **0.1** is used, but this is a hyperparameter that we need to adjust through experimentation. Moreover, the topology of the decision trees can differ between the iterations. Models are added sequentially until no further improvement in the performance can be made. A good intuitive example is to think of a golfer whacking a golf ball toward a hole. After each shot, the golfer needs to compute the distance between their current position and the actual position of the hole. The calculated distance helps reassess the direction and magnitude of the next stroke to get closer to the hole. In this analogy, a stroke is like applying one of the **F0–F4** models and the distance is the residual.

It's now time to present the last boosting algorithm to be used for the main problem of this chapter.

Understanding XGBoost

XGBoost stands for **eXtreme Gradient Boosting**, a popular and efficient open source implementation of the gradient boosting tree algorithm. In recent years, it has been a favored choice in various Kaggle competitions, helping people win significant prizes. XGBoost can be used for regression, classification, and ranking problems. The method builds upon the concepts of supervised machine learning, decision trees, ensemble learning, and gradient boosting already presented throughout the book. To understand the mechanics behind the algorithm, let's examine it in more detail with an example.

> **Tip**
>
> **Kaggle** is an online community of data scientists and machine learning enthusiasts. It offers a platform for sharing ideas, learning through examples, competing against other practitioners, accessing real-world datasets, and much more. Consider creating an active Kaggle profile to gain exposure to the community and recruiters.

Once again, we use a minimal toy dataset to facilitate the computations. *Table 8.2* shows five instances of students that relate them passing a particular exam and the hours spent studying:

student	hours	pass	P_1	residuals_1	P_2	residuals_2
1	40	1	0.5	0.5	0.55	0.45
2	25	0	0.5	-0.5	0.35	-0.35
3	35	0	0.5	-0.5	0.35	-0.35
4	73	0	0.5	-0.5	0.35	-0.35
5	57	1	0.5	0.5	0.55	0.45

Table 8.2 – Instances for determining student success based on studying time

Too much studying can also be a reason for failure, as the instance for the fourth student demonstrates. As we did in the previous section, we start with the base model. As we are dealing with a binary classification problem, there are only two possible outcomes, **0** (fail) and **1** (pass). A common approach, in this case, is to choose their average as the initial prediction of the base model (P_1). So, the model predicts a 50% chance of passing the exam – not very useful information! Next, we calculate the residuals by subtracting from the **pass** column the P_1 one. The result is stored in **residuals_1**. Let's now fit a tree to the residuals, putting at the root the **hours** attribute. There are various options to consider for its threshold, and two of them are shown in *Figure 8.10*:

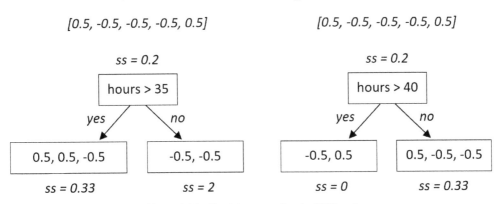

Figure 8.10 – Decision trees for the XGBoost

So, which of the two should we use? As we did in the *Contracting a decision tree* section of *Chapter 3, Classifying Topics of Newsgroup Posts*, we need to calculate some gain value. In the XGBoost case, we utilize a quantity named **similarity score**, given by the following equation:

$$Similarity\ score = \frac{(\sum Residuals)^2}{\sum[P \cdot (1 - P)] + \lambda}$$

The term λ is a regularization parameter, and for convenience, let's make it zero. Regularization, as we already know, reduces the model's sensitivity to individual observations and therefore decreases overfitting. The probably P is the previous prediction of the model (initially the base model), equal to 0.5 in our example. For the lower leaf of the left tree, the equation yields the following:

$$Similarity\ score = \frac{(0.5 + 0.5 - 0.5)^2}{0.5 \cdot (1 - 0.5) + 0.5 \cdot (1 - 0.5) + 0.5 \cdot (1 - 0.5) + 0} = 0.33$$

Figure 8.10 includes all the other similarity scores. To determine the best split in the tree, we compute the gain defined as the following:

$$Gain = Left\ Similarity + Right\ Similarity - Root\ Similarity$$

So, for the left tree, the gain is equal to $0.33 + 2 - 0.2 = 2.13$, and for the right tree, equal to $0 + 0.33 - 0.2 = 0.13$. Based on this information, the tree with the higher gain is chosen, but we must experiment with many thresholds to elicit the best option. The used dataset is very simple, so we obtain a shallow tree. In practice, however, the datasets contain many features, resulting in very deep trees that must be pruned. A relevant metric, in this case, is given by the following equation:

$$Cover\ value = \sum[P \cdot (1 - P)]$$

The **cover value** determines whether the pruning of a branch should take place. So, if the gain is greater than the cover, we can continue further splitting the branch; otherwise, the branch is cut. Note again that P is the previously predicted probability (=0.5 in the example). For the left lower leaf in the figure, the cover value is equal to $0.5 \cdot (1 - 0.5) + 0.5 \cdot (1 - 0.5) + 0.5 \cdot (1 - 0.5) = 0.75$. The outcome is less than the gain, so we can move on to splitting the branch, either using another threshold for the same feature or another feature if present in the dataset.

It's now time to extract the new predictions using the left tree of *Figure 8.10* and the following formula for the outputs of the model:

$$Output = \frac{\sum Residuals}{\sum[P \cdot (1 - P)] + \lambda}$$

The outputs of the two branches are, therefore, the following:

$$Output_{left} = \frac{0.5 + 0.5 - 0.5}{0.5 \cdot (1 - 0.5) + 0.5 \cdot (1 - 0.5) + 0.5 \cdot (1 - 0.5) + 0} = 0.66$$

$$Output_{right} = \frac{-0.5 - 0.5}{0.5 \cdot (1 - 0.5) + 0.5 \cdot (1 - 0.5) + 0} = -2$$

As we did with gradient boosting, we have to add the output of the tree scaled by a learning rate (=0.3 by default) to the initial prediction. In this case, however, we need to convert the latter to **log odds** using the following equation:

$$\log(odds) = \log\left(\frac{P}{1 - P}\right) = \log\left(\frac{0.5}{1 - 0.5}\right) = 0$$

So, the new predicted value for the first student is the following:

$$\log odds(new\_prediction) = \log odds\,(base\_prediction) + learning\_rate \cdot output = 0 + 0.3 \cdot 0.66$$
$$= 0.19$$

To convert the previous quantity back to a probability, we use the following formula:

$$new\ prediction = \frac{e^{\log (odds)}}{1 + e^{\log (odds)}} = \frac{e^{0.19}}{1 + e^{0.19}} = 0.55$$

The P_2 column contains the new prediction for each instance, which shows we are moving in the correct direction. The **residuals_2** column holds the difference between **pass** and P_2. In the next iteration, we train another tree to learn the residuals. As we did with gradient boosting, we can conclude the presentation of XGBoost here. Hopefully, all the previous numerical examples provide a better understanding of the algorithm. We can finally put XGBoost into action in the next section.

Classifying with XGBoost

Before using the method, we need to split our samples into a training set and a test set, using an 80:20 split:

```
import numpy as np
from sklearn.model_selection import train_test_split


# Create the train and test sets.
X_train, X_test, y_train, y_test = train_test_
```

```
split(data['pooled'], data['class'], test_size=0.2,
stratify=data['class'], random_state=123)

print("Number of samples in the training set:", len(X_train))
print("Number of samples in the test set:", len(X_test))
>>
Number of samples in the training set: 19826
Number of samples in the test set: 4957
```

Next, we create the model and fit it to the training data:

```
from xgboost import XGBClassifier
from sklearn.metrics import accuracy_score

# Fit the model to the training data.
model = XGBClassifier()
model.fit(np.vstack(X_train), y_train)
```

Finally, we can evaluate its performance:

```
# Extract the predictions using the test data.
y_pred = model.predict(np.vstack(X_test))
predictions = [round(value) for value in y_pred]

# Evaluate the predictions.
accuracy = accuracy_score(y_test, predictions)
print("Accuracy: %.2f%%" % (accuracy*100.0))
>> Accuracy: 83.92%
```

An accuracy equal to 83.93% is impressive, considering that we didn't apply any fine-tuning to the BERT model. The specific task is still pending, but before we move to that, let's present another crucial topic in machine learning.

Creating validation sets

Throughout the book, we mentioned many times that we need to experiment with multiple configurations of the models to find the optimal one. The most typical pipeline is adjusting the hyperparameters and the topology of deep learning architecture, training on a set of samples, and testing on another set. For that reason, machine learning is a highly iterative process. This strategy engenders a particular risk, however. Evaluating different model configurations with a given test set over multiple rounds leads to a model tuned to work well with the specific set. As the number of epochs increases, we implicitly fit the model to the peculiarities of the test set and consequently get a too-optimistic performance in the end.

We need a way to validate our model performance during training while leaving the test set for the final evaluation. This role is undertaken by the validation set that helps us tune the model's hyperparameters and configurations accordingly. As a result, the model learns the patterns from the training samples without overfitting. Recall that we cannot use the training set to test a model because it might have memorized the training samples. On the other hand, the validation set creates a model bias and is unsuitable for evaluating its generalization performance. The test set keeps unseen samples in the model until the very end, which is why it can offer an honest assessment of the final model.

Learning the myth of Icarus

To understand the synergies between the three sets, consider an analogy based on the famous myth of Daedalus and Icarus. Daedalus, the mythical master craftsman, created the Labyrinth for King Minos. His young son, Icarus, wanted to leave Crete but was prevented by Minos. For this reason, Daedalus created wings out of feathers and wax for his son to escape. Icarus, however, ignored his father's warnings and flew too close to the sun, causing his wings to melt and his subsequent fall into the sea. How does this story relate to the discussion of this section?

Based on his experience, the craftsman could approximate how close to the sun you could fly before the wings' wax melts. This information is the prior knowledge used to create a model and constitutes the training set. On the other hand, the wax melting point can be affected by other factors, such as environmental conditions during the flight. Therefore, we need a way to fine-tune the model's parameters over multiple iterations to compensate for those variations. At this point, the validation set comes into the scene and provides an unbiased evaluation of how well the model fits the data. Finally, the test set evaluates the model's performance on unseen data – in our analogy, the moment Icarus spreads his wing toward the sky and begins his last flight.

Based on the unfortunate outcome of the model (Icarus falling), we can deduce that both the training and validation sets were not representative enough for the wax-wing problem, underestimating the impulsive nature of youth.

Extracting the datasets

In Python, there is no direct way to extract the three datasets in one step, so we need to perform a small trick. First, we call the `train_test_split` method to get the training and test sets from the corpus and then call the same method on the training set to create the validation one. We have done the first step a few times already:

```
import numpy as np
from sklearn.model_selection import train_test_split


# Create the train and test sets.
X_train, X_test, y_train, y_test = train_test_
split(data['tweet'], data['class'], test_size=0.1,
stratify=data['class'], random_state=123)
```

Now, the training set contributes to the creation of the validation set:

```
# Split the train set into validation and smaller training
sets.
X_train, X_val, y_train, y_val = train_test_split(X_train, y_
train, test_size=0.1, stratify=y_train, random_state=123)


print("Number of samples in the training set:", len(X_train))
print("Number of samples in the validation set:", len(X_val))
print("Number of samples in the test set:", len(X_test))
>>
Number of samples in the training set: 20073
Number of samples in the validation set: 2231
Number of samples in the test set: 2479
```

So, at this point, we have at our disposal the three sets to continue the analysis. But how can they be used in practice? A typical technique is to contrast the model's performance on the training and validation sets before deciding on the various trade-offs. A convenient way to perform this task is by plotting the loss after each training round, as shown in *Figure 8.11*:

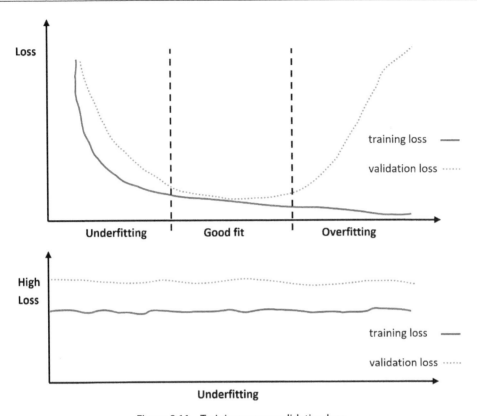

Figure 8.11 – Training versus validation loss

The plots present the conditions of underfitting, good fitting, and overfitting. When both losses steadily decrease, or when both remain flat and high, we face **Underfitting**. We can just let the model train for more time in the first case. In the second case, we can increase the model's number of parameters or its complexity and type. Conversely, **Overfitting** occurs when the two losses diverge; the training loss decreases while the validation increases. As a result, the model learns the training data very well but begins to lose its generalization capacity. Ideally, we would like to be in the area of **Good fit**, and for this to happen, we can halt the training process when the two losses start to diverge. This technique, a form of regularization, is known as **early stopping**.

Hopefully, you should be convinced about the utility of a validation set. But one more problem is still to be resolved, discussed in the next section.

Treating imbalanced datasets

The pending issue from the beginning of the chapter concerns the preliminary observation that the dataset is imbalanced. Specifically, the class distribution has a severe skew, as the offensive tweets prevail in the corpus. Training machine-learning models without mitigating this concern engenders the risk of having a strong bias toward the majority class. A possible strategy to address this problem is to perform **random oversampling** by randomly duplicating examples in the minority class. Conversely, we can randomly delete examples in the majority class using **random undersampling**. In both cases, applying re-sampling strategies leads to more balanced data distributions.

In this section, we attack the problem differently and use **class weighting**. Based on the number of instances in each class, we calculate weights that the model can use to pay more attention to examples from the underrepresented classes:

```
# Calculate the number of instances per class.
hate, offensive, neither = np.bincount(data['class'])
total = hate + offensive + neither


# Assign a weight per class.
weight_for_0 = (1 / hate)*(total)/3.0
weight_for_1 = (1 / offensive)*(total)/3.0
weight_for_2 = (1 / neither)*(total)/3.0
```

The weights are kept for later usage:

```
# Combine all weights into a dictionary.
class_weight = {0: weight_for_0, 1: weight_for_1, 2: weight_
for_2}

print('Weight for class 0: {:.2f}'.format(weight_for_0))
print('Weight for class 1: {:.2f}'.format(weight_for_1))
print('Weight for class 2: {:.2f}'.format(weight_for_2))
>>
Weight for class 0: 5.78
Weight for class 1: 0.43
Weight for class 2: 1.98
```

Based on the output, we observe that the underrepresented class for hate speech receives the highest weight (=5.78). In the next section, we combine the various topics presented so far to create a BERT model for classification.

Classifying with BERT

While BERT was put in action previously in the chapter, we didn't perform any fine-tuning tasks using our dataset. So, this step is part of the current section. Moreover, we need to create a neural architecture consisting of several parts to perform classification. The `build_classifier_model` method that follows shows the structure of the specific architecture:

```
# Method to build the classifier model.
def build_classifier_model():

    text_input = tf.keras.layers.Input(shape=(), dtype=tf.string,
name='text')
    preprocessing_layer = hub.KerasLayer(tfhub_handle_preprocess,
name='preprocessing')
    encoder_inputs = preprocessing_layer(text_input)
    encoder = hub.KerasLayer(tfhub_handle_encoder,
trainable=True, name='BERT_encoder')
    outputs = encoder(encoder_inputs)
    net = outputs['pooled_output']
    net = tf.keras.layers.Dropout(0.1)(net)
    net = tf.keras.layers.Dense(3, activation="softmax",
name='classifier')(net)

    return tf.keras.Model(text_input, net)
```

The structure of the model consists of an input layer, a preprocessing layer, a stack of encoders, a dropout layer, and a classification layer. Most of them should be familiar to you, so let's address a few key points. First, notice that BERT is fine-tuned by the text data included in `encoder_inputs`.

Dropout refers to dropping out units (both hidden and visible) in a neural network. More technically, dropout ignores randomly selected neurons during the forward and backward training passes. The reason for using this regularization technique is to attack overfitting by reducing the interdependent learning among the neurons. The dropout layer receives as input the embedding of each tweet (`pooled_output`).

The final dense layer takes the output of the dropout layer and normalizes the likelihood of each tweet being classified in one of the three classes using the `softmax` function. The number of trainable parameters in this setting is given here:

```
# Build the classifier model.
classifier_model = build_classifier_model()
```

```
classifier_model.summary()
>>
...
Total params: 28,765,188
Trainable params: 28,765,187
Non-trainable params: 1
```

We can also visualize the structure of the model and store the output in a file:

```
# Save the model architecture into a file.
tf.keras.utils.plot_model(classifier_model, to_file='./data/
bert-model.png')
```

The building blocks of the model are illustrated in *Figure 8.12*:

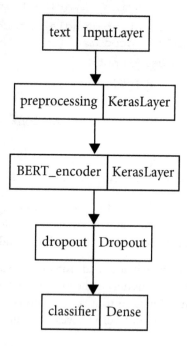

Figure 8.12 – Model architecture

Then, we convert the three datasets to a `tf.data` type because it provides flexibility in handling the data in TensorFlow:

```
# Create the three datasets.
train_ds = tf.data.Dataset.from_tensor_slices((X_train, y_
```

```
train))
val_ds = tf.data.Dataset.from_tensor_slices((X_val, y_val))
test_ds = tf.data.Dataset.from_tensor_slices((X_test, y_test))


# Combine consecutive samples into batches.
train_ds = train_ds.shuffle(len(X_train), seed=1).batch(32,
drop_remainder=False)
val_ds = val_ds.shuffle(len(X_val), seed=1).batch(32, drop_
remainder=False)
test_ds = test_ds.shuffle(len(X_test), seed=1).batch(32, drop_
remainder=False)
```

Let's define the loss function using accuracy as a metric. In this case, we compute the cross-entropy loss between the labels and predictions:

```
# Define the loss function and metric.
loss = tf.keras.losses.SparseCategoricalCrossentropy(from_
logits=False)
metrics = tf.keras.metrics.
SparseCategoricalAccuracy('accuracy')
```

Then, we set a few important parameters for the optimizer and proceed to the compilation of the model:

```
# Set the different parameters for the optimizer.
epochs = 15
steps_per_epoch = tf.data.experimental.cardinality(train_ds).
numpy()
num_train_steps = steps_per_epoch * epochs
num_warmup_steps = int(0.1*num_train_steps)


init_lr = 3e-5
optimizer = optimization.create_optimizer(init_lr=init_lr, num_
train_steps=num_train_steps, num_warmup_steps=num_warmup_steps,
optimizer_type='adamw')


# Compile the model.
classifier_model.compile(optimizer=optimizer, loss=loss,
metrics=metrics)
```

The model is now in place to proceed to the next step.

Training the classifier

Finally, we can start training the classifier. While fitting the model to the data, we use `class_weight` to make the classifier heavily weighted toward the minority classes:

```
print(f'Training model with {tfhub_handle_encoder}')
# Train the model.
history = classifier_model.fit(x=train_ds, validation_data=val_
ds, epochs=epochs, class_weight=class_weight)
>>
Training model with https://tfhub.dev/tensorflow/small_bert/
bert_en_uncased_L-4_H-512_A-8/1
Epoch 1/15
628/628 [==============================] - 744s 1s/step - loss:
0.8942 - accuracy: 0.6384 - val_loss: 0.6206 - val_accuracy:
0.7701

. . .

Epoch 7/15
628/628 [==============================] - 727s 1s/step - loss:
0.1926 - accuracy: 0.9498 - val_loss: 0.5015 - val_accuracy:
0.8714

. . .

Epoch 15/15
628/628 [==============================] - 740s 1s/step - loss:
0.0384 - accuracy: 0.9916 - val_loss: 0.7343 - val_accuracy:
0.8969
```

The performance after 15 epochs is as follows:

```
loss, accuracy = classifier_model.evaluate(test_ds)

print(f'Loss: {loss}')
print(f'Accuracy: {accuracy}')
>>
Loss: 0.7823630571365356
Accuracy: 0.8951190114021301
```

The accuracy is equal to 89.5%, which is better than the accuracy obtained in the *Classifying with XGBoost* section. We can also extract the model's prediction using three example tweets from the test set:

```
# Use three examples from the test set.
examples = [
```

```
     'I hate the ghetto trash at the special school across
the street from my building. All of them will grow up to be
criminals.',
     'God my tweets are so ghetto',
     'i wanna go to the ghetto club tonight.']


# Predict the classes of the examples.
result = classifier_model.predict(examples)
y_pred = np.argmax(result, axis=-1)
print(y_pred)
>>
[0 1 2]
```

The output suggests that all three examples received the correct label. The first example is classified with the hate speech label (=0), the second as offensive speech (=1), and the third as neither (=2).

Applying early stopping

However, did we perhaps miss an important step and forget applying early stopping? In the code that follows, we generate the loss and accuracy plots for the training and validation sets:

```
# Print the training and validation accuracy and loss.
history_dict = history.history

acc = history_dict['accuracy']
val_acc = history_dict['val_accuracy']
loss = history_dict['loss']
val_loss = history_dict['val_loss']

epochs = range(1, len(acc)+1)

# Show the first plot.
plt.plot(epochs, loss, 'r', label='Training loss')
plt.plot(epochs, val_loss, 'b', linestyle='None', marker='o',
label='Validation loss')

# Show the second plot.
plt.plot(epochs, acc, 'r', label='Training acc')
```

```
plt.plot(epochs, val_acc, 'b', linestyle='None', marker='o',
label='Validation acc')
```

The output is shown in *Figure 8.13*:

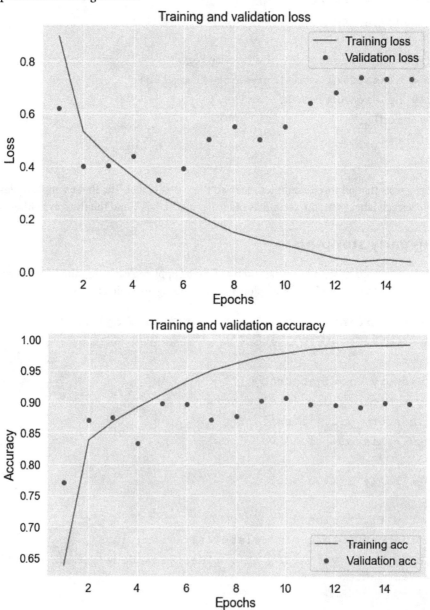

Figure 8.13 – Plots of the training and validation loss and accuracy

According to the previous output, we should apply early stopping after the seventh epoch, when the validation loss starts to increase. At this point, the accuracy for the training set is 94.98% (recheck the output after training the model). Another interesting observation comes from the second plot. Although the loss for the validation set increases, the relevant accuracy remains the same. How can this be correct?

To decipher this mystery, we need to understand what each quantity measures. Loss computes the difference between the prediction and the actual value. Accuracy, however, measures the difference between a threshold and the actual value. For accuracy to change, we need to move above or under the threshold, making it more resilient to changes. So, as the model overfits, the loss increases in the validation set, but the model can still predict correctly the same instances.

The following section concludes the current chapter and discusses an important neural network.

Understanding CNN

A **convolutional neural network** (**CNN** or **ConvNet**) is a category of neural network. It can include one or more convolutional layers capable of efficiently processing spatial patterns in data with a grid-like topology. Therefore, CNNs find extensive utility in image-processing applications that work with two-dimensional image data. The layers are arranged in such a way as to detect simpler or more complex patterns.

For example, in an image classification task, the first layers can identify simpler features such as lines and arcs. In contrast, the layers, further along, can detect patterns such as part of a face or an object. So, a CNN made of a single layer can only learn low-level features, and in typical applications, we stack more than one. The plot in *Figure 8.14* illustrates this process:

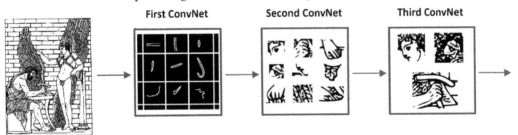

Figure 8.14 – Stacking convolutional layers

Each convolutional layer of the network includes a set of *kernels*, also known as *filters*, that aim to extract different features from the input. In **First ConvNet**, for example, we observe six filters to detect the different edges of the image. Their output is fed to **Second ConvNet** to identify higher-level features, such as an eye or fingers. Finally, the last layer can detect more complex patterns based on the output of the second layer. Note that none of the filters are predefined, and it's up to the neural network to extract its kernels during the training phase. The developer can only set the number of filters, their size, and a few other parameters discussed later.

Let's now examine the function of each filter in more detail. A filter is essentially a small window that slides across an image, applying an operation called **convolution**. This is a linear operation, depicted with the * symbol, and involves the multiplication of the set of weights of the filter with the input. *Figure 8.15* presents an example of the specific operation:

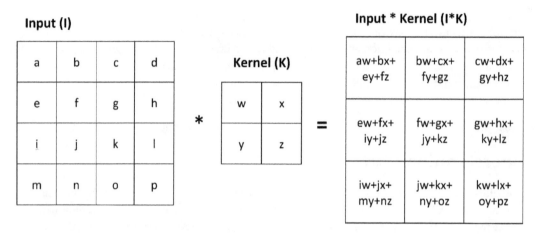

Figure 8.15 – The convolution operation

Imagine that **K** is superimposed over **I** and slides one step either horizontally or vertically at each time step. The cells of the output matrix (**I*K**) result from performing element-wise multiplication with the part of the input that the filter is on. Later, this quantity is summed. Multiple filters exist in each convolutional layer, and their weights can be learned through backpropagation. Apart from the kernel size (in the previous example, equal to two), we can also set two important hyperparameters, namely the *stride* and *padding*. Stride refers to the filter's step as it slides over the input. A stride equal to one was used in the previous example, while another standard option is a two-step stride. Incorporating too large values engenders the risk of skipping important information in the input matrix. On the other hand, there are fewer calculations, which increases speed.

In the example of *Figure 8.15*, the 4x4 input matrix convolved with the filter to produce a 3x3 output. If we wanted to obtain an output matrix that is the exact same size as the input one, we can apply a simple trick: pad the input with zeros around the edges. In this case, part of the kernel can overlay outside the initial input matrix and use the zero values for the convolution calculations. Adding padding allows a more accurate input data analysis and prevents shrinkage. On the other hand, applying convolution without padding reduces the dimensions of the output matrix in each CNN layer to the extent that it would not be able to extract any features in the data.

Equipped with the understanding of the convolution operation, let's examine in more detail the steps in a convolutional layer. Suppose we would like to process a 3x3 color image, which is just three matrices of pixels for each primary color: red, green, and blue. In the specific scenario, we incorporate one 3x3 kernel for each color channel, using padding and a stride equal to one. *Figure 8.16* demonstrates each of the steps:

Input (RGB)

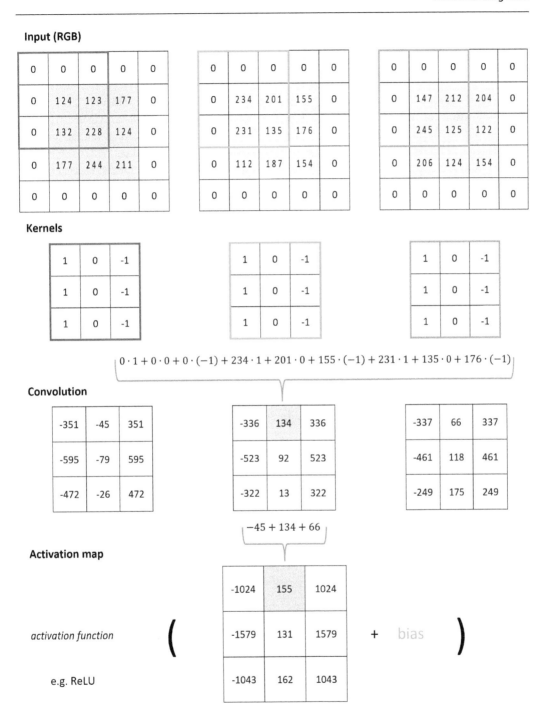

Figure 8.16 – Calculations in the convolutional layer

Each input matrix is convolved with the same filter that detects vertical lines in images. The output is summed and passed through an activation function, including a bias term. The result is an **activation map**, also known as a **feature map**, that defines which information is passed to the next layer.

Images offer a convenient way to understand how convolution works, but how can we intuitively relate the same function to text data? At first glance, this is not so straightforward. Texts have only one dimension, unlike images, and the convolution, in this case, is one-dimensional. As each filter detects a pattern such as a line or texture in an image, a text pattern can be a short phrase. You can think of these phrases as *n*-grams that activate the relevant filter. Therefore, using CNNs for text classification yields learning filters that can identify *n*-grams. Before using this layer to address the problem of this chapter, we need to introduce one more topic.

Adding pooling layers

Convolutional networks frequently work in tandem with another layer type called the **pooling** layer to generate less complex models. It aims to retain the important information of the features extracted from the ConvNet and discard the less important ones. In practice, this leads to fewer model parameters, speeding up computation and reducing the risk of overfitting. The most common variants of this method are *max*, *average*, and *sum* pooling.

In the case of max pooling, we define a spatial neighborhood and extract the largest value of the rectified feature map inside this area. We can also take the average of these numbers or their sum. In most practical applications, max pooling is chosen. An example is shown in *Figure 8.17*, using a 4x4 activation map, a 2x2 window, and a stride equal to **2**:

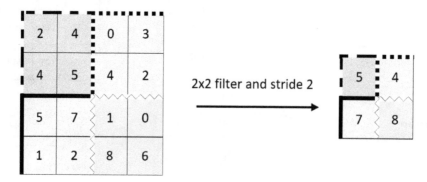

Figure 8.17 – The max pooling operation

To conclude, the convolution operation aims to extract matches with patterns while pooling aggregates of these matches over different positions. Let's now proceed to add the CNN layers to the model.

Including CNN layers

To incorporate the CNN layers, we will use the same structure for the neural network, including a few more components, as shown in the following code:

```
def build_classifier_model():

  ...

  outputs = encoder(encoder_inputs)
  net = sequence_output = outputs["sequence_output"]

  net = tf.keras.layers.Conv1D(128, (3), activation='relu')
(net)
  net = tf.keras.layers.Conv1D(64, (3), activation='relu')(net)
  net = tf.keras.layers.Conv1D(32, (3), activation='relu')(net)
  net = tf.keras.layers.GlobalMaxPool1D()(net)
  net = tf.keras.layers.Dense(512, activation="relu")(net)

  ...

  return tf.keras.Model(text_input, net)
```

Specifically, three 1D convolution layers are added, using 128, 64, and 32 filters respectively, and with a 3x3 kernel size. We also apply max pooling and feed the output to a dense layer with 512 units. Also, note the usage of `sequence_output` from the BERT output for experimenting with the new architecture. Next, we will plot the architecture of the model:

```
tf.keras.utils.plot_model(cnn_classifier_model, to_file='./
data/bert-cnn--model.png')
```

The output is shown in *Figure 8.18*:

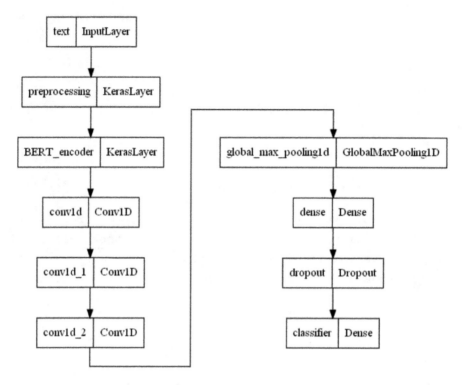

Figure 8.18 – Model architecture (CNN)

The rest of the code remains unaltered, and we can proceed to the training phase:

```
print(f'Training model with {tfhub_handle_encoder}')
# Train the model.
history = classifier_model.fit(x=train_ds, validation_data=val_
ds, epochs=epochs, class_weight=class_weight)
>>
...
Epoch 7/15
628/628 [==============================] - 753s 1s/step - loss:
0.2343 - accuracy: 0.9388 - val_loss: 0.3681 - val_accuracy:
0.8991
...
Epoch 15/15
628/628 [==============================] - 733s 1s/step - loss:
```

```
0.0566 - accuracy: 0.9890 - val_loss: 0.6212 - val_accuracy:
0.9014
```

As we did previously, we plot the loss for the training and validation sets, shown in *Figure 8.19*:

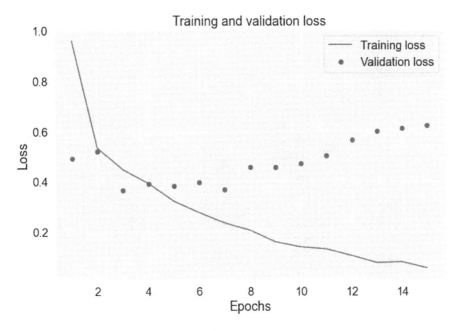

Figure 8.19 – The plot of the training and validation loss

We do not observe any significant difference, and the addition of CNN layers didn't offer any tangible improvement. As we have mentioned multiple times throughout the book, choosing the correct values for the hyperparameters and the neural network topology is a matter of experimentation. Coupled with the validation set, we have one more powerful tool to control the training process.

Summary

This chapter focused on identifying hateful and offensive language in tweets. Considering the intriguing nature of the specific task, we tried to provide a strong model from a technical perspective. In this respect, we had the opportunity to work with more advanced neural architectures and also strengthen our knowledge of new ML concepts.

Throughout the chapter, we had the chance to observe the benefits of transfer learning, which allow the construction of sophisticated applications with minimal effort. The BERT language model is a typical example and permits the fine-tuning of pre-trained models with our custom datasets. This chapter focused on more advanced techniques for text classification that belong to the family of boosting algorithms, particularly XGBoost, the hype of which was driven by its superior performance in various competitions.

The role of the validation set to fine-tune the model's hyperparameters and the strategies to deal with imbalanced data was an essential part of the chapter. Finally, we concluded with the presentation of convolutional layers, which are specialized to detect patterns in spatial data, such as images, but can also be applied in text processing.

The next chapter deals with another booming area in machine learning for text: *chatbots*.

9

Generating Text in Chatbots

Cutting-edge artificial intelligence applications can now produce uncannily humanlike creations, from written essays to music and drawings. These applications are a great promise toward artificial general intelligence, to the point where machines understand or learn any intellectual task that humans can perform. Unhindered conversation with a machine has always been at the forefront of this vision. Interestingly, the most common depiction of machine intelligence in popular culture is conversational agents that can mimic human dialogs. In this chapter, we will deal with a particular type: chatbots.

Chatbots have received much hype in recent years; in this chapter, we will discuss related topics from the perspective of natural language generation. Particular emphasis is given to language modeling, which is an integral part of modern chatbot deployments. First, we will look deeper at this core component of modern natural language processing and contrast two approaches based on the transformer architecture. Then, we will put this knowledge into action by building a language model from scratch and evaluating its performance on a publicly available corpus.

In the last section of this chapter, we will examine how to use pre-trained language models to create a chatbot. Transfer learning, in this case, is a safety net, allowing us to adjust these models for any custom application. In this context, we will perform fine-tuning using techniques such as reinforcement learning. By the end of this chapter, you will be capable of creating a language model or fine-tuning a pre-trained one.

We will go through the following topics:

- Understanding the different types of chatbots
- Understanding, building, and fine-tuning language models
- Applying the proper evaluation metrics for language models
- Using tools to visualize the machine learning workflow
- Implementing graphical user interfaces

Technical requirements

The chapter's code has been truncated in certain parts to facilitate reading the content. However, the entire code is available as different Jupyter notebooks in this book's GitHub repository: `https://github.com/PacktPublishing/Machine-Learning-Techniques-for-Text/tree/main/chapter-09`.

Understanding text generation

Our access to various services gradually evolves to become technology-driven rather than human-driven. Try to think of the last time you contacted the call center of a company, where an automated system probably answered your call. Replacing the human factor presents many competitive advantages in terms of cost and availability. However, these systems do not fully incorporate the communicative behaviors humans use and therefore are limited in reaching their full potential. The effort, in any case, is to create machines that are increasingly adept at sounding human and can pass the **Turing test**, which has long been a benchmark for machine intelligence.

> **Interesting fact**
>
> In 1950, the ingenious computer scientist Alan Turing introduced a test to check whether a machine can consistently fool an interviewer into believing it is a human. Today, the test refers to a more general behavioral benchmark for the presence of intelligence.

Natural language generation (**NLG**) is an emerging research area that uses artificial intelligence to generate human language, and it's a subcategory of natural language processing. NLG systems can be used in various contexts to describe an image with a short sentence, generate news feeds, or even spread personalized propaganda and misinformation. In this chapter, we will tackle the generative processes in natural language processing with a particular focus on conversational agents, also known as chatbots.

Chatbots find extensive usage in various tasks; for example, in large organizations, they answer customer queries; in education, they assist in teaching a new language; and in research, they gather data from real humans. Their input and output can utilize different communication channels, such as speech, text, or even facial expressions and gestures. Broadly, they can be categorized into two main types: **retrieval** and **generative-based chatbots**. Agents in the first category are used in closed-domain scenarios and rely on a collection of predefined responses to the user input. On the other hand, generative chatbots produce original combinations of phrases rather than selecting them from a list of options. As this chapter unfolds, we will present both types while focusing more on the second category.

The coding examples incorporate **PyTorch** (`https://pytorch.org`), another prevailing machine learning framework. Moreover, to facilitate the work on language modeling, we will utilize **Hugging Face** (`https://huggingface.co/`), which offers many state-of-the-art pre-trained models and datasets. In this way, you will significantly enhance your machine learning toolbox and skillset.

Let's begin by creating a retrieval chatbot.

Creating a retrieval-based chatbot

The implementation in this section is inspired by **ELIZA** (https://web.njit.edu/~ronkowit/eliza.html), an early chatbot, and one of the first programs capable of attempting the Turing test. It simulated a psychotherapist in an initial psychiatric interview to demonstrate the superficiality of the communication between man and machine. The client performed the conversation using pattern matching and substitution methodology.

First, we need to set a list with possible patterns and the relevant responses using the code in the chatbot.ipynb notebook:

```
from nltk.chat.util import import Chat, reflections


# Pairs of patterns and responses.
pairs = (
    (
        r"I need (.*)",
        (
            "Why do you need %1?",
            "Would it really help you to get %1?",
            "Are you sure you need %1?",
        ),
    ),
    (
        r"Why don\'t you (.*)",
        (
            "Do you really think I don't %1?",
...
```

The reason for using more than one answer (chosen randomly by the nltk module) is to make the dialog a little more engaging. Observe the %1 notation, which displays the match pattern inside, (.*). The more patterns are included in the list, the more *intelligent* the interaction becomes. At the same time, however, it complicates how the chatbot can be managed. While crafting the translation rules in *Chapter 6, Teaching Machines to Translate*, we saw similar challenges. Both suffer from the same shortcoming: relying on scarce and costly human knowledge.

Next, to make the interaction even more interesting, we will define a set of substitution words:

```
# Substitute words in the string, according to the specified
reflections, e.g. "I'm" -> "you are".
reflections = {
    "i am": "you are",
    "i was": "you were",
    "i": "you",
    "i'm": "you are",
    "i'd": "you would",
    "i've": "you have",
    "i'll": "you will",
    "my": "your",
...
```

For example, when the chatbot encounters the string *I am* in the input, it flips it to *you are* in the response. Now, let's define the main method for chatting:

```
# Create the bot.
eliza = Chat(pairs, reflections)

# The main chat method.
def eliza_chat():
    print("Chat with Eliza!")
    print('Enter "quit" to stop.')
    print("---")
    print("Hello. How are you feeling today?")


    eliza.converse()
```

Finally, we can begin the conversation with the bot:

```
# Begin to chat.
eliza_chat()
>>
Chat with Eliza!
Enter "quit" to stop.
---
Hello. How are you feeling today?
```

```
>I am feeling good!
Did you come to me because you are feeling good?
>Yes
You seem quite sure.
> I'm
Why do you say that you are?
>quit
Thank you for talking with me.
```

Here, we can observe `reflections` in action. The response to *I'm* ends with the phrase *you are*. Unfortunately, `eliza` is an elementary chatbot, which can hardly be scaled to support unhindered communication. So, in the rest of this chapter, we will explore state-of-the-art solutions for constructing conversational agents. As we have done several times already, we will begin with the necessary context before proceeding to the implementation. In the following section, the discussion is around the critical topic of language modeling.

Understanding language modeling

Language models are key ingredients for creating chatbots and many natural language processing applications. In the *Modeling the translation problem* section of *Chapter 6*, *Teaching Machines to Translate*, we stated that a language model expresses our confidence that a sentence is probable in the target language. Probability in this context does not necessarily refer to whether a sentence is grammatically correct but how it resembles how people write. Essentially, a language model learns from text resources, which can contain ungrammatical sentences, misspelled words, slang, biases, and so forth. Therefore, it is a probability distribution over words or word sequences derived from the training corpus.

In simple terms, the objective is to predict the next word, given all previous words within some text. A familiar example is the autocomplete feature in Google's search bar, which allows you to construct search queries. In this chapter, we will revisit language models to provide a broader understanding of this fundamental concept in natural language processing. Again, the focus is on text generation systems, which is where these models shine.

In *Chapter 8*, *Detecting Hateful and Offensive Language*, we discussed how state-of-the-art models, such as BERT, can be incorporated into a neural network to facilitate text classification. While BERT utilizes a stack of encoders to create the model, other architectures are very similar to the decoder-only transformer. One of the most prominent options is **Generative Pre-Trained Transformer 2 (GPT-2)**, with 1.5 billion parameters trained on a corpus of 8 million scraped web pages. As in BERT, there are many variants of GPT-2 in terms of size, the smaller of which takes up 500 MB of storage, while the largest is 6.5 GB. Besides their main difference in using either an encoder or a decoder architecture, the two models differ in another significant way.

GPT-2 works like a traditional language model as it outputs one token at a time. This output token is added to the sequence of inputs in the next time step. Models, where the observations from the previous time steps are used to predict the value at the current one, are called **autoregressive**. On the other hand, BERT is not autoregressive, as it uses the entire surrounding context. The masking mechanism that's incorporated during the training phase corrupts a few input tokens and directs BERT to find the words that better predict the masked ones. Reconstructing the initial input is what autoencoders do, so BERT is an **autoencoding** model. A relevant discussion can be found in the *Introducing autoencoders* section of *Chapter 5, Recommending Music Titles*.

You are probably wondering which option is better for a given problem. Without providing a conclusive answer, the natural application for the autoencoding models is text classification because they build a bidirectional representation of the input. By contrast, the autoregressive models only know what they have seen so far in the input, so they are suitable for text generation. In this chapter, we will use the second option to create our chatbots. But first, let's discuss a related topic.

Understanding perplexity

In the previous chapters, we came across various automatic metrics for assessing the performance of natural language processing systems, such as the **Word Error Rate (WER)** and the **Recall-Oriented Understudy for Gisting Evaluation (ROUGE)** scores. On the other hand, recruiting human subjects is an attractive alternative because it permits measuring performance using specific target groups on real-world tasks. For example, professional translators can better access the translation quality instead of a metric such as the **BiLingual Evaluation Understudy (BLEU)** score. Nevertheless, this manual assessment comes with a price, as human evaluations are costly, slow, and often generate inconsistent results. As a result, it is not uncommon to use both automatic and manual approaches to assess the intermediary and the final objectives of an NLP system, known as **intrinsic** and **extrinsic evaluation**, respectively.

In language modeling, we can perform an extrinsic evaluation by letting the model generate a large number of sentences and asking human annotators to rate each one. In this case, the main challenge is deciding which of the model's different variants to evaluate based on their configuration. Adjusting the model's hyperparameters, an essential part of the training phase, leads to a new set of output sentences that needs to be rated. In practice, we can carry out a small fraction of human evaluations, making it hard to elicit the most efficient language model.

A convenient alternative, in this case, is some intrinsic property of the model to estimate its quality independently of the tasks it has to perform. Consider the following analogy: a small number of college students must be selected for the basketball team. Height is an intrinsic property of each student. An increased height does not guarantee higher basketball performance but correlates well. Therefore, first, we can evaluate all students solely on their height and pick a small fraction for the actual draft on the court.

A commonly used intrinsic metric to evaluate language models is **perplexity (PPL)**. Intuitively, it tells us how perplexed the model is after encountering a piece of text. The smaller the model's surprise, the better its performance. Measuring the complexity using PPL is suitable because it lets us compare different models on the same corpus. In the next section, we will consider an example to clarify this concept.

Introducing a numerical example

Suppose that we have a slot machine with five vertical reels that spin, as shown in *Figure 9.1*:

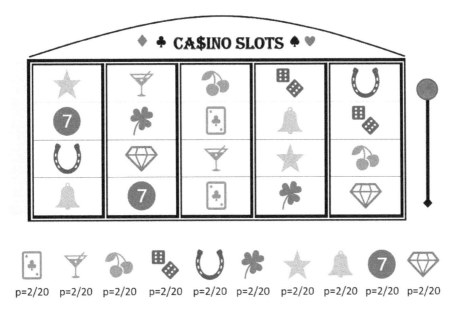

Figure 9.1 – Slot machine with equiprobable symbols

The slot machine is a model that can output a discrete random variable using 10 different symbols in each reel (such as cherries, dice, and so on). So, we can say that the *vocabulary* of the slot machine is equal to 10. The number of possible next symbols that can follow any symbol is equal to the vocabulary size, and it's called the **branching factor**. In the simplest scenario, the output in each reel is independent of the other, just like in a unigram language model.

Four possible outcomes of this process are shown in the preceding figure, which constitutes a tiny training set for the model. The random variable has a uniform probability distribution, as each symbol has an equal chance of appearing in the sequences (=**2/20**). In general, rare symbols (low probability) are more surprising than common symbols (high probability). To determine how *surprised* the model is upon encountering one of the symbols – for example, cherries – we can use a quantity that expresses the fact that surprising events provide more information:

$$information(cherries) = -\log_2(p(cherries)) = -\log_2\left(\frac{2}{20}\right) = 3.32$$

Then, we can perform the same calculation for all symbols and combine the output to extract the entropy measure. Recall the discussion on measuring uncertainty in the *Contracting a decision tree* section of *Chapter 3*, *Classifying Topics of Newsgroup Posts*. The following formula gives us the entropy:

$$E(S) = -\sum_{i=1}^{c} p_i log_2 p_i$$

In our case, the equiprobable symbols yield the following value:

$$E(S) = -\left(\frac{2}{20} \cdot log_2\left(\frac{2}{20}\right) + \frac{2}{20} \cdot log_2\left(\frac{2}{20}\right) + \frac{2}{20} \cdot log_2\left(\frac{2}{20}\right) + \frac{2}{20} \cdot log_2\left(\frac{2}{20}\right) + \frac{2}{20}\right.$$
$$\cdot log_2\left(\frac{2}{20}\right) + \frac{2}{20} \cdot log_2\left(\frac{2}{20}\right) + \frac{2}{20} \cdot log_2\left(\frac{2}{20}\right) + \frac{2}{20} \cdot log_2\left(\frac{2}{20}\right) + \frac{2}{20}$$
$$\left.\cdot log_2\left(\frac{2}{20}\right) + \frac{2}{20} \cdot log_2\left(\frac{2}{20}\right)\right) = 3.32$$

Finally, the perplexity is calculated by exponentiating entropy:

$$PPL(X) = 2^{E(s)} = 2^{3.32} = 10$$

What does the previous result tell us? PPL, in this case, is equal to the initial vocabulary size. The model (slot machine) is as perplexed as if it had to choose randomly between 10 options. Therefore, PPL can be considered the model's average branching factor.

Now, let's see what happens when the symbols stop having the same probability, as shown in *Figure 9.2*:

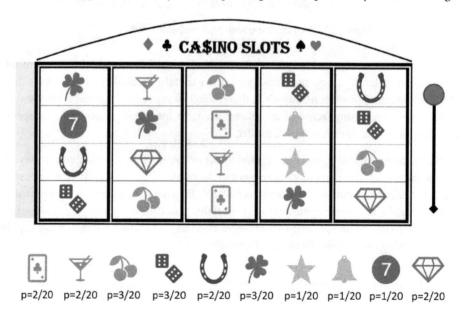

Figure 9.2 – Slot machine with non-equiprobable symbols

The new entropy is as follows:

$$E(S) = -\left(\frac{2}{20} \cdot \log_2\left(\frac{2}{20}\right) + \frac{2}{20} \cdot \log_2\left(\frac{2}{20}\right) + \frac{3}{20} \cdot \log_2\left(\frac{3}{20}\right) + \frac{3}{20} \cdot \log_2\left(\frac{3}{20}\right) + \frac{2}{20}\right.$$
$$\cdot \log_2\left(\frac{2}{20}\right) + \frac{3}{20} \cdot \log_2\left(\frac{3}{20}\right) + \frac{1}{20} \cdot \log_2\left(\frac{1}{20}\right) + \frac{1}{20} \cdot \log_2\left(\frac{1}{20}\right) + \frac{1}{20}$$
$$\left.\cdot \log_2\left(\frac{1}{20}\right) + \frac{2}{20} \cdot \log_2\left(\frac{2}{20}\right)\right) = 1.43$$

The perplexity now becomes this:

$$PPL(X) = 2^{E(s)} = 2^{1.43} = 2.69$$

The result suggests that the new model is much less perplexed as if it had to pick between 2.69 words at each reel. In general, obtaining models with lower PPL correlates well with better quality.

Understanding the perplexity of language models

The probability distributions for the different events were set in the previously contrived numerical example. However, a language model is an abstract, idealized description of the data-generating process in mathematical terms that tries to estimate the real probability distributions. For that reason, we must extract a revised formula for perplexity.

The first quantity to be calculated is the likelihood of a sequence with m tokens, which is the product of each token's probability using the language model:

$$P(X) = \prod_{i=0}^{m} p(x_i|x_{<i})$$

For example, considering the phrase *I love pizza*, we can calculate its likelihood:

$$\prod_{i=0}^{2} p(x_i|x_{<i}) = p("pizza"|"I", "love") \cdot p("love"|"I") \cdot p("I")$$

Notice that a common problem when multiplying small quantities, such as probabilities, is that the number can become too small to be represented by a computer (causing an underflow). Thus, the trick is to transform multiplication into addition by taking the log of the likelihood:

$$log_2 \prod_{i=0}^{m} p(x_i|x_{<i}) = \sum_{i=0}^{m} log_2 p(x_i|x_{<i})$$

Normalizing the result, we get the **cross-entropy loss** function:

$$CE = -\frac{1}{m}\sum_{i=0}^{m} log_2 p(x_i|x_{<i})$$

Recall from the *Introducing linear regression* section of *Chapter 4, Extracting Sentiments from Product Reviews*, that loss functions intuitively inform us about some cost associated with a decision. Furthermore, cross-entropy in language modeling helps while predicting the tokens. By exponentiating the previous quantity, we obtain perplexity:

$$PPL(X) = b^{CE(X)} = b^{-\frac{1}{m}\Sigma_{i=0}^{m} log_b p(x_i|x_{<i})}$$

While cross-entropy traditionally uses logarithm base 2 (b=2), deep learning frameworks such as PyTorch use the natural logarithm e (b=e).

Now that we're equipped with a good understanding of the essential elements of perplexity, we can proceed to the coding part. To demonstrate these steps, we will calculate the PPL of a model available from Hugging Face.

Calculating perplexity

In the code included in the `perplexity.ipynb` notebook, we measure the PPL of the `gpt2` model using three datasets:

```
import torch
from transformers import GPT2LMHeadModel, GPT2TokenizerFast

device = torch.device("cuda" if torch.cuda.is_available() else
"cpu")

# Load the models.
model_name = "gpt2"

model = GPT2LMHeadModel.from_pretrained(model_name).to(device)
tokenizer = GPT2TokenizerFast.from_pretrained(model_name)
```

The PPL calculation consists of different steps:

1. First, we define a few initialization variables and then the appropriate method:

    ```
    from tqdm import tqdm
    ```

```
max_len = model.config.n_positions
#  Use at least 512 tokens for context.
stride = 512

# Calculate the perplexity of the model.
def calc_perplexity(encodings):
    stack = []
```

2. Then, we start reading the data using a sliding window for the context:

```
for i in tqdm(range(0, encodings.input_ids.size(1),
stride)):
        start_pos = max(stride-max_len+i, 0)
        end_pos = min(i+stride, encodings.input_ids.
size(1))
        trg_len = end_pos - i
        inp_ids = encodings.input_ids[:, start_pos:end_
pos].to(device)
        trg_ids = inp_ids.clone()
        trg_ids[:, :-trg_len] = -100
```

3. Now, we can calculate the negative log-likelihood:

```
# Calculate the negative log likelihood.
with torch.no_grad():
    out = model(inp_ids, labels=trg_ids)
    nll = out[0] * trg_len

# Negative log-likelihood stack.
stack.append(nll)
```

4. Finally, the method returns the calculated perplexity:

```
return torch.exp(torch.stack(stack).sum()/end_pos)
```

Next, it's time to evaluate the model on the three diverse datasets:

```
from datasets import load_dataset

# Load the dataset.
testset = load_dataset("wikitext", "wikitext-2-raw-v1",
```

```
split="test")
encodings = tokenizer("\n\n".join(testset["text"]), return_
tensors="pt")
print("The perplexity of the model: %.2f" % calc_
perplexity(encodings).item())


# Load the dataset.
testset = load_dataset("tiny_shakespeare", "default",
split="test")
...


# Load the dataset.
testset = load_dataset("iamholmes/tiny-imdb", "iamholmes--tiny-
imdb", split="test")
...
```

The results are as follows:

```
The perplexity of the wikitext model is: 25.17
The perplexity of the tiny_shakespeare model is: 49.12
The perplexity of the tiny-imdb model is: 42.82
```

As GPT-2 was trained on Wikipedia data, we can observe that the measure on the relevant dataset is lower than the other two. However, notice that this can be partially attributed to the different vocabulary of the datasets, which artificially inflates perplexity. The main disadvantage of PPL is that making meaningful comparisons across datasets is not easy. Generally, each dataset has a distribution of words, and each model has different parameters. So, instead, we often contrast different models trained on the same dataset.

The takeaway message of this section is that PPL measures the model's confidence, not its accuracy. So, it's a proxy for calculating the model's quality. It offers a convenient way to narrow the number of candidate models for a given problem, but it's better to involve real subjects in the final evaluation. We can now proceed with implementing a language model from scratch.

Building a language model

First, we must choose an appropriate model architecture and a sufficiently large dataset to build a language model. This section's implementation is based on the transformer architecture, which has proven to be very efficient for many sequence-to-sequence tasks. Thus, we will adopt the steps from the following tutorial: https://pytorch.org/tutorials/beginner/transformer_tutorial. html. Using an off-the-shelf solution for the encoder layers abstracts many implementation details, making the code less dense and more comprehensible. Notice that all the steps are symmetrical with those presented in the *Introducing transformers* section of *Chapter 7, Summarizing Wikipedia Articles*, and you can always refer there for a quick revision. Finally, we will use the `WikiText2` dataset, which is conveniently available from the `torchtext` library. The corpus is a collection of over 100M tokens extracted from various Wikipedia articles (`https://blog.salesforceairesearch.com/the-wikitext-long-term-dependency-language-modeling-dataset/`).

To save some space, we haven't included all the implementation details that can be found in the `language_modeling.ipynb` notebook, but we will discuss a few highlights that require more attention. First, let's see the architecture of the transformer model:

```
class TransformerModel(nn.Module):
    def __init__(self, voc_size: int, emb_size: int, att_head:
int, ffn_dim: int, layers_num: int, dropout: float = 0.5):
        self.model_type = 'Transformer'
        self.pos_encoder = PositionalEncoding(emb_size,
dropout)
        encoder_layers = TransformerEncoderLayer(emb_size, att_
head, ffn_dim, dropout)
        self.transformer_encoder = TransformerEncoder(encoder_
layers, layers_num)
        self.encoder = nn.Embedding(voc_size, emb_size)
        self.emb_size = emb_size
        self.decoder = nn.Linear(emb_size, voc_size)
...
```

In this setting, we use only specific components from the modular transformer architecture of PyTorch. The network consists of an embedding layer, followed by the positional encoder. Next, two encoder layers are engaged (`layers_num=2`), while the linear layer with a log-softmax function emits the probability distribution of the output words. Recall that the aim here is to create a model that can assign a probability for a word's likelihood to follow a specific word sequence.

To train the model, we will once again use cross-entropy loss and stochastic gradient descent as the optimizer. Specifically, the criterion computes the cross-entropy loss between the input and the target:

```
# Set the criterion.
criterion = nn.CrossEntropyLoss()
# Set the learning rate.
lr = 5.0
# Set the optimizer.
optimizer = torch.optim.SGD(model.parameters(), lr=lr)
```

The original `WikiText2` dataset is organized in pairs of input/target sequences in the form shown in *Figure 9.3*:

Input	Target
If it ain't broke, don't fix it.	Necessity is the mother of invention.
Necessity is the mother of invention.	When in Rome, do as the Romans do.
When in Rome, do as the Romans do.	Beggars can't be choosers.

Figure 9.3 – Input/target pairs for training the model

In this case, the target is the same as the input shifted by one step (the second input sentence becomes the first target). Once more, we want the model to learn to output the correct word based on previous tokens. That is why we have this shift in the training pairs. The code that extracts the input and the target uses chunks of 35 sentences instead of three in the preceding figure:

```
bptt = 35
def obtain_batch(data: Tensor, i: int) -> Tuple[Tensor,
Tensor]:
    chunk_len = min(bptt, len(data) - 1 - i)
    input = data[i:i+chunk_len]
    target = data[i+1:i+1+chunk_len].reshape(-1)
    return input, target
```

During training, we also store the best transformer model based on its performance on the validation set:

```
if val_loss < best_val_loss:
    best_val_loss = val_loss
    best_transformer = copy.deepcopy(model)
```

The `deepcopy` method ensures that a new compound object is created (`best_transformer`) in which we recursively add copies of the items found in the original. A simple (shallow) copy engenders the risk of having changes in the model's inner objects during training that affect the reference variables in the previously stored `best_transformer` object. Finally, the notebook includes two interesting techniques to facilitate the training process. We will examine both in the next two sections.

Dealing with the variations of gradient learning

The first technique applies to deep neural networks that use gradient learning and backpropagation. In the *Understanding long short-term memory units* section of *Chapter 6, Teaching Machines to Translate*, we discussed the vanishing gradient problem, where the partial derivatives traversing the network backward tend to become very small. This problem has a direct impact on the learning of the model's parameters. As a result, earlier layers of the network learn slower than the later ones; in extreme cases, the training process can stop completely. For a long time, this was a major hurdle when training large deep neural networks.

A similar problem arises when the network generates some large loss during the training phase. This situation can lead to very large gradients that generate significant updates to the model's parameters and instability for the network. Again, in extreme cases, we can encounter an overflow in the values of the parameters. One of the remedies to circumvent an **exploding gradient** is to use a technique called **gradient clipping**. As the name suggests, we can clip the gradients during backpropagation to keep them below a certain threshold. Moreover, instead of clipping the values in the gradient vectors, we clip by the norm of the vector. For example, using a clip norm equal to 1.0 rescales the values inside the vector so that its norm equals 1.0; the vector [0.9, 100.0] is clipped to [0.00899, 0.999995].

The relevant step in Python is shown here:

```
torch.nn.utils.clip_grad_norm_(model.parameters(), 0.5)
```

Inside the `train` method, we use `clip_grad_norm_` to keep the gradients within a specific range, a hyperparameter that's configured by trial and error.

Setting the learning rate

The second technique that's used in the notebook concerns the learning rate. In the *Training the model* section of *Chapter 7, Summarizing Wikipedia Articles*, we dealt with the concept of the learning rate and how to choose its value. The strategy was to move fast at the beginning of the training process (high rate) and slow down as we reached the minimum of the loss (low rate). A similar approach has been adopted in this section, where the learning rate decays at each epoch by the gamma parameter:

```
scheduler = torch.optim.lr_scheduler.StepLR(optimizer, 1.0,
gamma=0.95)
```

As we saw earlier, the learning rate for the first epoch is equal to 0.5. By multiplying this number with gamma, we get 4.75, which is the second epoch's learning rate. During the third epoch, it is $4.75 \cdot 0.95 = 4.51$, and so forth.

After training the model for 20 epochs, we achieve the following performance:

```
...
    print('valid loss: %5.2f, valid ppl: %8.2f, time: %5.2fs' %
(val_loss, val_ppl, elapsed))
>>
...
-------------------------------------------------------------
valid loss: 5.56, valid ppl: 260.72, time: 1631.64s
-------------------------------------------------------------
```

Notice that both the validation loss and the model's perplexity are reported in the output. In addition, the increased time to complete this experiment indicates how resource-hungry the training process is. So, you should wait a while before running this code fragment on your computer entirely. The next section discusses a convenient tool for visualizing various parameters while creating a new model.

Using TensorBoard

Despite the astonishing results achieved by models based on deep learning, there is a frequent complaint that their high performance is not easily interpretable. Especially in industries that require clear explanations of the features involved, such as financial institutions, there is an urgent need for tools that shed light on the internals of the models. Moreover, sharing the outcome of the training and evaluation phases is critical for many businesses and research groups. This section presents a tool that can perform the previous tasks seamlessly and be customized according to our needs.

TensorBoard is an open-source tool that can track the output of machine learning experiments and visualize different quantities during the workflow. In addition, it helps us interactively understand the training progress better and choose the appropriate model between competing implementations. Originally, the tool was part of TensorFlow, but now, it's a separate project that can also be incorporated into PyTorch. In this section, we will describe the most basic steps.

Initially, we must create a `writer` object to log various information. By default, all the logged data is placed under the `runs` directory inside a folder named with the current date and time:

```
from torch.utils.tensorboard import SummaryWriter


# Writer will output to ./runs/ directory by default
writer = SummaryWriter()


print('Current run is: ' + writer.get_logdir())
>>
Current run is: runs\Sep20_19-28-21_CL-5CG10472MV
```

The following code snippet demonstrates the way to create the conceptual graph of our model's structure (more about this graph shortly):

```
# Create a sample input for the transformer.
inputs, targets = obtain_batch(val_data, 0)
input_mask = generate_square_subsequent_mask(bptt).to(device)
# Log the graph of the model.
writer.add_graph(model, (data.to(device), input_mask))
```

After each training iteration, `writer` logs the current values for three measures – `Loss`, `Time`, and `Perplexity`:

```
. . .
            print('epoch: %3d, %5d/%5d batches, lr: %02.2f, ms/
batch: %5.2f, loss: %5.2f, ppl: %8.2f' % (epoch, batch, num_
batches, lr, ms_per_batch, cur_loss, ppl))

            # Log the summary for the loss.
            writer.add_scalar('Loss/train', cur_loss, (epoch-
1)*num_batches+batch)

            # Log the summary for the time.
            writer.add_scalar('Time/train', ms_per_batch,
(epoch-1)*num_batches+batch)

            # Log the summary for the time.
            writer.add_scalar('Perplexity/train', ppl, (epoch-
1)*num_batches+batch)
. . .
```

The three real numbers are stored using the `add_scalar` method. Then, we can monitor the training progress inside the browser. TensorBoard includes a built-in web server for this task that we can launch like so:

```
%load_ext tensorboard

%tensorboard --logdir runs/
>> Reusing TensorBoard on port 6006
```

After a few seconds, the web server that hosts the framework will start listening on port 6006. Then, TensorBoard can be accessed at `http://localhost:6006/`. Finally, the output in *Figure 9.4* helps us monitor how the different quantities change over time:

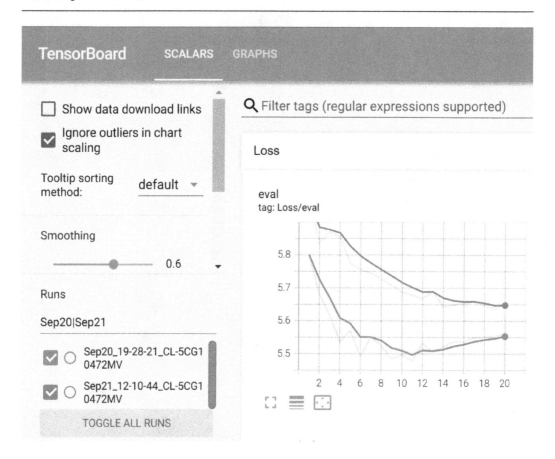

Figure 9.4 – Evaluation loss for two runs in TensorBoard

In this visualization, we are contrasting two versions of the candidate models filtered from the list of **Runs** using the **Sep20|Sep21** regular expression. The comparison is based on the evaluation loss shown in the two plots. The model from the **Sep20** experiment exhibits better performance. An interesting observation concerns the knee point of the evaluation loss in the tenth epoch. At this point, loss receives its lowest value, after which it starts to rise again. Does this ring a bell? In the *Creating validation sets* section of *Chapter 8, Detecting Hateful and Offensive Language*, we had a similar discussion on how validation sets help identify the most efficient model version. Fortunately, the code saves the best version after each epoch, so we can easily apply the early stopping technique.

We can also interact with the conceptual graph of the model. The graph visualizes the different components and how they are interconnected. Therefore, it is a convenient way to examine the model's structure and ensure it conforms to our intended design. For example, in *Figure 9.5*, we can see the two encoder layers included in the network. Clicking on each box allows us to examine their internal structures:

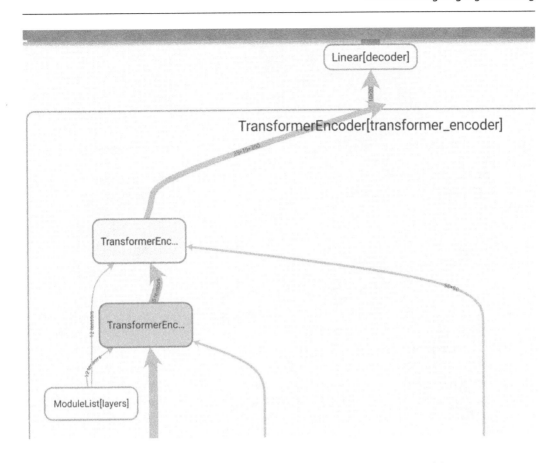

Figure 9.5 – Part of the conceptual graph of the transformer model

Besides being a tool for scrutinizing models and getting better insights, TensorBoard has another role. In today's working environments, sharing the work between different stakeholders is critical because it enables better visibility, reproducibility, and collaboration. *TensorBoard.dev* is a free public service that can host our experiments online. Executing the following command initiates the process of gathering all the relevant files from the local repository and uploading them to the service:

```
!tensorboard dev upload \
  --logdir runs \
  --name "My ML4Text experiment" \
  --description "Comparing two language models" \
  --one_shot
>>
***** TensorBoard Uploader *****
```

```
This will upload your TensorBoard logs to https://tensorboard.
dev/ from the following directory:

runs

. . .
```

At this point, a URL is created so that you can upload your TensorBoard logs and obtain a permalink:

```
Please visit this URL to authorize this application: https://
accounts.google.com/o/oauth2/auth?response_type=code&client_
id=XXX

New experiment created. View your TensorBoard at: https://
tensorboard.dev/experiment/D62fZGL4S66Q08C2alEvoQ/

. . .
```

Using the previous link, we can share our work with others, who can visit and interact with TensorBoard, and the training output runs without the need to install any additional software. The link provided in this example allows us to examine the two experiments in this section. However, beware that we have only scratched the tool's surface. TensorBoard can offer many more functionalities, such as representing graphically high dimensional embeddings, multimedia, and many more. Note that another frequently used tool with similar functionality is **Weights & Biases** (https://wandb.ai/). Next, we will present a way to add a more informal and perhaps funny style to our visualizations.

Visualizing using XKCD

Before we conclude this section, let's create two visualizations related to the previous language model using the xkcd plots from matplotlib. XKCD (https://xkcd.com/) is a famous webcomic based on statements on life and love, and mathematical, programming, and scientific inside jokes. We can use the XKCD style to present the validation loss for each epoch and include an annotation that points to the best model. First, we will consider 20 sample validation losses:

```
# Sample validation loss for 20 epochs.
val_loss_array = [5.79, 5.63, 5.599, 5.603, 5.502, 5.503, 5.52,
5.523, 5.52, 5.477, 5.49, 5.513, 5.511, 5.533, 5.518, 5.549,
5.509, 5.533, 5.539, 5.542]
```

Then, we will plot the data points along with the annotation for the best model:

```
with plt.xkcd():

    fig = plt.figure()
```

```
ax = fig.add_axes((0.1, 0.2, 0.8, 0.7))
ax.set_yticks([5.5, 5.6, 5.7, 5.8])
plt.xticks(np.arange(20), np.arange(1, 21))
ax.set_ylim([5.4, 5.9])


# Include an annotation pointing to the best model.
ax.annotate(
    'HERE YOU WILL FIND\nTHE BEST MODEL!',
    xy=(9, 5.5), arrowprops=dict(arrowstyle='->'),
xytext=(5, 5.7))
```

The output is shown in *Figure 9.6*:

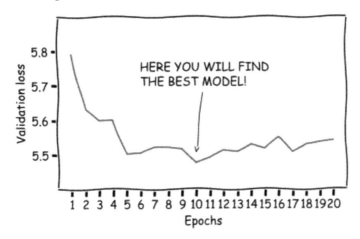

Figure 9.6 – Validation loss in each epoch

We can also print the architecture of the model that was created earlier using the XKCD style:

```
# Create an xkcd plot that shows the model's architecture.
with plt.xkcd():


    fig, ax = plt.subplots(figsize=(12, 11))
    ax.axis('off')
    ax.set_xticks([])
    ax.set_yticks([])


    # Include an annotation with the model's architecture.
```

```
    ax.annotate(best_model, xy=(0.2, 0.))


    # Draw the figure.
    stick_figure(ax, x=.03, y=.6, radius=.02, quote='What a
model!')
```

Figure 9.7 shows part of the visualization:

```
TransformerModel(
  (pos_encoder): PositionalEncoding(
    (dropout): Dropout(p=0.4, inplace=False)
  )
  (transformer_encoder): TransformerEncoder(
    (layers): ModuleList(
      (0): TransformerEncoderLayer(
        (self_attn): MultiheadAttention(
          (out_proj): NonDynamicallyQuantizableLinear(in_features=200, out_features=200, bias=True)
        )
        (linear1): Linear(in_features=200, out_features=200, bias=True)
        (dropout): Dropout(p=0.4, inplace=False)
        (linear2): Linear(in_features=200, out_features=200, bias=True)
        (norm1): LayerNorm((200,), eps=1e-05, elementwise_affine=True)
        (norm2): LayerNorm((200,), eps=1e-05, elementwise_affine=True)
        (dropout1): Dropout(p=0.4, inplace=False)
        (dropout2): Dropout(p=0.4, inplace=False)
      )
      (1): TransformerEncoderLayer(
        (self_attn): MultiheadAttention(
          (out_proj): NonDynamicallyQuantizableLinear(in_features=200, out_features=200, bias=True)
        )
        (linear1): Linear(in_features=200, out_features=200, bias=True)
        (dropout): Dropout(p=0.4, inplace=False)
        (linear2): Linear(in_features=200, out_features=200, bias=True)
```

Figure 9.7 – The language model's architecture

Observe the two encoder layers that are part of the model's structure. XKCD plots can be handy for generating humorous graphs or used instead of hand-drawn sketches. A significant portion of this book was dedicated to how to create visualizations of the data, models, or obtained results. So, you are now fully equipped to use this knowledge for your work. In the next section, we will put a pre-trained language model into action to create a generative chatbot.

Creating a generative chatbot

After our previous short journey on language modeling, let's focus on the second type of conversational agent and implement a generative chatbot. To make the interaction more enjoyable, we will use a pre-trained model that has been specifically designed for this task. Additionally, we will wrap the implementation around two **graphical user interfaces (GUIs)** that facilitate the interaction with the model. Finally, we will discuss the steps for tuning the pre-trained model on a different dataset.

Using a pre-trained model

The lack of sufficiently large datasets, processing power, and time are often decisive factors in resorting to a pre-trained model. More importantly, tweaking language models is far from a modest task and requires much expertise. Thus, to create the chatbot, we will utilize *DialoGPT* (https://huggingface. co/docs/transformers/model_doc/dialogpt), a tunable neural conversational response generation model for multiturn conversations. DialoGPT is trained on 147M multi-turn dialogs. The responses generated by the model are comparable to human response quality under a single-turn conversation Turing test. In addition, for efficiency, we will leverage a smaller version of the model (https://huggingface.co/microsoft/DialoGPT-medium).

So, let's load both the actual model and its tokenizer, the module that converts the text into numerical inputs for the neural network and vice versa. The code is included in the chatbot-pretrained. ipynb notebook:

```
import torch
from transformers import AutoModelForCausalLM, AutoTokenizer

# Load the models.
model_name = "microsoft/DialoGPT-medium"

gpt2_tokenizer = AutoTokenizer.from_pretrained(model_name)
gpt2_model = AutoModelForCausalLM.from_pretrained(model_name)
```

The following chat method is responsible for receiving the user input, along with the previous history, and generating a response from the bot:

```
def chat(input, history=[], gen_kwargs=[]):
    # Tokenize the input.
    input_ids = gpt2_tokenizer.encode(input+gpt2_tokenizer.eos_
token, return_tensors='pt')

    # Update the dialogue history.
    bot_input_ids = torch.cat([torch.LongTensor(history),
input_ids], dim=-1)

    # Generate the response of the bot.
    new_history = gpt2_model.generate(bot_input_ids, **gen_
kwargs).tolist()s

    # Convert the tokens to text.
```

```
    output = gpt2_tokenizer.decode(new_history[0]).
split("<|endoftext|>")
    output = [(output[i], output[i+1]) for i in range(0,
len(output)-1, 2)]


    return output, new_history
```

Notice the use of gpt2_tokenizer for the encoding and decoding steps. Additionally, the model receives both the user input and the previous dialog history as context, which shows the ability of DialoGPT to generate context-consistent responses.

Next, we will simulate a multi-turn dialog generation requesting advice from the chatbot:

```
# Simulate the chat.
me = ["What is your best advice?", "Does money buy happiness?",
"Do you have money?", "Did you buy happiness?", "Well done..."]
history = []

for user_input in me:
    output, history = chat(user_input, history, gen_kwargs)
    print("Me:\t", user_input)
    print("Bot:\t", output[len(output)-1][1])
    print("---------------")
```

The output dialog is as follows:

```
Me:     What is your best advice?
Bot:    Don't be a loser.
---------------
Me:     Does money buy happiness?
Bot:    It does if you're a loser.
---------------
Me:     Do you have money?
Bot:    I have a lot of money.
---------------
Me:     Did you buy happiness?
Bot:    I bought happiness.
---------------
Me:     Well done...
```

```
Bot:    I'm a happy guy.
    ---------------
```

After the previous conversation on money and happiness, we can create an interface to allow a smoother interaction with the model.

Creating the GUI

A GUI is an interface with interactive visual components through which users can interact with computer software. Wrapping an interface around the language model makes its usage much more accessible. The following code snippet shows one of the visual components, which is the text entry box:

```
import textwrap
import datetime as dt
from tkinter import *

# A GUI for the chat application.
class Chatty:
    ...
        # Add an input entry box.
        self.input_entry = Entry(bottom_label, bg="#6a747e",
fg="#EAECEE", font="Helvetica 14")
        self.input_entry.place(relwidth=0.74, relheight=0.07,
rely=0.0, relx=0.0)
        self.input_entry.focus()
        self.input_entry.bind("<Return>", self.on_enter_
pressed)
    ...
```

The specific widget is bound with the on_enter_pressed method. When the user presses *Enter* while typing in the text box, the specific method is called:

```
    # Method to capture the press of the Enter button.
    def on_enter_pressed(self, event):
        msg = self.input_entry.get()
        self.chatbot(msg)
```

The user input is now retrieved, and the chatbot method is engaged:

```
    # Chat with the bot.
    def chatbot(self, msg):
```

```
...
        # Get the bot's response.
        output, self.history = chat(msg, self.history, gen_
kwargs)
        response = f"{output[len(output)-1][1]}\n\n"


        # Show the response on the GUI.
        self.text_area.configure(state=NORMAL)
        self.text_area.tag_config('response', justify='right',
foreground="black", background="lightgreen", wrap='word',
rmargin=10)
        self.text_area.insert(END, response, 'response')
        self.text_area.configure(state=DISABLED)


        self.text_area.see(END)
...
```

Among other tasks, the method retrieves a prediction for the `DialoGPT-medium` model. The output is the interface shown in *Figure 9.8*:

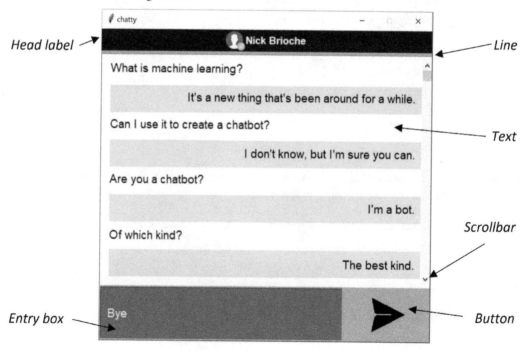

Figure 9.8 – GUI for the chat application

For better understanding, try to associate each visual element from the Jupyter notebook and the GUI in the preceding figure. We can now type a message in the **Entry box** area and obtain a response from the model. If necessary, we can scroll through the whole history of the conversation. Undoubtedly, the interaction is far better, but there is a critical drawback of GUIs created in this way; they cannot be shared easily. So, in the next section, we will discuss deploying the same chatbot on the web.

Creating the web chatbot

The effort for creating the web version of the GUI is minimal, as we just need to use one of the many libraries that allow us to create interactive web applications in Python. Gradio (https://gradio. app/) is one of the possible options, and in this section, we will adapt the Python code so that it includes HTML tags:

```
# Chat with the bot using a new input and the previous history.
# Return a basic HTML including the dialogue.
def chat_html(input, history=[]):

    # Skip empty input.
    if not input: return

    output, history = chat(input, history, gen_kwargs)

    # Create the HTML text.
    html_text = "<div class='chatbot'>"
    for tuple in output:
        for i, sen in enumerate(tuple):
            turn = "user" if i%2 == 0 else "bot"
            html_text += "<div class='msg {}'> {}</div>".
format(turn, sen)
        html_text += "</div>"

    return html_text, history
```

Using the specifics of the gradio module, we can run the chat application on a local web server:

```
import gradio as gr


# Launch the interface.
gr.Interface(fn=chat_html, theme="default", inputs=[gr.inputs.
```

```
Textbox(placeholder="Hello!"), "state"], outputs=["html",
"state"], css=css).launch()
>>
Running on local URL:  http://127.0.0.1:7861
```

The chatbot can be accessed using the previous URL, which leads to the interface shown in *Figure 9.9*:

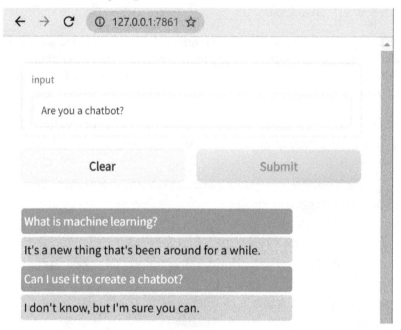

Figure 9.9 – GUI for the chat application in the browser

You can now incorporate a similar interface in your Jupyter notebook and allow other people to interact with your models. For example, *Google Colaboratory* (https://colab.research. google.com/) is an excellent choice for hosting your notebook for online access. If the notebook is available from a public code repository (for instance, GitHub), you can also use *MyBinder* (https:// mybinder.org/).

We can now proceed to the last section, which deals with how to tune a pre-trained model.

Fine-tuning a pre-trained model

Adjusting a pre-trained model to our needs is the most frequent path when building a language model. The hard work of optimizing the model's parameters has already been done for us, and we only need a customized dataset to fine-tune it. This is essentially the task in this section. We will focus less on a performance-oriented solution, aiming to provide an educational exercise that sheds light on this important theme.

For this task, we will incorporate the Cornell Movie-Dialogs Corpus (https://www.cs.cornell. edu/~cristian/Cornell_Movie-Dialogs_Corpus.html), a large collection of fictional conversations extracted from raw movie scripts. The corpus is available from the convokit toolkit, which we loaded in the fine_tuning_LM.ipynb notebook:

```
import convokit
from convokit import Corpus, download


# Load the corpus.
corpus = Corpus(download('movie-corpus'))
```

For each conversation, we will extract the sentences and store the results in a training and validation file. Notice that for this exercise, we only keep 1,000 conversations for training and 300 for validation. For clarity, we will skip a few steps, but the code in the notebook should be self-explanatory. The following extract_dialogs method provides the sentences for each dialog:

```
def extract_dialogs(corpus, split=None):
    dialogs = []

    # Iterate over all conversations.
    for convo in corpus.iter_conversations():
        # Consider only conversations in the specified split of
the data.
        if split is None or convo.meta['split'] == split:

            dialog_str = ""

            # Get the sentences in the conversation.
            for utterance in convo.iter_utterances():
                dialog_str = dialog_str + " " + utterance.text

            dialogs.append(dialog_str)

    return dialogs
```

Now, we can call the method and obtain our samples:

```
samples = extract_dialogs(corpus)
```

The data from the previous step is stored in a training and validation file. Next, we will reload the instances and print an example dialog:

```
from datasets import load_dataset

# Load the data from the text files.
data = load_dataset("text", data_files={"train": "./data/
cornell_train.csv", "validation": "./data/cornell_val.csv"})

data["train"][15]
>>
{'text': ' Do you know how much I missed you? Welcome home.'}
```

In this case, the conversation consists of only two sentences. To speed up the training process, we will incorporate the small version of the DialoGPT model and tokenize the input data:

```
from transformers import AutoTokenizer

# Setup tokenization.
model_name = "microsoft/DialoGPT-small"
tokenizer = AutoTokenizer.from_pretrained(model_name, use_
fast=True)

def perform_tokenization(samples):
    return tokenizer(samples["text"])

tokenized_data = data.map(perform_tokenization, batched=True,
num_proc=4, remove_columns=["text"])
```

The critical element is to use the `Trainer` class, which provides a suitable training and evaluation loop in PyTorch, optimized for the Hugging Face transformers:

```
from transformers import AutoModelForCausalLM
from transformers import Trainer, TrainingArguments

# Load the model to be tuned.
model = AutoModelForCausalLM.from_pretrained(model_name)
```

```
name = model_name.split("/")[-1]


# Define the training arguments.
training_args = TrainingArguments(
    f"{name}-finetuned-cornell",
    evaluation_strategy = "epoch",
    learning_rate=2e-5,
    weight_decay=0.01,
    push_to_hub=False,
)
```

Finally, we can instantiate the trainer and initiate the training process:

```
# Create the trainer.
trainer = Trainer(
    model=model,
    args=training_args,
    train_dataset=new_dataset["train"],
    eval_dataset=new_dataset["validation"],
)


# Start training the model.
trainer.train()
>>
Epoch    Training Loss  Validation Loss
1        No log         7.098641
2        No log         5.578784
3        No log         5.300162
```

The process was only performed for three epochs, but we can still observe that the validation loss constantly decreases. Narrowing the experiment to three epochs and utilizing a reduced movie corpus dataset does not provide exciting results. Hopefully, you understood the basic steps of the fine-tuning process and can apply them in another setting. The following section concludes this chapter with an alternative approach to performing the same task.

Tuning using reinforcement learning

So far, the methods we've incorporated for building or tuning language models have attacked the problem from a certain angle. Using an encoder/decoder architecture variant, we trained models to map an input sequence to a response. This approach works well for chit-chat chatbots, but other methods are more appropriate when a specific user goal is involved, such as booking a ticket or finding a reservation. The reinforcement learning paradigm is a promising avenue for this task, which is why it has gained significant attention in recent years.

Reinforcement learning describes a class of problems where the model learns using rewards from a sequence of actions. Instead of telling the agent which actions to take, its role is to discover the actions that yield the most reward by trial and error. For a quick recap, you can refer to the *Reinforcement learning* section of *Chapter 1, Introducing Machine Learning for Text*.

In this section, we will utilize the *Transformer Reinforcement Learning* (*trl*) library, which allows us to train transformer language models with **proximal policy optimization (PPO)**. PPO is a state-of-the-art technique that provides instructions to the reinforcement learning agent in terms of what actions it must follow based on the state of the environment it is currently in. Its benefit is that it performs comparably or better than other methods, while its simplicity makes it easy to implement and tune.

The following example is included in the `fine_tuning_LM-RL.ipynb` notebook and provides a gentle introduction to the topic. Again, we will implement a few basic steps to tune a language model and, as we did previously, we will use `DialoGPT-small`:

```
# Load the models.
model_name = "microsoft/DialoGPT-small"

model = GPT2HeadWithValueModel.from_pretrained(model_name)
model_ref = GPT2HeadWithValueModel.from_pretrained(model_name)
tokenizer = GPT2Tokenizer.from_pretrained(model_name)

# Chat with the bot using a new input and the previous history.
def chat(input, history=[], gen_kwargs=[]):
...
```

The `chat` method's body is the same as the one in the *Using a pre-trained model* section. Please refer to that section for the details. Next, we will create the trainer and define the query:

```
# Initialize the policy and the trainer.
ppo_config = {'batch_size': 1, 'forward_batch_size': 1}
ppo_trainer = PPOTrainer(model, model_ref, tokenizer, **ppo_
```

```
config)

# Encode a query.
query_text = "Does money buy happiness?"
query_tensor = tokenizer.encode(query_text+tokenizer.eos_token,
return_tensors="pt")
```

Notice the usage of `model_ref`, which keeps the original model as a reference. The training process is repeated for five interactions:

```
for x in range(5):
    response_tensors = []
    pipe_outputs = []

    # Get a response from the chatbot.
    result, history = chat(query_text, [], gen_kwargs)
    response_text = result[0][1]
    response_tensor = tokenizer.encode(response_text+tokenizer.
eos_token, return_tensors="pt")
```

Calling the `chat` method with the query generates a response that is evaluated with a reward. The polarity of the reward is determined by the presence of certain words in the response. For instance, when it contains the word `happy`, `happiness`, or `fun`, the reward is positive and equal to `1.0`:

```
    # Positive reward.
    if response_text.find('happy') >= 0 or response_text.
find('happiness') >= 0 or response_text.find('fun') >= 0:
        print("+ reward: " + response_text)
        reward = [torch.tensor(1.0)]
    # Negative reward.
    else:
        print("- reward: " + response_text)
        reward = [torch.tensor(-1.0)]
```

Finally, the model can be trained using PPO for each interaction:

```
    # Train the model with the PPO algorithm.
    ppo_trainer.step([query_tensor[0]], [response_tensor[0]],
reward)
>>
```

```
+ reward: Money doesn't buy happiness.
+ reward: Buy happiness
- reward: Why am I here?
- reward: Money is so great!
+ reward: So much money... such happiness...
```

As in the previous fine-tuning task, this small exercise does not provide tangible results but is sufficient for educational purposes. Based on the reward function, `gpt2_model` should now contain the necessary changes, which are very few. In our example, the reward was basic and had to do with the presence of certain keywords in the output of the language model. In goal-oriented tasks, we need to define the appropriate reward that makes sense for the current problem.

In concluding this section, you learned how to create generative chatbots, using either pre-trained language models or by creating one from scratch. While compiling a new application-oriented model seems preferable, it poses many practical challenges regarding the significant effort involved. For that reason, fine-tuning pre-trained language models exploits the benefits of transfer learning and is often the preferred choice. Finally, based on the problem under study, by aiming for goal-oriented or free-conversation chatbots, we can incorporate a different approach to fine-tune the language models.

Summary

This chapter focused on yet another exciting field in natural language processing related to text generation. In this context, we examined chatbots as a convenient case study. In addition, the content included many references to previous chapters to urge you to revisit specific topics from a different perspective.

The power of the transformer architecture and the abundance of data has paved the way for more elaborate language models. We presented how to create such a model from scratch or fine-tune a pre-trained model. During this discussion, we also applied a third type of learning: reinforcement learning.

Evaluation metrics are a constant theme throughout this book; this chapter was no exception. We used perplexity as an evaluation metric and discussed TensorBoard, which helps us shed light on the internal mechanics of deep neural networks. Finally, we worked on creating user interfaces in Python.

The next chapter is the final chapter of this book and deals with another cutting-edge theme in machine learning: *text clustering*.

10

Clustering Speech-to-Text Transcriptions

When dealing with real-world datasets, the most common situation is that they come unlabeled—manually labeling each sample is often unrealistic in terms of time and cost. Therefore, it is imperative to incorporate methods that can handle datasets of this type. Unsupervised learning algorithms are applicable in this case and, in this chapter, we deal with a particular kind for grouping similar data under the same category. Expressly, we incorporate clustering methods that allow the transformation of raw data into possible actionable insights, for instance, identifying the general theme in each cluster.

While the previous chapters focused mainly on supervised learning techniques, we dedicate the current one solely to unsupervised methods. Another differentiation is the creation of the text corpus using speech-to-text technology. Next, as the chapter unfolds, we present hard and soft clustering techniques, providing insight into their mechanics and putting them into action. Finally, we discuss how to evaluate the clustering result.

By the end of the chapter, you will be capable of applying different clustering methods to pertinent problems and also understand how to tune their hyperparameters.

In this chapter, we will go through the following topics:

- Understanding the different techniques for text clustering
- Implementing and configuring the methods for text clustering
- Assessing the performance of the implemented systems
- Applying and evaluating speech-to-text for creating data

Technical requirements

The chapter's code has been truncated in certain parts to facilitate reading the content. However, the whole code is available as different Jupyter notebooks in the book's GitHub repository:

`https://github.com/PacktPublishing/Machine-Learning-Techniques-for-Text/tree/main/chapter-10`.

Understanding text clustering

Until now, our primary goal was to assign a predefined label to a piece of text so that we could categorize it as spam or ham, label its topic, identify its sentiment, and so forth. In all of those cases, the labels were predetermined, which is the distinctive feature of supervised learning. In many other situations, however, the labels are not known from the beginning. Consider, for example, collecting feedback about a service or product using surveys. Responses to open-ended questions are essential to most questionnaires, but detecting similar themes from the answers is tedious if done manually. Other examples include news topics, customer call transcriptions, user tweets, and many more. In all the previous cases, businesses benefit from discovering insights in the chaos of unstructured data and seizing potential opportunities.

Algorithms that learn the structure of the data without any assistance (no labels or classes given) are part of unsupervised learning. We already got a flavor of these methods when discussing dimensionality reduction techniques for visualization or feature selection in *Chapter 3, Classifying Topics of Newsgroup Posts*, and *Chapter 5, Recommending Music Titles*. This chapter examines problems from this perspective, intending to cluster text data into different categories automatically. Specifically, **text clustering** is the process of dividing a population of samples into various groups such that the data points in the same category are more similar than those in other ones—the aim is to locate functional patterns within each group and decipher why this happens.

In general, clustering can be divided into two major subgroups:

- **Hard clustering** is about grouping each data observation into a different cluster. For example, in a marketing survey, each customer is assigned to just one of the market segments.

- **Soft clustering** is about grouping each observation in more than one category, providing a probability or likelihood for each cluster. For example, a recommender system based on customer reviews can associate a new user with more than one cluster of products.

Throughout the current chapter, we present methods for both types of clustering. Moreover, using speech-to-text, we create the text corpus to be used when incorporating the methods. The audio files and the transcriptions are part of the *LJ Speech Dataset* (`https://keithito.com/LJ-Speech-Dataset/`) consisting of 13,100 short audio clips of a single speaker reading passages from seven non-fiction books. In our coding examples, we employ a subset of the available corpus. Let's begin with the essential step of preprocessing the input data.

Preprocessing the data

The first task is to read the file with the meta-information about the corpus. The `metadata.csv` file includes one column with the audio filename and one with its transcription, separated by the | symbol. The relevant code is included in the `text-clustering.ipynb` notebook:

```
import pandas as pd


# Read the data from the reduced csv file.
data = pd.read_csv('./data/metadata.csv', usecols=range(2),
names=['audiofile', 'transcription'], sep="|")
data.head()
>>   audiofile   transcription
0    LJ001-0001  Printing, in the only sense with which ...
1    LJ001-0002  in being comparatively modern.
2    LJ001-0003  For although the Chinese took impressio...
3    LJ001-0004  produced the block books, which were th...
4    LJ001-0005  the invention of movable metal letters ...
```

Unfortunately, the dataset lacks any information about the text source of each audio transcription. So, we extract this information by first downloading the content of the seven books:

```
import os
import requests
from fuzzysearch import find_near_matches


# Download the content of each book.
response = requests.get("https://archive.org/stream/
artscraftsessays00artsrich/artscraftsessays00artsrich_djvu.
txt")
book1 = response.text.replace("\n", " ").replace("   ", " ")
...
```

Let's create a method to help us identify the source of each transcription. We employ the `find_near_matches` method, which performs a fuzzy search of a string against a reference text (*fuzzy*, in this case, means that it matches patterns approximately):

```
# Find the book each sentence belongs to.
def which_book(input):
...
```

```
            books = ['book1', 'book2', 'book3', 'book4',
    'book5', 'book6', 'book7']
            found = False

        while (found == False):
            # An input may appear in various books.
            for book in books:
                # Check the input against all books.
                if (len(find_near_matches(input,
    eval(book), max_l_dist=mld)) > 0):
                    found = True
                    res.append(book)
    ...
```

Next, we iterate in the list of transcriptions and obtain the identifier of the relevant book:

```
    # Find the book id(s) per transcription.
    for excerpt in data["transcription"]:
        id = which_book(excerpt)
        book_df = book_df.appen'({'book'id':id[0]}, ignore_
    index=True)
```

We can now print the number of input sentences per book title:

```
# Store the book ids.
data['book_id'] = book_df

# Calculate the number of transcriptions per book.
data['book_id'].value_counts()
>>
book2        5281
book7        4453
unknown      1442
book3         689
book6         489
book5         485
book1         164
book4          97
Name: book_id, dtype: int64
```

We observe that the dataset is not balanced as most transcriptions come from book2 and book7. Moreover, many samples are not matched with any books (1442 instances). Using a more relaxed criterion for the fuzzy search (max_l_dist) can possibly reduce the number of unknown book identifiers. In the *Performing exploratory data analysis* section of *Chapter 3, Classifying Topics of Newsgroup Posts*, and the *Treating imbalanced datasets* section of *Chapter 8, Detecting Hateful and Offensive Language*, we discussed the issues related to instances monopolizing the dataset. To avoid this annoying situation, we balance the corpus and extract the same amount of observations for each book:

```
# Use a subset of the examples.
data_red = pd.DataFrame()


# Iterate over all books and keep 95 samples for each one.
for i in range(7):
    data_red = data_red.append(data[data.book_id=='book'+
str(i+1)].sample(n=95, random_state=123))
data_red = data_red.reset_index(drop=True)
data_red.shape
>> (665, 3)
```

Let's now focus on the audio files, extracting the features of one of them:

```
from pydub import AudioSegment
from pydub.playback import play


# Pick an audio file.
uri = "./data/wav/" + data_red['audiofile'][30] + ".wav"


# Import the audio file.
wav_file = AudioSegment.from_file(file=uri, format="wav")


# Play the audio file.
play(wav_file)


# Print the file's frame rate.
print("Frame rate: " + str(wav_file.frame_rate) + " Hz")


# Print the number of bytes per sample.
print("Bytes per sample: " + str(wav_file.sample_width))
>>
```

```
Frame rate: 22050 Hz
Bytes per sample: 2
```

The frame rate and the bytes per sample suggest that the audio file is high quality. Next, we extract the audio samples and plot the waveform:

```python
import matplotlib.pyplot as plt
import numpy as np
import seaborn as sns

# Get the samples of the audio file.
samples = wav_file.get_array_of_samples()
time = np.arange(0, wav_file.duration_seconds,1/wav_file.frame_
rate)

# Create the waveform with its data.
waveform_df = pd.DataFrame(columns=['time', 'samples'])

waveform_df['time'] = time
waveform_df['samples'] = samples

# Plot the waveform.
ax = sns.lineplot(data=waveform_df, x=time, y=samples)
```

The output is the sound wave presented in *Figure 10.1*:

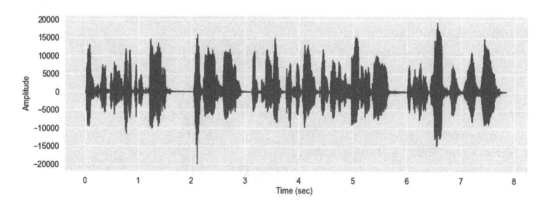

Figure 10.1 – Waveform of the audio file

The *x* axis shows the duration of the file (around 8 seconds), and the *y* axis is the signal's amplitude. We can also extract a few more interesting statistics for all waveforms, such as their duration, maximum amplitude, and word count:

```
import re
# Store the audio statistics in a dataframe.
statistics_df = pd.DataFrame(columns=['duration_seconds',
'max', 'word_num', 'book_id'])
i = 1


for index, row in data_red.iterrows():
    i+=1
    wav_file = AudioSegment.from_file(file="./data/wav/" +
row["audiofile"] + ".wav", format="wav")
    # Store the following as features.
    statistics_df = statistics_df.append({'duration_
seconds':wav_file.duration_seconds,'max':wav_file.max,'word_
num':len(row["transcription"].split()),'book_id':row["book_
id"]}, ignore_index=True)
```

We can now print the relevant statistics:

```
statistics_df.head()
>>   duration_seconds      max        word_num      book_id
0    6.392608              18888      16            book1
1    5.788889              20927      19            book1
2    5.150340              29599      17            book1
3    3.455283              29092      10            book1
4    4.952971              22680      16            book1
```

The specific values can be presented in an elegant way using a **pairplot**, which allows the plot of pairwise relationships between the variables of a dataset in a single figure. So, let's create a pairplot contrasting the statistics calculated previously for each one of the seven books:

```
# Plot the statistics information.
g = sns.pairplot(statistics_df, hue="book_id",
palette="Paired", markers=[".", "v", "^", "<", ">", "*", "X"])
```

Figure 10.2 shows the specific visualization:

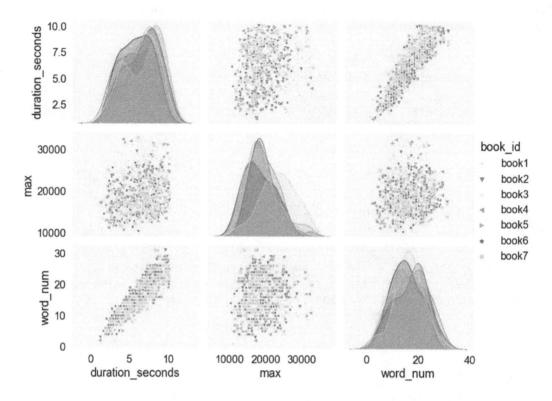

Figure 10.2 – Pairplot of the audio statistics

Based on the previous plots, we do not observe any significant differences among the seven books, except for the distribution of the max amplitude for **book1**. The specific graph is slightly to the right compared to the other ones. Next, we proceed with the creation of the dataset. Although the *LJ Speech Dataset* includes the transcriptions of the audio content, we would like to simulate a frequent scenario in real-world settings where we have to deal with speech-to-text results.

Using speech-to-text

Speech-to-text, also known as **speech recognition**, is a forefront technology that allows the accurate conversion of speech into text in real-time or batch mode. The recent advances in machine learning have led to state-of-the-art systems that can understand natural speech in many languages. Deep neural networks have proven to be very efficient for speech recognition, and current systems have an error rate of between 3%-5%, depending on the task. As a point of reference, humans achieve similar error rates when asked to transcribe recorded audio. Deep neural networks have worked so well for the task because of the data's compositional nature; waveforms can be cut into phonemes, which are the building blocks of words. Then, words can be combined to create sentences. We have seen a similar concept during the discussion in the *Understanding CNN* section of *Chapter 8, Detecting Hateful and Offensive Language*. Processing an image using a convolutional neural network relies on layers of low- to high-level features. Let's see now how to employ speech-to-text to create our dataset.

> **Interesting fact**
>
> Radio Rex, launched in 1922, was the first commercial toy to respond to voice commands. Using a one-word vocabulary was enough to make a celluloid dog exit his house. The word *Rex* could trigger the release of a spring attached to an electromagnetic circuit resonant to 500 Hz (the frequency of *E*). Unfortunately, the toy had a terrible false-rejection rate.

First, we import the necessary module and set up the recognizer:

```
import speech_recognition as sr


# Create an instance of the recognizer.
recognizer = sr.Recognizer()
# Set the energy threshold.
recognizer.energy_threshold = 300
```

Iterating over all input files in the dataset, we transcribe the audio using the *Google Speech Recognition API* (https://cloud.google.com/speech-to-text), which is a cloud service for several languages that receives audio and transcribes it into text:

```
# Start the speech-to-text process.
for file in data_red["audiofile"]:
    i+=1
    # Read the audio file.
    audio_file = sr.AudioFile("./data/wav/" + file + ".wav")
    # Extract the file's audiodata.
    with audio_file as source:
        # Record the audio.
        file_audio_data = recognizer.record(source)
    try:
        # Transcribe speech using Google web API.
        hypothesis.append(recognizer.recognize_google(
audio_data=file_audio_data, language="en-US"))
```

It usually takes several minutes to transcribe all sentences. Hence, to avoid repeating the same processing, we store the hypotheses of the recognizer in a file:

```
# Save the hypotheses.
hypothesis_df = pd.DataFrame(hypothesis,
columns=['hypothesis'])
hypothesis_df.to_csv("data/hypothesis.csv", line_
terminator='\n', index=False)
```

Speech recognition is far from the perfect process and often returns erroneous transcriptions. Transcribers who listen to each audio file create ground truth transcriptions manually by writing down what is said. Besides being time-consuming, the transcription process can also be erroneous due to background noise, slang and accent, mumbling, and so on. Nevertheless, comparing the correct human transcriptions with the hypotheses returned by the recognizer is straightforward.

First, we apply a few preprocessing steps in both ground truth transcriptions and the hypotheses:

```
# Preprocess the ground truth transcriptions and hypotheses.
ground_truth = data_red["transcription"].to_list()


# Remove the following symbols.
symbols = ",.!?;"
for i in range(len(ground_truth)):
    ground_truth[i] = ground_truth[i].lower()
    for c in symbols:
        ground_truth[i].replace(c, "")
hypothesis = hypothesis_df['hypothesis'].to_list()
for i in range(len(hypothesis)):
    hypothesis[i] = hypothesis[i].lower()
```

At last, we can calculate the error of the recognizer using the most typical metric for the task. The **word error rate** (**WER**) expresses the average number of word mistakes considering three error factors. First, *substitution* errors occur when a reference word gets replaced by another word. Then, *insertion* errors happen when a word that was never spoken is added to the hypothesis. Finally, we have *deletion* errors when reference words are left out of the recognizer's hypothesis. WER is defined according to this formula:

$$WER = \frac{substitutions + deletions + insertions}{word\ count}$$

The denominator expresses the total number of reference words. Notice that the metric can take values above one, for instance, when the number of insertions exceeds the number of reference words. Next, we measure the WER for our dataset:

```
from jiwer import wer

# Calculate the WER.
error = wer(ground_truth, hypothesis)
print(error)
>> 0.14171767761083287
```

Based on the previous output, the recognizer has a 14% WER. The speech recognition task is indeed very challenging! The analysis that follows is based on the hypotheses of the recognizer. Still, you can easily repeat the same process using ground truth transcriptions. In the following section, we introduce the most well-known clustering algorithm.

Introducing the K-means algorithm

The **K-means** algorithm is a predominant unsupervised learning algorithm for clustering data due to its simplicity and efficiency. It aims to group similar items in the form of K clusters. After selecting K random centroids, it repeatedly moves them around to group the most similar samples to the center of each cluster. As a similarity measure, we can use metrics such as the Euclidean distance, cosine similarity (check the *Calculating vector similarity* section in *Chapter 2, Detecting Spam Emails*), Pearson correlation coefficients (discussed in the *Understanding the Pearson correlation* section of *Chapter 5, Recommending Music Titles*), and so forth. An example can help us to understand the algorithm better. Suppose that you are given the dataset shown in the upper-left plot of *Figure 10.3*:

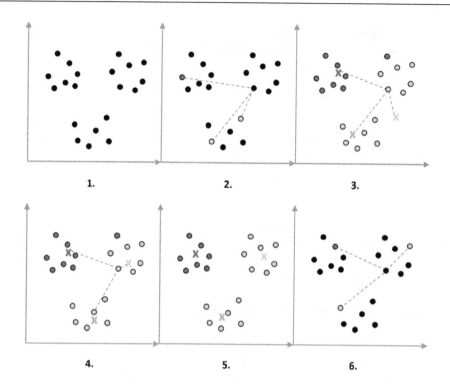

Figure 10.3 – K-means basic steps

It's straightforward to identify that the data points can be grouped into three clusters. Unfortunately, K-means does not possess any visual capacity to spot the clusters easily, and it needs to follow a series of steps to reach the same assumption. These are summarized as follows:

1. Select the number of clusters, K, that we want to identify. Suppose that in this example, $K=3$.

2. Randomly select three distinct data points as the cluster centroids and measure the distance from all points to the centroids.

3. Assign each point to the closest cluster centroid and calculate the mean of the newly created cluster (depicted with the X symbol).

4. Repeat *steps 2* and *3* using the mean values as centroids.

5. Stop the iterations when the clusters no longer change or the maximum number of iterations is reached.

6. Repeat from *step 2* using a new set of random points.

The last step should seem redundant as, in the previous example, we obtain the perfect clustering in *step 5*, right? Well, this is obvious for a human to deduce, but not for the algorithm per se. K-means should repeat the same process multiple times to ascertain that the best possible clustering is achieved.

After finishing *step 5*, the algorithm calculates the variation within each cluster. The less variation within clusters, the more homogeneous the data points are inside each cluster. Therefore, the solution that offers less variation is the chosen one. Let's expand this discussion a little bit further.

We need a score that measures how well the model clusters the dataset to calculate variation. The specific score is called **inertia** or **within-cluster sum-of-squares**. It is defined as the sum of distances of all the points within a cluster from the cluster centroid. Thus, the K-means algorithm aims to minimize the following quantity:

$$\sum_{i=0}^{n} min_{\mu_j \in C}(\|x_i - \mu_j\|^2)$$

Where, the following applies:

- μ_j = the jth cluster centroid
- x_i = the ith point in the cluster
- n = the total number of points in the cluster
- C = the set of cluster centroids

Generally, a cluster with small inertia is more compact than a cluster with a large sum of squares. The inertia calculation is done for each cluster and data points within the cluster. The results are added together to measure the inertia of each iteration.

In the previous example, the choice of K is deduced indirectly after the visualization of the dataset, and in practice, we commonly resort to this approach. However, a more elegant way to extract the number of candidate clusters is presented in the following section. Before incorporating K-means, notice that the number of clusters, K, and the number of iterations are hyperparameters for the algorithm.

Putting K-means into action

It's time to set things in place to cluster the dataset. First, we load the speech-to-text hypotheses from the CSV file (data/hypothesis.csv), filtering those samples with an error:

```
from sklearn.feature_extraction.text import TfidfVectorizer
from sklearn.preprocessing import normalize


# Read the hypotheses from the speech-to-text.
hypothesis_df = pd.read_csv('data/hypothesis.csv',
names=['hypothesis'])
hypothesis_df = hypothesis_df[hypothesis_df['hypothesis'] !=
```

```
"<ERROR>"]
data = hypothesis_df['hypothesis']
```

Next, using `tf_idf`, we vectorize the input sentences:

```
# Vectorize the hypotheses.
tf_idf_vectorizor = TfidfVectorizer(stop_words='english', max_
features = 5000)
tf_idf = tf_idf_vectorizor.fit_transform(data)
tf_idf_norm = normalize(tf_idf)
tf_idf_array = tf_idf_norm.toarray()
```

We can now apply the principal component analysis to reduce the dimensions of the feature space:

```
from sklearn.decomposition import PCA


# Perform PCA to reduce the dimensions of the feature space
with two principal components.
pca = PCA(n_components=2)
pcaComponents = pca.fit_transform(tf_idf_array)
```

Before incorporating K-means, there is still an unsolved problem pending from the previous section: how to decide the optimal number of clusters for the algorithm.

Finding the optimal number of clusters

As already discussed, the K-means algorithm aims to minimize inertia while simultaneously acquiring meaningful clusters. Inertia becomes zero when we pick the number of centroids equal to the dataset size. In this case, every distance is equal to zero (the point and centroid match), which obviously doesn't provide any helpful insight into the data. Thus, we apply a handy technique called the **elbow method** to balance the tradeoff between coherent and meaningful clusters. The method relies on constructing a graph, where the x axis represents the number of clusters and the y axis is the inertia score.

First, we train a model with a small cluster value and calculate the inertia. Then, we increase the cluster number by one and repeat the same process. The following code shows the relevant steps in Python using one to seven clusters:

```
from sklearn.cluster import kMeans


# Use the elbow method to extract the optimal number of
clusters.
```

```
num_clusters = range(1, 7)

k_means = [kMeans(n_clusters=i, max_iter = 600) for i in num_
clusters]

inertia = [k_means[i].fit(pcaComponents).inertia_ for i in
range(len(k_means))]

plt.plot(num_clusters, inertia)
```

The output is shown in *Figure 10.4*:

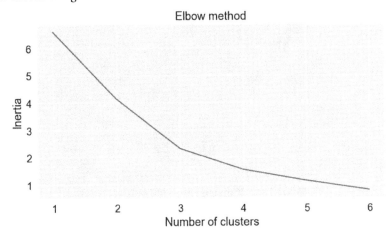

Figure 10.4 – Extracting the optimal number of clusters using the elbow method

Observe that between points **3** and **4** on the *x* axis, the curve's slope changes sharply, thus creating an elbow shape. The *K* value corresponding to this point is the optimal number of clusters, in our case, equal to three. Next, we utilize the specific outcome to train a K-means model using 10,000 iterations. The created model allows the prediction of the cluster for each point:

```
# Perform the clustering.
k_means = kMeans(n_clusters=3, max_iter=10000, algorithm =
'full', n_init=200)
kmeans_model = k_means.fit(pcaComponents)
kmeans_pred = k_means.predict(pcaComponents)

# Plot the clusters.
plt.scatter(pcaComponents[:, 0], pcaComponents[:, 1], c=kmeans_
```

```
pred, s=50, cmap='Paired')

# Plot the cluster centers.
centers = kmeans_model.cluster_centers_
plt.scatter(centers[:, 0], centers[:, 1], c='black', s=300,
alpha=0.6)
```

Figure 10.5 shows the outcome of this step:

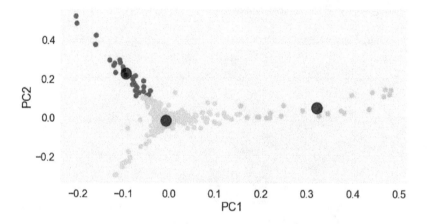

Figure 10.5 – K-means clustering output

As expected, each sample is clustered into one of three groups. Alright, assigning each point to a cluster is one thing, but how can we interpret the outcome of this process?

Interpreting the clustering result

In most clustering tasks, specific domain knowledge is required to transform the clustering result into meaningful knowledge. An experienced data scientist can provide valuable insight in this case. When text data is involved, we can extract the most relevant cluster words to obtain some intuition of the contents of each group. The cluster_top_words method extracts the indices of the predictions in each cluster, calculates the mean tf_idf vector of the corresponding predictions, and returns the most relevant words. Let's examine the different steps:

1. First, we define the method and get the unique labels:

```
# Get top words (=num) per cluster.
def cluster_top_words(tf_idf_array, prediction, num):

    # Get the unique labels.
```

```
    labels = np.unique(prediction)
    top_words = []
```

2. Then, we start iterating over all unique labels:

```
for label in labels:
        # Indices for each cluster.
        idx = np.where(prediction==label)
        # Mean feature values across cluster.
        x_means = np.mean(tf_idf_array[idx], axis = 0)
        # Get the indices to sort x_means.
        sorted = np.argsort(x_means)[::-1][:num]
        # Get the list of words.
        words = tf_idf_vectorizor.get_feature_names()
```

3. Finally, we extract the top words and return the result:

```
        top = [(words[i], x_means[i]) for i in sorted]
        df = pd.DataFrame(top, columns = ['features',
    'score'])
        top_words.append(df)

    return top_words
```

We can now call the previous method for obtaining the 15 most relevant words per cluster:

```
# Get the 15 top words per cluster.
top_words = cluster_top_words(tf_idf_array, kmeans_pred, 15)
```

The outcome of this step can be visualized using the following code:

```
# Plot the top words per cluster.
x = np.arange(len(top_words[0]))

for i, df in enumerate(top_words):
    ax = fig.add_subplot(1, len(top_words), i+1)
    ax.barh(x, df.score, align='center', color='#0a7ff2')
```

The bar plots of *Figure 10.6* inform us about the top words in each cluster:

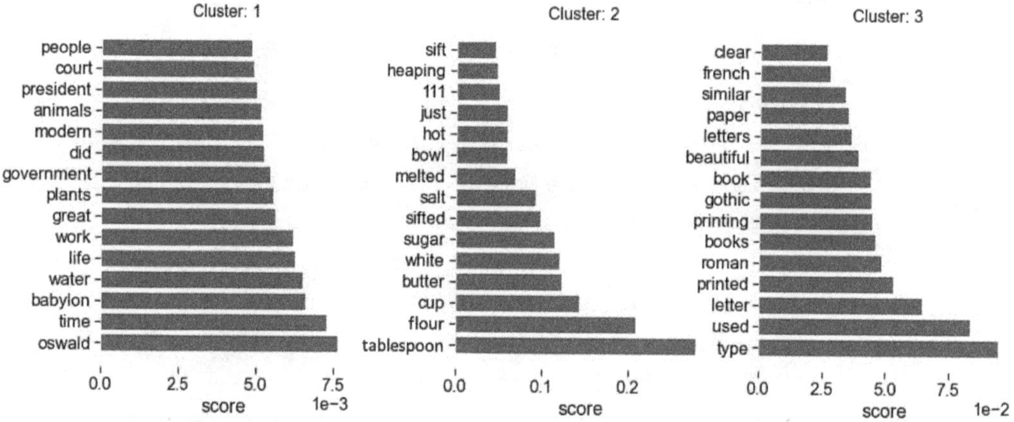

Figure 10.6 – Top words per cluster

The first cluster includes words such as **court**, **president**, **government**, and **oswald**, which suggests that there is a topic about the assassination of President Kennedy. Indeed, one of the books is entitled *The Warren Report: The Official Report on the Assassination of President John F. Kennedy*. The topic in the second cluster seems to be related to cooking due to the prevailing words such as **bowl**, **melted**, **salt**, **sugar**, **butter**, **cup**, **flour**, and **tablespoon**. Once again, the book entitled *Marion Harland's Cookery for Beginners* is part of the corpus. Finally, the third cluster includes words such as **french**, **gothic**, and **roman**, most probably from the *Arts and Crafts Essays* book, which discusses decorative arts.

In the next section, we present another commonly used method for clustering.

Introducing DBSCAN

The basic idea behind the **density-based spatial clustering of applications with noise (DBSCAN)** algorithm is that clusters are regions of high point density, separated from other clusters by low point density regions. The algorithm takes each point in the dataset to identify the high-density regions and checks whether its neighborhood contains a minimum number of points. Unlike K-means, DBSCAN does not require manually specifying the number of clusters; it is more immune to outliers and more appropriate when the clusters have complex shapes.

To employ the algorithm, we need to set two hyperparameters:

- *epsilon* is the radius of the circle to be created around each point to check the region's density
- *minPts* determines the minimum number of data points within the circle to label its center as a *core* point

All the data points with less than *minPts* but more than one point in their neighborhood are called *border* points. Finally, data points without any other close neighbor than themselves are known as *outliers*, or *noise* points.

Notice that the points can be partially located in the previous circle and that *minPts* includes the point itself. Also, when the data space has more the two dimensions, *epsilon* becomes the radius of a hypersphere. In this case, *minPts* is the minimum number of points in the specific hypersphere.

As in the case of K-means, we show the basic steps of DBSCAN using as input the data points in the upper-left plot of *Figure 10.7*:

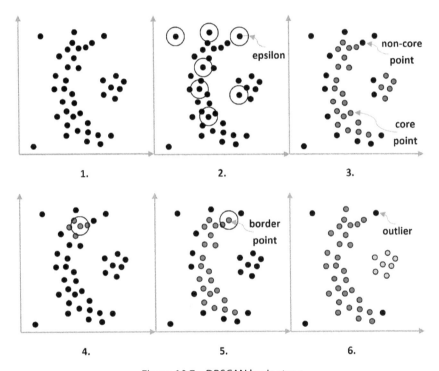

Figure 10.7 – DBSCAN basic steps

Looking again at the specific plot, how many clusters can you identify? Most probably two, one big and one smaller nested one. The steps of the method are summarized here:

1. Select a value for *epsilon* and *minPts*. Suppose that in this example, *epsilon*=1 and *minPts*=3.

2. Choose a random point and check whether the minimum points criterion applies within the *epsilon* radius.

3. If the answer to *step 2* is positive, label the point as a core point. Otherwise, it is a non-core one.

4. Choose a random core point and cluster together all core points inside the radius. Then, move to a core point close to the expanding cluster and repeat.

5. A non-core point is part of the same cluster only if it contains at least one core point. In this case, it is called a *border* point.

6. Repeat the process for the next cluster starting from *step 2*. Points not part of any group are considered outliers (noise).

We can now proceed and incorporate the algorithm.

Putting DBSCAN into action

DBSCAN is sensitive to the initial values of the hyperparameters and, as in related situations, domain knowledge and experimentation are required. Similar to the elbow method in K-means, we can employ another implementation of the same technique using the `kneed` module. The method allows the estimation of *epsilon*, but contrary to the elbow method, we do not solely rely on the plot to extract the parameter's value. It is often difficult to visually identify the knee/elbow point, and the `kneed` module provides its exact value.

In the following code, we use **k-nearest neighbors (KNN)** to extract the distances between each point in the dataset and its five nearest neighbors. Then, we sort the distances in ascending values and create the plot to get the point of maximum curvature:

```
from sklearn.neighbors import NearestNeighbors
from kneed import KneeLocator


# Perform 5-nn to extract the distances.
nn = NearestNeighbors(n_neighbors=5).fit(pcaComponents)
distances, idx = nn.kneighbors(pcaComponents)
distances = np.sort(distances, axis=0)
distances = distances[:,1]


# Find the knee point.
i = np.arange(len(distances))
knee = KneeLocator(i, distances, S=0, curve='convex',
direction='increasing', interp_method='polynomial')


# Plot the knee.
knee.plot_knee()
```

The knee point in *Figure 10.8* resides at the intersection of the curve and the dashed vertical line:

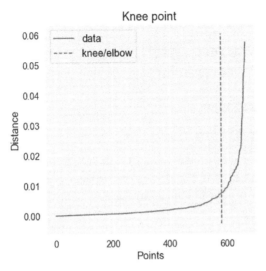

Figure 10.8 – Knee point calculation

Next, we print its exact value:

```
print("Knee point: " + str(distances[knee.knee]))
>> Knee point: 0.007346658772005564
```

Before using DBSCAN, we must assign a value for the *minPts* parameter. As a general rule, its value should be greater than or equal to the dimensionality of the dataset. Also, the minimum value must be chosen to be at least equal to 3. A value set to 1 wouldn't make sense, as any single point becomes a cluster of its own. Using *minPts* equal to 2 yields the method we will present in the next section. The larger or noisier the dataset is, the larger value of *minPts* is required. A commonly used heuristic is to set the value $2 \times dimensions$ for the parameter. In the following code, we adopt the heuristic and set min_samples equal to 4 (2×2):

```
from sklearn.cluster import DBSCAN


# Perform the clustering.
db = DBSCAN(eps=distances[knee.knee], min_samples=4, n_jobs=-
1).fit(pcaComponents)
# Get the cluster labels.
labels = db.labels_
# Count the total number of clusters.
num_clusters = len(set(labels)) - (1 if -1 in labels else 0)
```

```
# Count the total number of noise points.
num_noise = list(labels).count(-1)

print('Number of clusters: %d' % num_clusters)
print('Number of noise points: %d' % num_noise)
>>
Number of clusters: 7
Number of noise points: 132
```

According to the output, there are 7 clusters and 132 outliers. Many noisy points suggest that the algorithm is not performing very well. The chosen *epsilon* value is extremely small, so most of the points do not lie in the neighborhood of other points and are treated as outliers.

Assessing DBSCAN

Let's employ a few metrics to assess the quality of the DBSCAN model better. First, we calculate the **silhouette coefficient**, which quantifies how dense and well-separated the clusters are. The coefficient measures the average distance of a point in the cluster to all the other points within the same cluster. For the same point, we also calculate the average distance to the points of the closest cluster. Intuitively, we would like that the first quantity is as small as possible (density) and the second to be as large as possible (separability). Consider the example of *Figure 10.9* containing three clusters:

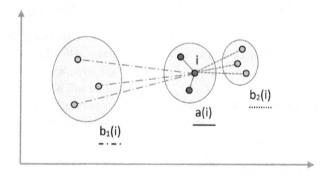

Figure 10.9 – Average distances for the silhouette coefficient

For an individual point, *i*, we calculate the silhouette coefficient, *s(i)*, using the following formulas:

$$s(i) = \frac{b(i) - a(i)}{\max\{a(i), b(i)\}} \; and \; b(i) = \min\{b_1(i), b_2(i)\}$$

Where, the following applies:

- $a(i)$ = the average distance of point i to the points in the cluster
- $b(i)$ = the average distance of point i to the closest cluster
- $b_1(i)$ = the average distance of point i to cluster 1
- $b_2(i)$ = the average distance of point i to cluster 2

In ML terminology, $a(i)$ is called **cohesion** and is an intra-cluster metric, measuring the similarity of the points in the same cluster. Conversely, $b(i)$ is called **separation** and is an inter-cluster metric. It refers to the degree to which the clusters don't overlap. The range of the silhouette coefficient is between -1 to 1. As the coefficient approaches the value of 1, the cohesion and separation of the clusters as a whole increase. When the coefficient approaches 0, it's unclear whether point i should belong to the right cluster or the one in the middle. Finally, a value close to -1 signifies that point i is likely misclassified. The same process is applied to all the other samples in the dataset.

Calculating the coefficient for our example demands just one line of code:

```
from sklearn import metrics


# Print the model results.
print("Silhouette Coefficient: %0.3f" % metrics.silhouette_
score(pcaComponents, labels))
>> Silhouette Coefficient: 0.231
```

The output suggests that the score is closer to 0, and there is an overlap between the clusters. In this section, we use the silhouette coefficient to assess the quality of the clustering model. Still, the coefficient can also be employed to identify the optimal number of clusters for K-means. Notice that the elbow method uses only intra-cluster distances in its scoring function, while the silhouette coefficient uses both inter- and intra-cluster distances.

Another indicative result of the created DBSCAN model is the distribution of the data points in each cluster. The following code shows the specific calculation:

```
# Get the sample counts in each cluster
counts = np.bincount(labels[labels>=0])
print (counts)
>> [507    5    4    4    4    4    4]
```

As we can observe, the first cluster includes almost all data points. Another indication of the low performance of the algorithm. Finally, let's plot the clusters as we did with the K-means case:

```
# Plot the clusters.
colors = ['blue', 'yellow', 'green', 'red', 'black']
```

```
vectorizer = np.vectorize(lambda x: colors[x % len(colors)])

plt.scatter(pcaComponents[:,0], pcaComponents[:,1],
c=vectorizer(labels))
```

Figure 10.10 shows the outcome of this step:

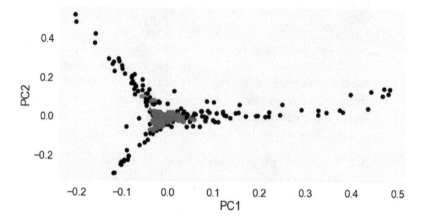

Figure 10.10 – DBSCAN clustering output

One of the clusters in the middle monopolizes the data, while there are many outliers depicted in black color. Looking at the plot, we observe a large dense area in the middle. Conversely, the three edges are less dense. DBSCAN is not a good option in this setting, as there is no drop in the density of data points in the middle to detect the boundaries between the clusters, hence the problem with the silhouette coefficient we saw earlier. Finally, the algorithm struggles with clusters of varying density, leaving out too many extraneous outliers in the more dense clusters.

Let's now move to the third clustering method presented in the chapter.

Introducing the hierarchical clustering algorithm

Hierarchical clustering is another unsupervised machine learning algorithm that seeks to build a hierarchy of clusters. To achieve this aim, it constructs a tree-like structure called a **dendrogram** that shows the hierarchical relationship between objects in a dataset. Typically, there are two ways to construct the dendrogram: the **agglomerative clustering** approach or the **divisive clustering** one. The first option is more common and follows a bottom-up approach by sequentially merging similar clusters. In divisive clustering, we put all observations in one big cluster and then successively split the clusters. A top-down approach is adopted in this case. *Figure 10.11* shows an example of a dendrogram with the fusions or divisions made at each successive stage:

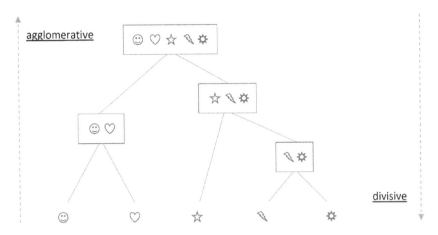

Figure 10.11 – Hierarchical clustering dendrogram

Next, we examine the basic steps of agglomerative clustering. To facilitate understanding, we reuse the example from the *Extracting word embedding representation* section of *Chapter 3, Classifying Topics of Newsgroup Posts*. Again, we visualize the personality traits of users with a personalized grayscale vector consisting of five elements (each for each trait). This time we aim to cluster four user profiles, as shown in *Figure 10.12*:

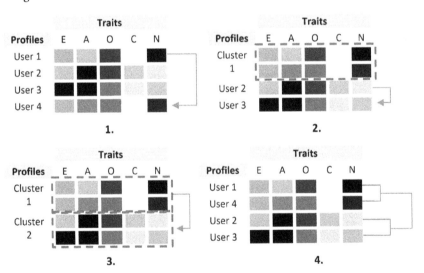

Figure 10.12 – Hierarchical clustering steps

The basic steps of the process are summarized as follows:

1. Compare each user vector with the others and find the most similar pair. In our example, **User 1** and **User 4** are more similar than any other combination (you can visually compare the grayscale values in their vectors).

2. Merge the two profiles under the same cluster (**Cluster 1**). Repeat *step 1* and use the profile vectors and the merged cluster for the comparisons. The pair of **User 3** and **User 4** is now the most similar combination.

3. Merge the two profiles under the same cluster (**Cluster 2**). As there are only two remaining clusters, we stop the iterations.

4. Merge **Cluster 1** and **Cluster 2** to build the dendrogram. Notice the height of the branches, which signifies the order that the clusters were formed. The cluster of **User 1** and **User 2** is created earlier than the one for **User 3** and **User 4**. The smaller the height of a branch, the more similar the clusters underneath.

Hopefully, this simplistic visual example provides a basic intuition of the algorithm. Once more, we encounter the concept of similarity between two objects. Euclidean distance is often the selected distance measure in hierarchical clustering, but most algorithm implementations allow the selection of other metrics. After choosing a distance metric, we must also determine where the distance between two clusters is measured.

There are a few different options for this task, such as *complete linkage*, the longest distance between two points in each cluster. *Single linkage* is the shortest distance between two points in each cluster. Finally, the *average linkage* is the average distance between all points of one cluster to all points of another one. These different options are part of the **linkage function** we need to set before executing the hierarchical clustering algorithm. In the next section, we see how to incorporate a linkage function after putting the algorithm into action.

Putting hierarchical clustering into action

First, let's create the dendrogram for our dataset using agglomerative clustering and `ward` as the linkage function:

```
from scipy.cluster import hierarchy


dendro = hierarchy.dendrogram(hierarchy.linkage(pcaComponents,
method='ward'))
# Cut at 1.5 to get 3 clusters.
plt.axhline(y=1.5, color='black', linestyle='--')
```

Instead of measuring the distance directly, `ward` analyzes clusters' variance to generate groups that minimize the within-cluster variance. The output dendrogram is illustrated in *Figure 10.13*:

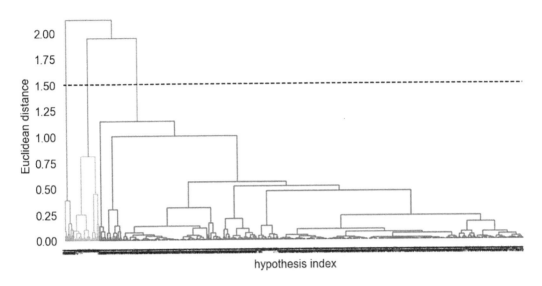

Figure 10.13 – Hierarchical clustering output

By default, the Euclidean distance is used as a distance metric. Due to the size of the dataset, much of the information in the lower part of the dendrogram is crammed. As a reference, the *x* axis includes 664 points that we cannot see. Notice how the cluster pairs are formed and the different heights of the branches. Based on the visualization, we can cut the tree horizontally at any value of the Euclidean distance and acquire a specific number of clusters. In the example, the horizontal dashed line at **1.5** yields three clusters.

As with the K-means case, we extract the top words per cluster. In the following code snippet, we create an agglomerative clustering model and predict the cluster for each hypothesis:

```
from sklearn.cluster import AgglomerativeClustering

# Perform the clustering.
agg = AgglomerativeClustering(n_clusters=3,
affinity='euclidean', linkage='ward')
agg_model = agg.fit_predict(pcaComponents)
```

Then, we proceed to the extraction of the 15 top words per cluster:

```
# Get the 15 top words per cluster.
top_words = cluster_top_words(tf_idf_array, agg.labels_, 15)
```

The following code provides the visualization of the results:

```
# Plot the top words per cluster.
x = np.arange(len(top_words[0]))

for i, df in enumerate(top_words):
    ax = fig.add_subplot(1, len(top_words), i+1)
    ax.barh(x, df.score, align='center', color='#0a7ff2')
```

Finally, the output is shown in *Figure 10.14*:

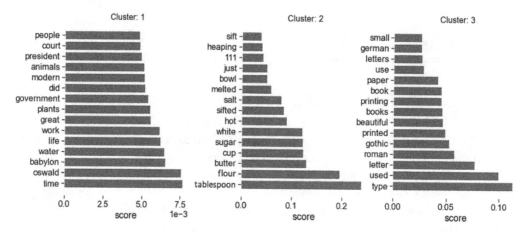

Figure 10.14 – Top words per cluster

The results are similar to the one for K-means, and we did not become wiser with the result of DBSCAN. However, perhaps getting similar output from two different methods makes us more confident in the validity of the claims we can make later in the analysis. Until now, we discussed three methods for hard clustering. The key takeaway is that it allows us to put each sample in one of several clusters. You must determine which information is included in each cluster and give it a label. In the final section, the focus moves to an algorithm for soft clustering.

Introducing the LDA algorithm

In *Chapter 3, Classifying Topics of Newsgroup Posts*, we examined how to classify the instances of a newsgroup dataset into predefined topics. A related situation is encountered when we want to assign a topic label to a piece of text without prior knowledge of the available topics. **Topic modeling** refers to the task of identifying groups of items, in our case words, that best describes a collection of documents or sentences. The topics emerge during the specific process; hence they are called *latent*.

A popular topic modeling technique to extract the hidden topics from a given corpus is the **latent dirichlet allocation (LDA)**. Strictly speaking, LDA is not a clustering algorithm because it produces a distribution of groupings over the sentences being processed. However, as a document can be a part of multiple topics, LDA resembles a soft clustering algorithm in which each data point belongs to more than one cluster. For this reason, we made it part of this chapter. As in the case of hard clustering, we need the expert opinion of humans to evaluate the outcome of LDA.

The main idea behind the algorithm is that each document can be described as a distribution of topics and each topic as a distribution of words. LDA aims to find the topics of a document based on the words in it. Starting with M documents and a set of N words included in the documents, we can create the left plot of *Figure 10.15*:

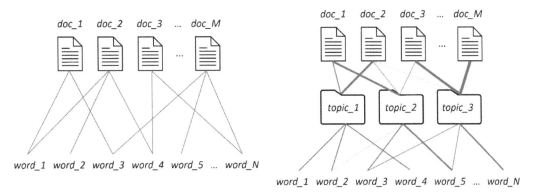

Figure 10.15 – The main idea behind LDA

The plot shows the connections of each document to the words it contains. Identifying the topics requires checking all the possible connections for all documents. This task is not practical, and to alleviate this limitation, we introduce a latent layer with three topics, as illustrated in the right plot. The number of connections is reduced as the documents connect only to topics and the latter to words. LDA must find the weight of the connections, which are depicted schematically with the different thickness levels of each connection line. For example, **doc_2** may consist of the following mix: 42% **topic_1**, 36% **topic_2**, and 22% **topic_3**. The most important hyperparameter for the algorithm is the number of clusters to aim for. In the next section, we incorporate LDA to solve the main problem of this chapter.

Putting LDA into action

First, by using the code in the `topic-modeling.ipynb` notebook, we obtain a fresh copy of the dataset from the CSV file:

```
# Read the hypotheses from the speech-to-text.
hypothesis_df = pd.read_csv('data/hypothesis.csv',
```

```
names=['hypothesis'], skiprows=1)
corpus = hypothesis_df[hypothesis_df['hypothesis'] !=
"<ERROR>"]
```

Next, we tokenize the sentences and perform a light preprocessing of the words:

```
# Tokenize the input text.
def tokenize(text):
    tokens = []
    doc = nlp(text)

    for word in doc:
        # Checks whether the word consists of whitespace.
        if word.orth_.isspace(): continue
        # Does the word resemble to a URL?
        elif word.like_url: tokens.append('URL')
        # Does the word resemble to an email?
        elif word.like_email: tokens.append('EMAIL')
        else: tokens.append(word.lower_)

    return tokens
```

We can also load a set of stop words, for cleaning the dataset later:

```
import spacy


sp = spacy.load("en_core_web_sm")


# Define the list of stopwords.
stop_words = sp.Defaults.stop_words
```

Let's define the standard method for lemmatization:

```
# Lemmatize the input word.
def lemmatize(text):
    sentence = sp(text)
    lemma = ''
    for token in sentence:
```

```
        lemma += token.lemma_ + ' '

    return lemma.strip()
```

An important design decision for this test is to focus solely on nouns and adjectives for the input:

```
# Keep only the nouns and adjectives.
def filter_nouns_adj(text):
    sentence = sp(text.lower())
    nouns_adj = ''
    for token in sentence:
        if token.pos_ == "NOUN" or token.pos_ == "ADJ":
            nouns_adj += token.text + ' '

    return nouns_adj.strip()
```

The `extract_text_for_lda` method sequentially calls the previously presented methods to process the input:

```
# Extract the text for LDA.
def extract_text_for_lda(text):
    filtered_text = filter_nouns_adj(text)
    tokens = tokenize(filtered_text)
    tokens = [t for t in tokens if t not in stop_words]
    tokens = [lemmatize(t) for t in tokens]
    tokens = [t for t in tokens if len(t) > 4]

    return tokens
```

Then, we use the method to parse the data from the corpus:

```
text_data = []

# Parse all data from the corpus.
for row, col in corpus.iterrows():
    tokens = extract_text_for_lda(col.hypothesis)
    text_data.append(tokens)
```

We are now ready to incorporate LDA, but first, a necessary transformation is required:

```
import gensim
import pickle


# Transform the data for gensim.
dictionary = gensim.corpora.Dictionary(text_data)
corpus = [dictionary.doc2bow(text) for text in text_data]


# Save the data in a file.
pickle.dump(corpus, open('./data/corpus.pkl', 'wb'))
dictionary.save('./data/dictionary.gensim')
```

Finally, we can create the LDA model using three clusters and obtain the four most common words for each topic:

```
# Create and save the model for 3 topics.
ldamodel = gensim.models.ldamodel.LdaModel(corpus, num_
topics=3, id2word=dictionary, passes=15, random_state=123)
ldamodel.save('./data/model3.gensim')


# Get the 4 most common words per topic.
topics = ldamodel.print_topics(num_words=4)
for t in topics:
    print(t)
>>
(0, '0.007*"court" + 0.006*"government" + 0.006*"public" +
0.006*"morning"')
(1, '0.011*"great" + 0.008*"paper" + 0.006*"modern" +
0.006*"service"')
(2, '0.019*"letter" + 0.012*"plant" + 0.012*"water" +
0.009*"animal"')
```

The first topic seems to be related to the assassination of President Kennedy. To verify this assumption, let's extract the distribution of topics for a random input text related to this event:

```
# Text to identify a topic.
test = 'the assassination of president kennedy took place at
dallas, texas'
test = extract_text_for_lda(test)
test_bow = dictionary.doc2bow(test)


print(ldamodel.get_document_topics(test_bow))
>> [(0, 0.6977441), (1, 0.11669667), (2, 0.18555923)]
```

Indeed, the sentence consists of a mix: 70% topic 1, 12% topic 2, and 18% topic 3. Next, we create a handy interactive visualization to examine the newly constructed LDA model:

```
import pyLDAvis
import pyLDAvis.gensim_models


# Load the corpus.
dictionary = gensim.corpora.Dictionary.load('./data/dictionary.
gensim')
corpus = pickle.load(open('./data/corpus.pkl', 'rb'))


# Read the LDA model, store and show the visualization in HTML.
lda = gensim.models.ldamodel.LdaModel.load('./data/model3.
gensim')
lda_display = pyLDAvis.gensim_models.prepare(lda, corpus,
dictionary, sort_topics=False)
pyLDAvis.save_html(lda_display, './data/lda-3-topics.html')
pyLDAvis.display(lda_display)
```

The output is an HTML page that can be loaded in any web browser, as illustrated in *Figure 10.16*:

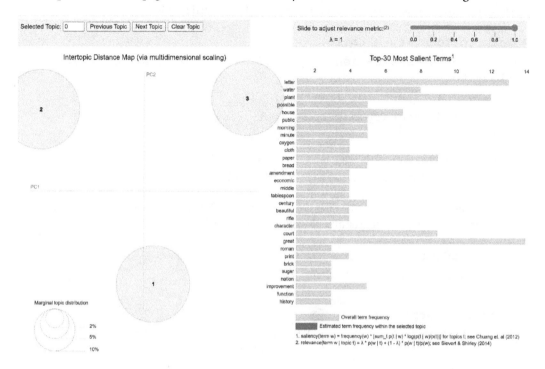

Figure 10.16 – Interactive visualization of the LDA model output

The specific web page is interactive and offers a visual interpretation of the different topics. Although the text is not clear enough, we can immediately identify a few basic elements. First, there are three clusters (circles), which are pretty much spaced apart. Circles that are closer signify similar topics, while the cluster size measures the topic's importance relative to the whole dataset. Finally, we can hover over each circle and observe which terms are most frequent in that topic.

After the presentation of LDA, we have reached the end of the chapter. The aim was to avoid excessive mathematical formulation for the different methods and provide a more intuitive explanation of their mechanics. Hopefully, you should be sufficiently equipped to understand the major design choices when incorporating each clustering method.

Summary

This chapter focused on text clustering, intending to segregate samples with distinct characteristics and assign them to different groups. Clustering is one of the most important areas in data science simply because most datasets come unlabeled. Here, we tried to provide a good overview of the topic, but in reality, we only scratched the tip of this gigantic iceberg.

In this context, we presented both hard and soft clustering methods to categorize speech-to-text transcriptions. Specifically, speech recognition, often coupled with the techniques presented in this book, provides a convenient way to gather text data. Finally, we presented methods that allow the automatic configuration of the clustering algorithms, along with metrics, to assess their performance.

We have finally reached the end of the book! But stay tuned, as much more excitement is waiting for the years to come!

Index

X

XKCD
used, for visualizing 360-362
XML Path Language (XPath) 273

Z

zero-frequency problem 53
example 53, 54
ZeroR 93

Packt.com

Subscribe to our online digital library for full access to over 7,000 books and videos, as well as industry leading tools to help you plan your personal development and advance your career. For more information, please visit our website.

Why subscribe?

- Spend less time learning and more time coding with practical eBooks and Videos from over 4,000 industry professionals

- Improve your learning with Skill Plans built especially for you

- Get a free eBook or video every month

- Fully searchable for easy access to vital information

- Copy and paste, print, and bookmark content

Did you know that Packt offers eBook versions of every book published, with PDF and ePub files available? You can upgrade to the eBook version at packt.com and as a print book customer, you are entitled to a discount on the eBook copy. Get in touch with us at customercare@packtpub.com for more details.

At www.packt.com, you can also read a collection of free technical articles, sign up for a range of free newsletters, and receive exclusive discounts and offers on Packt books and eBooks.

Other Books You May Enjoy

If you enjoyed this book, you may be interested in these other books by Packt:

Production-Ready Applied Deep Learning

Tomasz Palczewski, Jaejun (Brandon) Lee, Lenin Mookiah

ISBN: 9781803243665

- Understand how to develop a deep learning model using PyTorch and TensorFlow
- Convert a proof-of-concept model into a production-ready application
- Discover how to set up a deep learning pipeline in an efficient way using AWS
- Explore different ways to compress a model for various deployment requirements
- Develop Android and iOS applications that run deep learning on mobile devices
- Monitor a system with a deep learning model in production
- Choose the right system architecture for developing and deploying a model

Data Cleaning and Exploration with Machine Learning

Michael Walker

ISBN: 9781803241678

- Explore essential data cleaning and exploration techniques to be used before running the most popular machine learning algorithms
- Understand how to perform preprocessing and feature selection, and how to set up the data for testing and validation
- Model continuous targets with supervised learning algorithms
- Model binary and multiclass targets with supervised learning algorithms
- Execute clustering and dimension reduction with unsupervised learning algorithms
- Understand how to use regression trees to model a continuous target

Packt is searching for authors like you

If you're interested in becoming an author for Packt, please visit `authors.packtpub.com` and apply today. We have worked with thousands of developers and tech professionals, just like you, to help them share their insight with the global tech community. You can make a general application, apply for a specific hot topic that we are recruiting an author for, or submit your own idea.

Share Your Thoughts

Now you've finished *Machine Learning Techniques for Text*, we'd love to hear your thoughts! Scan the QR code below to go straight to the Amazon review page for this book and share your feedback or leave a review on the site that you purchased it from.

`https://packt.link/r/1-803-24238-8`

Your review is important to us and the tech community and will help us make sure we're delivering excellent quality content.

Download a free PDF copy of this book

Thanks for purchasing this book!

Do you like to read on the go but are unable to carry your print books everywhere?

Is your eBook purchase not compatible with the device of your choice?

Don't worry, now with every Packt book you get a DRM-free PDF version of that book at no cost.

Read anywhere, any place, on any device. Search, copy, and paste code from your favorite technical books directly into your application.

The perks don't stop there, you can get exclusive access to discounts, newsletters, and great free content in your inbox daily!

Follow these simple steps to get the benefits:

1. Scan the QR code or visit the link below:

https://packt.link/free-ebook/9781803242385

2. Submit your proof of purchase
3. That's it! We'll send your free PDF and other benefits to your email directly

CPSIA information can be obtained
at www.ICGtesting.com
Printed in the USA
LVHW061106230723
753125LV00002B/34